WOMEN IN CONCERT

WOMEN IN CONCERT

An Anthology of Bengali Muslim Women's Writings (1904-1938)

Edited by

SHAHEEN AKHTAR and MOUSHUMI BHOWMIK

Translated by STREE

Foreword by

FIRDOUS AZIM

Stree

This English translation, *Concert of Women: An Anthology of Bengali Muslim Women's Writings, 1904-1938,* was first published in October 2008 by STREE, an imprint of Bhatkal and Sen, 16 Southern Avenue, Kolkata 700 026

The translation is from the Bengali original text, *Zenana Mehfil: Bangali Musalman Lekhikader Nirbachita Rachana 1904-1938,* edited by Shaheen Akhtar and Moushumi Bhowmik, published by Stree, 1998.

ISBN 81-85604-57-6
Rs600.00

Design by STREE; typesetting by Krishna Gopal Das, 74T Sultan Alam Road, Kolkata 700 033, and printed by Arunima Printing Works, 81 Simla Street, Kolkata 700 006.

Published by Mandira Sen for STREE, An imprint of Bhatkal and Sen, 16 Southern Avenue, Kolkata 700 026

In memory of Sufia Kamal

Contents

Foreword

Putting together anthologies of women's writings continues and remains part of the feminist literary project of unearthing women's voices. The effect of such anthologies is to highlight, every time, the notion of a separate sphere of women's writing. Do women write differently from men? Does the rewriting of literary history contribute to our understanding of women's social and cultural position? These questions acquire a double significance in *Women in Concert: An Anthology of Bengali Muslim Women's Writings, 1904-1938,* the English translation of the Bengali book, *Zenana Mehfil:Bangali Musalman Lekhikader Nirbachita Rachana, 1904-1938* (Stree, 1998).

The complexities in the way of looking at the categories of Muslim and women, and social transformation, or negotiations with a nationalist modernity, can perhaps best be encapsulated with a quote from the anthology itself. Abul Fazl, reviewing *Niyantrita* (translated as *A Woman Bound by Destiny* in this volume) says:

> There are many difficulties in the way of writing Muslim fiction. The main among these is the custom of seclusion. . . . The lives of men and women are the foundation of literature—there is no way for Muslim writers of either sex to find out about each other's lives. Their vision bounces off from the high walls surrounding them. (p 207)

While this review bemoans the fact of seclusion, and the difficulties of writing a 'complete' Muslim fiction, this fact of seclusion also helps to create that separate space—which this collection of writings has made into *Women in Concert*—a gathering of women, a woman's space. The trajectory traced here—

from Begum Rokeya Sakhawat Hossain to Shamsunnahar Mahmud—traverses the first half of the last century and includes a wide range of writings as Bengali Muslim women struggle to carve a space for themselves within the modernizing and nationalist discourses that marked that period in this region.

The Bengali Muslim negotiation with modernity and even with anti-colonial struggles has not been well recorded. Most accounts speak of 'backwardness', where the Bengali Muslim 'renaissance' takes place about fifty years after the Bengal renaissance. Women's position is a special marker of this backwardness. The early twentieth century is celebrated as the period in which the Muslim community along with women were awakened into modernity, through education, writing and publishing, social and political work, and so on (Amin 1995). There is a way of reading this negotiation differently, pointing out the variegated and differentiated elements that had to be taken into consideration. Perhaps the most vivid description of this is to be found in Anisuzzaman's introduction to *Muslim Manosh O Bangla Sahitya* (The Mind of the Muslims and Bengali Literature, 2001), where the differences in the routes that Hindus and Muslims in Bengal traversed are recorded. Interestingly, this text does not ascribe Muslim 'backwardness' to the British divide-and-rule policy, but shows how an economic placement made the recovery from colonial domination more difficult. It was the failure to build up a strong economic base that can account for the different route that Muslim Bengal has chalked out for itself. What is of further interest is that the base for the Muslim middle class seems to have rested on a rural gentry, making it more difficult to access or identify the 'modernizing' urban forces.

Economic factors along with the fact of geographical location helped to separate the social and political profile of Hindus and Muslims in Bengal. The place of women then has to be looked at from within this prism. In South Asian history in general, women's placement in nationalist discourse has been problematized. The 1989 collection of essays in *Recasting Women* (1989) perhaps laid the foundation, or at least gathered together the strand of thinking that marks such a questioning. In this complex terrain, the figure of the Muslim woman is made to become the emblem of many contradictory elements. First she becomes the symbol of the backwardness of the community as a whole, and practices such as purdah, or the wearing of the burqa, or keeping women away from vernacular and secular education are seen as part of this process. She also becomes a symbol of mystery, hiding behind the veil a potent sexuality, a mystery to be unearthed. For women to write and voice their own concerns, their feelings and emotions from within this site, which is loaded with meaning, becomes very difficult.

While one way of looking at the position of Muslim women in Bengal in the first half of the twentieth century aligns them to the modernizing and nationalist impulses effecting India as a whole, the modernizing efforts in the Middle East and the so-called Muslim world had a great influence on Muslims in Bengal. Kazi Nazrul Islam's famous paean to Kemal Ataturk shows how a pan-Islamic discourse was being created during that era. The debate around the veil—the covering of the head and/or face—was one of the main issues around which this modernizing effort was centred. Turkey and Iran outright banned the donning of the veil in public institutions. Leila Ahmed (1992) has perhaps best encapsulated this debate, and shown how the discourse drew on both 'Islamic' sources (in the sense of bringing in the Koranic verses on the necessity of veiling) and was a direct influence of Western cultural forces. Women were left to negotiate their way through contradictory forces and to form spaces for themselves. Seclusion, purdah and burqa form part of the discourse that women themselves were weaving, as evinced most notably in Begum Rokeya Sakhawat Hossain's writings. That this debate was, however, an ongoing one among Bengali Muslims is well shown when we look at a series of issues of *Saugat*, mainly during the year 1936. These writings, coming after Rokeya's *Abarodh-Bashini* or *Padmaraag*, reports on happenings in Turkey, Iran and

Afghanistan to widen the parameters of the Muslim woman's question. Contemporary examples can also be drawn from Egypt or Indonesia to show how new positions and roles were being envisioned for the new Muslim woman.

This collection of writings has indeed performed a very significant task. This is a bold attempt, drawing attention to the various and *different* trajectories through which a history of Bengali women can be put together. One can imagine the other trajectories that can be drawn, and a pluralistic reading of history enabled. By adding contemporary reviews, letters and comments, the collection has put these writings into context, helping the reader evaluate the writings in their own times, and creating a terrain for a writing of women's history in the process. The main issues that emerge through the writings in this collection can thus be seen as part of the historical and political processes through which a community of women was seeking to place themselves within an emerging social order, in the emergent new post-colonial nations.

To begin with: Rokeya Sakhawat Hossein has rightly become an iconic symbol for the awakening of Muslim women. As such, it is difficult to say anything new about her. However this anthology puts together, if not little-known, less anthologized pieces from that writer. The first piece, 'The Degradation of Women', which introduces the collection, speaks of women's 'enslavement'. A civilizing impetus is at work here. The metaphor of slavery portrays this situation as not peculiar to Muslim women alone. It calls for liberty and freedom. Our enslaving devices are our very ornaments, and the call to awakening could be made to any group of women. The question of religion, however, cannot be ignored, especially as the censored portions of this essay dealt with the way that religious interpretations were keeping women outside the purview of modern civilization. Rokeya's words echo through the centuries, as contemporary women's groups in Bangladesh use these very same censored words of Rokeya to mount their own campaign for a secular polity. Rokeya is well known for her protest against moribund social mores, where sometimes with humour as in *Abarodh-Bashini* (The Secluded Ones) and sometimes with reason and rationality, as in 'Burqa', she points out the inequities of the position of women.

These words of awakening echo in different forms throughout the volume: Fazilatunnesa, writing in 1929, expresses this beautifully as the 'tumultuous winds [that] have managed to raise a flutter in the hearts of Muslim women *who have been asleep for ages*' (p 219). This is one of the problems that I think all these writers face: as they exhort women to forge a new path for themselves, they invariably repeat an image of backwardness. Nowhere is this more prominent than in the call for women's education. Again, this is most evident in Rokeya's writings. 'The Need for Women's Education among Muslims' is typical of the spirit represented by all these women writers. The choice of material that has been used in this anthology, however, not only highlights this 'need', but goes beyond that to look at the ways in which women themselves struggled with providing that education. The Rokeya letters in this volume give the impression of someone who worked hard gathering money and ideas from all kinds of sources to make her school a true centre of learning. The very next writer, Khairunnesa Khatun, widens the educational project to look at rural schools. She points to many problems including the paucity of suitable female teachers and the lack of funds for such schools. Histories of Muslim women's education tend to focus on the Sakhawat Memorial School, and the many strategies that Rokeya adopted to ensure the smooth running of her school. That there was a larger issue at stake here has been well illustrated by the inclusion of this wonderful essay by Khairunnesa Khatun entitled 'The Obstacles to Our Education'. The need for women's education is highlighted by every writer in this volume, and what is brought out is not only an exhortation to send daughters to school, but the practical considerations: of teachers, of resources, of the nature of the curriculum and so on.

These writings were published in *Saugat* or *Nabanoor*, publications that promoted Muslim writers in Bengal. These publications were involved in a form of nation-making as well. Were the contours of the nation imagined in these journals that of a Muslim Bengal? How did the writers envisage the position of the Bengali Muslim in the post-colonial national structure? Our women writers display a kind of ambiguity in this regard. Writing in Bengali itself, it must be noted, for the Bengali Muslim, is suggestive of placement within a secular mould of identity. We have seen that the language debates of the past had devised a *dobhashi* Bengali, in which there was a strong admixture of Arabic and Persian words. While this kind of Bengali is usually termed as *musulmani* Bengali, Anisuzzaman (2001) has pointed out that this was not the language really spoken by Bengali Muslims, peasantry or otherwise. This was a deliberately constructed literary Bengali that made it easier to transmit Arabic-Persian tales or evolved during a period of linguistic experimentation.

Many of our women writers received formal instruction in Arabic or Persian, and we know from Rokeya's story how difficult it was for girls to get a secular education in Bengali. The picture had considerably changed by the time of Shamsunnahar Mahmud; being taught Bengali and even writing in that language had become totally acceptable among the Muslim Bengali intelligentsia. The terrain on which notions of the emerging nation were being germinated was crisscrossed with linguistic and religious differences, and our writers' envisioning of the nation traversed across this very difficult territory. Khairunnesa in her essay translated as *For the Love of the Motherland* (1905) calls on her 'sisters' to sacrifice for the motherland, which seems to be a united Bengal. She brings in the example of kshatriya women of the past and exhorts women to give up British and European goods, their finery and ornaments, for the 'resurrection of India's dormant industries' (p 60). An image of a wider nation, going beyond community and sometimes even class, is drawn, and the place of women within that nation is debated and a feeling given that women have to ensure their place within the new nation. Literary endeavours such as the piece entitled *The Labourer* by Razia Khatun Chowdhurani, anthologized here (pp252-58), brings in the story of the working classes, and the complete separation of middle class families and the newly emerging professional classes, who depended so much on being able to work. The stepping beyond middle-class concerns to bring in other classes of people shows the limitations of the world that writing and writers draw, and gestures towards a more variegated citizenry, where notions of inclusion and exclusion will have to be considered. These concerns are perhaps best encapsulated in the excerpt from *A Woman's Responsibility towards the Village Community* by Mahmuda Khatun Siddiqua (pp232-33), where women's responsibility to life outside the home is highlighted. Interestingly enough, the essay begins with a quotation from the Koran.

The debate on women and nation becomes part of a discussion on women and writing or women's creativity. Razia Khatun Chowdhurani has an essay entitled *The Literary Endeavours of Muslim Women* (pp249-51). By 1928, when this essay was published in *Saugat,* it seems that there was enough of a body of writing by women to warrant such a title. It is interesting to look at what she expects from such writing. She reiterates the gendered division of labour, and associates with women's writing 'motherly' qualities. Women are to write the 'words of consolation that people want to hear in times of distress'. Not only is this a reiteration of a separate sphere of women's writing, but ascribes to it a different purpose. Virginia Woolf's contemporary theory of androgyny had talked about the extinction of the author's gendered concerns, but the effort here is to exploit gender differences, to create a special field for women and writing. We have seen earlier that Abul Fazl had blamed the system of purdah for the lack of understanding men and women have of each others' lives, and hence the very incomplete literary representations. A different use of this seclusion is being made, as the missing motherly and comforting qualities can now be interjected into the literary sphere through women's writing. Women's special contribution to literature and life is discussed again in *Literature and Art* (pp224-31), by Mahmuda Khatun Siddiqua, written in the same year *Mohammedi,* 1928. The ethical purposes of writing are debated here, and the continuities and dissonances between a woman's public and private life are pointed out. This can also be extended to look at woman's place within modernity, the reconciliations between accepted mores of living, and the new territory that the contemporary woman writer was charting for herself. Mahmuda Khatun Siddiqua's poems, as anthologized here, reveal a sensuality that makes us wonder about the veiled nature of literary language that permits many a thought to be uttered, and many a desire to be expressed.

The inclusion of letters and anecdotes about the writers enliven the kind of publishing endeavours that women were involved in. Description of manuscripts arriving in the offices of *Saugat*, a sudden meeting with an author, and so on, bring to life for the readers of this volume the world in which these women wrote and published. The emerging woman writer, both in the creative and intellectual fields, is made visible through the inclusion of letters and reviews.

An anthology of women's writing helps to create a conversation amongst women, as each writer echoes or carries forward themes and issues highlighted by her sisters. Canon-making has its virtues, and in any canon of Bengali writing, it is Begum Rokeya who will stand out as the beacon carrier. The inclusion of excerpts from Rokeya's biography by Shamsunnahar Mahmud wonderfully draws the various threads together. This trend of women writing a woman's biography had been set into motion perhaps by Elizabeth Gaskell when she wrote the life of Charlotte Bronte in 1857. Women writers influence each other, act as inspirations for each other, and form a sisterhood of writing. Even more crucially, they help us trace a line of descent—a history in which to place ourselves. 'For we write through our mothers, if we are women', wrote Virginia Woolf. Perhaps the success of *Women in Concert* lies in this—that it has drawn a history of women's writing, of Muslim women's writing in Bengal. This book will indeed be inspirational to newer generations of writers.

The trajectory followed in this volume is a reiteration of modern nation-making: education, writing, print media, the formation of a community or nation through these means. Our writers even while taking part in this modern nation-making process constantly bring in images of what is left outside the purview of this imagined or emerging nation: the poor, the labourer, the village, and finally the veiled woman, deprived of education, enslaved by tradition and religion. Even while separating themselves from these women, while taking off the veil as it were, our writers cannot look away completely. That is why there are constant calls for awakening, passionate exhortations to throw away the bonds of slavery, and crucially to accept an identification with other marginalized groups. The call for education lists the difficulties of running village schools, the picture of the new middle class homes include the people who are paid to work within them, and the 'modern' woman writer has constantly to grapple with her own straddling between two worlds.

A NOTE ON THE TRANSLATION

The debate on language and the apt language for literature as we have seen had acquired another dimension when it came to Muslim writers from Bengal. The formulation of a 'modern' Bengali, tried to eradicate these differences, to create a less differentiated, and even mode of expression. The translations have aptly conveyed the impression of a language in transition—be it in the essays, poetry or fiction. That Bengali had become in the hands of the writers anthologized, and in the larger community, a truly secular language where 'Muslim' concerns of namaz or purdah could be dealt with as easily as political and social concerns of poverty, backwardness or education, is well illustrated in this volume. The translations, done by a host of translators, make for easy reading, and do reflect to a great extent, the differences and commonalities of usage.

Dhaka, May 2008

Firdous Azim
Chairperson of the Department of
English and Humanities
BRAC University, Dhaka

References

Ahmed, Leila, *Women and Gender in Islam,* New Haven: Yale University Press, 1992.

Amin, Sonia Nishat, *The World of Muslim Women in Colonial Bengal 1876-1939*, Leyden: Brill Academic Press, 1995.

Anisuzzaman, *Muslim Manosh O Bangla Sahitya,* 1757-1918, Dhaka: Papyrus, 2001.

Sangari, Kumkum, and Sudesh Vaid, eds, *Recasting Women: Essays in Colonial History,* Delhi: Kali for Women, 1989.

Woolf, Virginia, *A Room of One's Own* (Harmondsworth: Penguin, 1976 [1928].

Acknowledgements

As editors, we owe debts on behalf of the original Bengali *Zenana Mehfil*, of which *Women in Concert* is a translation, to many people: authors and family members of authors, scholars, researchers, translators, compositors, designers and publishers. Some of them are no more. For this English edition we must thank again all who helped us to put the original anthology together ten years ago and also those who made the English edition possible now.

In 1997 we were extremely fortunate to meet Sufia Kamal and she helped us in many ways to understand the time we were studying, for she had belonged to it. Sufia Kamal passed away in 1999, but her spirit to fight for justice remains. Prior to formally starting the book, Shaheen Akhtar had interviewed Mohammad Nasiruddin, editor of the legendary journal *Saugat*, a couple of years before his death in 1993. It is an honour for the book to carry an interview with a man such as him who played a key role in giving voice to the early literary pursuits of the Bengali Muslim woman. We were also extremely fortunate to meet Selina Bahar Zaman and Rokeya Rahman Kabir, who gave us glimpses into the lives of our authors, M. Fatema Khanam and Akhtar Mahal Syeda Khatun, respectively. They too have passed away during the past ten years. Writer Akhtaruzzaman Elias, who had helped us with his insight and wit, had died even before we could finish work on the Bengali *Zenana Mehfil*. To him we still owe so much. Novelist Umartul Fazl of Chittagong had very kindly talked with us about writing as a Bengali Muslim woman when we went to see her in 1996. She too has passed away since the Bengali edition was published.

Historian Sonia Nishat Amin's book *The World of Muslim Women in Colonial Bengal 1870-1939* had given us a starting point for our own research, and we thank her for sharing her work with us. Yasmin Hossain had studied Bengali Muslim women's early years of education and reform programmes for her Ph.D at the School of Oriental and African Studies in London, and she very generously had lent us support when we were working on the Bengali book. We have learnt much from her and even now our book rests on her work, albeit indirectly.

We must specially thank writer Syed Mustafa Siraj, editor Nurjahan Begum and former lecturer Hamida Khanam for their interviews, which are included in Part II, Conversations. To Razia Khatun Chowdhurani's daughter Rabeya Khatun Chowdhury, Nurunnesa Khatun Vidyavinodini's granddaughter Shama Qader, Mrs. M. Rahman's grandniece Siddiqua Zaman, who was deputy librarian, Institute of Business Administration, University of Dhaka, Abul Fazl and Umartul Fazl's sons, Abul Momen and Abul Mansur, historian Salauddin Ahmed, Mahmuda Khatun Siddiqua's niece, photographer Syeda Khanam and journalist Abul Maqsud we are grateful for sharing their personal remembrances of the authors and in some cases also their research with us.

We are sincerely grateful to the panel of translators who translated individual chapters of the Bengali book, without whose efforts the book would not have come about. We owe an enormous debt to Firdous Azim of BRAC University, Dhaka, who has taken special care not only to write the Foreword but also to point out flaws and gaps in our work and help with corrections with exemplary patience. Neshat Quaiser of Jamia Millia Islamia University has enabled us to understand some of the Arabic and Persian words and phrases and Islamic allusions and has helped to write some of the endnotes. To Mahua Sarkar of Binghamton University, SUNY, we owe special thanks for her support to the translation project and her valuable advice on revisions in general and also on the Notes by the Editors.

Dhaka and Kolkata, May 2008 S.A. and M.B.

Notes by the Editors

FINDING THEIR OWN PATH Shaheen Akhtar

The presence of Muslim writers in the history of Bengali literature was not so apparent for almost the first half of colonial rule in India. However, research and a closer reading of literary history reveals their presence, and we even come across some women writers from that period. For example, the poet Rahimunnesa (estimated dates, 1760-1800) was writing at this time. Between the middle of the eighteenth century to the second half of the nineteenth, Muslim writers used a form of language which has come to be known as *dobhashi*, in which Bengali was liberally peppered with Arabic and Persian words. The genres they wrote in included theology, history, biography, poetry, tales of romance, and so on. This school of writing flourished outside the purview of British imperialism, maintaining a tenuous link with the past. The content and style of these writings drew on local and indigenous sources and influences. These poets did not enjoy even the patronage of local zamindars, but were totally dependent on the people, and their charming lyrics survived and were disseminated because of popular support. Garibullah and Syed Hamza who wrote in the eighteenth century were pioneers of this school of poetry. The rest of the dobhashi writers belonged to the nineteenth century, during which period the *punthis* written in Bengali-Arabic began losing their appeal and were counted among the *Battala* variety of pulp literature.[1] This was largely due to the growth of 'modern' forms of writing that emerged during the nineteenth century. However, a large number of *punthis* continued to be written in Bangladesh and, in fact, such writing is still practised in a limited way. In 2005, when I was compiling an anthology of women's writing, I located a few *punthis,* including significant ones such as *Gazi Kalu O Champabati* and *Banbibir Kissa.*

The year 1870 is significant, as it is around this time that Bengali Muslims made a significantly noticeable progress in receiving modern education. This is also the period when 'modern' forms of writing started being practised by the new Muslim writers. Judging by literary merit the foremost among them was Mir Mosharraf Hossein. This was the golden age of Bengali modern literature. This contribution by Muslim writers who came in late into the publishing arena was largely ignored by literary historians. They never got their due from contemporary Hindu writers and intellectuals. Probably this is why Muslim writers started to look for a platform of their own—in papers, presses, literary meets, books and anthologies. This effort helped to convey the newly-forged sense of a modern identity to the people of their community. Muslim women began writing in these papers from the early twentieth century, and this anthology is a compilation of writings by eleven of them.

The movement to reform the status of Bengali women begun in the third decade of the nineteenth century was Hindu-oriented—evident in the laws that reformists tried to bring into effect. At the same time there was a massive drive to educate elite women. We might refer to a comment by Geraldine Forbes about the reform movement, quoted by Yasmin Hossein in the *Prekshapat* (Foreword) in the original Bengali book *Zenana Mehfil* (1998). Geraldine Forbes wrote that while reformers aimed at raising the position and general standards of the women at home, none of them wanted women to have economic and legal freedom. The comment is equally applicable to that section of Muslim society that had exposure to modern education. When Muslims began advocating women's education towards the end of the nineteenth century, they too aimed at bringing about a reform in the inner quarters—creating educated mothers and housewives.

When Begum Rokeya took up the pen at the beginning of the twentieth century, one might say that Muslim women had become active participants in the reform movement. The desire to have women receive modern education was top priority in Begum Rokeya's agenda. However, her goal was wider—enabling women to earn and achieve economic independence. Her writing combines women's envisaged roles with marriage, conjugal life and household matters. A glowing example of this may be found in the novel *Padmaraag*.

In her writing, she sharply reacted against the discrimination perpetrated on women in the name of religion. Gradually, Muslim society in Bengal accepted the reformist programme outlined by Begum Rokeya, and once the traditional roles played by women as daughters, wives and mothers were contested, the image of the 'modern' woman, as posed by the reform movement, took on a wider dimension.

Running a girls' school and a women's organization, writing continuously about women's emancipation, it is no wonder that Begum Rokeya shines in the field of women's writing in Bengal. But it is good to remember that she was not the only one. Many other Muslim women followed up on the issues raised by her in their writing. The women writers of that period featured in this anthology are—Begum Rokeya Sakhawat Hossain, Mrs. M. Rahman, Khairunnesa Khatun, Nurunnesa Khatun Vidyavinodini, M. Fatema Khanam, Razia Khatun Chowdhurani, Akhtar Mahal Syeda Khatun, Fazilatunnesa, Mahmuda Khatun Siddiqua, Shamsunnahar Mahmud and Sufia Kamal.

2

In the mid-1990s, when we had begun work on *Zenana Mehfil,* I was often asked in Dhaka why we were including only Bengali Muslim women writers in the anthology. It was suggested that this was a communal act. Why were Hindu women writers left out? Truly, in Bangladesh there is hardly any instance of studying the communities separately in women's studies. Whether a pioneer among Bengali women was a Muslim or a Hindu did not make any difference to evaluating her contribution.

But the picture is somewhat different when it comes to literature. Although the works of contemporary writers are not anthologized on the basis of their religious identity, there is a trend, on either side of the border, of presenting writers—male or female—in terms of national identity, that is, as belonging to Bangladesh or West Bengal. Histories of literature usually dedicate a chapter on Muslim writers, covering six centuries, from the medieval age to the nineteenth century. This chapter would be slim in the books published in West Bengal and comparatively thicker in those published in Bangladesh, although Bengali literature in this period was enriched by the contributions of both Hindu and Muslim writers. Moushumi Bhowmik in her editorial note, which follows, has talked about the scant space given to pre-Partition Muslim women writers in the anthologies published in Kolkata—a major reason why *Zenana Mehfil* included only Muslim women writers. We are aware that be it political or literary history, domineering interests marginalize, sometimes even obliterate, other histories. Entire schools of poets, writers and artists can disappear as a result. Muslims writers, irrespective of whether they are male or female, it goes without saying, have been largely ignored by most literary histories. In this context *Zenana Mehfil* and its English translation are necessary interventions in the rewriting of literary history.

The publication of the Bangladesh edition of *Zenana Mehfil* by the University Press of Dhaka was greeted with unexpected enthusiasm. The amount of discussion and criticism generated proved that readers in Bangladesh, assuming that the writers featured were their own, forgave the errors and embraced the work. It was like finding a long-lost relative, and there was much praise for the endeavour.

3

Zenana Mehfil, published, as mentioned earlier, in January 1998, featured, significantly, a number of women writers who had been dropped from the annals of history. These were writers neglected in undivided Bengal, being Muslims and being women. And probably because they were women, the neglect continued in Pakistan after Partition and even in present-day Bangladesh.

While putting the anthology together, when we could not locate the work of a particular writer in the Bangla Academy Library in Dhaka, we went looking in Calcutta's National Library, and maybe found it, finally, in tatters in an unknown library in Sylhet or Murshidabad. And even when one managed to locate a piece, there was no knowing who the writer was, that is, there was no information on her family, date and place of birth, year of death, and so on. It was difficult to find out about the personality or the private life of the woman who probably wrote in the flickering light of a candle. How could she make a story out of a square space enclosed by four walls in which she lived, and what inspired her to do so? We were left groping in the dark chambers of history. Most fortunately for us, some of the descendants of these near-forgotten writers—the custodians of their achievement and memory—were still alive.

When I was young, poems by Sufia Kamal and Begum Rokeya's writing were included in the textbooks we read. There was a note on Begum Rokeya which said that she would stay awake at night to read secretly by candlelight. I could not understand why a girl would want to spend her nights reading by candlelight, and that too clandestinely, at an age when I tried my utmost to break free of the monstrous grip of having to learn one's daily lessons, citing power cuts as an excuse. Besides publishing this information on her, textbook publishers would print images of Rokeya, in a full-sleeve blouse, head covered, heavy book in hand. This image, instead of being a source of inspiration to contemporary young women, acted more as deterrence.

We read a poem called *Chasha* (farmer), by Razia Khatun Chowdhurani, which went like this:

> The farmer of my country is the most devout of all.
> The liberation of the motherland is his only aim, he's our only hope.
> Was Dadhichi the saint more devout than he?
> It's difficult to outdo the good deeds accumulated by him.

We were made to write articles by elaborating the idea in school. We did not know whose lines these were that we had to build on to be able to score in the examinations. That was how Razia Khatun Chowdhurani had found a place in our textbooks, anonymously.

In Dhaka University, I lived in the Shamsunnahar Hall. Because of my familiarity with Nazrul Islam's works, I knew that Habibullah Bahar and Shamsunnahar were siblings about whom Nazrul wrote:

> Who's the best among you two?
> Bahar gets the finest flowers, Nahar the lights.

That was about it.

Rokeya Hall was next to the Shamsunnahar Hall. There would be a *milad mehfil* every year on 9 December, Rokeya's death anniversary. Women would wash their hands as part of the *wazu* ritual, put on a veil and participate in the service. The *milad* over, we would peep to see the maulana in a long beard and loose priest's robe, praying so that Rokeya's soul rests in peace. At precisely the same time, outside the academic institutions, the women's organizations in Dhaka had taken the veil off Rokeya and exposed her to the outside world. This was the mid-1980s. By that time already a few books had been published on Rokeya and *Abarodh-Bashini* had been translated into English. Gradually, a lot of posters were produced, quoting lines from Rokeya's radical writings. In 1988, General Ershad, who was the head of the armed forces, declared Islam the state religion of Bangladesh. Women, armed with posters and banners displaying images and words of Rokeya, took to the streets to protest. Rokeya supplied the words of resistance against the institutionalization of religion.

While the halo around Begum Rokeya grew brighter with each passing day, her contemporaries and juniors, with the exception of Sufia Kamal, remained in the shadows. True, Rokeya had ushered in a new era and steered it single-handedly. But there were other women assisting her on the journey who also rowed against the tide with her, trying their utmost to reach the other shore. Mrs. M. Rahman was one of the notable women writers who wrote in support of Rokeya. She elaborated on Rokeya's themes in her own style, thereby giving the latter's thesis an easy navigability. The repetition of Rokeya's ideas in the writings of her followers helped greatly to convince the reader. Quite a few writers included in the *Women in Concert*, like M. Fatema Khanam, taught at the Sakhawat Memorial School, Shamsunnahar Mahmud and Sufia Kamal worked in the organization, Anjuman-e-Khawatin-e-Islam—both founded by Rokeya—even after Rokeya's death and till the time of the Partition. While Rokeya was put on a pedestal and her fame has been thriving in Bangladesh, it would not be out of place to mention the women writers and activists who followed her in the same breath.

After Pakistan was created in 1947, there was a lot of enthusiasm towards recording the life stories of the Muslim litterateurs of the past and collecting their works. The only woman writer to have emerged out of that search was the eighteenth-century poet Rahimunnesa. Similarly, only four writers included in *Women in Concert* are featured in the biography series brought out by the government-run Bangla Academy, as against the biographies of 220 male writer-intellectuals published by them.

The four women writers are: Nurunnesa Khatun Vidyavinodini, M. Fatema Khanam, Shamsunnahar Mahmud and Mahmuda Khatun Siddiqua. There is no point lamenting the fact that Rokeya or Sufia were not included; their biographies are not difficult to come by. However, the rest of the writers in the book were not included in the Bangla Academy project which ran from 1986 till 1996. It is hard to say if they ever would be, the reason being that it is difficult to collect enough material on these writers for a biography. It does not look as if the project has the wherewithal—monetarily and in terms of preparation for research—to handle the work.

Fazilatunnesa's story, however, is different. She died in Dhaka in 1975. She did her undergraduate degree at Eden College, and took her MA degree from Dhaka University. Later, she became the principal of Eden College. Therefore there is no dearth of information on her life for prospective biographers. She was, besides, the first Muslim girl student at Dhaka University. She was placed first and got a first class in Applied Mathematics in 1927, a rare achievement for an Indian woman. She was pelted with stones on her way to the Dhaka University for not wearing a burqa. She went to England for higher studies. Isn't it rather strange that a woman who created so many milestones was left out of the Bangla Academy biography series?

Looking at the few biographies published as a part of the project, it seems the biographers spent considerable effort trying to ascertain how 'good' a woman these writers were. The same 'good' qualities have been attributed to each of them, turning the writers into clones of each other, in terms of behaviour, style and character. It is difficult to decipher what sort of people these writers were in real life. Fazilatunnesa's life certainly does not fit this pattern. She does not fit these slots—that of the ideal Muslim woman or the ideal Indian/Bengali woman. Rather than record the true story of her reckless and unconventional life, our biographers and publishers would prefer to consign Fazilatunnesa to the waves of oblivion.

4

Of all known Bengali Muslim women writers prior to Begum Rokeya, Rahimunnesa, who wrote in the eighteenth century, came first. Dr. Mohammad Enamul Haque discovered the manuscript of her poems in 1955, almost 150 years after it was written. He wrote, 'This discovery gives us a lot of hope that in this time of awakening, if the future researchers of Bengali literature went looking for ancient manuscripts in the ever-neglected huts in rural areas, they would find at least a few manuscripts written by Muslim women poets, if not more.' Twenty-two years later, in 1977, another manuscript, written by the poet Rahima of Chittagong, was discovered. In 1986 quite a few manuscripts penned by Zamirunnesa were collected from Chittagong. Collectors and researchers believe that Rahima and Zamirunnesa wrote in the first half of the nineteenth century. As they wrote outside the periphery of the reform movement, their writings did not come within sniffing distance of the printing press.

Taherunnesa comes next. She published a piece entitled '*Bamagoner Rachana*' (Writing by Women) in *Bamabodhini Patrika* in 1856. Taherunnesa is counted as the first Bengali Muslim woman writer of modern prose. There is not much information on her except that she studied in Boda School for Girls. Next in line is Nawab Faizunnesa (1834-1907). She was the zamindar of Hosnabad in Comilla, renowned for her dedication to social welfare, including founding schools for girls. She wrote a huge autobiographical work, *Rupjalal,* part poetry and part prose. There were stories within stories, on the lines of the *Arabian Nights.* The first edition of the book was published in Dhaka in 1876. She produced two books of poems—*Sangeet Saar* and *Sangeet Lahari*. Her fourth book, *Tattva O Jatiya Sangeet* (Theory and the National Songs), was published in 1887.

Chhahifa Banu (1850-1926) of Sylhet was a well-known composer of baul songs, gazals and narrative tales. Her book,

Chhahifa Sangeet (Songs of Chhahifa) was published in Sylhet in 1907, by Abdul Jabbar of Srihatta (Sylhet). She wrote three more books, including *Chhahebaner Jaari* and the Urdu *Yaadgaar-e Chhahifa.* The diary of Majeda Bibi Kulsum (1861?-1909), a writer who followed Chhahifa Banu, was discovered a few years back. In it she has expressed outrage at the many unwarranted developments in her conjugal and family life. Latifunnesa, who wrote towards the end of the nineteenth century, published the poem *'Bangiya Musalman Lekhikader Prati'* (To the Bengali Muslim Women Writers) in *Bamabodhini Patrika* in 1897. Next came Azizannesa. Her poem, '*Hamd Orthat Ishwar Stuti*' (In Praise of God) was published in the magazine *Islam Pracharak* in 1902. Azizannesa is counted as the first Muslim woman writer to have published in a Muslim-run publication.

There is a tradition of beginning any discussion or reading of women's literature with the nineteenth century or the modern age. *Women in Concert* spans the first four decades of the twentieth century but falls in line with the earlier tradition, maintaining a chronological order from Rokeya to Sufia Kamal. Most writers of this anthology, it goes without saying, came from rich and elitie families, were educated at home or in schools and colleges, imbibed modern sensibilities and were published in the papers of the time. Besides them there must have been other women, maybe not in great numbers, whose stories of protest and struggle and unpublished writings have remained outside the scope of *Women in Concert*, as only published and discussed women writers belonging to a particular time frame (1904-1938) were considered for this book. We hope the readers remember this while reading the book. We would like them to appreciate the efforts of these women, writing in the early days of the twentieth century—the writers who broke years of silence to write about women's education, employment, seclusion or marriage and broadened the horizons of the reform movement so that women could have an easier passage in the future. The joy of writing, the emotions involved, the grievances felt and protests registered are all present in this book.

Finally I would like to pay my respects to a man I have known—a man who lived long and in spite of being a man helped some of the women in *Women in Contert* to flower, nurturing their works with extraordinary affection and extreme tenderness even after they were dead. This gentleman was the *Saugat* editor Mohammad Nasiruddin.

May 2008, Dhaka

Translated by Chitralekha Basu

[1] Battala (north of Rabindra Sarani and Beadon Street) was the cultural hub of Calcutta in the mid-nineteenth century and had a vibrant publishing industry. Bengali religious texts, both Hindu and Islamic, illustrated with the striking wood-cut sketches—a fusion of biting satire and unrefined naiveté—were printed here, as were sketches, satires and fiction. The Bengali almanac or the *panjika,* often full of kitschy stories and illustrations, were bestsellers. Later, the term 'Battala' came to connote fringe publishing activity, covering the genres of thriller, crime, scandals and chapbooks – thin volumes, printed on cheap paper, with crude illustrations, written by authors with sleazy names, often adopted ones.

Bibliography

Akhtar, Shaheen, *Sati O Swatantara: Bangla Sahitye Nari*, 3 vols, Dhaka: Dibya Prakash and Water Lily, 2007

Anisuzzaman, *Muslim Manosh O Bangla Sahitya,* Dhaka: Papyrus, 2001.

Bandyopadhyay, Asit Kumar, *Bangla Sahityer Sampurna Itibritto,* Kolkata: Modern Book Agency, 1966.

Banu, Chhahifa, *Chhahifa Sangeet,* published by Abdul Jabbar of Srihatta (Sylhet), Saudagartula; printed by Muhammad Abdul Gani in Islamia

Press, Srihatta Bandarbazaar, 1907 (BS 1314).

Begum, Maleka, *Banglar Nari Andolan*, Dhaka: University Press, 1989.

Chaudhurani, Faizunnessa, *Rupjalal,* Dhaka: Girish Jantra, published by Sheikh Munshi Mula, 1876

Forbes, Geraldine, 'The Indian Women's Movement: A Struggle for Women's Rights or National Liberation?' in *The Extended Family: Women and Political Participation in India and Pakistan* edited by Gail Minault, Delhi: Chanakya, Delhi, 1981: 49-82.

Hai, Abdul Muhammad, and Syed Ali Ahsan, *Bangla Sahityer Itibritto*, Dhaka: Ahmad Publishing House, 1997.

Haque, Muhammad Enamul, 'Madhyajugiya Bangla Sahityer Ekmatro Muslim Mohila Kobi (Rahimunnesa)', *Bangla Academy Patrika,* 1 (Poush 1956 (BS 1363).

Khan, Shamsujjaman, *Mir Mosharraf Hossein: Natun Tathye Natun Bheshye*, Dhaka:, Abasar, 2004.

Hossein, Yasmin, Prekshapat, in *Zenana Mehfil:Bangali Musalman Lekhikader Nirbachito Rachana 1904-1938,* Kolkata: Stree 1998.

Murshid, Ghulam, 'Taherannesa: Prothom Muslim Gadya Lekhika', *Bangla Academy Gobeshana Patrika,* Magh-Asharh (Jan-June) 1977 (BS 1383-1384).

Nabanoor, Kartick (Nov-Dec) 1904 (BS 1311).

LOOKING BACK AT *ZENANA MEHFIL*

Moushumi Bhowmik

It was around 1994 that we started to discuss the idea of doing an anthology of the early writings in Bengali by Muslim women. We, co-editors of this volume, lived then as we do now on two sides of the West Bengal-Bangladesh border—Shaheen Akhtar in Dhaka and I, in Kolkata. Interestingly, we wanted to work on this collection of women's writings from a time when India had not been partitioned and hence Bengal was not divided. So, while our authors belonged to one nation, we belonged to two; our personal histories of struggle and achievement had been different, like the immediate history of our nations. Yet, the time to which our authors of *Women in Concert* (Bengali original edition, *Zenana Mehfil*) belonged was also our shared history and their writings our common inheritance. Besides, there were things in our current lives which connected us to this past; we shared many interests and concerns, especially for women, as women.

One of our main concerns at the time was the silence and invisibility of women in mainstream literary representation. Of course, there were different classes and communities of women and not everyone's situation was the same. Who was more silent and invisible where and who was less so, depended on the location and orientation of the listener/viewer. In my Introduction to the Bengali edition of *Zenana Mehfil*, I had written: 'a Hindu girl in West Bengal can grow up without having any contact at all with the Muslim community'; I was writing about my personal experience and was troubled by it. I worked then as the in-house editor of Stree and had to refer to anthologies like Susie Tharu and K. Lalitha's *Women Writing in India* and Ghulam Murshid's research on the early writings of Bengali women;[1] later we published Sambuddha Chakrabarti's *Andare Antare: The Bengali Bhadramahila in the Nineteenth Century* (Stree 1995).[2] What struck me as odd was the fact that the only Bengali Muslim woman who seemed to feature in these works with any consistency was Begum Rokeya Sakhawat Hossain. I felt the 'incompleteness' of these books, which is why I went on to pose this question in my Introduction: 'Were there no other Muslim women around Rokeya's time or before and after her who were also writing, just as there were other women writers in the days of [the Hindu] Rasasundari Devi [autobiography *Amar Jiban,* published in 1876] and [Brahmo] Swarnakumari Devi [1857-1932]?'

There were, indeed. My co-editor, Shaheen Akhtar had had glimpses into some of their works and lives while growing up in post-1971 Bangladesh. But she too was concerned with the incompleteness of what they had been told and taught and could guess at how much remained undiscovered and unacknowledged.

Thus we began to work on this anthology, keeping Begum Rokeya at the centre of our pursuit. We chose the date 1904 to start the anthology, because this was the year of publication of Rokeya's first article in *Nabanoor*.

1904-1932

We see Begum Rokeya as the beginning of an era in this book. The theme and style of her writings were so sharp and exceptional that they stirred up the entire Bengali Muslim world, including its inner quarters. Almost everyone included in this anthology was touched in one way or the other by Rokeya's brilliance. This is not to deny each individual author her uniqueness, yet it is also true that there are people who live in a certain time and leave their indelible mark on everything and everyone belonging to that time—either directly or indirectly. Rokeya was such a person.

Rokeya Sakhawat Hossain's *Amader Abanati (Our Degradation)*, her first published article, was included in 1905 in the collection of *Motichur*. She had renamed the piece *Streejatir Abanati* or *The Degradation of Women*, taking out five paragraphs from the earlier version. She was writing her last essay on the night before she died in 1932 but could not finish it. The piece was a critique of the exclusive right of the man in Islam, to pronounce the *talaq* or divorce: 'According to our religion, a marriage is solemnised with the consent of both the bride and the groom. God forbid, but if *talaq* or divorce must occur, should it not also be the prerogative of both husband and wife? Why does religion grant this right only to the man?'

In many of the writings included in this volume the authors criticize the mullahs (Muslim clergy) in the severest of language; they speak out against the rules of seclusion that are imposed on women. Yet many of the women also write in support of purdah or the veil, arguing that that is how they are meant to appear in public as Muslim women. They also write that Islam gives the woman many rights, but society does not allow her to enjoy them. The women in this volume write as women, mainly about being women; about the difficulties they face as women on the one hand and about their dreams and desires on the other. They write about learning to read and write and about the act of writing itself, about going out into the world to do the good deeds and supporting the big causes; about making good homes as good wives and mothers; also about love and longing. They seem to be part of a mission, at the core of which are questions of women's education and emancipation, social and religious reforms, nationalism and language and identity; this is a mission that is based in Muslim Bengal.

In the first four decades of the twentieth century Bengali Muslim women stepped out of the confines of home to participate in education and literary activities and also work for economic independence and social change. Well, it is not as though the Bengali Muslim woman had never before left home or worked for a living, because amongst the poor girls and women have always laboured outside their homes, where rules of seclusion and purdah were not necessarily in force. But that is not so much a question of the woman enjoying her rights; more of necessity. From Rokeya's time onwards the Bengali Muslim woman's rights and status began to be debated with a compulsion unknown in the past.

Our anthology ends with the publication of Sufia Kamal's first book of poems in 1938. Her first collection of short stories had been published the year before, in 1937, which was also the year of the publication of Rokeya's biography, written by her student and disciple, Shamsunnahar Mahmud. It was Shamsunnahar's tribute to the woman who had made it possible for her to come so far. A date is not really what matters, be it 1937 or 1938. Actually, by the end of the 1930s, Bengali Muslim women who had dared to be different were paving the way for others to join in the modernization process. In a limited sense Rokeya's dream was beginning to come alive. Shamsunnahar wrote in her biography of Begum Rokeya: 'Very often when I met Rokeya she would complain, "Why have you left your B.A. exams incomplete?"' Shamsunnahar says no one could have been happier than Rokeya on the day the results were out.

Rokeya had nicknamed Sufia Kamal 'Phoolkobi' or poet of flowers. She would say to her, it is not enough to write poems, you have to work for the good of the people too. In this anthology we have tried to see Sufia Kamal as the last representative of the Rokeya era. By the end of the 1930s, she had matured as a writer and a social worker. She no longer followed strict seclusion and alongside writing poetry, she was now also involved in women's organizational work. Moreover, the newly emerging urban middle class amongst Bengali Muslims was finding a voice in Sufia Kamal's short stories.

In 1939 Lady Brabourne College was founded in Kolkata 'mainly—but not exclusively—for Muslim girls. . . This gave institutional form to the struggle for women's educational rights,' says the historian Sonia Nishat Amin.[3] The founding of this college can be seen as a major achievement of the Rokeya era, because women's education was on the top of its agenda. In an interview, Hamida Khanam, former principal of the College of Home Economics in Dhaka, who also taught in Lady Brabourne College in 1945, said: 'Compared to our times, in the 1940s there were many more Bengali Muslim girls coming to college. Those who were staying in the hostel were not from Kolkata; they came from all over Bengal. Fazlul Huq had established Brabourne for the education of Bengali Muslim girls.'[4]

The fact that Muslim girls were coming out of seclusion and increasingly going to schools and colleges, some even entering different urban professions and politics too—these were undoubtedly signs of achievement for the first four decades of the twentieth century. Then came issues which were to change the social and political life of Bengal entirely: the Famine of 1943, impending Partition and increasing Hindu-Muslim conflicts. Interestingly, we do not hear the post-1940s woman's voice specifically addressing these issues as it had questions of seclusion or women's education. Could she not perceive how these changes would affect her life too? Or was it not necessary for the woman to concern herself with such matters?

Time for Transformations

Women in Concert is a weaving together of the writings of some rather extraordinary women, who lived in an extraordinary time of historical transformations in Bengal, and took part—sometimes consciously, but usually unconsciously—in these processes of transformation. Within the next few decades the land of Bengal and its people would get divided on religious and economic lines—class—resulting in the formation of two separate nations. Looking back, it seems now that everything then was actually moving in the direction of the break-up.

There are identity questions that the authors in *Women in Concert* are trying to deal with: what is it to be a Bengali Muslim woman? Should she wear the veil or discard it? Should a woman go out of the house? If so, to what extent should she do this? What is the point of education; should a woman go out into the outside world for education or should she wait till such time comes when separate arrangements will be made for her higher studies? There were pulls both ways—between the home and the outside world—which, typically, women always have to face, in all places and times. The *Saugat* editor, Mohammad Nasiruddin, had visually described Sufia Kamal's vacillation over the veil in the interview included in this anthology:

> 'Then one day, a young lady behind a velvety veil arrived with the aforementioned male relative at the *Saugat* office. Lifting her veil, the lady said, "I am Sufia. You have created havoc in my home by publishing my poem!"
>
> 'I said, "What does your husband say?"
>
> '"I have come at his insistence. He asked me to write more, and

> told me to do whatever you [Mohammad Nasiruddin] say. My husband says that he does not have any opinion about it."
>
> 'I said, "It is good that you have come. But I have an objection to something. Poets have a different style, they never wear a burqa. You are writing poems. You will become a poet. You will meet Rabindranath and Saratchandra. There are so many things that you have to do. Burqa does not suit you." She took off the burqa and gave it to her male relative. "What can I do, I have to abide by family norms. I, however, dislike burqas."
>
> 'After that she would frequently visit the *Saugat* office. She took off the burqa once she reached the second floor. Gradually, Sufia completely discarded her burqa, when her husband gave the nod. Sufia was the first poet who could break the walls of the zenana and the burqa and come to the *Saugat* office.'[5]

Women in Concert is by no means an attempt to present a 'complete' history of the Bengali Muslim woman's encounters with 'modernity' in the early decades of the twentieth century, as some reviewers of our Bengali edition have unfortunately thought, criticizing that this book ends up presenting an incomplete, even false picture of the Bengali Muslim woman's world and her struggles.[6] Indeed, there is neither one kind of Bengali Muslim woman, nor is 'modernity' a fixed category by which we can measure 'progress'. Besides, what book can claim to be a complete study on any subject? Indeed, the women in this book are confined to their own class and class interests, for them 'modernity', woman's empowerment through education, even employment, discarding the veil and such issues had a meaning that would probably be quite pointless in another social and economic context. This book merely shows slides of the small picture, but in so doing also conjures up a bigger picture of the time to which our authors belonged.

It was important for us as editors to focus on the micro—to see the writers as individuals, in the context of their everyday lives and environment. We tried to find family members and others who knew our authors and/or the time in which they lived. In studying the authors' works, we also included their private correspondence, which revealed things about them that their essays and stories and poems could not. These were women with grand public ambitions and intensely private griefs and longings. Begum Rokeya herself is an example of this: she had her dream of a successful school on one level while deep inside she wept for her lost niece Nuri. In Part II, Conversations, Syed Mustafa Siraj remembers his mother: 'When Ma [poet Anwara Begum] died, she was still very young; twenty-five or twenty-six maybe. I remember seeing her practise her handwriting. She wrote the letters round and neat, with a reed pen. She wrote things about me, called me her bird, "*Bharatpakhi*". Today my little bird did this; today he did that, she wrote; as though she were writing her diary.' So here was a woman who did not live long (why did so many of our authors die so young?); here was a young mother and her world of play with her child; here was someone who desired to read and write, a *woman* artiste, for she wrote as a woman, about her own world.

Looking Back: Time Upon Time

From the publication of the Bengali *Zenana Mehfil* to that of its translation, *Women in Concert*, much time has passed and major events have shaken the world, at the centre of which lie questions about Islam and women. Those events also affected our personal lives. Today, looking at *Women in Concert*, I feel more like its reader than editor, reading the book from the outside, trying to understand its importance in today's terms.

There is a complex layering of many different times in this book. First, there was that time when Begum Rokeya Sakhawat Hossain, Mrs. M. Rahman, Akhtar Mahal Syeda Khatun, Fazilatunnesa, M. Fatema Khanam and others wrote their essays, poems, novels, short stories and letters. Second, there was the time that our interviewees, Sufia Kamal, Mohammad Nasiruddin,

Mustafa Siraj, Nurjahan Begum and Hamida Khanam have reminisced about. Third, there was the time, about fifteen years ago, when we first started to work on this collection—thus the imperatives were different from what they are now. Fourth, now, more than ten years since the book was first published, when as editors we are somewhat distanced from the process of creating the book, it is being translated for a new reader. So a new time is getting inscribed on its body. Different times mean different politics of perception.

The book starts with the 'earlier historical moment when "new" women and men were talking about remaking women.'[7] But today when the remade woman is sometimes choosing to be re-remade, opting to move from unveiling to veiling, how do we look at some early writings in Bengali on the Muslim woman's awakening, need for religious reforms in Islam, seclusion/the veil and modernity? The original Bengali *Zenana Mehfil* had not included Begum Rokeya's essay '*Burqa*'. This English edition does. Veiling is such a complex issue—even in Rokeya's times it was difficult for someone as determined as Rokeya to decide what her stand on the question of the veil would be. So we get both the '*Burqa*' and '*Abarodh-Bashini*' (Living in Seclusion) from her; the more strongly anti-seclusion *Abarodh-Bashini* comes later though, in 1927-29. At the same time Rokeya chose to wear the veil to the end of her independent and active life. So, by including the '*Burqa*' in this collection now, *Women in Concert* tries to address the complexities surrounding the Bengali Muslim woman's 'modernization' question. The Muslim women's emancipation and encounters with modernity continue to be complex territories of debate even now.

After September 11, there was a proliferation of images of the veiled and oppressed Muslim woman in Western media, writes anthropologist Lila Abu-Lughod. These images were used to drum up support for the US intervention in Afghanistan. In her essay 'The Muslim Woman: the Power of Images and the Danger of Pity', Abu-Lughod says: 'I would argue that the use of these images has also been bad for us, in the countries of the West where they circulate, because of the deadening effect they have on our capacity to appreciate the complexity and diversity of Muslim women's lives—as human beings.'[8] At this same time, that is post-9/11, there has been a conscious and deliberate move towards some form of veiling among educated Muslim women both in the West and in the Islamic countries, as a political statement of their own separate identity. There is a whole range of reactions to this new veiling. A fourteen-year-old British-Bangladeshi schoolgirl told me during an interview in London in 2007, which I was taking as part of my research on migration, memory and music, that she preferred to wear the hijab because it gave her more confidence.[9] Her twenty-something sister, a Politics graduate of Goldsmiths' College, London, said that although she does not wear the hijab she believes in modest clothing, because that is what a Muslim girl is supposed to wear. She said the sari was not Islamic, although their mother wears it as traditional Bengali women's clothing. This girl said to me that the major problem for them, the Muslim youth, was the conflict between culture and religion. When I asked her if she ever wore a sari, she said, yes, during weddings and other festivals.

Historian Saba Mahmood wrote the following with anthropologist Chris Hirschkind in their essay 'Feminism, the Taliban and the Politics of Counterinsurgency':

> Women's voluntary adoption of what are considered to be patriarchal practices are often explained by feminists in terms of false consciousness, or an internalization of patriarchal social values that forces itself upon those who live within the asphyxiating confines of traditional societies. Even those analyses that demonstrate the workings of women's subversive agency in the enactment of social conventions remain circumscribed within the logic of subordination and insubordination. A Muslim woman can only be one of two things, either uncovered, therefore liberated, or veiled, and thus still, to some degree, subordinate. Can our bras, ties, pants, miniskirts, underwear,

> and bathing suits all be so easily arrayed on one or the other side of this divide? Can our daily activities and life decisions really be captured and understood within this logic of freedom or captivity? We need a way to think about the lives of Muslim women outside this simple opposition. Especially so in moments of crisis, such as today. . .[10]

This point of the need to go beyond the 'simple opposition' is also raised by Bangladeshi women's studies scholar Papreen Nahar. In a private correspondence with the artist Dhali Al-Mamoon, Nahar wrote,

> It is not easy to be either for or against the veil. However, I feel that the Muslim feminist position that upholds the veil is more concerned with the Muslim woman's identity and less with the question of her rights. In Bangladesh, such a movement that talks of women's freedom enacted within the boundaries of Islamic tradition was started over a hundred years ago by Begum Rokeya. It does not make sense to me any longer to say that Muslim women can do whatever they like while maintaining the purdah; I feel that it is a regression of sorts. And an appeasement of Islamic fundamentalist forces. At the same time I think that what happened in the French schools was wrong. Europe claims to believe in democracy. To discuss other people's clothing is for them a transgression of one's privacy. So, just as there can be no objection if someone rides a bus in a bikini, by the same logic you cannot stop a teacher in hijab from going into her classroom.[11]

To me *Zenana Mehfil* made into *Women in Concert* is no longer just a collection of essays, stories, letters, memoirs and critical analyses. While on the one hand it reflects on the 'complexity and diversity of the Muslim woman's life—as human beings', it also generates a body of criticism, which is very much a result of the politics and priorities of the time when it is being read. Sometimes the question of identity might seem more important that other questions of rights, sometimes the need to break away from tradition might seem more crucial. In the end, however, it is a string of little pictures that this anthology presents; stories of personal struggles and achievements from which we can draw inspiration. The processes of examination and analyses will keep changing of course; as more wars are fought and more acute polarizations take place in this world, the writings in this book will be read differently. What is important is that there still seems to be a point in reading them.

29 May 2008, Kolkata

Notes

1 Susie Tharu, and K .Lalitha, eds., *Women Writing in India: 600 B.C. to the Present* (2 vols.) (Delhi: Oxford University Press, 1991; 1993); Ghulam Murshid, *Sankocher Biwbhalata: Adhunikotar Abhighate Banglaramanir Pratikriya* (Dhaka: Bangla Academy, 1985); and *Rasasundari Theke Rokeya: Nari Pragatir Eksho Bachhar* (Dhaka: Bangla Academy, 1993).

2 Sambuddha, Chakrabarti, *Andare Antare: Unish Shatake Bangali Bhadromahila* (Kolkata: Stree, 1995). In this research on Bengali Hindu and Brahmo society in the nineteenth century, the author uses women's writings—poetry, essays, stories, songs, memoirs—to show that the agenda for social reform at that time was designed to reinforce an existing patriarchal framework.

3 Sonia Nishat Amin, *The World of Muslim Women in Colonial Bengal, 1876-1939* (Leiden: E.J.Brill, 1996), p.xiii.

4 See this volume, p 368.

5 See this anthology, pp 339-40.

6 Farida Akhtar, '*Banglar Narir Itihas: Rachanar Paddhati O Drishtibhongir Samasya*', Dhaka: *Bhorer Kagoj*, 11 September 1998. This article is a discussion on Bengali/Bangladeshi Muslim women's history of struggles and achievements that *Zenana Mehfil* had triggered off.

7 Lila Abu-Lughod, ed., 'Introduction' in *Remaking Women: Feminism and*

Modernity in the Middle-East (Princeton: Princeton University Press, 1998), p.4.

8 Lila Abu-Lughod, *The Muslim Woman: The Power of Images and the Danger of Pity,* published in *Eurozine:* network of European Cultural Journals, www.eurozine.com, 2006.

9 My research of the past six years has been on folk music, I on the theme of separation as it finds expression the folk repertoire of Bengal, for which reason I took a part of my work to the East End of London where a significant Bangladeshi community lives. This chapter of my research is titled 'Migration, Memory and Music', an ongoing project in audio documentation and the recordings of songs and interviews, including the one I am referring to here, which will be archived at the British Library's World and Traditional Music section. The younger sister is called Nazia Alom and the older sister, Nieema Alom.

10 Mahmood, Saba and Chris Hirschkind, 'Feminism, the Taliban and the Politics of Counterinsurgency' in University of Chicago Library Digital Collections, 2002, http://fathom.lib.uchicago.edu/1/777777190136/

11 I have been discussing the question of the veil and visible changes in the representation of women in contemporary Bangladesh with practising artist and teacher Dhali Al-Mamoon. It is in this context that Mamoon has shared with me his correspondence with Papreen Nahar of the department of Women's Studies, Dhaka University. I am grateful to Mamoon and Nahar for allowing me to use their e-mail correspondence of 20 May 2008 in this article.

List of Translators

Barnita Bagchi is Associate Professor in Human Sciences, Institute of Development Studies Kolkata.

Chitralekha Basu is an editor, creative writer, literary and film critic who contributes to *The Independent* and the *Times Literary Supplement*.

Sipra Bhattacharya is an independent translator, whose most recent translation was *A Prattler's Tale: Bengal, Marxism, Governance* by Ashok Mitra (Samya, 2007).

Anusuya Ghosh is Lecturer in English, St. Paul's Cathedral Mission College, Kolkata.

Nandini Guha is Reader at the College of Vocational Studies, University of Delhi. She received the Katha 2003 Award for translation from Bangla to English.

Adrita Mukherjee is a writer, and is based in New Zealand; she was formerly lecturer in English at Rabindra Bharati University, Lady Brabourne College and Visva-Bharati.

Rukmini Sen is Lecturer at the West Bengal National University of Juridical Sciences, Kolkata, teaching Sociology, Disability and Law, Law and Social Change.

The Bengali Calendar and Place Names

During the reign of the Mughal Emperor Akbar, the scholar Fatehullah Shirazi formulated the Bengali year on the basis of the lunar Hijri and the solar Bengali calendars. The new calendar was introduced in 1584 but was dated from Akbar's accession to the throne in 1556. The Bengali months are as follows:

Baisakh (mid-April to mid-May)
Jaishtha (mid-May to mid-June)
Asharh (mid-June to mid-July)
Sraban (mid-July to mid-August)
Bhadra (mid-August to mid-September)
Ashwin (mid-September to mid-October)
Kartik (mid-October to mid-November)
Agrahayan (mid-November to mid-December)
Paush (mid-December to mid-January)
Magh (mid-January to mid-February)
Phalgun (mid-February to mid-March)
Chaitra (mid-March to mid-April)

Place names in the authors' writings have been left as used in their times, for example, Dacca or Jessore. In the annotation provided by the editors, the usage post - 1971 has been retained: thus Dhaka, Joshor.

Part I

Women's Writings

1

Begum Rokeya Sakhawat Hossain (1880-1932): Feminism and Realism

Translated by Barnita Bagchi

In 1937, five years after Begum Rokeya's death, the writer and critic Mohitlal Majumdar read her biography and wrote:

> It's curious that the racial pride [that makes the Bengali race see themselves as a unified whole] should be embodied in a woman—that the spirit, conscience and intelligence of Bengali Muslim society should have expressed themselves in a female icon. In these times, such a woman is rare, even in Hindu society. But I, a Hindu, am not in the least ashamed about it, since Begum Rokeya is not just a Muslim woman. Having read her biography, I firmly believe that she was a Bengali woman in the truest sense.[1]

Mohitlal's idea of Rokeya, formed on the basis of reading her biography, were as follows: *(i)* she personified the spirit, conscience, and intelligence of Bengali Muslim society; *(ii)* she was more advanced than contemporary Hindu women; *(iii)* she was a true Bengali. Rokeya Sakhawat was both a writer and social worker. Her writing, establishing a school and running a women's organization were linked to one another. She plunged into a vast array of activities, with a view to achieving a definite goal—women's liberation.

In this anthology, we have been unable to deal exhaustively with the range and variety of Rokeya's life and works. Since the book deals with Bengali Muslim women's writing, primarily about women, in the first four decades of the twentieth century, the choice of articles is restricted to those which show why Rokeya Sakhawat Hossain was considered to have paved the way for women's liberation at the beginning of the twentieth century. In other words, we are concerned with the Rokeya whose writings on women's liberation transcend her own times. Based on the responses and evaluation made by readers and researchers who were her contemporaries or came later, we will try to present a brief account of Begum Rokeya.

Rokeya Sakhawat was born in 1880 in a family of zamindars, in Pairaband village, Rangpur district, now in Bangladesh. Her father's name was Zahir Mohammad Abu Ali Saber. He was against the education of women, especially women learning Bengali. The reason for this orthodox stance supposedly had to do with societal impositions at the time. Rokeya's elder sister Karimunnesa and elder brother Ibrahim Saber helped her to learn Bengali and English. She also knew Arabic, Persian, and Urdu. Brought up in strict seclusion, she never had the chance to be educated formally. Around the age of sixteen, Rokeya was married to Syed Sakhawat Hossain, a widower living in Bihar. He was a deputy magistrate who died on May 3, 1909. Rokeya died on December 9, 1932, at the age of fifty-three.

Even men who were in favour of women's awakening did not know how to react when they read Rokeya's essays. In 1905, after *Motichur* was published, Munshi Abdul Karim *Sahitya-Bisharad* and Syed Emdad Ali wrote:

> When the essays in *Motichur* were first published, it was as if our tolerance threshold gave way . . . When this excitement abated to an extent, we read the book again, this time taking a slightly more favourable idea about *Motichur* . . . Although not all, much of what the writer says is unalloyed truth and *Motichur* is, indeed, what its name suggests [a sweet made of grain flour beads that look like ground gems].

In that review, the two writers went on to write, 'It is one thing to reform society, quite another to keep attacking it indiscriminately. Whipping might leave scars on the social fabric, and it does not help to make up for a loss or lack in society. The writer of *Motichur* has been continuously hitting at society, and we cannot hope that any good will come of it.'[2]

Notably, most of Rokeya's writings 'hitting at society' were published in *Nabanoor*, edited by Syed Emdad Ali, one of the two critics just mentioned. Moreover, following the publication of *'Aamader Abanati'* (Our Degradation) in *Nabanoor*, in the issue dated Bhadra 1904,[3] letters of protest continued to be printed in the editions brought out in Ashwin and Kartik. The protests said: 'Women can never be equal to men in all respects—that would be going against nature.'[4] In another article, Nausher Ali Khan Yusufji wrote, 'Women readers! Do you really consider yourselves slaves? . . . Are the jewels [that you wear] really badges of your slavery? . . . Will true progress not happen unless you tear your clothes off and appear naked?'[5] Nearly twenty-four years after *'Aamader Abanati'* was published, Rokeya Sakhawat Hossain's *'Abarodh-Bashini'* (The Secluded Ones) was published in different issues of the *Masik Mohammadi* between 1927 and 1929.[6] In the 1930 issue[7] of *Masik Mohammadi*, a certain writer wrote, 'Perhaps the readers would have been more pleased if the writer had not dipped into undesirable stories while condemning the practice of seclusion.'

Rokeya was criticized in several ways for her writings, throughout. Even the 'progressive' men of the time failed to understand the import of her writings. Even if they wanted women's awakening, they perhaps did not want it to the extent that Rokeya did. To them Rokeya was guilty of making transgressions. There are hardly any precedents of cerebral writers ahead of their own times, especially if they are women, being let off without facing a challenge. And neither was Rokeya. Nearly fifty years after her death, Shibnarayan Ray wrote in *Bangalir Atmajijnasa* (The Self-Questioning of Bengalis), 'In her famous book, *Motichur* (vol 1, 1905; vol 2, 1921), she did not merely criticize society, but attacked religious beliefs as well. One does not know of any Hindu women among her contemporaries writing such essays.'[8]

In the first volume of *Motichur*, the title of the essay *'Aamader*

Abanati' was changed to *'Stree Jatir Abanati'* (The Degradation of Women). Five important paragraphs from the original essay were omitted.

For many years before and after her husband's death, Rokeya did not write anything. Ghulam Murshid commented in his essay, *'Pratham Naribadi Begum Rokeya'* (Rokeya: The First Feminist), when Rokeya started writing again in 1918, 'the volcanic heat' in her writing had died down, 'only the genuine enterprise of bringing about women's awakening was left.'[9] Abdul Qadir, the editor of *Begum Rokeya Rachanavali* (The Collected Works of Begum Rokeya) published by the Bangla Akademi of Dhaka, writes, 'I often like to think that it was the encouragement of the refined and calm Syed Sakhawat Hossain that inspired Rokeya to write *'Aamader Abanati'* and 'Sultana's Dream', and the reason why her sharp pen did not produce more such freethinking, fearless and stimulating writing was because of the absence of a congenial atmosphere.'[10]

Essays, written in two phases of Rokeya's life, are included in a compact form in this book, besides a few letters written by her to different people at various times. It is only in her letters that one is able to grasp Rokeya's sense of loneliness, grief, and the problems and difficulties that she had to face. Notably, Rokeya Sakhawat became a widow at just twenty-nine, and from then onwards she fought on alone. On the one hand, she was evicted from her husband's home in Bhagalpur because of a conspiracy hatched by her stepdaughter and son-in-law. On the other, running the Sakhawat Memorial School entailed a lifetime of struggle, waged entirely on her own. Running the school meant backbreaking work. It also meant having to make compromises in the way she lived. She spent her entire life behind a veil of sorts. In the memoirs of Mohammad Nasiruddin, the editor of *Saugat*, one finds that she did not meet men who were not related to her, talking to them from behind the purdah.[11] This was a norm she observed in order to save the Sakhawat Memorial School from the rage of fundamentalists. But she managed to rip across the barrier and be intimate with people in some of her personal letters. Some of these were written between 1912 and 1929, to a Pabna-based senior police inspector, Mohammad Yasin.

Rokeya was childless. She brought Nuri, her sister's daughter, to her place and raised her. Nuri, who went to Sakhawat Memorial, died at the tender age of twelve. In a letter to her cousin Mohsina Rahman (Mona), Rokeya wrote of her pain at having lived an unfulfilled married life and of her childlessness.

Rokeya travelled to various places in undivided India. She would set out during school vacations, whenever she had the chance. To her mountains were like sites of pilgrimage. In the novel *Padmaraag*, Siddiqua meets Latif in Kurseong. In her last years, tired and worn out, Rokeya would often return to Ghatshila, where a house was being built for her to spend the retirement years.

S.A.

The Degradation of Women[12]

Women readers! Have you ever thought about the sorry state you are in? What are we in this civilized twentieth-century world? Nothing but slaves! One hears that the slave trade has been abolished from the world, but are we free of slavery? Why are we still slaves? There are reasons for it.[13]

It is true that no one really knows how things were in antiquity. But one does feel that in the ancient times, when there was no civilization, nor social ties, our condition was not as bad as it is today. For reasons not yet known, as one part of humanity (men) began to gradually progress in various fields, the other (women), because they could not progress to a similar extent, instead of being comrades or companions of men, became their slaves.

Can anyone give reasons for our downfall, the world over? Perhaps the lack of opportunity is the major reason. Women, who did not get adequate opportunities, stopped participating in worldly activities. Men, finding that women were incapable and incompetent, started helping them. Gradually, the more men offered support, the more incompetent women became. Our state could well be compared with the beggars of our country. The more the wealthy philanthropists keep distributing alms for religious reasons the number of lowly beggars seems to increase. Gradually, begging became a part-time occupation for lazy people who are no longer ashamed to accept alms.

Similarly, we do not hesitate to accept charity, having lost our sense of self-respect. Therefore, we have become slaves of laziness, and, in a way, of men. Over time, even our minds have become enslaved.[14] And having acted as slaves for a very long time, we have become accustomed to slavery. In this way our mental faculties—self-reliance or courage—nipped in the bud over and over again for the lack of exercising them, now perhaps do not even germinate. So men find it easy to say, 'The five worst maladies that afflict the female mind are indocility, discontent, slander, jealousy and silliness. Such is the stupidity of her character, that it is incumbent on her, in every particular, to distrust herself and obey her husband.' *(Japan, the Land of the Rising Sun.)*[15]

And then certain people say, 'Exaggeration and lies are the ornaments of the female tongue.' Some say we 'lack intelligence' [*nakes-ul-akl*], while others call us 'unreasonable'.[16] Men begin to hold us in contempt, because of these faults. This is only natural. Take an example. In this country, a son-in-law is much cherished. Even a witch loves her son-in-law! Yet the man who lives with his in-laws after marriage is not loved to the same extent. Therefore, it is only when we lost the ability to distinguish between being free and dependent, progress and regress, that men, having so far been landlords and masters of the house,[17] ultimately started lording over us. Over time, we have begun to be counted as their household pets or a part of their valuable property.

With the coming of civilization and societal bonds, social norms were formulated in a way that pleased the heads of society! This too is natural. 'Might is right.' But now I would like to ask who is responsible for our degradation?

These jewels that we hold so dear are emblems of our slavery. It is true that now these are used in the hope of enhancing beauty; but in the opinion of many respected and distinguished people, jewellery was originally badges of slavery.[18] Prisoners are made to wear manacles of iron on their feet; whereas we (the loved ones) wear manacles of gold or silver—anklets. Their handcuffs are made of iron, while ours are bangles, made of gold or silver! Needless to add, women are made to wear bangles made of iron as well! Perhaps our gem-studded necklaces are made in imitation of dog-collars.[19] Like horses, elephants and various other animals, bound in chains, we too adorn our necks by wearing gold chains, thinking 'we have worn a necklace'. A keeper of cattle pierces the nose of a bullock to make it wear a 'nose-rope'. Similarly, in this country, our husbands put nose-rings on our noses! The nose-ring indicates that the husband is alive. Therefore, as you just saw, sisters, your precious jewels cannot be anything other than badges of slavery. Funnily enough, the more the number of these badges of slavery, the more respected and distinguished the wearer becomes in society!

How eager women are to acquire these jewels! It is as if their happiness and prosperity depend only on these! Women who are poor fulfil their lives of slavery by wearing glass bangles instead of gold and silver handcuffs. The widow, who is not entitled to wearing bangles, is supposedly the most unfortunate person. Custom seems to have tremendous power over human beings! Being accustomed to slavery makes one embrace the badges of slavery as well. Opium may be bitter to taste, but it is the addict's most favourite thing. However destructive alcohol may be, the drunkard would not want to give it up. Similarly, we consider ourselves glorified and swell with pride, wearing the emblems of slavery.

What I just said about jewellery might make some of the sisters I am addressing think that I am working as an agent of the men folk, that is, they might think that it is my strategy to make women despise jewellery so that men can spare themselves from paying the jeweller. But it is not so. I wish to say a few words only for your sake. If blowing one's husband's money is the reason why one wants to buy jewellery, there are several other ways of doing it. Let me suggest a way or two.

Put your gem-studded necklace around the neck of the spoilt pet dog in your house. When you go out for a drive in your carriage, you may put your precious necklace around the neck of the horse drawing it. Your bangles can be used as curtain-rings in your drawing room.[20] These are ideal ways of frittering away the money that would be most prized by the man who goes by the name of your husband. After all, jewellery is meant to display one's wealth. But why sport the badge of slavery on your body? When you make good use of your jewellery in the way I suggest, at first people will call you mad, but you could just ignore them.[21] Was there ever any good work accomplished in this benighted world without someone having to take the pains for it? The great Galileo was put in a lunatic asylum for saying 'the earth moves'. Which honest man has been able to speak his mind in this world without being condemned? So I say do not listen to what society says. In this world, good words or good deeds are not appreciated in the present times.

Indeed, jewels are nothing but badges of slavery. If one sees jewellery as a way of enhancing beauty rather than a badge of slavery, is that any less condemnable? Does not the very attempt to enhance one's beauty reveal that one is insecure? Men think of these tokens as a symbol of defeat. Often, while arguing, they would say, 'If what I say is proved false, I shall wear bangles.' The great poet Sadi, who wanted to inspire men, said, 'Heroes! Try [to be victorious] and do not wear women's garments.' In other words, they find it humiliating to wear our garments.

Now let us take a close look at what this garment in question is—for men's dress and ours are very similar. Does a dhoti at all differ from a sari in terms of length and breadth? In countries where men wear trousers, women wear them too. If we hear of 'ladies' jackets', we also hear of 'gentlemen's jackets'.[22] When one speaks of 'women's garments', one is probably referring to feminine weakness rather than clothes.

Men tend to say that they 'protect us by holding us close to their manly chests, taking the blows on our behalf and guarding us'. They frighten us by saying that we shall not get such love elsewhere in the wide world. This display of love makes us melt. Therefore, it is their charity that is destroying us. They imprison us in the cages of their hearts, depriving us of the ray of knowledge and pure air, thereby pushing us towards a slow death. They also say, 'We will carry the objects of pleasure for them [women] on our heads. Why should they take the pains to do something while we are here?' We thank the school of speakers who say so for their charitable remarks. But brothers! This benighted world is not an imaginary haven created by the poet's happy imagination—it is a complex, devious, hard world. It is the stuff of truth—not poetry:

> Not poetry, nor a novel, it's my life,
> Not a theatre, but my home.

Hence the difficulties! Otherwise, thanks to your blessings, there would be nothing to ask for. The maiden of Bengal, from being 'slender, soft-bodied, weak, trembling with fear,' in keeping with your imaginary descriptions, would acquire an aerial body, vaporize and disappear into the sky very easily.[23] But reality is not so happy. Therefore, this is my request to men: 'Please be charitable enough to not treat us with charity.'

Truly, many things are destroyed because of excessive care. Often the clothes that are packed and left with great care are fodder for termites. As the poet said aptly:

> Why did the light go out?
> I covered it with too much care,
> Wakeful through the nuptial night.
> Hence the light went out.

Therefore one can see that the excessive care shown to us by them [men] is the cause of our ruin. Well-protected as we are, always, from the danger-prone world, we have totally lost courage, faith and strength. We have stopped being self-reliant and become utterly dependent on our husbands. Faced with the dangers that are less than the least, we hide in a corner of our homes and rend the skies with our howling! And who does not know of our respected brothers ridiculing us because of our 'nasal weeping'? And we suffer such ridicule silently. I nearly die with shame and revulsion when I think how terribly cowardly we have become.[24]

We are quite overcome with fear when we see cockroaches or leeches, to say nothing of bears or tigers. Some of us might even faint. A little boy of nine or ten amuses himself by showing a leech trapped in a bottle to the women in the household who get scared. The women, who are weak, scream and run, as the boy laughs and runs behind them, bottle in hand. Have you not seen such a farce? I have—and it makes me want to die of shame. To tell the truth, I thought it was fun at the time of the incident; but now my blood boils at the thought. At whose feet have we sacrificed our bodily strength and fearless spirit? And now we lack the capability to even think about this sorry state of affairs.

I have shown you pictures of cowardice, now I shall show you pictures of physical weakness. We have become such inert, 'senseless material' that we are a little more than decorative objects in their [men's] drawing rooms. Reader! Have you ever seen the inert objects that they call wives or daughters in a rich Bihari Muslim family? Let me show you the image of a *begum saheba,* a daughter-in-law. If one could display her in a well-known museum, that would be the ideal way to show women the respect they deserved.

In a dark room with just two doors—one shut and the other open and therefore (probably for the sake of purdah) shutting out pure air and sun rays—the inert doll you see sitting next to a grand bed on a cot covered with red velvet, adorned with a variety of gold ornaments, lips reddened with betelnut juice, with a complacent expression, is the daughter-in-law of the begum. She is covered with jewellery worth Rs.10,240. I find it necessary to enumerate very clearly which part of the body carried exactly how many *bharis* of gold.[25]

1. On the head (adorning the parting of the hair), half a *seer*[26] (40 bharis)
2. On the ears, more than one *poa*[27] (25 bharis).
3. Round the neck, one and a half seers (120 *tolas*[28])
4. On the tender arms, nearly two seers (150 bharis).
5. Round the waist, nearly three poas (65 bharis).
6. And the weight of exactly three seers (240 bharis) of gold on the feet.

The nose-ring dangling from the begum's nose has a four-inch radius![29] Heavy embroidery made with sequins and pleats of all kinds are weighing down the poor salwar. And the poor wife is exhausted under the weight of the salwar and dupatta.

It is impossible to move carrying a weight of eight seers, so what can the hapless wife do except be an inert object? She always has a headache. The reasons for this are threefold: *(i)* the way her hair is pulled back tight, after putting fine-toothed combs in it; *(ii)* the heavy weight of jewels on her plait and her hair-parting; *(iii)* pieces of ground silver and sequins are glued, covering half her head and her eyebrows are covered with sequins. And on her forehead, stars and moons made of coloured foil are stuck with glue. The body is like an inert lump, the mind even more so.

To live one's life in this way, like an inert mass, is nothing but an ordeal. The begum's health gets utterly ruined for not engaging in any physical labour. Moving from one room to another tires her feet, making them ache. Her hands are totally incapable of doing any work. Indigestion and a lack of appetite are her constant companions. When the body lacks energy, so does the mind. So the minds and brains of these women are always diseased. And everyone knows how painful it is to carry the weight of a life that's forever suffering, given the state of one's health.

What does the picture make one think? What one learns by

thinking about one's own and others' physical condition is like religious instruction in the truest sense. The morals and knowledge that we sometimes gain from birds and animals living in the trees are superior to text-based learning. The knowledge that the great Newton gained from seeing the fall of a custard apple [*sic*] was not to be found in any book at the time. My thoughts about the daughter-in-law enabled me to paint this picture of our social condition. I felt very sorry for her and thought, 'Both this life and the next have been spoilt for this unfortunate woman.' If God does a stock-taking and asks her, 'Have you used your mind, brain, eyes, etc., well?' what will the begum say in reply?

I asked a girl of that house, 'How would you explain your not using your hands and feet to do any labour to Khuda?' She said, 'What you say is correct.' She told me that she does not waste time, engaging in constant movement instead. I told her again, 'Merely moving around is not physical exercise. Run for at least half an hour every day.' There was a roar of laughter at the mention of the word 'run'. I was sorry, however, and thought, 'You misunderstood it completely.' They were not even capable of gaining knowledge about anything. Hopes of our progress, it seems, are remote. God, the redeemer of the fallen, is our last resort.

Just as sunlight does not enter our bedrooms, the light of knowledge, too, cannot enter the chambers of our minds, since there are almost no schools and colleges good enough for us. Men can study as much as they want, but will the treasure-chest of ambrosial knowledge ever be fully open for us? If a great and liberal soul is kind enough to come forward and offer a helping hand, there are a thousand people to create obstacles in the way.

It is not the work of one person to push aside the obstacles raised by a thousand people and move forward. So the flicker of hope, even before it can catch the shine, tends to disappear in the darkness of everlasting hopelessness. Most people are so superstitious about the subject that whenever they hear the words 'women's education', they visualize a spectre in the future called 'the bad effects of women's education' and shudder. Society happily forgives a hundred faults of the uneducated woman, but when it comes to one who is only slightly educated, society magnifies some imagined fault of hers by a hundredfold, and foists the blame on her 'education', even if she is blameless. A hundred voices say in unison, most sarcastically, 'We bow our heads before female education.'

These days most people consider education only as a means of getting employment. It is impossible for women to take up jobs, hence in the eyes of these people female education is completely unnecessary. For hollow argument's sake, a native Christian might suggest that it was the woman's thirst for knowledge that caused the fall of man. This is because in the Book of Genesis one finds Eve, the first mother, ate the fruit of knowledge, for which both she and Adam were expelled from Paradise.[30]

In any case, 'education' does not signify the 'blind imitation' of any race or nation. Education is about developing the God-given knowledge or faculties through practice. It is our duty to make good use of these qualities, and a vice to misuse them. God has given us hands, feet, eyes, ears, a mind and an ability to think. If we strengthen our hands and feet through exercise, do good deeds with our hands, observe carefully with our eyes, listen attentively with our ears, practise analytical thinking by applying reason, that then is true education. I would not say true education is merely about passing examinations. Let me cite an example of the growth and flowering of one's ability to observe.

Where the uneducated eye sees just dust and mud, the scientist's informed eye can see many pleasing and wonderful things. The mud trampled under our feet that we consider no more than a mix of clay, sand, the murk of coal and watery substances and treat with disdain, when analysed by a scientist, will yield the following four substances. By analysing sand one gets opal; sifting mud will yield china clay or sapphire. From coal one gets diamonds and from water, ice! Therefore, Sister, as you can see, where the uneducated eye sees mud, the informed eye sees gems! How will we justify to Khuda the fact that we forever refuse to see?

Suppose you gave your maidservant a broom and told her, 'Go, make sure you keep my house clean.' The servant considered the broom to be a gift from you, wrapped it in a case made of gold lace, very carefully, put it in a high place and never used it! Meanwhile rubbish piled up in your house and it became uninhabitable. Afterwards, when you take account of your servant's work, what would you think seeing the sorry state your house was in? Would you be happy with her use of the broom to keep the house clean, or with her useless reverence to the object?

Our conscience is showing us the state of degradation we are in, most faithfully. Now it is our duty to try for our betterment. We should take the initiative to usher in progress. I have already said, 'God, the redeemer, is our only hope.' But one should remember that God, the redeemer, will not extend His hand, if one did not raise one's own in the first place. God helps those who help themselves. So I say, if we are not concerned about our condition, no one else will. Even if they do, it is not going to achieve a hundred per cent benefit for us.

Many people think that women tolerate the domination of men as they enjoy the wealth earned by men. This is largely true. It is possible that at the outset women, being incapable of physical labour, were compelled to share the wealth of others and therefore had to bow their heads before them. But now that women's minds have been enslaved as well, even in the case of poor women who sew or work as domestic helps to feed their husbands and sons, the incompetent husbands remain their 'lords'. Again, the man who marries an heiress to a huge property, instead of trying to make a living on his own, lords it over his wife too. And the wife does not object to his playing the master;[31] the reason being that since the higher faculties of women's minds were nipped in the bud, they have become 'slaves', internally, outwardly, in mind and heart. Now we have no independence or fire left in us or even a desire to acquire them! This is what I want to say:

We know awakening for the very first time could be difficult. We know that society would be outraged. We know that the Indian Muslims will slap a death sentence on us, and the Hindus will advocate death by fire![32] (And we also know that not too many of our sisters wish to be awakened!) But we need to wake up for the sake of the welfare of society. I have said that no good work can be done easily. Even after he came out of prison, Galileo said, ' . . . but nevertheless it [the earth] does move.' We too shall go through various tortures of that sort for the sake of awakening. Here I am giving the example of Parsi ladies. The following lines are translated from an Urdu newspaper:

> In these fifty years a lot has changed for Parsi women. Earlier, they did not even know the name of that Western civilization which they now practise. Like Muslims, they too lived in purdah (that is, in the inner chambers). They did not have the right to use umbrellas to protect themselves from the heat or rain. When the sun was too scorching, they would use their shoes as a shade! The cars they travelled in would have curtains. They could not talk to their husbands in front of others. But now Parsi women have relinquished the purdah! They ride in cars without curtains, talk to other men. They run their own shops. When, at first, a few gentlemen brought their wives out of purdah, there was a tremendous uproar all around. The white-haired intelligentsia said, 'The destruction of the world is at hand.'

But the world was not destroyed. So I say why don't you all, for once, move forward on the road towards freedom together? In time, all will be accepted. By freedom, I mean that the state of women should improve on a par with that of men.

Now the question may arise, how will the lost jewel be recovered? What must we do to become daughters befitting the stature of our nation? First, we need to have a wish and a strong intent to walk side by side with men in our daily lives. We must also believe that we are not slaves.

We shall do whatever needs to be done in order to be equal to men.[33] If being able to earn one's living makes us free, we shall do that. If necessary, we would work as lady-clerks, lady-magistrates, lady-barristers and lady-judges. Fifty years from now, we shall become lady-viceroys and make all the women of this country queens. Why must we be deprived of earning a living? Do we not have hands, feet, or intelligence? Why can't we put in the labour that we invest in running the households of our 'husband masters' to put up an independent business?[34]

If we cannot enter the world of government work, we shall enter the agricultural fields. Why do we lament the dearth of grooms when there is a daughter to marry off? Educate the daughters well and expose them to the professional fields, let them earn their own living. When it comes to the professional field, a man's labour is valued highly, while that of a woman comes cheap. If a lower class man gets two rupees a month for a certain work, a woman would get only one rupee. A male domestic servant is paid 3 rupees a month while a maidservant gets two rupees. At times, however, a woman might draw a higher salary than men.

If you say that we are weak-limbed, ignorant, unintelligent women, whose fault is that? Ours, of course: we have become dimwitted because we do not exercise our intelligence. Now we shall revitalize our intelligence through exercise. Can we not exercise and strengthen the arm that has been enfeebled by not doing any work? Now let us cultivate knowledge and see whether this dull head can be sharp again.[35]

Finally, let me say that we comprise half of the social body. If we lag behind, how will society rise? If you tie up a person's legs, how far can he limp along? The interests of men and women are not different—they are the same. The aims and goals of men are the same as ours. A child needs his father and mother equally. Be it the spiritual realm or quotidian life, we need qualities to help us walk beside men. At the outset they took rapid strides in the path of progress, while we remained behind. Now having reached the land of progress they find they are lonely without female companions. So now they have turned back, out of necessity. Societies where men are moving forward together with their female companions are reaching the summit of progress. It is our duty that instead of being a dead weight in the households of men we should become their companions, fellow workers, helpmates and so on, and cooperate with them. We have not been created to bear the burden of a good-for-nothing doll's life—that is certain.

I trust that our very able sisters will discuss this. Even if they do not launch a movement, they could think about this a little deeply.

Passages Omitted from the Essay 'Our Degradation'[36]

The major reason why we were never able to stand up against slavery even after reaching the nadir of degradation was perhaps because whenever a sister tried to do so, either religion or the scriptures were used as weapons against her, dealing out a severe blow. Of course, this cannot be stated with certainty, but this is what we surmise. Religious dictates make us embrace what we may not accept easily at first. Such is the sorry state of affairs that nowadays, the moment a girl is born, she is told, 'Down! You were born a slave, and you will remain a slave.' Thus it seems even our soul is enslaved.

When the mother tries to put her baby to sleep forcibly, and the baby, not feeling sleepy, raises her head and looks around, the mother says, 'Go to sleep quickly! There, the bogey is coming to get you!' Even if she is not sleepy, the child lies with closed eyes. So too whenever we raise our heads to do a survey of the past and present, society tells us immediately, 'Go back to sleep—

else, you will land up in hell!' Even if we do not believe that we rarely ever talk about it.

Men have published the books of religion, calling them God's written command, to keep us in the dark. It is not my object to discuss the esoteric truth of any particular religion or a spiritual subject. I shall only discuss the social rules and regulations that are codified in religion, so let those who are religious be reassured. In ancient times, the individual who became illustrious by virtue of his talent, revealed himself to be God or God's prophet, and tried to instruct the uncivilized barbarians. Gradually, as the world's people became more sensible, so did God's prophets (that is, the great men sent by God) and the Gods too became more and more intelligent.

So you see that these books of religion were no more than rules and regulations written by men. If a female sage had framed the rules, they may have been an antithesis of what the male seers wrote. But women did not seem qualified enough to be sages. Anyway, no one can say for certain whether religious scriptures were a gift from God. If God had sent a prophet in order to discipline women, then perhaps that prophet would not have remained confined to Asia. Why did the prophets not go to Europe? Why did God not make his command, 'women must remain subordinate to men', heard in America, the Arctic, and the Antarctic? Is God only the God of Asia? Did he not have dominion over America? The water and wind, which are God's gifts, could be found in all countries. Why then did the prophets not spread out among all nations? Certainly, we should no longer suffer with bowed heads men who lord over us unnecessarily in the name of religion. Moreover, mark the fact that rigid religious bindings lead to greater oppression of women. The proof of this is in the practice of sati.* Where the bonds of religion are loose, the progress of women is almost as good as that of men. Here,

* If a *kulin* Brahmin died, would not more than a hundred wives of his commit sati?

religion means the social regulations imposed by religion.

Someone might ask, 'Why bring in religion while speaking of social matters?' The answer to that is, 'religion' has, at the end of the day, bound us more strongly in chains of slavery. Men now dominate women in the name of religion, which is the reason why I had to bring in 'religion'. Let those who are truly religious forgive me for this.

Nabanoor, 2nd year, no. 5, 216-18.

The Burqa

For this English edition, I have included the essay 'Burqa', written by Rokeya Sakhawat Hossain in 1904.* It provides insights into the politics behind the imaging of Muslim women that is prevalent today, which has retained a continuity with the colonial times. The burqa is invoked to emphasize the barbaric nature of Islam. Interestingly, the view taken here differs considerably from that in *Abarodh-Bashini* and the Sketches where she is much more critical. In her essay, Rokeya challenges this myth propagated by the modernists. 'On many occasions when I meet my highly educated sisters, they advise me to give up the purdah. What is this thing called progress, may I ask? Does it only exist outside the purdah?' On being told that the burqa is too heavy for women she says that compared to the enormous hats worn by English ladies it is much lighter. The central argument of her essay was to ascertain that the system of purdah was not a hindrance to women's liberation. At the same time, she did oppose an artificial purdah as an impediment to women's

* This piece has been translated by Sipra Bhattacharya.

education and development. In certain families young girls never get to meet anybody except their very close female relatives. Given such a situation, from whom would they learn? 'Since this means they do not get to meet a cross-section of women, they remain extremely unaware of the world. It is desirable that more and more women should emerge from seclusion and mix with one another.' Knowledge can only be acquired from outside one's immediate environment. Rokeya recognized the need to dislodge a kind of male orthodoxy developed hundreds of years ago. She argued that the inner world of women must not be disrespected; rather it must be seen as valid, on a par with the men's world outside home. With this idea one may challenge men's monopolistic control over knowledge.

S.A.

The Burqa

I have often heard the opinion that our 'reprehensible' purdah system is apparently the real obstacle to our progress. On many occasions when I meet my highly educated sisters, they advise me to give up purdah. What is this thing called progress, may I ask? Does it only exist outside purdah? If that is so, we should take it that uneducated fisher women, the [low caste] Chamars and the Doms have attained much higher levels of progress than we have!

We believe that there is no real conflict between the purdah system and progress. Higher education is of course necessary for making progress. Some people say that in order to receive higher education, we should give up purdah and present ourselves at the University Hall to write our F.A. and B.A. examinations. Not a bad argument. But why? Is it impossible to set up a separate university for us women, with women examiners? Till such time as these arrangements are made, we can do without an examination-based education.

The practice of seclusion does not exist in the natural human state, but is based on what we make of morality. Animals do not practise seclusion, after all. As human beings became civilized, they adopted many 'unnatural' practices. While it is natural to walk, human beings have developed many modes of transport so that they do not need to walk. It is natural to cross a stream by swimming across it, but man has created many types of sailing vessels. With the help of these, oceans may be crossed easily, even if one does not know how to swim. Similarly, it is 'unnatural' human civilization that created the secluded space (or the inner rooms) meant for women.

The uncivilized tribes of our earth live in a semi-naked state. History tells us that in the past the uncivilized Britons lived in this state. Before that these people would paint their bodies. As they gradually grew civilized, they learnt to wear clothes.

Nowadays, the highly civilized European women and those of the Brahmo Samaj cover their entire bodies except the face when they go out. And Muslim women of other countries use another cloth to cover their face (burqa), thus perfecting the art of covering the body, when they go out of their homes. Even those who don't wear a burqa cover their faces.

Some feel that the burqa is very heavy. Compared with the enormous hats worn by English ladies, our burqa is less burdensome.

By 'purdah' we mean covering the body; not simply seclusion within the four walls of the women's quarters. Surely, not to cover the body properly means rejecting purdah. Those who go out of the house, to the market or elsewhere, properly clad, observe purdah far better than those who expose their bodies in a half-naked state to their servants, even though they are within the seclusion of their homes.

At present, European women have reached the pinnacle of

civilization. Who will accuse them of lack of modesty? No one can enter their bedrooms—even their drawing rooms—without permission. Is this seen as wrong? Certainly not! Indian sisters who have given up the practice of seclusion in imitation of Western civilization, have neither the European concept of privacy, especially in the bedroom, nor do they have our burqa!

It has been said: 'How ridiculous to hide a beautiful body from head to toe with an obnoxious covering like a burqa, creating a frightful effect! Surely, only those who have seen such a sight will readily appreciate how ghastly it is!' and so on. Yes, true. But it is my belief that no lady of a good family would like to attract attention to herself while standing on a railway platform, for instance. Hence, there is no harm in appearing ugly and inviting derision. High-born ladies would consider it wrong to show off their beauty and attract the attention of common bystanders.

English etiquette teaches us that ladies should be dressed simply, and especially when they are walking outside their homes they should not wear anything gaudy or opulent.[37]

While going out to attend functions, or when she is invited to other peoples' houses, a woman usually wears beautiful clothes and jewellery. However, a simple burqa is needed to cover her dress, ornaments and beauty from the gaze of the driver and other attendants as she gets down from the vehicle that has conveyed her. Likewise, a burqa or head-covering is required to keep her away from the public gaze while she is travelling by train.

Occasionally, even European ladies ask me, 'Why don't you give up purdah?' How tiresome this is! Can one really give up seclusion? According to these people, purdah means simply remaining indoors. If only they acknowledged that they too were unable to escape from their own need for privacy (which is the true meaning of purdah!), then they would not speak in this way. Their modesty is not truly preserved by their dress, especially their evening dress, which is truly objectionable. Still, it is superior to the finely spun, almost transparent, sari wound loosely about the body, which is what many of our young ladies wear these days.

Next comes the point of emerging from the secluded interiors: I am at a loss to understand what good this would achieve. On the other hand, it might be noted that even these independent ladies we spoke of have their privacy in their bedrooms!

On the whole, I believe that all the civilized people of the world enforce some form of seclusion. Had this practice not existed, what difference would there be between men and animals? I am thus unable to understand the words of the person who termed this pristine practice as 'reprehensible'.

Civilization creates greater need for privacy. Earlier, letters were simply folded, but nowadays these are placed within envelopes. The peasant does not cover his bowl of rice but we genteel folk place three or four plates of food on a tray and cover the entire tray. Those who are even more refined cover each dish separately. Many more such examples would be found: tables are covered with cloth, beds with bedcovers, pillows with pillow cases, and so on.

Though many of our sisters walk with bare feet, their more enlightened cousins encase their feet in socks and shoes. There are gloves to cover the hands as well. Therefore that there is no conflict between civilization and the practice of purdah.

But the practice of all rites must be within certain limits. The practice of purdah has become a bit too severe in our country. For example, young unmarried girls are made to observe purdah even in the presence of other women. A nine-year-old girl is reluctant to step outside her home in the fear that she might meet the lady next door. And being confined indoors takes a toll on her health. Secondly, this is an impediment to the education of girls. They never get to meet anybody except their very close female relatives. Whom would they learn from in such a case? The severity with which newly married girls are forced to observe purdah is equally objectionable; for the first few months after marriage they are forced to behave like inanimate dolls. Only the person who has actually experienced that enforced period of being blind and mute knows what terrible discomfort one has to endure. A bride of a noble family was forced to endure the painful torment of being stung by a scorpion on her back without raising a murmur. It was only during the ritual bath of the 'chauthi' on the third day that her relatives discovered the wound and sympathized with her. Nowadays, the family elders are often heard eloquently upholding the bride as an exemplary one. Possibly the scorpion's sting was not too poisonous!

Nevertheless, these artificial forms of purdah must be made more moderate. In many families, the ladies only visit the homes of very close relatives. Since this means they do not get to meet a cross-section of women, they remain extremely unaware of the world. It is desirable that more and more women should emerge from seclusion and mix with one another. Men get to know persons from all walks of life and we women should do the same. We should get to know any lady we consider refined and well-mannered—whatever her religion (Jew, Nasara, Butparast or any other).[38] We must give up the prevalent practice of maintaining a distance from people just because they are *ghayer mazhab* (of a different faith). Our religion is not so fragile that it would be destroyed if we communicated with women from other religions—why have such fears?

We will maintain the necessary practices of seclusion while giving up the wrong ones. If necessary we will wear the burqa and go for a stroll in the park, no harm in that. If we go to the hills on grounds of health, the burqa may accompany us. A burqa does not hamper free movement—but to move freely in it requires some practice. However, is there any task at all that can be perfected without practice?

A burqa is usually an unattractive, coarse garment. It must be made finer. Shoes and clothes have improved in quality, so should the burqa. This hapless article has come to this land all the way from distant Arabia—shall we reach the apex of progress simply by banishing it?

Of late, we have become enervated, narrow-minded and cowardly. But this is not because of the practice of seclusion—rather because of the lack of education. Because of this lack, our qualities of head and heart have been reduced and limited. The timidity of the women infects young boys as well. When a five-year old boy sees his mother fainting when she catches sight of an insect, why wouldn't he conclude that the insect must be a truly fearsome creature?

Let me hasten to add that we are not the only ones guilty of fainting on seeing insects crawling and flying about. Even the 'civilized' English ladies are not free from this phobia. In the book *Gulliver's Travels*, we read that when Dr. Gulliver reached the land of Brobdingnag, he hid timidly amidst the fields of grain. However, a Brobdingnagian found him, picked him up and took him home to show his wife the strange creature. Just as English ladies are frightened when they see spiders or other insects, the Brobdingnagian lady too started screaming when she saw Gulliver because to this enormous woman, the tiny Gulliver appeared to be an insect!! So we see that fear of insects is not necessarily destroyed if one gives up the burqa!

To free ourselves from arachnophobia and other such phobia, we require proper education so that our mind becomes cultivated. Unless we receive higher education, society will not achieve progress. As long as we are not equal to our men in the spiritual world, the mere hope of progress is nothing but a mirage. We must cultivate all branches of knowledge.

It is because of our lack of education that we are unfit to be independent. And being unfit, we have lost our independence. We were deprived of education in order to serve the interests of some short-sighted men. But now our brothers with foresight have realized that this situation has harmed them and retarded their progress. So they are now keen to wake up and to awaken us as well. I have said earlier, 'Man and woman together form one unit. Therefore one cannot reach the highest level of progress leaving the other behind.' I say the same thing now, and will repeat it a hundred times if necessary.

Now this is my request to my brothers: instead of blindly wasting money on buying objects like gold and pearl ornaments to deck up their daughters, an effort should be made to use that money for their education, which would indeed be a fitting ornament for them. Reading a book full of wisdom and knowledge brings immense happiness. One would not experience even a hundredth part of that happiness by wearing ten ornaments! Therefore, it is desirable that young women should show an eagerness to acquire the grace of knowledge rather than jewellery to enhance their physical beauty. Of this priceless ornament

Thieves cannot steal it,
Your family cannot take it away.
In giving, it is not reduced.
Knowledge is such treasure, they say.

I may add a few more lines:

Fire cannot burn it,
Water cannot drown,
Eternal and priceless gem
Forever decks your crown.

I repeat, let girls' schools be set up with the money kept aside for ornaments. But it is improbable that my sisters would be eager to exchange books for ornaments. It is unfortunate that my sisters are probably counted as household articles. That is why just as tables are decorated with flowers and windows with curtains, with garlands of flowers and beads, so does the mistress of the house feel it necessary to deck up her daughter-in-law with a load of ornaments. And the men too sometimes jeer at us, calling us 'stands to display gold and silver'. Yet 'thieves do not listen to moral tales!'

The purdah system does not stand as an obstacle in the path of education. We do not have lady teachers. If this deficiency is removed and separate schools and colleges for women are set up, higher education can be acquired despite the purdah. Possibly no Muslim would like to move forward on the path of education if this requires disobeying the necessary rules of purdah.[39]

I hope that my well-educated sisters are convinced that the burqa is not such a bad thing after all.

Nabanoor, 1904.

The Story of Creation[40]

It got quite late at night as we sat chatting. We were speaking of djinns, fairies and ghosts. Some of us had seen a white-bearded djinn reading the namaz, some a fairy dressed in white, and some others a ghost eating fried fish. Miss Nanibala Datta fell asleep, while I sat on a sofa. Zaheda Begum begged me to go to sleep, snuffed out the lamp, and went to her own room. Shirin Begum, instead of going to her room, slept in my bed. The lamp went out, but a candle burnt in one corner. In its light one could see clearly how the room had been done up. I cannot tell if sleep had taken over, but I believe I was awake. After a little while there was a terrible noise, at which Nanibala started and said, 'What was that sound?'

'I don't really know. I had seen a photograph in the newspaper a few days ago, of an amazing incident. Somewhere in Europe an aeroplane had broken down on top of a house, but the man inside had dropped right into the house and onto the bed straight, and without a single injury. Are you sure something like that hasn't happened here? Why don't you open the window and see?'

Mrs. Binapani Ghosh was enjoying the pleasures of deep sleep as she lay in bed. I turned to her and said, 'Wake up and get out of bed quickly!'

Before I could finish, she sat up with a start and asked, 'What's wrong?'

I repeated what I had said to Nani.

Nani said, 'It's raining cats and dogs. How will you open the window? Besides, it scares me. We have heard all these ghost stories tonight!'

Bina offered to open the window. As soon as she did, a gust of wind and rain swept in and drenched us—and along with it entered a huge meteor. We were rivetted at this sight. Shirin had woken up on hearing the din, from the other room Afsar came running—they, too, were dumbstruck. We could not decide whether to scream and rouse the whole household or flee. We continued to stare, amazed, at that ball of fire.

The ball of fire gradually became a radiant human figure. It seemed I had seen this great man somewhere at some point of time. But I could not quite recognize him. I do not remember human faces as a matter of habit, which has led to major embarrassments at times. The fiery stranger said:

'My dear young women! Are you all terribly frightened? Be assured, there is nothing to be afraid of.'

Shirin: 'The other day a police spy came to our place dressed as a dumb fakir, are you one of them?'

Nanibala: '[Ladies], you have taken a house near the maulana's, which is why you are beset by spies.'

The figure of fire: (fiercely) 'No, I am nothing of the sort. I am Tvasti, the creator of the world.'

As soon as they heard the name 'Tvasti', Bina and Nani stretched themselves out on the ground and paid their respects to him. Then I too remembered that when I was writing 'The Creation of Woman' in Calcutta, I had been visited by this radiant great soul. With due respect, we requested Lord Tvasti to take a seat. Bina said, 'May I ask why you have graced us with the dust of your feet (during monsoon, one should say 'the mud of your feet' rather than 'the dust of your feet') at this odd hour?'

Tvasti: 'Why? (pointing a finger towards me) Because of that girl.'

I said, with amazement, fear, and modesty, 'Me? What are you saying, great one?'

Tvasti: 'Yes, you! You have made a mess by translating the history of my creating woman into Bengali. But then, how can I blame you alone—it is also the fault of *Saugat's* office.'

Nani: 'How is that?'

Tvasti: 'Well, she wrote the article titled 'The Creation of Woman' for the monthly journal *Saugat*. At that point the editor was not in Calcutta; the fools in the office published it, omitting two footnotes written by her. Without these footnotes, the essay has become difficult to understand in places, and discerning readers, not being able to comprehend it fully, are dissatisfied. That's when they say, "Call that blighter Tvasti, let him come and explain where and what the mistakes are!" They summon me from heaven by doing a planchette at odd hours, bothering me every now and then.

'Listen to today's incident. Certain young men got caught up in the *satyagraha* movement. The ruling officials say, give up the eagerness for truth [*satyagraha*] and embrace the eagerness for lies [*mithyagraha*]. Two lawyers, who were harassed by the police since they did not embrace falsehood, have escaped to Ranchi. Their home is not far from yours. But you should know that robbers never listen to religious tales. Even in this unceasing rain and mud in Ranchi, they have no respite. During the day, they smear themselves with sand, bits of stone, mud and water, and devote themselves to propagating ideas about embracing truth, as against embracing falsehood, thereby spoiling the peace in the country by their lecturing! And at night the friends spoil the peace of heaven by doing planchettes! Till late night we are disturbed by the summons of the lawyers. At least in your mortal world there is the C.I.D. to punish young men for disturbing the peace, but there are no ways to subdue them in heaven.

My steam-driven chariot got entangled in a dome on your roof while I was returning late at night from the lawyers'. Luckily for me, there was a huge noise when I fell. It's not good for me to get drenched in this old age. So the moment the brave Bina opened the window, I entered the house.'

Nani: 'But Lord! There are iron bars in the window!'

Tvasti: 'Forget your termite-eaten bars! Nothing can shut me out.'

Nani: 'Lord! I am very curious to learn what are the elements you used to create man.'

Tvasti: 'No, child! I have no time. Now I shall take my leave. Please go back to sleep.'

But we cornered him. We would not let him go without knowing about the mystery behind the creation of man.

Shirin: 'You are soaked, you must drink a cup of hot tea. If you begin the story, I shall ask the maid to make tea.' Then she called in a loud voice, '*Maro*—['beat up']'

Tvasti (startled): 'What is this? Whom does she want to beat up?'

Shirin could not restrain her laughter. Covering her face with her sari border, she left quickly.

Tvasti: 'Did she go to call a hired lathi-wielding tough?'

Bina (restraining her laughter with difficulty), 'No, she went to call her maid, Maro'.[41]

Tvasti: 'Since you absolutely will not let me go, what can one do? I see that you women are no less than the lawyers! They, at least, abide by laws and regulations, but you disregard everything. But if you just listen, you will not remember. Therefore, Nani, you sit with pen and paper. I shall speak, while you write quickly. Take care to write very fast.'

While Nani was searching for a pen and inkwell, Bina came forward, pen and pencil in hand, and said, 'Lord! Do not worry about time. You speak, and I shall write it in shorthand. I can write three hundred words a minute in shorthand.' On hearing this, the great Tvasti was extremely pleased. He spoke, Bina wrote, as we watched and listened in silence.

We saw that poor Lord Tvasti was overwhelmed by sleep. At times he was speaking in a low voice while yawning, with eyelids nearly closed; and again he rubbed his eyes and spoke in a loud voice, testing whether Bina had written things down correctly. He made her cross out the mistakes and write again. It was as if he took recourse to a rhetorical flourish to prove that he was not assailed by sleep. At one point he roared: 'Do you know, my dears, I had no raw material in hand when I was creating woman: I had to collect the smell, taste and moisture from different sources. But while creating men, I did not have to worry at all. I had huge stocks of all the ingredients in the store. I put out my hand and used whatever it touched. For example, I used the poison-fang of snakes; including the root, to make teeth. To make hand and toe nails, I used tiger claws. I used a donkey's brain, entirely, to fill the brain cells of men.[42] I took heat from fire to create woman, I used only a piece of burning coal to make men. Write this down, child.'

Bina wrote, 'Burning coal.'

Tvasti: 'My dear girls! Pay attention. To make women I used only the cold of snow, while to make men I used chunks of ice, in fact, the whole Kanchendzongha peak. Did you write that down, Bina?'

Bina showed the paper: 'Ice, Kanchendzongha.'

Shirin: 'There is no doubt that both Vesuvius, the volcano, and Kanchendzongha were used, together. That's why here's how men describe themselves—

> The fire in the forehead blazed in bright flames,
> Stretching till nothingness, the patch grew full of fire,
> The terrible Shiva became the destroyer,
> He roared and took hold of his slaying trident.

And the next moment (although 'at the words of Parvati, Shiva dropped his aggressive demeanour')—

With smiling countenance, he said to Indra, Lord Slayer,
It is not right for me to kill the demon Vritra.

When the dictation was over the great Tvasti said, 'Note this, child, you must take particular care when writing this in ordinary language, so that not a word or punctuation mark is changed.'

Afterwards when Lord Tvasti took his leave everyone went to their respective beds. But when I was going to bed, I don't know how, I fell. I woke up with a start. Opening my eyes, I saw that I was still seated on that sofa. The candle burnt with a small flame in a corner of the house. Shirin and Bina slept like the dead! A cock's crowing was heard in the distance, and I realized that the night was over. Had I been dreaming all this while then?

Living in Seclusion[43]

Preface

By writing 'Living in Seclusion', the writer has opened up a new way of looking at women in society. Many have become famous by writing different kinds of history; but no one else has, so far, written the history of the miseries of the secluded women of India and Pakistan.

Reading the book, one is haunted by the thought of our tragic fall from the once-lofty state. It is perhaps not an exaggeration to say that a large part of that very Muslim society which had once been the world's ideal is now derided by almost the whole world.

While valiant women like Razia and Khawla have fought male warriors on horseback, the Bengali Muslim women surrendered everything to thieves and are shedding tears in silence. It is my firm conviction that the sleeping nation's rational eyes will be opened by reading 'Living in Seclusion.'

Finally, I thank the writer for her moral courage. I invite the generous gaze of male and female readers towards 'Living in Seclusion'.

Abdul Karim, B.A., M.L.C.

Sketch 12

A Hindu wife in western India went to bathe in the Ganges with her mother-in-law and husband. The bathing over, when she wished to return, she could not find her mother-in-law and her husband in the crowd. In the end she followed a certain gentleman. After a while, an uproar was created by the police. The constable caught hold of the concerned gentleman and said, 'You are abducting another man's wife.' He turned round, startled, and saw to his utter surprise that an unknown woman was walking behind him, holding on to the edge of his dhoti! When questioned, the wife said that she always had her head covered and therefore never had a good look at her husband. All she had seen was that her husband wore a dhoti with a yellow border; and she therefore followed the gentleman in question when she saw he too wore a yellow-bordered dhoti.

Sketch 29

Once I went to Aligarh to attend a certain ladies' conference. There I saw the delegates wearing all sorts of burqas. One of them wore a really peculiar burqa. After we were introduced, I praised her burqa, and she said, 'Don't say any more—I have suffered much humiliation because of this!' Afterwards, this is what she had to say about her humiliation:

She had once been invited to a wedding at a certain Bengali gentleman's house. On seeing her in a burqa, the children screamed in fear and did not know where to flee. Her husband knew other Bengali gentlemen, so she had to visit their houses.

Her visits to each of these houses caused the children to cry out in fear and create pandemonium. The children would tremble in panic.

Once she came to Calcutta. When she, along with four or five other women also clad in burqa, went for a drive in an open-top car, the boys on the street would say, 'O my God, what on earth are those?' One would say to the other, 'Be quiet! At this time of night, they can't be anything but ghosts.' When they saw the veil covering the face flutter a little in the breeze, they would say, 'Look, look! The ghosts are waving their trunks! Ooh! Let's run!'

One day the lady visited Darjeeling. She reached Ghoom station and saw that the assembled crowd was looking at a dwarf. The dwarf was as tall as a seven or eight-year-old boy, but had a young man's face, growing a moustache and beard. Suddenly, she noticed the crowd looking at her, highly entertained. The audience had forgotten about the dwarf and gazed at her, instead. Later, on reaching Darjeeling, they had lunch and went out sight-seeing on a rickshaw. They went to the Mall and found it was very crowded. Soldiers had returned from Tibet, and people gathered to watch them. The coolies drawing their rickshaw left the vehicle by the roadside and went to have a look at the show. After a little while, the lady saw the spectators peeping inside the rickshaw, one by one, to look at her.

When she went out on foot, the street dogs would bark and try to attack her. On seeing her, a couple of mountain horses, the riders still on the saddle, galloped about crazily. While visiting a tea garden she saw that a girl of three or four had picked up a large stone with which to hit her![44]

Another time, while roaming with four-to-five other Muslim women, they tripped on their burqas and fell in the muddy and pebble-infested soil beside a small waterfall. Some coolies came running from a nearby tea garden and pulled them up. In fond reproach, they said, 'As it is, you have put on shoes, moreover, you are wearing something like an enclosure. Given that you are in such a state, what do you expect but to roll on the ground?' Poor things! The elaborately embroidered dupattas of the women lay in the mud, while the burqas were soaked thoroughly!

And this is not all. People on the streets would silence their crying children by pointing to the burqa-clad women and say, 'Be quiet! Look, Mecca and Medina are passing by. There! See those witches covered from head to toe? That's Mecca and Medina!'

Sketch 38

A certain she-doctor I know, Miss Saratkumari Mitra, said, 'O dear! Visiting one of yours', I mean Muslim, homes is a lot of trouble. One can't even get a little hot water or a piece of cloth at the right time!'

One day someone who came to call her from a distant place informed that a married lady had toothache. She carried an adequate amount of medicine and equipment needed for tooth extraction with her. On her arrival, she found that it was not toothache that troubled her patient but labour pains. She was at a loss at what to do. Jamgaon was in the periphery of the city, almost like a village. It was difficult to find a horse-drawn carriage or a palanquin there. By the time she managed to get to Bhagalpur and returned with the necessary surgical instruments to Jamgaon, the patient was likely to expire. Miss Mitra asked the mistress of the house why she was not told the truth, and ended up making a pointless trip. The mistress of the house answered, 'Since I had sent a male servant to call a lady doctor, a toothache is all that I could tell him. For shame! How could I have told a man about what really happened? What kind of a female doctor are you that you don't understand what people mean?'

Sketch 39

It is not enough for society to just shut us up in our prison of seclusion. Apparently, Hazrat Mohammad's wife, Ayesha Siddiqua [the Prophet's wife] reached puberty at nine years. Therefore, once they are over eight, little girls in well-respected Muslim families are forbidden to laugh or speak loudly, run or jump and so on. In a nutshell, they are forbidden to make any movement. The girl is supposed to sit with her head bent in one corner of the house and engage in sewing; without stirring. She is not supposed to walk briskly.

One afternoon an eight-year-old girl belonging to a well-respected family came to the courtyard to find a small ladder resting against the thatched roof of the kitchen. For some reason, Tahera absentmindedly climbed two steps of the ladder. At that moment her father arrived. Seeing his daughter on the ladder, he lost all sense of proportion, and hauled her down with an abrupt jerk of his arm.

Tahera was a much-beloved only daughter of her father. She had only received love from her father; never seen him annoyed with her. Today, she was so terrified to see her father's terrible demeanour. The rude jerk with which he pulled her away caused her to tremble. She lost control and wet her clothes.

Since she was bathed late, at an unaccustomed hour, and overwhelmed by an excess of fear, she fell ill that night with a fever. As a rich man's daughter, and a very well-loved one at that, no pains were spared to get her the best medical treatment. A civil surgeon was brought in from a distant district headquarters. At that time (i.e. forty to forty-five years ago) it was not easy to call doctors home. It entailed paying up four times the doctor's fee, the cost of hiring a palanquin, and that of providing uncooked food and a constant supply of tobacco and betel leaves to the thirty-two palanquin bearers. It was a big affair.

In spite of all the care showered on her, Tahera's fever did not abate even on the third day. The doctor, finding the situation out of his control, took his leave. Giving a fittingly cruel reply to her father's rude behaviour, Tahera left, now free forever. *Innalillahi wa inna ilayhi raaji'oon*: Verily, we are for Allah and unto Him will we return.

Sketch 47

One would like to say in the words of the poet,

> It's not poetry nor a novel, it's my life
> It's not a theatre, but my home, in fact

About three years ago; the first motor-driven bus in our school was ready to take off. On the previous day, an Englishwoman, who was one of our teachers, visited the workshop and reported that it was terribly dark inside the bus. 'Oh no, I shall never travel by the bus' [she said]. When the bus arrived, one saw that there was a little bit of netting at the back of the bus over the door, some in front and at the top. Without these two pieces of netting, three inches in width and one and a half feet in length, the bus could have been termed 'fully airtight'.

On the first day the girls were taken home in the new bus, the maidservant returned and reported that the bus was getting too hot. Some of the girls had become restive on the journey back. Some had vomited. The little girls were scared of being in the dark and had wept.

On the second day, when she was sending the bus to get the girls, the English lady lowered the blind on the door and hung a coloured curtain there. Even so, when the students came to school, it was found that two or three among them had fainted, another two-three vomited, some had a headache, and so on. In the afternoon, the teacher in question lowered the blinds on either side of the bus and hung two curtains. That is how the girls were sent home.

That evening, Mrs. Mukherjee, an old friend of mine, came to see me. She was happy with the various improvements in the school, and said, 'Your bus is quite nice. When I first saw it on the road, I wondered whether it were a moving cupboard since all its four sides were fully closed. My nephew told me, "Aunty! Look, a moving black hole." How do girls manage to remain seated inside that?'

On the afternoon of the third day, the mothers of four or five students came to see me and said, 'Your bus is like Khuda's curse. You are burying the girls alive in a coffin.' I said in utter helplessness, 'What can I do? You would have said that the bus was without adequate cover, if I did not have it this way.' They grew very agitated and said, 'In that case, will you keep the purdah at the cost of lives? From tomorrow our daughters will not come to school.' Two or three girls fainted again on that day. Word was sent through the maidservants of different houses that girls would not come by the bus anymore.

After the evening had passed, I received four letters without the senders' addresses by post. The writer of the letter, which was in English, had signed himself 'Brother-in-Islam'. The other three were in Urdu—two anonymous and the fourth signed by five people. All the letters said the same thing—all of them had been kind enough to write, in the interest of the welfare of our school, that the curtains which had been hung on two sides of the bus fluttered in the wind, thus unveiling the bus. If proper measures were not taken by the next day, then they would, out of even greater kindness, spread slander about the school in Urdu dailies such as *Khabich* and *Palid.* They dared us to transport girls in vehicles that were not fully covered.

What a bother!

'If he doesn't catch the snake, the king will kill him, if he does, the snake will.'

Perhaps no one else had caught a live snake this way at the king's command. On behalf of the women imprisoned in seclusion, I wanted to say,

'Why, alas, did I come into this benighted mundane world,
Why was I born into a household that practised seclusion?'

Letters

86/A, Lower Circular Road, Calcutta
30-4-31

My dear Mona,[45]

May Allah the merciful bless all of you . . .

This time Nuri left us.[46] Nuri was prepared to go, she begged forgiveness from everyone. She asked that her salutations be sent to everyone.

Sister! What more shall I say of my hopes and hopelessness! I, of course, know the adage, 'Who would have thought that life was such a mistake?'

Like beaten snow, the desires of your childhood recede,
At the lashings of the stormy winds of scorched life.
The faded ambitions come from afar are left lying,
Like torn flags on the battlements of a ruined fort.

Ah! *'Kya Tiddi, kya Tiddi ka raan!'*[47] As it is, man is a small, puny little thing, so what is the point of his having lofty ambitions or setting great store by faith? Therefore, through our little lives, let us eat well, be comfortable, smile and play! That should be enough. And, if we can, let us pray to Allah with all our hearts! Unfortunately, I can't even pray. Perhaps no one as useless and unfortunate as me has been born yet.

In childhood, I did not get my father's love. As a married woman, I only nursed my husband in his illness. Everyday I checked his urine. I prepared his special diet, wrote to his doctor. Twice I became a mother, but I could not even dandle my children in my arms for long. One went at five months, another at four months. For the last twenty-two years I have been burning in the fire of widowhood. So how can Nuri make me weep too much? Her passing away was only a small addition to my huge burden of suffering. My failed life goes on, laughing and playing, and counting the days.

Your affectionate
Apa

2

14.12.31
1, Nripendra Lodge
Ghatsila P.O., Singbhum
B.N. Rly.

Dear Sister,[48]

May Allah the merciful bless you. It is now very pleasurable to walk about here. It is such fun to walk over the soft straw in the fields where the paddy has been cut. I walk around to my heart's content. I don't like to walk alone, though, and keep remembering you.

It would be such fun if you came with Bhaisahib, Rashida, and your baby girl and spent a few days here. Given that man's life is full of sorrow and struggle, it's enough to be able to laugh and have fun for just a few days. In my childhood, I had heard a song:

Laugh your fill, it's only for a few days,
A life full of sorrow remains.

Ghatshila seems to tell me something similar:

Walk your fill, it's only for a few days,
A life in the prison of the city remains.

That is why, I say, come here and give me pleasure for a few days. Compared to your Jalpaiguri bungalow, this house of mine is a cow-shed.

There is not much more time left before my fun days spent at

Ghatshila come to an end. If God wills, I shall go back on the 30th in the train that leaves at 12 noon. So on the 29th I shall have to tuck in my tail (that is, pack all my things!).

I remain in hope of getting a letter from you... Accept my heartfelt blessings.

Your loving sister
Rokeya

The following five letters, 3-7, were written by Rokeya Sakhawat Hossain in English.

3

13, European Asylum Lane
Calcutta
10. 9. 13

Dear Sir,[49]

Many thanks for your kind letters, received yesterday. These letters worked like some medicine which I required for my soul. Sometimes we yearn to tell somebody of our sorrows and difficulties. I hope you will come to Calcutta soon. I would like to tell you some of my . . .

4

1.10.13

I could not finish this letter yesterday, so I take up the writing again today. Fortune and misfortune are seldom in our hands, and not very often, as you say. Failure of a bank, for instance, can never be under one's control, but at the same time the poor depositor has to suffer the consequence for no fault of his own. We may well advise the depositor not to mind his loss! But who is to meet his unavoidable expenses? We cannot expect a hungry person to be satisfied and happy. Can you?

No, I am not unfortunate provided this school works well and I can achieve my literary talents. Only the other day I became very happy when I won the first prize in a rhyme-competition. There were some undergraduates and graduates and above all some English lady graduates too among the lady competitors. I enclose herewith a copy of my composition, which . . .

5

11.3.14

Dear Sir,

I got your letter dated the 18th, yesterday evening. I am sorry you did not get my last letter.

I am really very sorry to learn that you are not keeping well. Life is short, what is the use of pining over this and that? Human life does not always find smooth paths, but still I think a gentleman of your position need not be disheartened with life. After all, life is a very valuable thing and should not be wasted for nothing.

It is a pity you feel so lonely. But I fear your selection was not correct in choosing an ill-fated person like me whose life has been 'lost in misadventure', to write to.

Since two months I am suffering from some kind of fever—the fever is not much as the temperature never rises above 100 but I have become very weak. The weakness seems almost unbearable. I dread pen and paper; don't like even reading. I attend school with great difficulty: speaking to the girls tires me so much that many a time I let them have their own ways. I would very much like to write a nice letter to you but unfortunately I am unable to do so now.

More after hearing from you. Let me assure you that your letters are always welcome: so please write to me as often as you please. It was very kind of you to select me out of your so many friends; I feel honoured—rather proud of it, though I fear I do not deserve it.

Yours very truly,
R. S. Hossain

6

19.4.14

My dear Sir,

I am so thankful to you for your very kind letters dated the 19th & 31st March respectively. Your kind enquiries about me overjoyed me so much that I could not help addressing you as 'my dear Sir' and I hope I did no wrong in doing so. You are such a good friend, may God bless you with long life and prosperity. I am so helpless and friendless; even my nearest relatives are so heartless that they do not hesitate in trying to deprive me of my daily food! In this state of affairs, friends like you and Mr Ahmed Ali (the secretary of our school) are blessings of heaven.

Dear friend! Kindly pray to God to save me from my relatives.

Well, I must stop talking rubbish now. Our prize distribution has been postponed to the end of this month.

I do not get fever now but am dreadfully weak. I look fifteen years older than my actual age. I will consult a lady doctor again tomorrow.

Yes, the prize distribution of Suhrawardi Purdanashini [written in Bengali in the original] Madrassa is over. Have you read all the correspondence and note in 'Mussalman' and 'Comrade'?

Yes, God is sufficient for those only who know how to rely on Him. The difficulty is that we do not know how to stick to him. In my opinion I won't care for anything else if God were not sufficient!

The person about whose death Taifur and Baizid wrote to me was a first . . .

7

86A Lr Circular Rd
Calcutta
23.7.15

Dear Sir,

I owe you some apology for not replying to your kind letter earlier. I thought you would be in Calcutta soon and that I should get an opportunity of telling you everything in detail.

I sent a copy of our annual report and syllabus for your kind perusal. It took a long time and botheration to get this report printed. I hope one will excuse this unnecessary delay remembering that we are Mohammedans and the job was done by a Mohammedan press!

I cannot understand why you want to resign your post. Do you find the department very wicked? This world as a whole is wicked but the presence of some people like you is necessary to make an oasis in this desert.

Hoping this will find you and yours in good health and spirit.

Can Zeenat smile now? She will have to learn many things.

Sincerely yours,
R. S. Hossain

Notes

1 Review of Shamsunnahar's book *The Life of Rokeya*, published in *Saugat*, Jaishtha 1936.

2 'Book Review', *Nabanoor*, Bhadra 1905.

3 See the Bengali Calendar, Kinship Terms and Place Names, p. xlii.

4 S.A. Al-Musavi, *'Abanoti Prasange'*, (On Degradation), *Nabanoor*, Ashwin 1904.

5 *'Ekei Ki Bole Abanoti'*? (Is This What is Called Degradation?) *Nabanoor*, Kartik 1904.

6 B.S. 1335 and 1337.

7 B.S. 1338

8 *Purogami*, 16 February 1979.

9 *Rassundari Theke Rokeya* (Dhaka: Bangla Akademi, 1993), p. 156.

10 'Editor's Piece', *Begum Rokeya Rachanavali* (Dhaka: Bangla Akademi, 1984), p.16.

11 Mohammad Nasiruddin, *Bangla Sahitye Saugat Yug* (Dhaka: Noorjahan Begum, 1985), pp. 535-537.

12 This essay was published as 'Our Degradation' in Bhadra 1904 (mid August

to mid Sept. 1311) issue of *Nabanoor*. In 1905, when the first volume of *Motichur* was published, a modified version of the original essay, now given the title 'The Degradation of Women', was included.

[13] Rokeya's note to the original piece: Some might say that it is God's will that woman should be subordinate to man. He created man first, while woman was created afterwards, in order to care for and serve man. But here we shall not discuss any opinions found in religious texts. We shall only write what ordinary people can use their common sense to understand. In other words, I am expressing my individual opinion.

[14] 'Enslaved' in English in the original.

[15] This passage within quotes is in English in the original, and the Bengali meaning is provided by the author.

[16] 'Unreasonable' in English in the original.

[17] Rokeya's note: 'Although the Japanese wife is considered only the *first servant* [of] her husband, she is usually addressed in the house as the honourable mistress. Acquaintance with European customs has awakened among the more educated classes in Japan a desire to raise the position of women.' (Japan) [In English in the original and the Bengali meaning provided by the author, translator] Many ladies may object to the term 'servant' or 'slave'. But I ask, what does the word 'lord' (*swami*) mean? Just as one calls the giver a donor, one who takes has to be called a recipient. Likewise, if one party is called 'lord, master, god', what can one call the other except 'servant' or 'slave'? If you say that the wife becomes a servant by being bound to the husband in chains of love, indeed no one can object to a person accepting this vocation of servitude. But has the man too, by virtue of being bound by familial love, not accepted the duty of maintaining his family? Even the poorest labourer, when he gets the few pennies as wages in the evening having worked all day on an empty stomach, does not waste his money to satisfy the cravings of his own stomach, by filling it with puffed rice or sweet puffed rice. Rather, he buys rice and lentils with the money and gives it to his wife. When the wife, after cooking the food, gives her 'lord' a small amount that satisfies half his hunger, the poor husband is content with this. What a wonderful sacrifice! Even so, society calls the married man a 'lord' instead of 'love's slave'.

Oh yes, I remember another important thing. Do the hallowed women who object to wives being called 'servants' and cite Sita and Savitri at every turn not know that in Hindu society itself there is one (or more) class of *kulin* Brahmins who buy girls and marry them? What can you call someone who is bought against money other than a slave or a bought servant? Here some may mention the way the grooms' academic qualifications are up for sale, but ordinary folk do not speak of the 'sale of grooms', particularly because it is the groom's academic degrees which are being sold, not the groom himself. But this logic does not work when it comes to the sale of girls, since eight to twelve-year-old girls have no particular qualities or academic degrees that can be sold. So the girl herself is sold. Once when I was talking to a highly respectable Brahmin woman and this topic was raised, I asked her, 'Is there a dearth of kulin girls who match their stature that the men have to buy the girls they marry?' The lady replied, 'Not at all. Buying and selling is the norm with them. Just as one of them buys another's sister and marries her, his sister too will be bought and married by a third.'

We had absolutely no desire to name any particular social group or a distinct vice, but to stop the false reasoning offered by dubious debaters I was compelled to show proof that women servants and slaves existed. We are sorry about this. But it's mandatory to observe one's duty.

18 'Badges of slavery' in English in the original. Rokeya's note: a certain Shams-ul-Ulama (Zakauddin) says, 'A nose-ring is but a modified form of putting a rope through the nose.

19 In English in the original.

20 'Drawing-room' and 'curtain ring' in English in the original.

21 Rokeya's note: It is one and the same to wear jewellery and fritter away money. But one can hope that many will consider it more justified to spend money wisely, rather than fritter it away.

22 'Ladies' jackets' and 'gentlemen's jackets' in English in the original.

23 'Aerial body' in English in the original.

24 Rokeya's note: The other day (on 9 April) I read in an Urdu newspaper: The women of Turkey have complained to the Sultan, 'We have no occupation except remaining within the four walls. Let us be taught the use of guns and cannons, like men, so that, in times of war, we may protect our homes and cities.'

In the petition they have cited the following benefits: *(i)* The main benefit is preventing the loss which results because less number of soldiers are present in the battlefield as many of them are posted to guard the cities (the 'helpless' females will guard the cities instead). *(ii)* The children will become accustomed to war right from their infancy. If both father and mother are soldiers, children will not be scared or cowardly. *(iii) A* special variety of uniform, covering the entire body, except one's eyes and nose, will be made for women. *(iv)* To give the practice of seclusion its due honour, it has been decided that for at least three years the male soldiers in each family will teach warfare to their women. Afterwards, women who have been trained in warfare will visit households to teach warfare to women. The above-mentioned women have also written, 'We shall not bother the government to pay for our uniforms. We only hope that the government provides the guns and weapons.' Let us wait and see what his majesty the Sultan has to say to this petition.

The concerned newspaper is solely responsible vis-à-vis the truth in this news item. We believe it is not impossible for Turkish women to have such ambitions. History has it that earlier they would wage war. Turning the pages of sundry Islamic manuscripts, we might find descriptions of women going to war:

'When Jaigun, the daughter of the emperor, was imprisoned
And all the Arabian cavalry . . .'

I ask, what will the leaders of society in this country—who are shocked [in English in the original] to hear of 'lady clerks', who cannot imagine giving helpless females any arduous task except that of dressing up dolls and making garlands of flowers—do, if they hear of proposed lady-warriors? Will they not faint?

25 *Bhari*: A unit of weight equal to a little over 11 grams.

26 *Seer*: A measure of weight equal to about 2 lbs.

27 *Poa*: A measure of weight that is $1/4^{th}$ of a seer.

28 *Tola*: A measure of weight equal to about 12 grams.

29 Rokeya's note: Some of the nose-rings have a diameter of six inches and a circumference of at least 29 inches! The weight is one *chhatak*! (*Chhatak*: A measure of weight equal to about $^{1}/_{16}$ of a *seer*.)

30 Rokeya's note: Even so, Christians believe that Eve was truly cursed and it was Jesus Christ who freed womankind from that curse. They say,

'Through woman came curse and sin: and through woman came blessing and salvation also' (in English in the original, followed by Bengali translation by the author). Man did not become Christ's father, but woman was glorified as the status of Christ's mother was bestowed on her.

31 Rokeya's note: The freedom demanded by the women of certain social groups in Bengal is not true freedom—rather, only a hollow noise.

32 Rokeya's note: Reasonable men in society may not give the sentence of death, but 'unreasonable', helpless, innocent women (who don't go by reason or argumentation) would certainly give a sentence of execution by a hundred-faced, sharp, carving knives!

33 Rokeya's note: I am speaking of becoming equal to men to give an idea as to the way we should progress. What else could I compare it to? The state of men is our ideal. We want the kind of equality that should exist between boys and girls in a family. Since men are the sons of society, we are society's daughters! We do not say, 'put on the girl's head the same helmet that you would put on a boy's.' Rather, we say that as much care should be expended on making the veil that covers the young girl's head as is done in embellishing the young man's headdress.

34 Rokeya's note: But why should we have to do that? Why should the zamindar carry the plough on his shoulder when his farmer-tenant is around? Can we not do anything worthwhile other than being the king's servants? We cited clerks and so only as examples, just as in descriptions of paradise we have to say—there is no winter, no summer, only eternal spring. In the garden of paradise, flowers of diamond bloom on vines of emerald! So in order to qualify our high ambitions, what else could one compare work that is of high value with but that of a lady-viceroy's?

But let me also say that talk of becoming lady-clerks does not perhaps seem as shocking in other places the way it does in Bengal. There was a day when in Muslim societies in other countries, there was no dearth of 'women-poets, women philosophers, women historians, women scientists, women speakers, women doctors, women politicians', and so on. Only in Bengali Muslim society, we do not have such gems of women.

35 'Dull head' in English in the original.

36 Paragraphs 23-27 of 'Our Degradation'.

37 Rokeya's note: This statement echoes a sentiment similar to one in the *Sura*

Noor of the eighteenth 'paragraph' of the Holy Koran: 'Let the honourable ladies always keep their gaze lowered (not glance about playfully), and they should display their dress (only to particular persons), not to others.'

[38] In the Koran, Christians are often indicated with the word *Nasara*, i.e. Nazarenes. *Butparast* is idol-worshipper in Persian, but *But/Put/Pût* was also the Persian form of the Sanskrit *Buddha* so *Butparast* also means Buddhist.

[39] Rokeya's note: After writing this article I came across a lecture titled 'The purdah of ignorance' given by Sir Andrew Fraser (published in *The Telegraph*, 8 March). He said, 'Let the efforts of educationists be first directed to the instruction of our girls *within the purdah*, and let woman begin to exercise her chastening influence on society in spite of the system of seclusion, which only time can modify; and violent efforts to shake which can only arouse opposition to female education, instead of doing any immediate practical good in the direction of emancipation of women.' How similar his argument to ours!

[40] First published in the *Bangiya Musalman Sahitya Patrika*, Sravan 1919 with the title 'On the Creation of the Male'. The footnotes were written by Rokeya.

[41] Rokeya's note: The poor servant's beautiful name 'Mariam' has been distorted and transformed into 'Maro'. When I was in Bihar, I had the good fortune of hearing the names of a few women from highly respectable families, such as 'Hasho', 'Lato', 'Dallu', 'Ullu', 'Jubba' and so on. If one does not show what the names were in their original forms, one would be doing them an injustice and my sister readers may be afraid, like Lord Tvasti. Therefore, the original names were, 'Hashmat Ara', 'Latifunnesa', 'Daulatannesa', 'Aliunnesa', and 'Zubeida'.

[42] 'Cells' in English in the original.

[43] First published in the *Masik Mohammadi*, Kartik 1927; Bhadra 1927; Sravan 1929; Bhadra 1929.

[44] Rokeya's note: See the difference between Bengalis and Gurkhas. Whereas Bengali children screamed, ran here and there and fled the place, the Gurkha child picked up stones in self-defence, in order to hit the object of fear.

[45] Mohsina Rahman, the daughter of her paternal uncle.

[46] Rokeya's niece (sister's daughter) who died while studying in Sakhawat

Memorial School. Rokeya was bringing her up.

47 Urdu, literally meaning, 'How small the locust, how much smaller its thigh.' Metaphorically, speaking, 'How insignificant we human beings are, more so our grief.

48 Khanbahadur Tosaddak Ahmad, the assistant director of public instruction of undivided Bengal, was one of Rokeya's few well-wishers and advisors. This letter was written to his wife.

49 The letters written in English were to a police officer of Pabna District, Mohammad Yasin. We found the first letter (no 3) in Ghulam Murshid's book. In his *Rassundari theke Rokeya*, he writes (p. 159): 'In 1913, Rokeya wished to admit Syeda, a daughter of Mohammed Yasin, to her school. At that time the school had no facilities for boarding. At the same time Yasin could not find another place where she could stay. Whether or not Syeda could be admitted, Yasin and Rokeya became very close friends.'

2

Khairunnesa Khatun: The Educationist

Translated by Anusuya Ghosh

Among the writers included in this book, Khairunnesa Khatun seems to have been totally forgotten. We have not been able to disinter her birth and death dates. She was indeed a pioneer in women's education, a writer, and one can discern in her a swadeshi (the boycott of foreign goods in favour of Indian manufactured ones) or early nationalist identity. She sank into oblivion, in spite of playing a multifaceted role between 1890 and 1910. Was she forgotten so soon because she was a woman? We cannot but confront such a question after nearly a hundred years of her death, as the wilful negligence of a woman's role is a common feature cutting across cultures and time.

A slight reference to herself may be found in the footnotes to the essay, *'Amader Shikshar Antaray'* (Obstacles to Our Education, *Nabanoor*, issue 8, year 2), published in 1904. In it she sounds worried about the financial crisis affecting the running of Hosainpur Girls' School at Sirajganj, founded by Munshi Mohammed Meherullah. About twenty-two years later, Mohammed Abdul Hakim Bikrampuri writes in the essay *'Bangla Sahitye Muslim Mahila'* (Muslim Women in Bengali Literature, *Saugat*, Bhadra 1926), 'The late Khairunnesa Khatun Saheba had written a delightful book for women entitled *Satir Patibhakti* (The Devoted Wife).[1] She was the headmistress of Sirajganj Hosainpur Girls' High School. Those who have read her book, *Satir Patibhakti*, would have a fair idea of her writing skills and love for the Bengali language. Her venerable husband, Maulana Asiruddin Sahib, had urged and inspired her to write the book. The extent of the book's popularity may be gauged from the fact that it went into four editions. Her untimely death deprives us of the chance of reading any further contributions that she may have made had she lived longer. *Satir Patibhakti* was very well received by the Muslim society of the time. My maternal grandfather bought and read this book in the second decade of the twentieth century. The book pleased him so much that he named his first-born, my eldest aunt, Khairunnessa.

We find a little note on Khairunnessa in Professor Mansuruddin's *Bangla Sahitye Muslim Sadhana* (Muslim Endeavours in Bengali Literature), 1960, where it is mentioned that he received a copy of *Satir Patibhakti* by Khairunnessa Khatun, but without the title page, as a gift from a friend, and that 'there are only sixty-eight pages in this book'. An extract from Professor Mansuruddin's analysis of *Satir Patibhakti* follows:

> The authoress mentions in the preface to this book, 'I am merely an unlearned and simple Muslim woman; I have not written any other book. But when I was a teacher in a girls' school, I contributed some essays to newspapers.'[2]
>
> Although Khairunnessa calls herself unlearned and simple, her writings show that she was both educated and intelligent. She has studied the relationship between husband and wife, and the rearing and education of children at length, throwing considerable light on the subjects. Having lived in a conservative and reactionary atmosphere, Khairunnessa's thoughts and endeavours were neither contemporary nor progressive. However, even progressive minds would be able to make use of the ambience conjured up in this book and the food for thought that it provides. Her list of ideas on running the household is drawn from experience.
>
> *(i)* The inferior status of women in society is at the root of its decline.
>
> *(ii)* A family where the womenfolk suffer declines rapidly.
>
> *(iii)* A woman does not only give birth to children, she is also the bringer of all welfare.
>
> *(iv)* A family where the husband is content with the wife is guaranteed happiness.

(v) The glory of a respectful wife lies in encouraging the husband to do many great deeds.

On 25 January 1996, an article entitled *'Khairunnessa Khatun /Aarek Begum Rokeya'* (Khairunnessa Khatun/Another Begum Rokeya) by Syed Abul Maqsud, was published in the Bangladesh daily *Ittefak.* This article introduced us to the journalist and researcher Syed Abul Maqsud.[3] As a child, he had heard of Khairunnessa from his father. His grandfather, who died at the time of World War II, was a schoolteacher and a contemporary of Khairunnessa. While Khairunnessa taught in Hosainpur School, on the bank of the river Jamuna, Maqsud's grandfather was with the Teota School at Manikganj, beside the river Padma. Beginning 1979, Abul Maqsud became interested in Khairunnessa and began interviewing a few elder citizens of Sirajganj.

We could only trace a possible outline of Khairunnessa Khatun's profile against the backdrop of Muslim society as it was, and a developing Sirajganj (then a district headquarters, now a district), from our interview with Maqsud, taken on 10 October 1997, in Dhaka. The portrait was based entirely on the memories of people who, in turn, had heard of Khairunnessa from some of her contemporaries. Maqsud said: 'My grandfather, Syed Ziauddin Yusuf, taught at the Teota High School of Manikganj. This school was one of the first two high schools in Manikganj district. The founders of the school were Kiranshankar Ray and Kumudshankar Ray. Their village was near the Aricha ghat. They were renowned zamindars. My grandfather taught in that school at the end of the nineteenth century, in 1891-1892. At that time, the Bengali Muslims had begun to make their presence felt in the fields of publishing journals, education and literary activities. There were a few poets and litterateurs among them.

'What we refer to as the "secular" tradition of the Bengalis had not yet developed at the end of the nineteenth century. On one hand there were the Hindus who took their chosen path. They had progressed considerably. The Bengali Muslims, on the other hand, were left far behind. After the Hindus went far ahead, a group of Muslims felt that they too should do something about their community. There was a communal element in all this, but it had nothing to do with antagonism. Gradually, antagonism grew too, towards the end of the nineteenth century. Among the periodicals published by Muslims of that time, there were *Islam Pracharak*, *Mihir O Sudhakar*, *Mihir* and *Sudhakar* (independently). Only Muslims wrote in these periodicals. A certain amount of communal ideas, too, would get published. The Hindu periodicals published rejoinders to these discussions. Ismail Hosain Siraji wrote *Rainandini*, protesting against Bankim Chandra Chattopadhyay's *Durgeshnandini*. However, it does not look as if these writings caused much enmity among the two communities, as both knew that their common enemy was the British who had colonized the country. This was a view they held unequivocally. Communal hatred peaked at the time of the Partition of Bengal in 1905. Some Muslims did not support the Partition. Ismail Hosain Siraji was among them. He lived in Sirajganj; hence the suffix "Siraji" was added to his name.

'Khairunnessa too lived in Sirajganj. From what we know of her life and work, it seems that she began teaching at the end of the nineteenth century. She was associated with contemporary political activities. I have heard that she conducted a night school for girls as well. Even if she herself did not live in purdah [although her essay *'Aamader Shikshar Antaray'* gives one a feeling that she might have], her students were expected to do so. Since they would not come out during the day, she founded a night school, enabling girls to attend it as their coming and going would be more unobtrusive; avoid meeting people if they came out at night. Girls of eight and nine were not allowed to step out of their homes then.

'The Hosainpur school suffered from serious financial crises. I have heard that Khairunnessa went from door to door, requesting people to keep aside a fistful of rice at the time of cooking every day. In this way, a kilogram or even a kilo and a half of rice would be collected at the end of the month in each house, without putting any pressure on them. The accumulated rice would then be sold and the proceeds would go to the maintenance of the school.

'Khairunnessa belonged to a middle-class family. She chose to work in the villages. Her influence in propagating education, especially women's education, as we can see, could be felt in the entire Pabna district, Goalanda in Faridpur and parts of Manikganj; in other words, on both sides of the river Padma.

'You may have noticed that Congress agitation was at its peak in Sirajganj. A Congress session was held there. But Sirajganj was progressive even before the Congress session was held there. That was the time when Khairunnessa went from village to village on foot, to collect girl students and educate them in her night school. She played a huge role in the anti-Partition agitation of 1905. She had some connections with the Congress leaders of Sirajganj. It is also rumoured that Khairunnessa participated in the Congress-led processions in Sirajganj at the time. This perhaps made her unpopular among the Muslims.

'Hosainpur was very close to Sirajganj, located on the bank of the river Jamuna. The school now is under water, and Sirajganj town too has been subjected to continuous erosion. Khairunnessa died sometime between 1908 and 1911. She was alive in 1908 when *Satir Patibhakti* was first published. In the second edition of the book published in 1911, she is referred to as the deceased writer. I scanned the newspapers and periodicals of 1909 and thereafter and found no mention of the death of the lady who played a part in the anti-Partition movement of 1905 and made a huge contribution to women's education.'

S. A.

The Obstacles to Our Education

At present, there is a lot of interest in society in our [women's] education. Many highly-educated and noble persons have launched a campaign in favour of women's education. The country's newspapers are not silent on this issue either. It is believed unanimously that unless we are educated, there is no hope for total social development. There is, indeed, no doubt about the logic in this statement. A life without education is comparable to a world without the sun. An unlettered person can only be compared to an animal. If education makes men handsome and accomplished; why would it not enhance the beauty and pride of achievement in women who are naturally beautiful? If a woman of good character is also learned, the two qualities are likely to add to her beauty. Just as a sweet-scented breeze fills us human beings with a greater sense of contentment, similarly, a good-natured lady, who is also educated, would make a family happier. That both men and women must pursue education as a noble duty is mentioned in our *Hadis Sharif*: *'Talebal elme farizatan ala kulle moslemin o moslemat'*.[4] There is sanction of women's education in the Hindu scriptures as well, for example, *'Kanyapyevang palaniya shikshaniyatiyatnatah'*.[5] Hence, whichever way you look at it, there seems to be no doubt that it is our responsibility and an absolute necessity to be educated.

Men now realize that it is necessary to propagate women's education among the rich, poor, decent and not-so-cultured. Many of our fellow sisters have also understood its importance. Why then is there no development in women's education? Has anybody ever thought what the hurdles in the way of our education are and how we can make these barriers disappear? I do not seem to have heard or seen anything happening on this front! Must it be reiterated that unless we remove the problems and the obstacles at their roots, even a thousand lectures and hundreds of essays cannot extend the programme of education? Let us discuss some of the obstacles in the way of our education system and see how they could be overcome.

We are Muslims and we must abide by the dictates of Islam. It is not within our means to go beyond the limitations set by the benevolent Almighty at the time of our birth; and it is morally condemnable to do so. Unlike Hindu women, we do not have the licence to go to another village. Girls who have come of age are not allowed to go to another house without respecting the rules of purdah. Therefore, the first and major reason why education is not widespread among our girls is the absence of schools that are right for us in the right locations. Secondly, the Muslim community in Bengal is very poor. A lot of them find it difficult to provide for their families. They cannot afford the small amounts of money to pay for their sons' education, let alone their daughters'! There is a dearth of schools and also that of money. Granted, wealth might lead to waste, but these days it is impossible to get educated without paying for it. One needs books, slates to write on, paper and pens, to say nothing of school fees. In spite of the several good practices in Muslim society, one thing has not caught on yet. Had there been 1 percent of the encouragement and assistance that Hindus extend to each other vis-à-vis education, it would have served us well.

A Muslim boy's aspiration to be educated dies at the outset if he is not able to provide for himself. In such a situation, it is no wonder that a poor man's children remain uneducated. Even if a magnanimous soul establishes a school, unless he is rich, he cannot bear the school expenses alone and therefore cannot turn it into a 'free school'. He must rely on others for it to survive. While many of our countrymen donate freely elsewhere in the hope of securing inconsequential titles, when it comes to social welfare or a good cause they seem to run out of money! Contributions to the cause of education are indeed rare.[6] And it is not fair to expect that one will be able to sustain a school by begging for alms from the villagers! The reason why education cannot be spread to the desired extent must be more or less clear to all from these observations. Now I shall write about a few ways in which the pure light of education may be spread uniformly among the people.

First, we must establish schools that suit us in every city, village, and so on, as is necessary. Women teachers of good character will have to be posted in the city schools; and these schools must be situated in places that girls might attend without showing any disrespect to the norms of seclusion. Men must not be permitted within the premises of the school. Girls residing close to the school could be accompanied by a maidservant or may travel in groups of four or five to school. The older girls must be provided with transport, as it is not proper for them to walk in public places. There is no harm if there are no women teachers in the village schools, as of now. Sincere, aged and experienced Muslim male teachers would serve the purpose very well. If such a school is opened, the parents of older girls may not want to send their wards to it, but one does not see why a similar objection may be raised about the younger girls. Indeed, I feel society does not need to be so eager about the education of older girls at this moment. Their guardians—husbands, fathers or brothers—could take the decision on their behalf. The hope of progress in our society depends totally on the younger girls. Therefore, by educating them we might be able to achieve the ultimate goodness.

At this point it is imperative to decide that if established, who would take the responsibility of funding such schools? Many rich men dwell in cities. So it is not likely that the city schools will face a funds crunch. One could, if one so wished, run such a school, single-handedly, in the city. It could be run on donations as well. It is the village schools that face serious financial problems. In most villages it's difficult to find ten people who are well off. Even if one finds two or three affluent people among the illiterate low castes, they are against women's education. Can people who have had no connection with education for generations, be expected to spend money on women's education? The crux of the matter is that unless there is income from other sources, it is difficult to run a school on the money raised by the concerned village. I am not sure whether the regional Muslim education committee is troubled by this issue. Getting to know what is on their agenda would be interesting. The road to educating the hapless women of the country cannot be smooth without the benevolence of the rich zamindars and the veteran heads of society. Will they not, for the sake of the welfare of one's own society, come forward to ensure that the race of benighted women get educated? Do we have to spell it out that in order to have good, educated children one needs good and educated mothers first? The Muslims had once charmed the earth by ascending the zenith of knowledge. It is hard to believe that the women of this community should remain submerged under the darkness of ignorance. I cannot believe that Muslims would remain indifferent even after seeing this shameful and pathetic picture.

Nabanoor, 8th issue, 2nd year, 1904

For the Love of the Motherland

The kind of subjects that are being discussed and agitated about in these times augurs well for our country, which is in a state of decline. There is no doubt that the Partition of Bengal is at the root of these agitations. Today, in the towns and villages of every district, everybody—zamindars, lawyers, literate and illiterate—are organizing huge meetings, and making a firm pledge to not use foreign goods. I would like to say a few words about what the women who stay indoors ought to be doing at these times.

Sisters, do we not have any right to be concerned about the tasks in which our fathers, brothers and husbands are involved, the causes to which they have devoted their bodies and souls and the matters that are always on their minds? Of course, we have an equal right to participate in these matters! If we did not help them adequately and sympathize with them in moments of pain and hardship, we would be disrespecting the love shown to us by our fathers and brothers and giving our roles as wives and better halves a bad name.

We must not sit idle at the time of this great revolution. It is our responsibility to try to do as much as we can. Of course, I'm not asking you to arrange huge conferences or go to lectures at the Town Hall or on the streets. If we wish to, we would be able to help our men folk, even as we are sitting inside our houses. It is not much; we will only need to sacrifice certain things. Sisters, if your sacrifice helps our motherland, if it brings wealth and prosperity to the nation in abundance, if it results in the resurrection of India's dormant industries, then why would you be averse to making them? Why would you shy away from taking the pain resulting from such sacrifices? Come, let us be determined in sticking to our convictions, like our men. Let us prove to society that Indian women can do a lot of good to the country. Sisters, you may recall that kshatriya women had, in the past, made tremendous sacrifices when they gave up invaluable and bejewelled ornaments, clothes with gold embroidery and even cut off the beautiful hair adorning their crowns to make bowstrings to help men who would use them in battle. Why then should we hesitate to make such little sacrifices? Today, if we turn away from helping our men in these small matters and fail to encourage them, even as we are by their side, will not God Almighty curse the race of women?

Sisters! Come, let us pledge to give up saris made from foreign cloth; scorn British bodices, chemises and socks; start using rose water and attar instead of lavender, and free ourselves from wearing shoes meant for foreign ladies that make us stumble. Only then will we be able to benefit our country. A huge variety of dhotis, silk saris and fine cloth are manufactured in Bombay, Dhaka, Pabna, Nadia and Murshidabad. These clothes are both glamorous and durable. If we used these materials, our money would stay within the country, artistic activity would get a boost and the poor weavers and labourers would be able to earn themselves a frugal meal through work. Perhaps men are not as effective as women when it comes to striving for the development of our country. If we did not allow them to bring home foreign goods, would men be able to do so? We have more control at home. Even if a man favours foreign products, could we not make an earnest appeal to make him give up the idea? It is certainly possible. How can we call ourselves their better halves, if we cannot do this?

A considerable amount of cotton and silk are produced in our country, but we hardly appreciate this fact. Foreigners buy the material at a low price and take it home. What we get instead are highly-priced, imported foreign clothes. If we started using indigenous cloth, it would support a number of textile manufacturing units in the country. And if the cotton and silk we grew were utilized in our own country, foreigners would never be able to ruin us by taking shiploads of our money across the seven seas.

See what harm enamelled utensils have brought upon us! In the past we were accustomed to using utensils and pots made of bell metal [alloy of copper and tin], brass and copper. Suddenly, these showy yet highly-brittle new utensils have infiltrated from nowhere and filled up our homes. Indigenous utensils can be sold at half their price even when broken, but sisters, have you ever seen broken enamelled utensils fetching any resale value? A householder possessing ten utensils of bell metal or copper might regard these as property, which could be sold or pawned to get funds in times of distress. But enamelled utensils are not considered worth any value. Since these are used mainly by us, could men force us to do so if we refused? Come, my sisters, let us pledge not to touch these enamelled utensils! Let us see if we can revive the use of indigenous bell metal and copper.

Sisters, can't you see how utterly degenerated we have become? Could the merchants from across the seven seas have cheated us by offering ornaments made of German silver and bangles of bevelled glass and taken home shiploads of Indian wealth and rice if we weren't gullible? And we still think we have gained priceless stuff! Are these not enough to bring ruin on us? If we think calmly, it would not be an exaggeration to say that these foreigners are, in a way, robbing us. India alone can produce for almost the entire world; which means, whatever one might procure from all over the world is available here in India. Have you thought for a moment why then are we, who live in the very same India, on a course of steady decline? Seeing that we are such simpletons, the merchants of America, England, Scotland, Germany, Australia, Switzerland and Japan are constantly trading paltry articles for the crops we produce with hard labour, taking them home, even as we go begging from door to door for a fistful of rice! Unless we liberate ourselves from the dishonest clutches of these merchants, we will continue to remain in this abyss of despair!

Most people in the country keep a cow or two for milk and almost everyone drinks milk every day. But tea prepared without imported tinned milk does not seem to taste as good. What a calamity! One is utterly disheartened thinking about such things! A country is pushed into such a sorry state of affairs at a time when the degeneration is complete. Sisters! You drink tea and feed the tinned milk to suckling infants, assuming it is absolutely pure, but do you ever pause to think if this milk is from an ass or a horse? It is only luckless Indians who would think that the milk produced beyond the seven seas is better than the fresh cows' milk available at home. I do not suppose people from any other country would think so.

Our country produces huge amounts of *gur* [molasses], sugar and sugar candy. Indians were content with having gur and sugar before the British came to our country. Now we hate to consume indigenous molasses, unrefined sugar and candy. We cannot do without refined sugar. We spot impurities in the home-grown sugar and molasses. Every year we import refined sugar worth Rs.55,000,000 to India. Sisters, if we could keep this huge sum of money at home, wouldn't the country have benefited hugely? We never think of this for a moment. Is it not possible to have the home-made molasses refined if one so wants? Certainly it is. Come, let us, for once, start consuming indigenous molasses and sugar.

Much of our wealth is going abroad in connection with another disastrous activity—smoking cigars and cigarettes. We produce fine varieties of tobacco as well, but the school and college-going boys in our country hanker after cigars and cigarettes from abroad. I really do not understand why; I think it may be a part of their affecting a luxurious way of life. About Rs.3,000,000 spent annually on cigars and cigarettes go outside the country. Investing the money in growing tobacco and other essential ingredients at home would have been a better idea. It would have helped to keep the money in the country. Sisters, do we ever notice how our children are damaging their health by smoking these foreign-made and poisonous cigarettes from a young age? It is a pity that being indulgent mothers, instead of dissuading them from smoking the poisonous cigarettes, we encourage them indirectly. Can we not free our children from the clutches of this poisonous stuff, if we try now? If we put a strict ban, asking our children not to touch cigarettes, will they not listen to us? Does a mother's command have no value?

Dear sisters, today I mentioned just a few things. I hope all of you will try your utmost to bring about our country's welfare. If you choose to spend your days in everlasting slumber, there is no hope for poor India. This is the time to wake up. If we opened our eyes even now, I hope, much could be accomplished through our efforts.

Nabanoor, Ashwin 1905

Notes

1 We could not procure a copy of *Satir Patibhakti* in spite of our best efforts. Neither Bangla Akademi, Dhaka, nor National Library, Kolkata, had a copy. There may be one in a private collection or less-known library, which a reader might know of.

2 'Of these essays we were able to trace just two, published in *Nabanoor* and included in this collection.

3 Syed Abul Maqsud is a writer, journalist and researcher. He lives in Dhaka.

Among his better known books are, *Maulana Abdul Hamid Khan Vasani*; *Harishchandra Mitra* and *Syed Waliullahar Jiban O Sahitya* (The Life and Works of Syed Waliullaha). He was awarded the 'Bangla Akademi Purashkar' in 1995 in recognition of his research. At present, Maqsud works as the news editor of Bangladesh News Agency, in Dhaka.

4 'It is the duty of every Muslim to seek knowledge; it is their *farz*.'

5 'One should always endeavour to educate one's daughters'; source unknown.

6 Khairunnesa's note: The fact that contributions to good causes are rare is evident from the plight of Sirajganj Hosainpur Girls' School. It was founded by Munshi Mohammed Meherullah, about eight or nine years back. Though the said Munshi sahib is financially unsound, he has been managing the finances of the school single-handedly all this while. No tuition fees are charged from the students. Instead, they are given books, paper, pens and stationery, occasionally. Most people of this village are very poor and therefore unable to help. There is a serious shortage of furniture, benches and tables in the school. In spite of several applications sent to the raja, nawab, zamindar and several wealthy and titled men, not a single paisa could be procured. This shows where the priorities of the people of this country lie.

3

Mrs. M. Rahman (1885-1926): A Portrait of Courage

Translated by Anusuya Ghosh

When it comes to spirited and inspirational writing, Mrs. M. (Masuda) Rahman is second only to Rokeya Sakhawat The arrival, sojourn and departure of this writer, who produced a small body of work were as spectacular and brief as a meteorite's. Unfortunately, very little about Mrs. M. Rahman—one of the most noteworthy writers of the second decade of the twentieth century—can be known from her books and the notes she left. As she died at the young age of forty-one, it was difficult getting any information from the living members of her family who hardly have any memory of her.

At the time of Mrs. M. Rahman's death, her daughter, Mahfuza Khatun, and her grandson, the six-year-old Muhammad Aziz Sultan Kamruzzaman Chowdhury, were her only heirs. After Partition in 1947, her relatives and acquaintances got scattered on either side of the border. Now after more than sixty years, the links between them are rather tenuous. For such reasons, the life story of such a remarkable woman remains rather indistinct. We shall try to construct a biographical picture of Rahman from *Bangla Sahitye Saugat Yug* (The Age of *Saugat* in Bengali Literature), based on the information gathered from her sister's granddaughter, Siddiqua Zaman.

Masuda Rahman was born in a village called Sherpur in Hooghly district in 1885. Her father, Khan Bahadur Mazharul Anwar Chowdhury, was a distinguished lawyer of the Hooghly Judges' Court. He was a member of the Standing Council, headed by the Lieutenant Governor. His family owned a zamindari in Sherpur. Masuda's mother was called Begum Moizatunnesa. As the daughter of a prosperous, educated family in Hooghly, Masuda learnt how to read the Koran, and some Bengali and Urdu in her paternal home. She was the eldest of eight brothers and sisters. Masuda was married off at a very young age of eleven (eight or nine, according to some), to the zamindar of Furfura, Kazi Mahmudur Rahman; who was the registrar of Calcutta at that time.

Looking at the publication dates of Rahman's writings, it seems that she began writing after the First World War. At the same time she had met the poet Nazrul Islam. Prior to this, the explosive articles of Rokeya Sakhawat, published in *Nabanoor*, had a deep impact on her mind and probably inspired her to write. Rahman got to know Rokeya Sakhawat Hossain and corresponded with her. Probably that is why Rokeya's thoughts on women's issues resonate in the writings of Rahman. Added to that was her own propensity to recklessly fling angry words about in her writings. The essay *'Amader Dabi'* (Our Demands) included in this collection, for instance, ends like this:

> Do you expect those who had stripped the venerable woman in an open court,[1] those who snatched the veils of the universally respected, bereaved women in the fields of Karbala,[2] those who called their mothers bloodthirsty tigresses without a qualm (the extent of humiliation that women go through in these times is almost unutterable) to show you respect? One who never receives the respect of fellow human beings keeps sinking into the depths of moral degradation. The humiliation, accumulated through aeons together, has not only transformed us into tigresses, but venomous snakes as well. As bloodthirsty tigresses, we shall suck dry the hearts of those who humiliated us and thus apply a balm to our aggrieved souls. As the mauled serpents, we shall let out spurts of venom, sting the offenders over and over again and make them suffer so that the intense humiliation meted out to us might be avenged.

An example of her curt and outspoken style may be found in the same essay: 'Even if a dutiful father tries very hard, all he does is teach the Koran by rote and thereby feels a sense of self-aggrandizement. Thus, he can say, 'My daughter is *Khatam-Koran* [Koran-literate]', although she might not be able to make sense of a single word in the book.'

Mrs. M. Rahman did not hesitate to hit out at the male guardians in a Muslim family as well as the Bengali Muslim society of the time, in general, through her incendiary writings. She almost managed to shred them apart for their biased and unjust attitude vis-à-vis education, marriage and purdah. Like the other Muslim writers who were contemporaries of Rokeya Sakhawat Hossain and arrived immediately afterwards, Rahman's writings were mainly centred on the realization of the rights of women as sanctioned by Islam. It is her recklessness that marks her apart. Her use of abrasive words and aggressive views makes her a rebel, quite different from her contemporaries. She writes in an article in *Saugat*, Ashwin 1926, 'I never received a Bengali education. Sorrows and pain, hitting hard against each other, have ignited the flint of my soul; and the tip of my pen sometimes reflects sparks of this fire.'[3]

What was Mrs.. M. Rahman like? Since she has been dead for over eighty years, it is not possible to get an exact picture of what she was like. Siddiqua Zaman, granddaughter of Mrs. M. Rahman's third sister, Marzina Begum, was born fourteen years after her grandaunt's death.[4] She had heard that her grandmother's sisters were self-willed and free thinkers. They possessed characteristics that were rare in contemporary Muslim society. It's possible to get an idea of Mrs. M. Rahman, the person, from Siddiqua Zaman's recollection of her grandmother as she knew her in childhood.

> 'At that time we lived first in Kareya Road [in Calcutta] and then in Balu Hakkak Lane. As my brother and I were among the eldest, our paternal grandmother often took us along to various places. In the mornings, she usually went to New Market. I remember going there with her a few times. In the afternoons, after lunch, she went to matinee shows. I remember the last film I saw with her starred Kanan Devi and Ashok Kumar. In the evening, she sometimes went out to listen to music. But, I never knew where she went; until later. She loved listening to kirtans [devotional songs]. When a good programme of kirtan was on, she

attended on her own, even at night. On the days she rested after lunch, I noticed that she either listened to songs or read novels. It was curious to see that while my paternal grandfather never smoked cigarettes, my grandmother did so, in a holder, after lunch. She would not smoke many, just one or two a day. I heard from my father that she knew the Hindu *Puranas* very well. I noticed a difference between her and my grandfather. He was not much attracted to the Bengali language or culture, but my grandmother always listened to Bengali songs. She never wore the burqa, just a sari and used its end to cover her head.'

Siddiqua Zaman could share only a lone anecdote about Mrs. Rahman:

'I heard from the granddaughter of my grandmother's sister, that their relation with their father [Mrs. Rahman's father] was never very amicable. When the poet Nazrul was about to be arrested and there was a buzz to that effect, Masuda Rahman had no way but to appeal to her father for Nazrul's release. She perhaps felt that her father, being a Khan Bahadur and friendly with the British, might help her. But her father refused to speak to the British magistrate in this matter. Masuda, was very upset over this and said that she would never return to her father's house while she lived and stuck to her word.

Kazi Nazrul Islam referred to Masuda Rahman as his Ma or mother. It was she who organized Nazrul's wedding with a Hindu girl, Pramila Sengupta, of Comilla district, on 24 April 1924. She also arranged Nazrul and his wife's visit to Hooghly. Nazrul wrote a rather long elegy, entitled 'Mrs. M. Rahman' when he heard about her death. This mournful elegy was published along with a letter in *Saugat*, Magh 1926.[5] Here is an extract from the letter in question to the editor of *Saugat*, Mohammad Nasiruddin:

'I was writing a poem on the imprisoned state of Gazi Abdul Karim when the news of Ma's [Mrs. M. Rahman] death threw me into confusion. Many were weeping at home. She loved me more than her own son. I could not give her anything in return. I feel desolate, friendless, like a

> destitute, merely staring at the ebb and flow of life's tide. I am miserable. Please publish the poem written in memory of Ma, in the opening pages of *Saugat's* Magh issue. I am not requesting you to do this because she loved me, but on the merit of her literary achievements, which deserve to make such a claim. I shall be happy if you publish this. Ma too would perhaps rest in peace, when she sees the belated appreciation of her neglected talent.'

Mrs. M. Rahman died on 20 December 1926. An article in *Saugat* said 'We hereby state, with grief-stricken souls, the demise of one of the greatest writers of Muslim society, Mrs. M. Rahman, who was only forty-one. She was suffering from the formidable disease of small pox *(inna lillahi . . . raaji'oon)*, verily we are for Allah and unto Him will we return. She was concerned with protecting the rights of women at all times and her writings strongly condemned the injustices meted out to women . . . The loss of a talented writer like Mrs. M. Rahman has truly impoverished Muslim society.'

In an article entitled *'Mrs. M. Rahman Smarane'* (In Memory of Mrs. M. Rahman), Shamsunnahar Mahmud writes in *Nauroz* Asharh 1927, Bengal's fiery serpent, Mrs. M. Rahman, is no longer with us—she left for the other, darker world at a very untimely hour. She came at a time that was very difficult for Muslim women, and inspired them to follow the path of liberation, making them taste the heady delights of freedom. Indeed, it seemed that the sorrows of women down the ages were embodied in her. . . . The hurt that collected in her 'wronged bosom', like a poison froth might have scorched all wrongs and untruths [done to women].

We have come to know, from Mrs. Rahman's familial sources, that she wore khadi [indigenous spun cloth] as a mark of her anti-British views. In fact, following her last wishes, her shroud too was made of khadi.

She wrote a novel entitled *Ma O Meye* (Mother and Daughter), which her family says is autobiographical). This novel was serialised in *Saugat* in Agrahayan 1930. Rahman's only published book is *Chanachur* and we have been able to procure it. Some of the essays in it vary slightly from their original versions. We find another book by Rahman mentioned in *Bangla Muslim Granthapanji* (List of Bengali Muslim Works, Dhaka: Bangla Akademi, 1985, collected by Ali Ahmed, p.618). This book, entitled *Muktir Mulya* (The Price of Freedom) was advertised in *Masik Mohammadi,* in Sravan-Bhadra 1944. *Chanachur* was published by her husband, Kazi Mahmudur Rahman, in Agrahayan 1927, in other words, a year after she had died. The flyleaf of this book contains a dedication by her only child, Mahfuza Khatun:

> 'For my venerable mother
> one who had boundless love
> one who taught me to love my motherland and her people—
>
> To that great lady of Bengal,
> at the feet of the honourable Mrs. R. S. Hossain Sahiba—
> under the direction of my father, Maulavi Kazi Mahmudur Rahman Sahib,
> I hereby pledge my respects—to my heavenly mother.'

It is noteworthy that after reading Rokeya Sakhawat Hossain's book of the same name, Mrs. M. Rahman wrote a poem entitled *'Motichur',* expressing her admiration for Begum Rokeya's book. The poem was published in the periodical *Sahachar* in Asharh 1922.

S.A.

The Great Fire

Respected editor of *Bijoli*! I have heard that Deshbandhu Chittaranjan Das has cited the examples of the *Vedas, Upanishads,* the Koran and *Gita* to show that 'all wolves bark in the same tone', that is, they all have the same objective. Even if he wanted to be direct, was this the best way of putting it? When the Vedas and the Koran become one, one might hear Shiva's horn and Israfil's trumpet blow in unison.[6] And that would be a real problem. Never mind the instrument that is played [to celebrate the occasion], I am not going to budge an inch before I have seen what I desire.

Was Chittaranjan so desperate to spill the beans that he had no fear of the mob? Does he not fear the brahmins cursing him, tearing at their sacred threads, or the mullahs wagging their beard at him censoriously? They are not the sort who would let him go without a protest. Having successfully concealed the truth for a long time, now they will not remain quiet when there is a lot of hue and cry over the issue!

They live with untruths, the reason why their preaching is so rigid and dry. Religion is supposed to lead to people's welfare. Society is an institution that establishes peace and discipline, vanquishes evil, respects courtesy and brings about an overall welfare. They say a state is destroyed by the sins of a king, and man is destroyed by the sins of a wife. I would say fools who pass themselves off as pundits—thus bringing shame on the community of learned men—and society leaders taking recourse to whimsy are breeding beasts instead of human beings. The country is declining. The nation is on the verge of a collapse.

Suddenly we hear the call of the nation. It is strange and indeed hopeless to think that a handful of people would liberate the country from [this sorry state] overnight, like the way giants might dig up a tank or build a pleasure park for a princess! One must first earn the right to be free, to become more seasoned by suffering for one's mistakes. To propagate the Mahatma's words, the late poet Satyendranath Dutta wrote the following:

> O Swaraj-seeking people awake!
> Swaraj we must get.
> We give up all to gain this wealth
> That freedom we so crave.

But can those who are unable to satisfy neighbours expect to satisfy their countrymen? Can those who never learnt to exercise self-control rule the country? Can the frail and emaciated carry the flag of freedom? That requires a lot of strength and courage. Stubbornness alone cannot help one hold on to the flagstaff. One is likely to drop down on the ground, if one tried doing that.

Pack the conservative old men off to the forests with their rosaries, snatch the religious texts from the hands of the hypocrites and lawyers, drive the offenders away from the sacred podium of this temple we call society. Preach the words of our creator for the benefit of mankind.

Koran, Koran Sharif, Kalame Mazid . . . reading matter to feed my demonic appetite with, a cool drink quenching my thirst on the lethal fields of Karbala—I have not yet understood you fully. I would like to make sense of you, know you. I would like to devour you entirely.

My elders have not initiated me to the Koran, they concealed the voice of the bountiful, merciful, and benevolent Hazrat Mohammad from me.

An irreligious and anti-motherhood society has decreed that women must always satisfy desires, cook delicious food, give birth to babies every year like bitches do, must abide by all its selfish dictates with bowed heads and offer their devotion, blindly, at its feet.

We are goddesses, women, and vicious witches, all in one. Beware—it is not as if we have lost all sense of self-respect because we play mothers to you.

If you do not have the so-called sacred thread around your neck you will not be able to pronounce the words of God! If you do not have a few strands of hair like a goat on your chin, you will not be able to expound on the Koran! If you do not have the stamp of a *tol* or madrasa,[7] your ideas will never be accepted even if you are wise! Do you expect those blinded by self-interests and so narrow-minded to make high-thinking and selfless workers?

Dear women, do you have any idea as to how petty-minded and slavish your own mothers were? What do you expect of the sons of women who, in this age of new awareness, remain content with jewellery enough to cover one's entire body and vaults full of money, forgetting their duties as women? How could they be any different from those who put chains on their fellow brethren and lead them to the gallows? Their daughters can hardly ever become mothers in the true sense.

My fellow workers! You are running after wealth, but where will you keep the accumulated treasure? The treasury full of jewels has vanished into thin air by the powers of a magic charm. You have pledged to achieve the flag of liberation, courted all kinds of hardship and oppression for that reason, but where will you hoist this flag of freedom? The forts that once stood erect have been razed to the ground! Want to raise a golden temple? Where would you find such a place? Our beautiful country now looks like a cremation ground—a place for evil spirits to prowl around, a ground for vultures to keep their eternal vigil. The air is putrid with the poisonous smell of decay! Is this a suitable place to erect a shrine of gold? We have to destroy, burn and erase all that is there to create anew.

You cannot cleanse and purify this abhorred land, now full of waste, without our help. You work very hard to bring home the golden harvest every year, but we are the ones who do the threshing, separating the grains from the husk. Do not add to the garbage by engaging in violent fights. Let us do the job that is ours. The flames of a hundred Vesuvius are stored in our chests, our hearts are tempestuous with the power of a thousand cyclones, and our eyes contain the unfathomable waters of ten thousand oceans.

Come, my sisters, let us prepare the ground for our darling sons to lay the foundations of a liberated country. Let us set fire to all that is bad, fake and heinous. Let the great fire stored in our hearts go up in flames, consuming this heap of ignominious rubbish. We will let these ashes fly away and wash the residue with tears of happiness.

And the golden shrine with a diamond diadem will finally be erected in our country. On top would soar the flag of liberation, high above, kissing the skies. There would be new life. The picture will feature brave mothers, raising brave sons, active brothers will be accompanied by dedicated sisters and proud wives would appear beside men, brave as lions.

For centuries together, Indians will live under the flag of liberation, in this golden structure and the bosom of the motherland.

It is not enough to imagine such a glorious spectacle. The parched heart is unable to quench its tremendous thirst merely with a vision. We must see this in reality. Come my sisters, let us pray that it happens:

> This wish, this toil, may it all come true,
> This and only this, O Bountiful, I ask of you.

Bijoli, Chaitra 1922

An Honest Agenda: 'Words Versus Work'

Deeds are necessarily preceded by talk. But if deeds do not begin at the end of all that talk, one must understand that the words were spent merely as a futile exercise or a pretext for whiling away some time.

According to many bashful women, 'to roam around shamelessly in the neighbourhood may be an excuse to break up homes', but it is also true that the women of the house may work for the nation by coming out of their houses uninhibitedly. My closest friend, Mrs. Rashad, is an example of the fact that women can work towards social welfare without being 'shameless'. She was concerned about the abject state of women for a very long time. The fact that women do not get enough to eat is among the chief signs of the disrespect shown to us, and she felt it keenly. That was a long time ago, when she was a married woman.

Just after she became a widow, her prime concern was the

state of the *bhadramahila*—the 'respectable women'—vis-à-vis that of the unfortunate common women entrammelled by the many varied concerns of life. The latter are illiterate. On top of that, they are plagued by the many ills of the purdah. They must put up with much humiliation even from the members of their own family, for a mere morsel of food and a piece of cloth.

Given the situation, it was imperative that those who enjoyed some economic freedom and were driven by a sense of altruism had to step in. Thus Mrs. Rashad, her elder sister, the silent Mrs. Sakhawat Hossain, founder of Sakhawat Smriti Balika Vidyalaya, and I—the four of us went from door to door, visiting different neighbours. One man tried to test her guts by trying to scare her, and then lauded her. He promised to offer help and even donate Rs. 200 for the good work. (But that was about it! We did not get a reply to the letter that we wrote him.)

Even after ignoring the threats and sarcastic comments of the so-called well-wishers, it was possible for her, by the grace of God Almighty, to begin a workshop last October. She has named it 'Zenana Talimgaha or Nari Shilpa Vidyalaya'. Here, girls will be taught the art of spinning cotton yarns from the charka or spinning wheel, weaving, do all kinds of sewing, book binding, learn to make boxes, hats and various kinds of pickles.

Widows, as well as married and unmarried girls can secure admission here. Affluent ladies can come to the school from their respective homes or stay as boarders by paying a fee. Destitute girls can live in the school premises, like adopted daughters of the founder. Their children, if any, can also stay with their mothers.

Only three students have been admitted so far. Mrs. Rashad is teaching them to sew and spin the charka. She will appoint a trainer when she has about ten students. This is the moment when we need the help and sympathy of our countrymen. We do not need money right now, not until we have ten students. Sympathy and effort are needed now to help us get students, especially since Mrs. Rashad is always frail and the mother of a child. Had I not been entangled with personal duties, I would not have urged people to collectively do the legwork. Any lady can approach her without hesitation.

I appeal to my sympathetic brothers to collect some students.

My progressive and affectionate sisters! Let us turn this race of women who are provided for by others into self-sufficient practitioners of art. Let us emancipate the helpless captives! Let us create women-power to awaken the vital life forces in women.

Will you still sleep even in this age of awakening? We too are humans, and we must get all the rights befitting humans. I have said this before, and I repeat: no one is served the good things on a platter. These could only be achieved by force and through hard work. Whatever other human beings are capable of, we too are.

Bijoli, 30 March 1922

Peace and Power

Do you know why bizarre thoughts come to our minds? So bizarre and grotesque are these thoughts that even the thought of these make the *Mahabharata* seem impure! One must seal one's ears when such thoughts are voiced.

But habit never dies! The more I want to remove these thoughts from my mind, the more they get crystallized, solidifying into writing on stone, as it were.

What shall I do? I am helpless. Why does a ray of hope shine in the dark corners of a weak, sequestered and naïve Bengali girl's heart? Handcuffed as she is, from where will she muster the courage of breaking free? Why do the liberating winds of the Arabian desert penetrate the barriers of the purdah? Why does the storm of rebellion rise from the heart of a woman, ignored and deprived of her rights? Who shall provide the answers to these queries?

I wonder what kind of thoughts pass through the minds of

women who are treated merely as men's pleasure partners, more like a household pet of some kind and are 'plagued to the bones with torture'?

There is a slight difference between licking the boss's boots after being kicked and pouncing on him in full force. It is how they behave that marks one quadruped from another.

I have heard since my childhood that the patriotic Aryans pledged all that they had for the progress of the country. Some of those who proudly wear chains as if these were jewellery and dance around in glory were once so passionate about their motherland that they had embraced imprisonment. That was a long time ago when they did not think of explaining things to their countrymen.

Thus, when the people awoke to the tune of 'Bande Mataram' after Lord Curzon's Partition of Bengal, at that moment, good or bad, a black cloud rose in the western horizon of my heart. A voice rose from the innermost quarters of my heart to cry out, O my devoted worker! Look at the clan of mothers. Did you teach your women, sisters and wives to give up their children before you sounded the clarion call to boys and young men to become patriots? Do you want to have roses blossom in a thorn bush?

Great men, both real and mythical, feel that women fulfil their duties by giving birth to sons.[8] So, down the ages, women have fulfilled their duty. But are they capable of producing sons who would live long enough? They give births to offspring who are already half-dead.

Uma, daughter of Nagendra, had a peaceful family life with her husband, Shiva, the attendants, Nandi and Bhringi, her children and the pet bull. But why did such a peaceful girl transform herself into the spectacle of a nude demoness, wearing a necklace of human heads, standing atop her husband's chest? Why did the beloved Mohammad's daughter, the queen of all goddesses, Fatema Zohra, want to break open the kafunra[9]? Why? It is because there is a limit to tolerance, because strength and power can grow even amidst peace and quiet.

When a man wants to show manly prowess, he does not mind bowing down at the feet of these very 'portals of hell', no matter if it is a goddess or human being. The clan of women does not react unless they have been hit real hard. And I have already mentioned that it is women who bring life to earth.

Could anybody act against one's nature? Could women, being mothers, ever abandon their natural love and affection? Some might begin with that prejudice and try to argue that 'women would never progress,' but such people are not even worth a serious mention.

Dhumketu, Agrahayan 1922

Our True Nature

All around, there is a call, urging people to awaken. Everyone is saying, wake up! True, but how long are people supposed to suffer from this delusion? The respected Parimal Kumar Ghosh has written:

> 'Hail woman! Arise for the glory and good of all.
> Bengal's sister, mother of Bengal,
> Caged at home, selfish pawn
> Pleasure-giver, decor alone
> . . . rights-less, awake you all!
> Bengal's sister, mother of Bengal.

Let the merciful God give the poet a long life. This is my sole prayer.

Now, the question is, what shall we do after we do awaken? One can hardly rest quiet in such an awakened state, there are a myriad things left to be done. Should one sit around like a cripple when God has given us a pair of hands, limbs and heads?

Awake we must, arise we must,
Set out to work,
We must set out.

But what shall we work with? We have no education, no experience, no freedom. People might say that the will to work would automatically win over obstacles. One must possess considerable mental strength to by-pass these hurdles. One must be self-sacrificing.

We must first know who are the ones to have deprived us, and by whom are we being humiliated. Is it society? Whenever one thinks of society, many questions come to mind. Who make this society? Aren't they our own people?

No matter who its members are, we must destroy this demon called 'society'. How long must women, posing as reticent simpletons or pleasure girls, be devoured by these demons? For how long must women continue to ignite the fires of male lust?

[Dear women], once and for all forsake your matronly cares and concerns. You have already meted that out quite generously, the result being that men have spoilt themselves, driven by excessive greed.

We have been hearing the following perhaps since even before we were born:

'Father is our dharma, father our heaven
Father our eternal God.'

And indeed it is so. Even as unborn children in the womb we have been told that the 'the husband is one's greatest guru'. The same thing is inscribed everywhere—on combs made in Germany, borders of handkerchiefs, towels and saris, made in Manchester, vermillion boxes—and the list continues.

'Wherever I turn my eyes to
I see my one and only Lord . . .'

But these shoe-wearing species are wicked (please excuse the language of this uneducated woman)!

Dear Sisters! How far did your fathers and husbands fulfil what they were duty-bound—morally and legally—to have done for you? I am just an illiterate, little-known sister of yours, but believe me I have suffered. I have tested them all and feel defeated. Our only hope is God Almighty! Mothers, do see to it that your daughters get education, develop integrity of character, are religious and able to make good use of their hands, limbs and brains so that they may be independent and self-reliant.

Marriage is another problematic issue! I thought Hindu and Muslim girls were keen to get married, but now it seems that even educated Christian and Brahmo girls long for the proverbial sweet that is damning—whether or not one actually tastes it. When the union between the two principles of creation—man and woman—is inevitable and endorsed by the Creator Himself, it will certainly take place. Why rush it?

The first task is to equip the girl in question so that she is ready to handle married life. Young widows often remain celibate all their lives, although widow re-marriage is sanctioned in different communities (except the Hindu). Why cannot unmarried girls do the same for a little longer? Indeed they would, if only their parents allowed them to do so.

There are a thousand other ways women could achieve fulfilment, besides getting married.

Indeed, there are; let the girls achieve these first.

Nothing can be achieved without collective strength. One must be able to proceed with whatever strength one has, to each her own.

True dedication will surely lead to success. There are many women zamindars in the Muslim community. They have sufficient economic independence. There are many educated women in the Hindu community. Our Christian sisters are educated as well as independent. And above all, we expect a bit more from our educated and capable Brahmo sisters. They have endured much hardship, much deprivation and attracted the admiration and respect of all by sheer hard work and dedication.

One's religious identity does not matter; it is more important to realize that we all are the children of the sole Creator.

We are humiliated, deprived womankind, robbed of our rights. Let us pray to the God Almighty together. [Dear God], please make our lives successful and worthwhile, give us freedom and emancipation. (Amen)

Has your father taught you anything? Did he give you enough education for you to win life's battles? Has he given you anything more than unconditional paternal love—a material gift to make you self-sufficient? Has he given you away to an educated, good-natured, warm and sympathetic man?

(Dutiful fathers are indeed worthy of our veneration.)

What did your husbands give you? Are you their life partners and housekeepers, their friends and the mothers of their children, or are you like household pets, ready to endure insults and abuse, the kicks and the stick, for the sake of a piece of leftover fish and milk? Or are you just a partner in his pursuit of worldly pleasures?

Shame on you! It is better to commit suicide if your life is such a slur on womanhood.

(Let God's blessings be showered upon the happy couples.)

You are the daughters of wealthy zamindars, wives of judges. Your fathers and husbands own marble palaces that are a feast for the eyes; they have properties worth thousands. And they have you, the repository, the mobile lockers of all their diamonds and gems—mere decorative furniture pieces to adorn their palaces.

Do you have anything to give? The men spend a lot of money on inconsequential luxuries and some of them go bankrupt as well. Could you donate funds towards the making of a free nation or to an orphanage? Could you establish a school for girls or a home for widows? Could you set up a workshop where thousands of hungry women who earn their livelihoods through sin could do vocational courses and become self-sufficient?

No, you can do nothing. You are penniless beggars, and like domestic pets are dependent on the mercies of the master of the house. You were born to be servants, and will bear that burden for the rest of your lives.

Say [with me], 'No, we shall never do so. Nothing remains constant for a long time in a fast-changing world.'

> Allah does not help change people unless they initiate the change themselves.
>
> (Koran, Surahbad)

Why should we follow the social dictum and continue to bear the burden of slavery? [I urge you to] make fun of this wicked society and break the shackles it has put on us. Do not sleep any longer. Open your eyes, look at the writing on the clear blue sky, it says 'work and peace'. One can hear the birds cooing the songs of liberation! Therefore, do wake up!

There is a lot to be done. But can we who are not well-educated, self-reliant, self-sufficient or free do anything? A French countess once said: 'When you do not possess a penny, how can your mind be free?' Quite so. How can people without financial independence ever do any work?

But do we sit tight in that case? No, we cannot do so; we must have it by force, we must achieve it at the cost of hard work and loss. You will not get it if you demand it from men; they are incapable of giving, as I have said earlier. And how can they show you any respect in the first place? They, after all, are giving their fellows exactly the kind of respect and rights that they get from the king's men. Poor things! Let us not blame them. They are the ones who should be pitied.

In conclusion, I would like to say to my sisters the world over, please do fulfil the request of this little-known sister of yours. In this society where injustice and a law of the jungle prevail, rise like tormented serpents in the image of the destroyer. Respond to the call of your sister by roaring like thunder, my sisters, as you flash like a streak of lightning!

Dhumketu, Ashwin 1922

What We Want

If one utters the truth it may anger the fool, and one may even run the risk of losing one's friends; but I say that it hardly matters. If truth antagonizes a friend, I would rather forsake the concerned friend with hatred. Such a loss would not sadden me. At least I shall be true to my God, I shall not be embarrassed to face him. Nowadays one comes across new phrases, such as 'manly woman', 'boorish woman' and 'the woman rules', and so on, all because women have begun to speak out what is true and justified. But should we not speak the truth regardless? If we do not protest, the torture would only increase, never abate. It is not as if no one has tried to protest; but can a rotten, scavenger of a dog that feeds on carcasses alter its habits? So many great men arrived down the ages; so many reformers were born. They did protest but could not achieve anything that lasted. People, whose arrival was like a balm of perfumed air, soothing us with a sense of freedom and peace left us. Their demise transformed that cool breeze into a tremendous cyclone and wrought anarchy.

In the age of prophets, it is said, whenever people became irreligious and licentious, a prophet was born in their midst and guided them to the path of justice and spirituality.

When the Arabs considered it their duty to kill their daughters, it was Hazrat Mohammad who showed us through his daughter, Fatema, how precious a daughter could be. He did not rest at that, but made the son and daughter equal by law. As the daughter goes to her husband's house she would get a little less of her father's property, that is, two daughters' share would equal that of a son's. If the father wishes, he can disown a son, but cannot deprive a daughter of her shares.

Both men and women must acquire knowledge and education. No discrimination is made between a son and a daughter in this respect. In spite of this, the less-than-human followers of Mohammad treat sons as the guide who will lead them to deliverance, and daughters like garbage. The son inherits his father's property, entirely, while the daughter does not get a penny.

A considerable amount is spent on the son's education, but no one remembers to educate the daughter. Even if a dutiful father exerts himself too much, all he does is makes the daughter learn a little from the Koran by rote and rests complacent at having fulfilled his duty. Thus both parents say with visible pride, 'My daughter knows the Koran,' when she does not understand the meaning of a single word of what she has learnt by heart.

When the son becomes a lawyer, an attorney or a judge and builds a fourth storey above a three-storied house, rules over a whole district, adds a few more honorifics acquired from the British rulers to the degrees acquired from the university beside his name, moving around the zenith of happiness and honour, the daughter remains uneducated, illiterate and leads the life of a dependent, like an unhappy slave. Most of them are also denied the love of their husbands. The selfish, inconsiderate father often gives his daughter away to a drunkard, a licentious rake given to prostitution or to a crude, heartless and vicious man, instead of one who is sympathetic and good natured.

They keep harping on the same refrain, 'We become penniless by marrying off our daughters, how could we spend money on her education? Whatever we spend on a daughter's marriage is more than her due.'

Heartless people, fools! Whom do you benefit by spending on your daughter's wedding? You merely convert her into an example of slavery, complete with jewellery so that she could be put up as an exhibit in the drawing room of another insensitive man like yourself.

Marriage establishes the institution of the family. To be able to do that one needs a certain level of education. Marriage would make sense only if you educated the girl and gave her away to a decent person. It hardly makes sense if you give away an ignorant girl to be tortured to death by the fires of uncertain domesticity and then say, 'I spent ten thousand rupees on my daughter's wedding.' O unlucky fool!

These fools greatly abide by their Prophet's sayings only in one respect. Do you know what it is? They make it a point to take new wives all through their lives, from a very young age to the fag end. They say with a mild, complacence, 'The Hazrat has laid down that one can marry till the age of seventy.' This seems true enough, for He knew that the Almighty God has sent these men to planet Earth with a dog's nature and also the fact that they would never be able to shed the despicable dog-like behaviour. Hence, they have only abided by what the Almighty has besought them with, after much thought.

Society was created by men, and the religious texts created by them are destroying us little by little. Unless we rebel and point out their lapses, they would never be conscious of their wrongdoings.

They have ruined us by depriving us of knowledge, which is invaluable. They often ask us to go away. Sometimes they also ask why we do not go, in spite of their repeatedly telling us to do so.

The great litterateur Dr. Lutfur Rahman Sahib, who is like a dear brother to me, has expressed this beautifully, 'It is essential to see that a man never dares to send a woman away. If a man really sends a woman away, may she not be pushed completely into the dark. Just because a woman's mobility is restricted, she has to endure so much pain, and such untruths.'

So amazingly true! Just because there is death, life has such lasting appeal; otherwise life by itself would have no value. Men know very well that we cannot go very far. That is why they ask us to go away, repeatedly. If we could go away, if there was a place for us to go to, then they would never have uttered such a thought.

Will they who, since the times of the *Mahabharata,* could not give away land even the size of the head of a needle to their brothers without bloodshed, ever give us our rights?!

> The land held on the tip
> Of a sharp needle.
> I shall not give to the Pandavas
> Without a battle.

Dear Sisters! 'The Kohinoor is worth five slaps with your slippers.' Let us give them five slaps and take our rights by force.

In fact, we too are in the wrong. We ask for our rights from men—the same men who do not have any rights themselves, who want to become big even as they behave like beggars, who have entrammelled themselves in the serpentine coils of slavery and shrunk their ideals smaller and smaller, they whose very souls have become slaves. Are they in a position to give us our rights? Can they help us achieve emancipation? Are you crazy?

Will the unfortunate people of this hapless country ever be able to respect us?

Those who had stripped a respectable woman in the open court, had unveiled the universally respected but bereaved women in the fields of Karbala, did not wince while calling mothers bloodthirsty tigresses (the humiliation of women at the present time is almost unutterable)—those very people, you suppose, would honour you! One who never receives the respect of fellow human beings always sinks into the depths of moral degradation. The accumulated humiliation of aeons has made tigresses and serpents of us. As bloodthirsty tigresses, we shall suck dry the hearts of those who humiliated us and quieten our aggrieved souls; as repressed serpents we shall empty our venom and soothe our anguished hearts through successive stings.

Dhumketu, September 1922

Notes

1 Refers to Draupadi, the wife of the five Pandava brothers in the epic *Mahabharata*. At the Kaurava court the eldest brother, Yudhisthira, played games of dice with Shakuni, losing all the possessions of the Pandavas until only their wife, Draupadi, was, left. He bet on her and lost her to the Kauravas. Duhshashana, one of the Kaurava brothers, ordered Draupadi, who had accompanied her five lords and was with the Kaurava women, to come to the court, where he tried disrobing her. The Pandavas watched in silence and shame but did not protest. Draupadi was finally saved by Krishna, who supplied her with a magical sari that kept her clad even as Duhshashana unravelled it.

2 The Battle of Karbala took place in A.D. 680, in present day Iraq, between Prophet Mohammad's grandson Hussain ibn Ali and the army of Yazid I, the Umayyad caliph. Hussain was killed in the battle and his family was taken prisoner. It is said that the women and children, who were waiting in the tents while the men fought, were captured and marched to Yazid I's court; and that the exhausted, hungry and thirsty captives were humiliated and harassed.

3 From the essay *'Bhul Bhanga'* (The End of a Mistake). This was published as a protest against the essay *'Banga Sahitye Musalman Mahila'* (Muslim Women in Bengali Literature) by Muhammad Abdul Hakim Bikrampuri, published in *Saugat*, Bhadra 1926.

4 Siddiqua Zaman retired as librarian, Institute of Business Administration, University of Dhaka.

5 This long poem by Nazrul begins in this way:
'Muharram's moon is still further away,
Yet, what woes of Karbala smite me thus?'

6 In Islam, Israfil is the angel . . . who will blow the trumpet from a holy rock

in Jerusalem to announce the Day of Resurrection. The trumpet is constantly poised at his lips, ready to be blown when God so orders. Lord Shiva, both creator and destroyer, possesses a horn that signifies this duality: it sounds the destruction of evil and the creation of all that is beautiful and good.

7 Tol and madrasa, respectively, Hindu and Muslim schools, where traditional education is imparted; including of the scriptures.

8 The original quotation *'Putrarthe kriyate bharya':* One should marry for the sake of begetting sons. *Manusmriti,* the ancient lawbook of the Hindus.

9 Uma is another name of the goddess Durga.

4

M. Fatema Khanam (1894-1957): A Short-Story Writer

Translated by Adrita Mukherjee

In 1964, seven years after the death of Mamlukul Fatema Khanam, Bulbul Publishing House, Dhaka, brought out a collection of seven of her short stories. The collection was called *Saptarshi* (The Seven Stars). The late Selina Bahar Chowdhury, the moving spirit behind the publication, was a descendant both of the 'Bulbul' family as well as Fatema Khanam's.[1] In 1933 the magazine *Bulbul* and publishing house were established as a result of the combined effort of Selina Bahar's father, Habibullah Bahar and her aunt Shamsunnahar Mahmud. Fatema Khanam was also an aunt of Selina's mother, Anwara Bahar Chowdhury. Thus Fatema Khanam was Selina's great aunt.

Selina Zaman (née Bahar) had a strange fondness for this great aunt (nanu). While in college, she would save up her pocket money, hoping to publish her nanu's book some day. She also, perhaps, nursed a sense of hurt for a long time, which she hinted at while speaking to us during an interview in 1997: Bulbul had published so many authors. Why did it take such a long time to publish Fatema Khanam? In the Introduction to *Saptarshi*, Selina wrote, 'Having talent is not enough. One needs an encouraging environment and connections in order to flourish. Rokeya Sakhawat Hossain and Shamsunnahar Mahmud, for instance, had found that environment and the necessary connections. But Fatema Khanam was not as fortunate.'

It is not as if Fatema Khanam lacked this 'environment' and 'connections' from the outset. She studied, played, and enjoyed life like any other ordinary child. But her life took an unexpected turn around 1906, when twelve-year-old Fatema was married off into a family of *pirs* or holy men. Pitched into such a conservative, unsympathetic environment, Fatema spent a lifetime torn between living with adversities and not being able to cope with them.

Fatema Khanam was born in 1894 in a village called Tachhbidanga in the Manikganj subdivision in Dhaka. Her father, Raisuddin Ahmed, was an inspector with the railway police, and travelled on work to different places in Bengal and Bihar. As a child, Fatema accompanied her father frequently on his trips. She did not attend school, but her education began with learning different languages at home. Raisuddin Ahmed had employed an English lady to give lessons to his wife Akhtarunnesa. He had taught his daughter Fatema to wear breeches and ride a horse. Evidently, he was a freedom-loving man with liberated ideas. He had left town once supposedly to avoid arresting freedom fighters Prafulla Chaki and Kshudiram Bose. It is a mystery why such a man married off his young daughter of barely twelve years to Abdur Rahman, son of the pir Abdul Gani of Garpota village in Manikganj. When she spoke to us, Selina Bahar Zaman too regretted the marriage.

Whatever be the reason why Raisudddin took such a step, there is no doubt that from this time on Fatema's life became a long saga of unrelenting struggle. Her husband was a doctor. 'Her parents-in-law were educated but not in favour of educating women. Getting caught with a book would fetch severe reprimands. Fatema used to read books by Michael Madhusudan Dutt, Bankim Chandra Chattopadhyay, Hem Chandra Bandopadhyay and Nabin Chandra Sen on the sly . . . At times, to avoid being called names, she would, very cautiously, crouch in front of the stove as something cooked on it, place her notebook on one knee and touch up her story with a pencil, using her other knee to hide the act. Most of her early manuscripts are written in pencil.'[2]

Fatema's father-in-law died a few years after her marriage. The joint family collapsed and a few years later Fatema and her husband set up a separate household. Soon, when her doctor husband left his profession to be a pir, like his father, Fatema, who found it difficult to reconcile the differences with her husband and cope with financial worries, went to live in Dhaka with her sons in 1920. Her first job in

Dhaka was at a primary school called the Aga Nawab Deuri School. A few months later, Fatema was transferred to Posta Girls' School where she worked until 1926. In 1927, she started teaching at the Muslim Training School, but frequent disagreements with the 'arrogant headmistress' made her leave and join Sakhawat Memorial Girls' School the same year.[3] In 1921, Fatema Khanam's first short story *'Shesh Anurodh'* (The Last Request) came out in the half-yearly *Dhrubatara* magazine published from Joshor. The editor of the magazine, Dr. Narul Wahab, was a distant relative.

Around 1930, Fatema Khanam's busy life came to an abrupt halt when she became seriously ill with a gall stone problem. Gradually, her health was ruined completely; the reason being a lack of adequate medical facilities at the time. In fact, she was almost totally inactive in the last twenty years or so of her life.

Fatema Khanam's writing career actually spans just one decade, beginning with *'Shesh Anurodh'* published in 1921, as mentioned earlier, and ending with the article, *'Taruner Daitwa'* (The Duty of the Youth) which came out in 1929 in the annual *Shikha*—the mouthpiece of contemporary Bengali Muslim literature. In between her stories and essays were published in several journals like *Manasi o Marmabani, Matrimandir, Saugat, Masik Sanchay*—all published from Calcutta, *Al-Farukh* and *Shikha* published from Dhaka, and *Juger Alo* from Yangon.

Around the time when Fatema Khanam came over to Dhaka with her sons in 1920, her younger sister, Kanij Fatema, died suddenly. Kanij Fatema's daughter Anwara (Khuki) was only two years old at that time. Fatema Khanam brought up Anwara as her own daughter, and spent the last years of her life with her. Anwara was married to the writer and politician Habibullah Bahar. After Fatema Khanam's death, author Abul Fazl wrote to Anwara Bahar from Chittagong,

> 'It is a devastating loss for you. But for her [Fatema Khanam], you wouldn't have been what you are today. She shaped your life for you—and it's not nearly enough to say that . . . you could pursue your studies and career without a hitch only because she was always there to support you. You

> didn't have much trouble bringing up your children [because of Fatema Khanam's presence]. All her wishes, hopes and dreams revolved around you.'[4]

It is perhaps easier to find a clue to Fatema Khanam's 'wishes, hopes and dreams' by looking closely at the world she inhabited rather than in the stories she wrote. The characters in Fatema Khanam's stories seem to have been created for a fictional space alone. The real Fatema Khanam, however, is still alive in the memory of the people associated with her world in different ways: niece Anwara Bahar, grandniece Selina, brother-in-law Nurul Momen, authors Abul Fazl and Didarul Alam, and so on.

It does not seem likely that Fatema Khanam wished to model her women characters in *Saptarshi* on herself. They seem to follow the trodden path, as directed by society: a path that is shaded by the love of a husband or lover. The women are upset if the screen is moved even slightly away. Some women, Chameli, for instance, may be strong-willed but are ultimately soft and feminine, perhaps even somewhat dependant on men. When it came to her personal life Fatema Khanam was not one who would despair easily. She had a tremendous innate ability to fight back. She could invest ugliness with beauty. At the time of her unrelenting struggle in the 1920s, it is likely that her 88 Urdu Road house was dogged by want, but she never failed to entertain her young writer friends there.[5] She had never been to a school, but started going to a coaching class rather late in life, to help 'Khuki' (Anwara) with her studies, and even began taking painting lessons. Otherwise, she thought, she would 'never be able to teach her [Khuki] anything. Society wouldn't let me.'[6]

One cannot help thinking whether Fatema Khanam's women characters were idealized versions of herself. Did she, secretly, long for a perfect, happy life, the sort her creations led? It is difficult to find a satisfactory answer to this question, for the fictional world of her short stories coexisted with a deeply emotional feeling towards independent and bold women like Begum Rokeya and Fazilatunnesa.[7] She had wanted to write the biography of Begum Rokeya,[8] and had nurtured a humble wish to invite Fazilatunnesa to a home-cooked dinner.[9] Perhaps she was content to find fulfilment of her hopes and desires in the lives of her niece Anwara and her daughter Selina. Selina Bahar Zaman had reminisced a day in her youth when back from college she found her Nanu—quite seriously ill at the time—scribbling unsteady lines with a pencil on a scrap of paper:

> 'Behold the morning sun rising in a glory of light
> Darkness starts and melts away, as if in fright.'[10]

Fatema Khanam once wrote to Mohammad Nasiruddin, the editor of *Saugat* magazine, 'There's nothing very special in my life that warrants writing a short history.' Indeed, it was this unassuming demeanour which made Fatema Khanam's life special. Otherwise, she would not have been able to express her secular sentiments so quietly while speaking at the condolence meeting in memory of the young writer Didarul Alam. The friendly relationship she shared with her brother-in-law Nurul Momen was also unusual. She wrote to Momen in a letter:

> 'Whenever I spent time chatting with you, it felt as if I had gone back in time—I felt light and carefree, as if I entered the playroom of my childhood.'

The influence of Saratchandra Chattopadhyay and Rabindranath Tagore is evident in Fatema Khanam's style and language, which she herself acknowledged.[11] This, however, does not mean that she was eclipsed completely by the shadow of the great writers. She occupied a unique position as a woman writer, and as one within the Bengali Muslim tradition. She was able to convey the distinctive features of her experience through the small details in her writing.

> Sitting in that tiny room, as the midday sun shone bright outside, Helen tried to push the long days to their end with great effort, almost physically, as if with both hands, by reading, knitting laces, embroidering flowers

> on a handkerchief. If she heard someone was going to Calcutta, she would start at once to pack things for Selim—little things like pure ghee, molasses made from dates, halwa, murabba [pieces of fruit soaked in syrup].[12]

Abul Fazl comments, 'Perhaps as a writer, Fatema Khanam was not one of the greats.' There is no doubt that he is right. But one cannot help wondering if, considering her time and her personal constraints, Fatema Khanam did not, at least, deserve a place beside the other women writers of her age? Couldn't she too have been remembered alongside the Sita Devi, Shanta Devi and Shailabala Sarkars?

M. B.

Chameli

One fine day, Chameli disappeared—Chameli, the girl who dressed like a man and hung around with men. The neighbours said, 'Born of a cook and growing up with Mirzapur ruffians—how can a girl like that stay in purdah?'

Chhoto Bibi did not utter a word. The slur hit her hard. She may not have carried Chameli in her womb but she had raised her since she was a small infant, like her own. Chhoto Sahib took his car out and made useless rounds of almost all the lanes of Calcutta for the next few days. Time passed, its relentless cycle squashing season after season. Chameli was almost forgotten.

Salmu came in playing a bamboo flute, holding a balloon and a ten-rupee note in the other hand.

'Ma, Chameli gave you this money,' he said.

'Chameli? Where is she? Run along, bring her over to me right now.'

'But she's gone.'

'Gone? Silly boy, did the flute make you forget all else? Why didn't you bring her over?'

'But she didn't want to come. She just walked away, down the lane next to Patal's house.'

'Didn't she say anything to you?'

'Yes, of course. She said, "Give this money to Ma, I got paid today." '

Malek was Chameli's friend from her childhood days. They would play cards, argue noisily for no apparent reason, and smoke bidis together. Often other young loafers from the locality would join them.

The other day a public announcement was being made to the sound of drums, about a meeting where a maulana would explain the Koran. 'We've got to attend,' said Chameli's gang.

The maulana quoted a verse from the Koran and explained, 'The most pious deed for a Muslim is to bring those unfortunate souls who have lost faith back in the fold.'

Malek ran his eyes keenly all over Chameli, who was sitting next to him. He would bring this prodigal daughter, clad in a man's long shirt and pleated dhoti, back into the fold of holy Islam, at any cost.

The gang broke up. Chameli had disappeared. Malek worked as a film operator with Madan Company. To him the daring heroines on the screen looked like spitting images of Chameli. The speeches of the maulana rang like gunshots in his ears.

Chameli started a business of selling cardboard boxes. She had a shop at one of the crossings near lake Champa and employed a few young men to help her.

'So when did you quit your job at the office, Chameli?' asked Malek, offering her the bidi he was smoking.

'Oh, a long time ago,' Chameli replied. 'Who the hell cares about a handyman's job that pays a measly fifteen rupees a month and comes with a boss constantly yelling at me? See my shop? I've got my own business now, earning between twenty and thirty rupees a month.'

'Oh, is that why you went to Darjeeling—to get new orders?'

'Of course. And it's not just Darjeeling. I went to all sorts of other places too—Delhi, Lahore, Ceylon—all within the past year.'

Malek suddenly became quiet. 'Why are you wasting your life like this, Chameli?' he asked. 'Why don't you get married?'

Chameli grinned. 'Marry? Marry whom?'

'Why not me, for instance?'

'You?' Chameli said angrily. 'Why on earth should I marry you? Am I not a man? If I hear you utter that word again I'm going to screw up your future with one kick of this shoe-clad foot.'

Malek turned away dejectedly. Chameli had wrapped the fake skin too tight on her body. It would not be easy to tear it off.

'Amma, O Amma!'

Chhoto Bibi turned. It was Chameli. She was carrying a bundle. Inside it were a couple of cauliflowers, a kilo of mutton and a huge fish-head. Chameli had not eaten food cooked by her mother for a long time, and planned to do so today.

'Chameli, you're back! Why did you leave us, dear?'

Her brothers crowded around. 'Chameli Bu, please don't go away again. Please!'

Chameli could almost hear the chains clanking around her ankles. In front of her was her mother—the image of unconditional love. Chameli touched the glorious woman's feet just once and turned back, scared.

'Chameli, wait a minute, let me at least cook something for you.'

Chameli did not stop. In the wink of an eye she was lost in the enormous sea of people on Harrison Road.

It was three weeks later that Chameli opened her eyes. This was the first time since her illness that the spark of life had returned to her eyes. All her fair-weather friends had beat a retreat during her illness. It was Malek alone who sat by her sick bed round the clock, fighting death with all his might.

Two months later, Chameli was completely cured. She went to the market on her own and cooked lunch. When Malek sat down to lunch, instead of fighting with him for the choicest portions of fish and meat, Chameli passed them on, filling up Malek's plate. Unlike other times, Chameli did not even try to keep them for herself.

'You'd better stop cooking, Chameli,' Malek said. 'I'll be in trouble, if you fall ill again.'

Chameli did not reply. She looked a different person. After lunch, when Malek offered her his cigarette, Chameli threw it away.

'What's wrong? Don't you want it?' Malek asked, surprised.

'I've given up smoking,' said Chameli.

Entering his room at night, Malek was dumbstruck. Chameli had swapped men's clothes—the sort she had been wearing since the day she was born—for a woman's garb. She draped the sari end nicely over her head, covering the manly side-parting. Fragrant flowers adorned her hair, neck and arms. She was looking like a new bride, overcome with coyness.

'Chameli, what a surprise to see you in a sari! You look beautiful,' Malek said. 'Will you always wear this? Promise me that you won't ever wear men's clothes again.'

'Will that make you happy?' Chameli asked demurely, casting a sideways glance at Malek that was both sweet and intense.

Malek looked at the impenetrable darkness outside and nodded quietly. 'Yes,' he said.

Masik Sanchay, Magh 1928.

The Bond

Mukhujye Mashay stood at the fashionable gate—embellished with flowers, fruits and twigs—of the beautiful white bungalow and called out, applying all the force that he could muster, 'Halim! O Halim! Open the door, please.'

It was almost midnight. The still shadow of quiet slumber hung heavy on the railway employees' quarters. Only those unfortunate souls who had night duty were awake, ready to flag off trains and run home. Occasionally sounds of prolonged whistles and the steady chugging of a train that had not gone too far yet resonated across the stillness.

Finally, after several calls went unanswered, Mukhujye Mashay knocked forcefully on the door. A young woman stood beside him with downcast eyes, her face half-concealed by her sari. The door opened. Halim appeared, a handsome young man just roused from his sleep, a lantern in hand. The sub-engineer had been newly transferred to this place. Everyone at the station respectfully called him 'Halim Sahib' but his relationship with Mukhujye Mashay was somewhat different. Mukhujye Mashay was from the same village as Halim's father-in-law. Halim's wife and her brothers and sisters all called Mukhujye Mashay Thakurda (grandpa) and the old man himself had revealed this to Halim enthusiastically when they first met. Since that day he was Thakurda to Halim as well.

'Thakurda! At such an hour?' asked Halim, putting the lantern down.

'I'll explain everything tomorrow morning. I've brought a maid for you. Show her in.'

Surprised, Halim lifted the lantern and looked at the woman with sleepy eyes. What a lovely face that was, how fair and graceful! Its composed, soft and youthful glow was clearly visible with the light turned on her. Perhaps the thought that a maid trying to hide her face was an unpardonable offence—however beautiful she may be—had prompted the woman to draw the sari anchal back, revealing her forehead. Halim lowered the lamp quickly. It was as if someone had opened the floodgates of memories held in his heart for years together, and he trembled.

'Where did you find her so late at night, Thakurda?' he asked, trying to brush the sleep away from his eyes.

'How can an old man like me get lucky enough to 'find' anyone like her?' said Mukhujye Mashay, shaking his salt-and-pepper head. 'I went to see my wife. When she heard you desperately needed someone to cook and clean for you, she sent this girl.'

'Please thank Thakurma for me,' Halim said, embarrassment showing in his smile. 'But really, this . . .

'Young lady, eh?'

'So she is, Thakurda.'

'Worried? You shouldn't be. I know you're a perfect gentleman. Your heart is a hundred feet above anything mean.'

'Maybe, but one can't ignore the gravitational pull, can one?'

Mukhujye Mashay turned the lamp on the girl. It seemed for a moment that the heat of the unnecessary banter between the two men had singed her loveliness. She stood looking at the ground, biting her lower lip, her bent head drooping even more.

'Foolish man!' Mukhujye Mashay said, grimacing in mock-anger. 'What sterling courage! Do you suppose just because the poor girl has to work for her living, she doesn't come from a decent family? How can you talk like that about her, Halim? I wouldn't have come to you at all had she been from my community! I'd have kept her in my house with due honour.'

Halim, now embarrassed, began scratching his head. 'Why don't you ask the lady if she'd be comfortable living here? After all, there's no woman in my house.'

Mukhujye Mashay swung his hands and raised his voice. 'Lady! That's a promotion awarded too soon. It's all very well, but don't overdo it. She's after all your maid.' He turned to face the girl. 'Why don't you just walk past him and enter the house, my dear. It's no use arguing with this cheeky young man.'

But the girl did not move. She stood there, inert, as if turned to stone. Mukhujye Mashay said impatiently, 'Look at this now! I can't possibly leave her on your doorstep at this late hour, when hounds and jackals come out to prey. Why don't you ask her to come in, Halim?'

'All right,' Halim said, looking somewhat wan with worry. 'Come in.' He picked up the lantern and went in. The girl followed him hesitantly.

'It's going to be all right,' Mukhujye Mashay called out from outside. 'You will thank this old man when you find your heart turned to gold at the magic touch of this lovely girl.'

Halim did not hear him. He had gone back to bed.

Even though his sleep was disturbed, Halim woke up early next morning and left for work. The morning was spent checking mail, signing a stack of papers brought by the clerk, and following up a few urgent things. By the time he returned to the bungalow, the new maid had finished the morning's work. It was a pleasant surprise to return home. The familiar house seemed to have got a new lease of life and was smiling out of sheer bliss. Halim went past the rooms, as if in a dream. The drawing room and study looked delightful. The young woman had given a completely new look to household articles such as the writing table, bracket, chairs and the sofa set. The articles proudly wore the touch of two skilful hands that bore the mark of refined taste and had treated them with great care. Halim lay down on the sofa, using his hands to support the head, struck suddenly by the arid loneliness of his life which revealed itself before his introspective eye like a harsh monstrosity, for the first time. Halim felt the greedy stirrings of a desire, a feeble thirst in a remote corner of his heart, for a womanly presence. So far he had thought women were utterly inconsequential and had ignored them rather snobbishly.

He would probably have sat in silence for a while, but the reverie was broken by his young Bihari servant, Khusia. 'Breakfast is ready, Sir,' said the boy.

'Is it so?' Halim stopped dreaming and got up. The young woman of last night was standing beside the table, applying jam on a biscuit. Halim pulled a chair and sat down. He was quite overwhelmed to find that there was a lot of food on the table: tea and biscuits, paneer, parathas, halwa, kofta and the like, the cutlery laid out perfectly too. He had tried hard for the past one year to train his Bihari servant, without much success.

'Has the cook prepared all this?' he asked Khusia.

'No, Sir,' said the boy. 'It was Madam.'

'Madam? Who's Madam?' Halim was shocked.

The young woman was about to leave, quietly, like a shadow. Khusia pointed to her and said, 'The lady.'

'And who asked you to call her 'Madam'?' Halim asked hotly.

'It was Mukhujye Thakur, Sir,' Khusia said, frightened. 'He came over in the morning and told the cook and me about Madam.'

Halim was embarrassed. 'Really, what a nuisance! Thakurda will drive me mad,' he muttered, almost involuntarily.

The Sun God was preparing to lie down at the farthest point of the horizon. Halim lay on a sofa in his drawing room, reading a book. The young woman entered and said, 'Please get up. You shouldn't read in the falling light, it's almost evening.'

'Yes, I was just going to get up,' Halim said, softening towards the girl. He was about to add something, but seemed to think better of it.

'Did you want to say something?' said the girl, smiling slightly.

Halim paused for a while and said, 'Actually, I haven't had a chance to talk to you properly since you arrived. What's your name? Or shouldn't I ask?'

The young woman smiled. 'Why not? I've come to work as your maid, after all. But please don't speak so formally with me.'

'All right,' said Halim, still slightly inhibited. 'But you didn't tell me your name.'

The girl understood that he was trying to get a hint about her family background. 'My name is Pari,' she said, not revealing her real name or anything else about her family. A mischievous smile danced around her lips for a second and disappeared. No more words were exchanged. Halim handed the book over to her and got up.

Everyone at the office—from the clerk to the trolley man—noticed that their boss had changed. He remained a little unmindful these days, but was quieter, polite and more tolerant of their mistakes. The clerks working at the station noticed another change in Halim. His thin frame was filling up and he looked healthier these days.

One day Mukhujye Mashay came over for a visit. 'Does this old man look familiar at all?' he teased.

'Just a little,' replied Halim with a smile. He thought for a while and asked, 'Tell me something, Thakurda. The young woman Thakurma sent—is she really a maid?'

'Of course,' Mukhujye Mashay laughed loud. 'But maid or not, she's from a decent family. Never forget this, my boy,' he added seriously.

Halim looked suspiciously at the old man. Mukhujye Mashay suddenly remembered he had a lot of very important things to attend to, and escaped before Halim could ask him any other question.

Halim was invited to dinner at the zamindar's house. Returning home at almost one o'clock at night, he was surprised to find the light in Pari's room still burning, which meant she was awake. Curious, he tiptoed to her window and peeped in. Pari was bending over an English newspaper spread over her pillow, a little smile playing on her rosy lips. Halim knocked on her door and entered.

'Can you read English, Pari?' he asked, amazed.

Pari dropped the paper quickly and said, 'No, of course not. I was only looking at the lovely pictures.'

'I'm afraid I can't believe that, Pari,' said Halim. 'I know that there's a news item in today's paper about a Jewish woman who told her husband that she was going to meet a friend and stepped out in the evening. When she didn't return home her husband started looking for her only to find that she got married to another man the night before. The editor has presented the story with funny asides, and it's hard to keep a straight face when one reads it. I saw clearly that your eyes were on the report and you were smiling.'

'You're mistaken,' Pari shook her head, smiling. I learnt a little Bengali from Thakurma when I was little. You probably heard the saying that even the weavers in Bikrampur can read and write a bit. If I was really learned, or if I knew English, I could have become a teacher in a girls' school. Why would I come here to work as a maid?'

Halim was a little hurt. 'Yes, that's true,' he said, with a sigh. 'But why don't you keep a chair in your room, Pari? There are so many around here.' he said, changing the subject.

'What's the point? You'll never come in here. We could go to your drawing room if you like.'

'But it's not as if I alone can sit on a chair,' said Halim, even as they walked towards the drawing room. 'Bring two chairs and a table into your room sometime tomorrow. I'll give you English lessons from time to time.'

Hope had presented itself unexpectedly. Pari had not expected anything so kind. She followed him silently.

Halim took off his coat and hung it from the wall bracket. Then he lay down on the easy chair. Pari squatted near his feet. 'Let me take off your shoes,' she offered.

Halim's fingers stopped on his tie-pin. 'No, not you,' he said. 'I'll call Khusia.'

'Khusia and I are both your servants. What difference does it make?' Pari asked, looking downwards as she untied his shoelaces.

Halim hung his tie against the chair, leaned back and shut his eyes. A little later he said, 'Khusia gets paid, but you don't take money from me, Pari.'

'You've never offered me any. I was scared to ask for it lest you asked me to leave.'

'If only I could, Pari,' Halim said, failing to stifle a deep sigh. 'How much do you want?' he asked a little later.

'Whatever you think best.'

'Why don't you take charge of my money from this month? I hate to keep track of every penny that is spent.'

'What if I stole from you?'

'Go ahead.'

'All right,' Pari said with a mischievous smile. 'But you didn't tell me what you had for dinner at the zamindar's.'

'Nothing,' said Halim, suddenly sitting up. 'I forgot to tell you.'

'But I thought you had a great memory when you were a student,' said Pari, smiling sweetly, her voice resonating with excitement

Halim was taken aback. He looked at her, mute for a moment, and said, 'How did you know?'

'I'm clairvoyant,' Pari said. 'But let's not talk about that. Instead, tell me why you didn't eat anything.'

Halim closed his eyes and lay back. 'Dinner at a rich man's house is always served late, and there's usually more to drink than eat, quite an excess, in fact, when a dance performance is on. It's quite horrible, it would probably put off any decent human being. So I escaped.'

Pari's beautiful face glowed with an overwhelming sense of respect as she listened to Halim. She could not help losing her heart, dropping it like a bouquet of flowers on the feet of her object of worship, who was young, with no woman to tie him down and yet capable of such extraordinary self-control.

'It's strange,' Halim said, half-asleep, 'Thakurda still revels in such company, even at this ripe old age.'

Pari ignored the remark, bowed her head at his feet quickly, with great caution, and stood up. 'But you can't go to bed without having dinner.' she said. 'I promise to get something for you to eat within half an hour. Watch the clock.'

It was a rude jolt. Halim was suddenly wide awake. 'Don't bother,' he hastened to say. 'Just get me some halwa please, if there's any left.'

'Whatever you like. I will see you in the dining room.'

In about half an hour, Pari entered the room with a tray loaded with rice and four to five side dishes. Her countenance had changed. The storm that was raging in her heart had subsided. Affection, goodness and love flowed like a river inside her. She looked the image of the ideal woman, calm, serene and eager to serve, glowing with sheer feminine grace, almost like a Goddess—a far cry from the youthful and restless beauty that she normally was. Halim, still reclining in his easy chair, looked at her, mesmerized, 'I'm not going to eat,' he said teasingly, 'it's been more than half an hour since you went.' He looked at his watch. 'Exactly two minutes and ten seconds more.'

Pari put the tray down on the table. 'That's not the fault of my cooking,' she said. 'The extra time went in loading the tray.'

Halim pretended he had not heard, shut his eyes again and lay there, enjoying the moment of peace and comfort. Pari came over and shook the arm of his chair forcefully, saying, 'What's on your mind? Still thinking of ways to punish me for the delay? The food is waiting.'

'I was just wondering why you took so much trouble.'

'Maybe you had more trouble hunched up in the chair like that.'

'Not quite, I wasn't too badly off. I didn't have to sit in front of two stoves burning like hellfire and take the heat.'

'But you must have been awfully hungry!' Pari was slightly exasperated, 'That's enough. Come, get up. The food will get cold.'

Halim had no option but to get up. After he finished eating, Pari offered him a paan. When he finally reached his bed the chilly breeze of an early winter dawn had started to blow in from the window. The sweet holy music of the morning azan reverberated through the breeze. Pari said, 'There's no point in going to bed now. Today is Friday. You'd better read the namaz.'

'Namaz! But I've never done that, Pari.'

'Why? Don't you believe in saying your prayers?'

'Of course I do. Won't my soul be damned if I didn't?'

'Then you'd better do it now.'

'That's a strange command,' Halim said, scratching his head. 'I'm not sure I remember all the words.'

'Not a command,' Pari said, smiling softly. 'It's just a request, a prayer. I shall remind you the words if necessary.'

Pari seemed to have a curious influence over Halim's heart and soul. Halim was incapable of ignoring any request that came from her.

Halim returned home by the ten o'clock train after a week-long official tour. It was a very strenuous trip, and his whole body seemed to be aching with exhaustion. He finished dinner quickly and reclined on his bed with a newspaper. Pari sat beside his bed, slowly fanning him. Her lovely face seemed clouded over with worry as she gazed at him.

Halim finished scanning the headlines of the paper. Pari suggested, 'Why don't you try to get some sleep now?'

'I'm not sleepy at all. But you've been fanning me for a long time. You must be tired.'

'I wouldn't be tired even I fan you the whole night,' Pari said, lifting her eyes shyly to his. 'But if you don't put the paper down you won't get the rest you need.'

'All right, then. I won't read the paper anymore. Let's hear your story instead.'

Pari was suddenly very quiet. Halim said contritely, 'Did I say anything to hurt you, Pari?'

Pari looked up silently. It looked as if she was trying to say something but couldn't bring herself to talk. After a long time she asked Halim, 'May I ask you something?'

'Of course.'

'I want a truthful answer.'

'If I know it, you shall have it.'

'Yes, you do know it.' Pari sat down at the foot of the bed and gently lifted Halim's feet on her lap. She leant forward and asked urgently, 'Promise me now that you will tell me the truth.'

The sudden touch was like a streak of lightning passing through his entire body. Halim felt goose pimples sprout on his skin. He shut his eyes. For the past two months he had lived in the same house as Pari. At times he had spent the whole night talking to her, but she always kept her distance. She had taken off his shoes when he returned home, massaged his forehead if he had a headache, but always seemed to shy away from any kind of closeness. This sudden intimacy amazed Halim. His feet, resting close to Pari's breast, trembled as he tried to keep his voice steady. 'Yes, Pari, I can't lie while I'm touching you. I promise you, I shall answer you truthfully.'

Pari looked at him steadily. 'Are you married?' she asked.

Halim was surprised. 'Is that all? Yes, of course. Have you ever heard of a twenty-five year old Bengali man who wasn't married yet?'

'Is your wife alive?'

'Probably,' replied Halim after a pause.

'Strange! Don't you know for sure?'

Halim's face lost colour. 'Yes—no—but why do you want to know, Pari?'

'Isn't it natural for me to want to know about the life of my master, especially since he's so good as to be almost divine?' Pari replied at once.

'Maybe. But—well, take it that she's dead.'

Pari smiled and shook her head. 'It's only possible for men to speak of someone living as dead. Men can forget about their wives easily, but we women are different.'

Halim stared at the ceiling emptily. 'I've promised to tell you everything, haven't I, Pari?'

'Yes,' said Pari. 'But maybe you've forgotten the details.'

'No. Well, here's the story. It was a long time ago. I was only twelve years old then, studying in Class Eight. Our family had an ancient and proud history—my father was a descendant of the Syeds. But he was poor. My father-in-law, on the other hand, was rich, but his family wasn't anything like ours. He lived in the village next to ours. I was very good at studies, and got the best student's prize every year. My father-in-law thought I would be a good catch and proposed marriage between his daughter, Naim Khanam, and me. Naim was a child of five at that time. My father agreed to the proposal because my father-in-law promised to pay for my education. He kept his promise for three years but when I was in my second year in college he suddenly stopped sending money. I managed somehow to finish college because I had got a scholarship in my entrance exam and a distant uncle had also chipped in with some money. When I got another scholarship in my graduation, my father admitted me to the Shibpur Engineering College. But the professional course was much more expensive than we expected. And then my uncle stopped his contribution. My father was desperate. He brought my wife over to our house, sold her jewellery and deposited the money in a bank. He started to send me an amount every month from that money.

'That was the first time since my wedding that my wife came to our house. My father-in-law wouldn't allow her to come because she was still a child. Soon after my father sold her jewellery my father-in-law heard about it. He took his daughter back forthwith and wrote an extremely insulting letter to my father. Even after all this, my father went to bring my wife back, but he was insulted and packed off empty-handed. I didn't know any of this until my father wrote to me, explaining everything. During my vacations, I myself went to bring my wife back. My father-in-law had been transferred to Rajshahi. I went to see him there. My father-in-law behaved abominably with me. I was treated like an outcast and wasn't even allowed to meet my wife. I'd only seen her once—at the wedding. You can understand, Pari, can't you, how terrible this experience must have been for us?

'Well, the money in the bank ran out soon. I managed to finish my studies and get a job. I've been working for the last seven years. My parents had tried very hard to get me married again. But my experience with marriage was so bitter that I just couldn't bring myself to fulfil their wish. My mother has passed away. She made me promise at her deathbed that I'd never have anything to do with my father-in-law or his daughter. Last year my father, too, passed away. He expressed the same wish as my mother before his death.'

Halim stopped. He was slightly breathless. The story was not unknown to Pari. She had wanted to check what Halim really felt about his father-in-law and wife. She found that he had not exaggerated anything and was strictly truthful. She picked up the fan again.

'So you're going to get married again?' she asked.

'No.'

'In that case, will you accept her?'

'No.'

Pari's face fell. She sought to hide her anxiety from him by covering her head with her sari. 'But do you think it is right to leave your wife without judging if she's guilty or innocent? Aren't you punishing her for a fault that's not hers?' she asked, her voice trembling slightly.

'I don't know. I'm not judging her, merely following my parents' last wishes.'

'But is that right? Maybe your wife will wait for the rest of her life with the hope of coming back to you.'

'I don't think so.' Halim smiled bitterly. 'If that was so, she'd try to meet me once at least.'

Pari was silent for a while. Then she said softly, 'Do you trust me?'

'Yes, of course.'

'Are you going to believe what I tell you?'

'Yes.'

'I am from the same village as your father-in-law.'

'I know.'

'My mother lives in your father-in-law's house.'

'Really?' Halim asked, surprised.

'Yes. I've been a companion to your wife since we were both ten years old.'

Halim sat up and held Pari's hand. 'You've seen her, then?'

'Of course, as I told you, we were friends.'

'Does she remember me?'

'All the time,' Pari said firmly. 'She looks at your photograph and cries over it. Not a moment passes when she doesn't remember you.'

Halim let go of Pari's hand. An involuntary sound of pain escaped his lips. He turned on his side, shutting his eyes. Pari felt an excruciating agony stabbing her heart but she sat still without speaking a word, her eyes heavy with unshed tears. Halim did not turn to face her.

Pari switched off the light. She could not bear to leave him there alone and go to her own room. Quietly, she dropped down on the floor and lay there. Time passed. Much later, when the drawing room clock chimed the hour, Halim stirred and murmured, 'Pari, switch on the light, please.'

Pari got up and switched it on. Her hair, free of all restraints, was wet with her tears, and her eyes reddened from weeping.

'Were you crying, Pari?' Halim asked.

'Yes.'

'But why?'

'You didn't let me finish what I wanted to say,' Pari said.

'But you didn't say anything else.'

'May I say it now?'

Halim nodded.

'Are you really not going to accept your wife again?'

'How can I? It was my parents' last wish.'

'But I'm sure they said that only because they were so badly insulted. It is a sin to reject your wife out of anger. No one can make you do that either.'

'Yes, I know.'

'Isn't it a very wrong thing to do?'

'I agree, Pari. But there's nothing I can do. She's not going to come back.'

'Of course she will.'

'Do you know what a terrible father she has?'

'Yes. But I also believe that if she's devoted to her husband, Allah Himself will bring them together.'

Halim marvelled at the passion and sincerity in her voice. Pari continued, 'She might come over to see you secretly, without telling her father.'

'That's impossible,' Halim shook his head.

'No, it's not. She could take the help of Thakurda and Thakurma to come over and meet you secretly.'

Halim sat up on the bed, excited. 'If she's so much in love with me, if she really comes away secretly, I shall accept her with all the respect that's due to her. I give you my word, Pari, I shall definitely do that, no matter whatever punishment I receive from Allah after my death for breaking my promise to my parents.'

Pari was trembling within. 'She has come to you,' she said, fighting to keep her voice steady. 'She is here, in this house.'

'Where is she?' Halim asked disbelievingly, his face flushed with anticipation. Pari's legs suddenly felt heavy. She sat down on the bed and bowed her head at Halim's feet. 'I am the unfortunate woman—your rejected wife.' The words were barely out when she fell at his feet in a dead faint.

Pari regained her senses a little later. She felt her head resting on Halim's lap. He was fanning her lovingly. Tears fell uncontrollably from his eyes, wetting Pari's face.

Juger Alo, Sravan 1925

The Genius of Didarul Alam

I had met Didarul Alam only once.[13] But that particular day will always remain etched in my memory. Didarul was the editor of *Sammilani* and *Juger Alo*—two journals published from Rangoon. I came to know him when I started writing for *Juger Alo*. Later he wrote a couple of letters to me. I do not suppose I will ever forget his childlike candour in addressing me as Mother.

This young author had appeared on the horizon of Bengali literature like the young sun at dawn. The serialised novel *Foyar Deshe* (In the Land of Foya) and other stories and essays written by Didarul bear evidence to a budding talent. There was a saint-like purity and integrity in Didarul. The most striking quality in him was a genuine desire to bring about Hindu-Muslim unity. Indeed, I do not know of many journalists, young or old, who aspired as passionately as Didarul towards this. At that time, there were riots all over Bengal. While every newspaper and magazine published gruesome reports that were ghastly enough to send shivers down the spine of young mothers, Didarul alone held on to his steadfast belief that the two communities would eventually come to peaceful terms. He never carried any such provocative report in his paper, neither did he accuse or find fault with anyone. He tried his best to bring together these two blind, fighting communities. Indeed, his integrity, honesty and sterling liberalism amazed many at that time.

Didarul is with us no more. The cruel hand of death has snatched him away, and no force—neither a mother's love nor his love for literature or his country—was strong enough to hold him back. His talent, which was like a budding flower, never had the chance to bloom. He left work unfinished, songs unsung. His life has come to an untimely end, but he will remain alive in the memory of his family and friends, and the passion for his unfinished work will remain ablaze in our hearts like a flame of lightning for ever.

Masik Sanchay, Phalgun-Chaitra 1928

Fatema Khanam

by Abul Fazl

(Abridged)

After a long and painful illness, Fatema Khanam passed away on 1 July 1957, at the age of sixty-four.

The name of Fatema Khanam would not be familiar to the modern reader of Bengali fiction. Fatema's writing career was over before many of today's writers were born. The main reason for this was her prolonged ill health, the other probably being poverty.

About thirty years ago, a small and short-lived monthly magazine called *Tarun Patra* was published from Dhaka. It was edited by Fazlul Karim Mullick, but the person behind the magazine was the late Abul Hossain. Every issue of the magazine used to be full of Abul Sahib's writing—written either under his own name or pseudonyms.

During 1925-26, I was a student at Dhaka University. Some of us, newly initiated into literary activity, were quite heady with the zeal of creative writing. The passion of youth and the devotion to literature had made us quite unstoppable and, at times, even arrogant. We were particularly inspired when a new magazine was born. We chased authors, ran errands for the editor and haunted the office of the magazine at all hours. My passion for *Tarun Patra* was soon rewarded when one of my quite immature pieces was published in it, and, unbelievable though it may seem, my name appeared as the 'Assistant Editor'. Such eminence was bound to go to a budding author's head. I was no exception; I was floating in air.

It was during this period, when I was almost ready to lay down my life for *Tarun Patra*, that I discovered Fatema Khanam. I met her when I went to collect one of her pieces for the paper. Later, this acquaintance deepened into a relationship that was stronger than the ties of blood. The reason behind this was probably something that had a wider implication. I had started writing stories since my student days at Muslim Hall. But when

I actually got down to it, I found to my dismay that I did not know my own society very well, particularly the homely and domestic aspect of it. I realized that in order to pursue a serious writing career I could not merely rely on my own limited experience and the second-hand stories recounted by a handful of relatives and friends. The same thought had occurred to my fellow writers and friends. Naturally, we became quite eloquent about the need to penetrate the purdah. I went so far as to write an essay with the grandiose title 'The Disadvantages of the Purdah System in Literature' and it was read out with great fanfare at the meeting of the Muslim Hall Literary Club.

The liberals were pleased with my essay but the traditionalists reached the inevitable conclusion that I was a demon come to ruin the citadel of Muslim society. It did not help matters that soon afterwards we established an organization called the Anti-Purdah League with the best student of Muslim Hall, Mr Naziruddin, as its secretary. At that time the sole Muslim woman student at the university was Fazilatunnesa. The women whose happy voices are heard today in the lecture halls of the university probably do not stop to think how their road to freedom was paved, inch by inch, by our little efforts. Fazilatunnesa, particularly, had made a unique and historical contribution to this.

The aforementioned essay of mine argued that we cannot create authentic vignettes of Muslim society in our literature because we lack knowledge of Muslim domestic life. As a result we, the young writers, started to haunt the houses of women we knew, forging relationships where they did not exist. I had already come to know that Fatema Khanam wrote secretly and that she had a soft spot for writers. Naturally it was not difficult for me to make inroads into her house and heart by taking advantage of her motherly affection.

When I saw Fatema Khanam for the first time she had a very fair complexion and enjoyed good health. Later, of course, she lost her health and good looks to prolonged illness. Fatema

Khanam had started to write much before I came to know her, though she had not had the chance to publish anything. It was not that all women were behind the purdah then, but their writing inevitably was. Often even their family members did not know about their writing. The notebooks were hidden in some bottomless trunk or a tightly shut drawer. They made stealthy appearances on quiet afternoons or at the dead of night, when the whole house would go to sleep. The trepidation the women felt was usually transmitted into their writing. It was hesitant, tentative and apprehensive.

Before I came to know Fatema Khanam, her notebook, too, had been banished into the darkness of secrecy. I was fortunate enough to be able to bring some of her writing into light. At that time she was living at 88 Urdu Road in Dacca. She probably inherited the house from her father. Her elderly mother, two sons, a brother, and a nephew and a niece who had lost their mother lived with her. I never saw her husband, nor did I ever hear her mention him. Perhaps she had a deep sadness in her heart about this, which she bore silently and alone. I never heard her complain about anything or indulge in self-pity. She taught at a girls' school close to her house and the house was probably run on her earnings. It could not have been very easy to run the house on a limited income, but, surprisingly, I have never seen the mistress of the house or her family members flustered or untidy.

I have had numerous meals at her house. At times our whole gang of friends would land up there for a feast. We loved to eat. Just one instance would suffice to illustrate how passionate this love was. We had started a club at Muslim Hall called 'Eating Club', and the sole activity of this club had to do with the sheer fun of eating. Mr. Abdul Haq, now president of the East Pakistan Secondary Education Board, deserves all credit for conceptualizing and creating this unique institution. Needless to say, he was the founder-president of the club and also its secretary—we members were just humble eaters.

Fatema Khanam had a spontaneous affection for Muslim society members who also wrote. She would often regret the fact that Muslim girls lagged behind in studies. She had never had the chance to study in a school or a college, but learnt Bengali and Urdu at home and had a working knowledge of English. The occasional English word or phrase she used in her conversation or writing was always correct and apt. Her knowledge of Urdu was very good indeed: she could speak and write in the language quite effortlessly. Fatema Khanam was not merely concerned in a general way about the education of Muslim girls, but particularly about the future of her niece who lived with her. This niece was Begum Anwara Chowdhury, B.A., B.T. The following excerpt from Fatema's letter dated 5 October, 1928, illustrates her anxiety over Anwara's education:

> 'I've started to attend a coaching class at this age, and take lessons in painting too. As a result I don't have much time in my hands nowadays. I have to do all this for Khuki [Anwara], otherwise I shall never be able to teach her anything. Society wouldn't let me.' (She was planning to sit for the Matriculation Examination around this time.)

Fatema Khanam worked closely with the founder of Sakhawat Memorial Girls' School and the leader of the Bengali Muslim women's emancipation movement, Mrs. Rokeya Sakhawat Hossain. Begum Rokeya was very fond of Fatema, and Fatema, too, held Begum Rokeya in very high esteem. The following excerpt from her letter written to me from No. 43, Mirzapur, probably sometime in 1927 (this letter is undated, but her previous letter is dated 4 March 1927) bears evidence to this:

> '... I have quit the job that brought me here. I could not get along with the arrogant Anglo-Indian headmistress of the school. I thought of going back to Dacca, but Mrs. R. S. Hossain just would not let me. She made me take up a post at her school. So I am still here. Mrs. M. Rahman's daughter is living with her now. ... Mrs. R. S. Hossain is

> going to give a speech at the All Bengal Women's Association. I am very keen to join the Association. I shall write to you later about this. Indeed, no one else has done half as much for the women of the idle and useless Muslim society as this widowed and elderly lady. But the pity of it is that despite her efforts, she's not being able to awaken the Bengali Muslims from their slumber of ignorance. At her school, girls are taught not only the Koran and subjects like Bengali, English, Urdu, Persian, but also domestic skills like cooking, home-nursing, first aid, sewing and embroidery. It's a pity that while the girls from the western parts of the country are flocking to the school, Bengali Muslim girls are sadly oblivious to a need for education. Out of a total strength of 114, only two girls are Bengali. You can surely realize what this must mean for Bengal.'

Fatema Khanam's letter to me dated 14 July 1932 has an interesting snippet, which is worth a mention. This mysterious bit of news may be of interest to readers of Bengali literature, especially to Nazrul enthusiasts.

> 'I have not received any letter from you after returning from Dacca. Hope you are keeping well. I met Jahanara [a girl from the school] recently. She is quite good-looking and sings very well. She would be a little over eighteen . . . I heard a rumour that Jahanara's book was actually written by Kazi Sahib [Nazrul Islam]. Of course, I don't know if this is true or not. A girl from the family of the poet Sufia N. Hossain (now Begum Sufia Kamal) told me that Jahanara was a favourite student of Kazi Sahib's. It was from him that she learnt music.'

On 5 October 1928 Fatema Khanam wrote a letter to me from her house on Urdu Road in Dacca.

> 'I hope never to submit my work to *Saugat*. I am not overly concerned about this, since my work is obviously not good enough to be published. Did you ask for the article on Nazrul Islam? Haven't they given it to you?'

Fatema Khanam wrote a long article on Nazrul Islam and sent it to *Saugat*. For some reason, *Saugat* did not bring it out, perhaps the reason why she was a little annoyed with the magazine. Thinking about it now, I am ashamed to say that I cannot recall what ultimately happened to the article, or, indeed, if I was able to dig it out from the *Saugat* office at all.

The last letter Fatema Khanam sent me was dated 3 May 1936. She wrote this letter from 41 Haranath Ghosh Road, Dacca. She was seriously ill at that time. It must have been quite an effort to write—her handwriting was crooked and almost illegible in places. It was obvious that her fingers were trembling violently as she wrote. I guessed that she was not going to live long. But surprisingly, Fatema Khanam lived on for another twenty-one years after this. However, she never really recovered fully. We did not exchange letters after this, and I never got to see her again.

As I have mentioned before, Fazilatunnesa was our only contemporary Muslim woman student at the university. She was the first Muslim woman to pursue higher studies, successfully overcoming the numerous obstacles that she had to encounter. Consequently, she was the symbol of progress in our eyes. Fatema Khanam shared our admiration of Fazilatunnesa. Once she told me, 'I wish to invite Fazilatunnesa to my house and to treat her to home-cooked food. Could you please carry my invitation to her?'

At that time Fazilatunnesa was living at a hostel run by Christian Missionaries, near the Dacca General Post Office. I met her and conveyed the invitation. Fazilatunnesa accepted it. Fatema Khanam was absolutely thrilled to hear this. She started to make arrangements for a proper feast. Unfortunately, due to some unavoidable reason, Fazilatunnesa had to cancel the dinner engagement at the last moment. I still remember how deeply hurt and disappointed Fatema Khanam was that day. Incidentally, the food did not go to waste, as my friends and I ate it up easily.

Fatema Khanam was very fond of my friend Didarul Alam. On 28 December 1929, Didarul died of tuberculosis at the age of 26. His untimely death was a great shock to Fatema Khanam. The *Masik Sanchay* magazine of Dacca brought out a special 'Didarul issue' that month, under the initiative of the poet Abdul Qadir. Among the writers who contributed articles were Dr. Niharranjan Ray, Kazi Abdul Wadud, Shamsul Olama Kamaluddin Ahmad, Jasimuddin, Naimuddin, Sufi Motahar Hossain, Nazrul Islam and Habibullah Bahar. The short piece Fatema Khanam contributed illustrates not merely her deep affection for the young writer, but also her ability to write beautiful prose.

About thirty years ago, an article written by Fatema Khanam entitled 'Letter from a Muslim Lady' was published in a monthly magazine called *Matri Mandir*. The piece illustrates her deep religious conviction, a sharp analytical mind and a uniquely individual style. A portion of the article revealing her thoughts on the purdah system follows:

> I obey only the purdah that's imposed by my own conscience. This purdah does not come in the way of regular everyday work. This is not a 'purdah', but actually a restraint on the self, exercised by an invisible power. I firmly believe that we have to keep purdah alive despite all obstacles. I think this realization elevates a woman to the status of a goddess—a woman who commands respect. She is the universal mother, in front of whom the world kneels down. A woman can be highly educated or wise, she can work side by side with men in every sphere of life, she may even become a conqueror like Emperor Alexander—but without this power she can never be called a woman in the truest sense of the term. I also believe that the women of Europe and America would have been able to create a new heaven in this world, had they not been masquerading as men by sacrificing their true womanliness. A woman must not lose sight of her feminine side. And in order to do that one cannot afford to ignore the purdah totally. What we need to do is to clean up the filth that clings to it.

. . . In her stories *'Sagar Sanjog'* (The Bond) and *'Asray'* (The Haven), Fatema Khanam has drawn an authentic picture of our familiar domestic environment, and described the everyday hopes, desires, joys and sorrows of ordinary people in an easy and simple style, in a language devoid of ornamentation. She has never been daring, never entered unfamiliar territory. She wrote about the life she knew intimately and empathized with—her stories are sketches of people she knew. Maybe they recount incidents she herself encountered.

As a writer Fatema Khanam was probably not one of the great ones. She could not leave behind as many pieces as would merit a careful consideration of her writing abilities when she died. I have tried to look for a reason for this towards the beginning of this article. She left us only a limited number of pieces. But as a human being Fatema Khanam was definitely extraordinary. Whoever came in touch with her was impressed by her unusual generosity, dignity and self-respect. Fatema Khanam did not have an easy life, but nothing could ever curb her inherent dignity and self-respect.

Samakal, 1957

Notes

1 Selina Bahar Zaman (née Chowdhury): writer, researcher on Kazi Nazrul Islam who had greatly helped us at the time of working on the original *Zinana Mehfil* passed away in 2001. In her lifetime she was in charge of the Bulbul Publishing House after retirement from the department of mathematics, Jagannath College, Dhaka. Books written/edited by her include *Smritisudhay* (Sweet Memories), (Dhaka: Bulbul Publishing House, 1991) and *Nazrul Pandulipi* (The Nazrul Manuscript) (Dhaka: Bangla Akademi, 1994).

[2] Selina Chowdhury, 'A Few Words from the Publisher', *Saptarshi* (Dhaka: Bulbul Publishing House, 1964).

[3] See Siddiqua Mahmuda, *M. Fatema Khanam: 1894-1957* (Dhaka: Bangla Akademi, 1989), p.15, excerpt from letter written to Abul Fazal.

[4] Quoted in ibid, p. 35.

[5] Abul Fazl, Fatema Khanam (*Samakal*, Paush-Magh, 1950). See this volume.

[6] Abul Fazl, *'Parichiti'*, *Saptarshi*, see note 5.

[7] See Chapters 1 and 7, this volume.

[8] In this connection, Fatema Khanam wrote to Begum Rokeya in a letter: '. . . You wished to know the history of my life. My life is less than nothing— it's like the saying "a dog has nothing to do, it never walks but runs." I am exactly like that useless dog. This is why I didn't reply to your request.' (9 December 1926). Writer Abul Fazl, too, mentions in a letter to his friend Didarul Alam, 16 July 1926, that Fatema Khanam has requested 'Mrs. R. S. Hossain for her permission to let her write her biography.' (See Siddiqua Mahmuda, *Fatema Khanam*, p.26.)

[9] Abul Fazl, *Fatema Khanam*,.

[10] Quoted, Siddiqua Mahmuda, *Fatema Khanam*, p.34.

[11] Selina Chowdhury writes in the Introduction to *Saptarshi*: 'I have heard [from Fatema Khanam] that . . . "Tagore and Saratchandra Chattopadhyay have helped to bring my literary sensibilities out into the open . . . Naturally, it is quite possible that my style and language would be influenced by them."'

[12] Chowdhury, 'Matrihara', *Saptarshi*, p.41.

[13] Writer Didarul Alam started to publish the magazine *Juger Alo* from Rangoon in 1923. He was a close friend of Abul Fazl, a writer from Chittagong. Fatema Khanam had met Didarul Alam through Abul Fazl, and two of her short stories were published in *Juger Alo* in 1926. Didarul died an untimely death in 1929. Fatema Khanam wrote this short piece after his death. Didarul's younger brother Wahidul Alam writes: 'She [Fatema Khanam] was very fond of Didar. Once she was invited to his house in Dhaka, and appreciated the dinner greatly.' Quoted, Siddiqua Mahmuda, Fatema Khanam, pp. 26-27.

5

Nurunnesa Khatun Vidyavinodini (1894-1975): A Novelist

Translated by Adrita Mukherjee

'I wish I too could write books! But it seems impossible—I don't dare attempt it.' Nurunnesa Khatun had once, in an intimate moment, confessed to her younger sister Fatema. Nurunnesa was eighteen then, visiting her father's house after her marriage. She had discovered some writings by her sister, 'perfect pieces of prose', which had surprised and delighted her. Fatema gave her elder sister the encouragement Nurunnesa needed then. 'Why should it be impossible?' Fatema had said, 'You can make it possible if you make an effort. Go on trying, Sejo bubu, and I'm sure you'll be able to write a book.'[1]

It seems, indeed, that 'effort' had a very important role to play in the life of Nurunnesa Khatun. Throughout her life she tried to reinvent herself. All her 'efforts' were conscious endeavours; her 'wishes', natural inclinations. When did Nurunnesa first 'wish' that she, too, would like to write? How did a girl born into an orthodox and respectable Muslim family from Murshidabad learn to dream about writing a book? Getting satisfactory answers to such questions is difficult. We can but try to conjecture.

Nurunnesa was born in 1894 in the Khondkar family of Shahpur (or Sahapur) village in Murshidabad district. The family had an ancient lineage: the famous pir, Shah Taher, was the ancestor of Nurunnesa's father, Khondkar Habibus Sobhan. Her mother's name was Sadikatunnesa. Nurunnesa had three brothers, at least two of whom were known to have done some writing. One was a journalist who lived in Chittagong; another, Khondkar Rakibus Sultan, published two volumes of poetry.[2] Nurunnesa's sister Fatema also wrote as Nurunnesa mentions in the dedication to her novel, *Swapnadrishta* (The Dreams Vision).

We come to know from the scant material available on Nurunnesa Khatun that she had learnt some Persian from her maternal grandfather, Syed Siyadat Hossain. Nurunnesa herself recalls this gratefully in the introduction to her novella *Bhagyachakra* (The Wheel of Fortune).[3] Girls from 'ancient respectable Muslim families', she says, had very limited opportunities to study. A little Arabic, Persian and Bengali, and a bit of the Koran were all that they had access to. If anyone wanted to proceed beyond that, she needed both 'effort' and a strong 'wish'. Nurunnesa had never in her life 'tasted the pleasure of sitting down on a library bench'. The very use of the word 'tasted' indicates how intense this desire must have been. 'I never sat down in front of a teacher with a book. I picked up the alphabet to satisfy my curiosity and ultimately managed to read a few books.'[4]

Purdah was very strictly observed in the house. 'I was hardly aware of the social and worldly realities due to the strict observance of purdah in our family. To tell the truth, in my father's house, I had not known the beauty of nature except for the moon-and-star-studded night sky, like a canopy overhead.'[5]

The strictures of purdah were relaxed a bit in 1921, after Nurunnesa was given in marriage to Kazi Golam Mohammad, a lawyer from Serampore. Keeping in mind the times, Golam Mohammad seems highly romantic. He had liberal ideas, a taste for literature, and was fond of travelling. 'From the Bengali year 1319 [1912], I began to accompany my husband on his tours, like a basket tied to a fisherman's waist. Thus the strict purdah was, automatically, relaxed a bit.'[6] It is possible that the experiences Nurunnesa gathered while travelling with her husband helped her to realize the aspiration of becoming a writer. Her first novel *Swapnadrishta* was published in 1923.[7]

On an October morning in 1997, Shama Qader, the second child of Nurunnesa's youngest daughter Khaleda Manzoor-e-Khuda, sat talking to us at her school at Dhanmondi in Dhaka. Shama talked about the people in her family—her grandparents and her mother. Although Shama had seen little of Nurunnesa, she had heard a lot about her nanu from her mother, aunts and uncles and had formed a fairly clear picture of Nurunnesa in her mind. She thought her grandfather contributed significantly to her grandmother's literary career. 'Ultimately, Nanu can be said to be successful largely because of my nana. Granted, Nanu did the writing. But to collect all her work, arrange them systematically and publish them in books was where Nana came in. It was not very easy in those days.'

Nurunnesa herself has talked about her husband's contribution in her writing. In the Acknowledgements to her novel *Janaki Bai*, she says: 'My dear husband! . . . This historical novel would never have been written without your genuine help and efforts; and I am ever grateful to you for that.'[8]

Nurunnesa Khatun's career spans a meagre six years, which passed like a whirlwind, with books closely following each other. She won recognition for her work almost as soon as she began to publish. Her first novel was brought out in 1923. In 1929 the last short story *Niyati* (Fate) was published. In the intervening time she wrote a novel entitled *Atmadaan* (Sacrifice), a historical novel called *Janaki Bai, ba Bharate Muslim Biratwa* (*Janaki Bai, or, the Tale of Muslim Bravery in India*), two long novellas called *Bhagyachakra* (The Wheel of Fortune) and *Bidhilipi* (Destiny), the last included in this volume. Her *Collected Works* came out in 1929. The Nikhil Banga Sahitya Samiti conferred on her the title of 'Vidyavinodini' for her contribution to Bengali literature. The Nikhil Bharat Sahitya Sangha followed suit with the title of 'Sahitya Saraswati'. In 1923 Nurunnesa read an essay called '*Banga Sahitye Musalman*' (Muslims in Bengali Literature) at the sixteenth session of Bangiya Sahitya Sammelan held in Munshiganj. The president of the convention, Sri Jagadindranath Ray, the maharaja of Natore, was very impressed with Nurunnesa's essay. In the month of Poush in 1925, Nurunnesa was offered the presidentship of the Bangiya Musalman Mahila Sangha (The Bengal Muslim Women's Association). She delivered a lecture at the association's meeting, which was published later that year in the Magh number of *Saugat* magazine.

After the Partition of Bengal, the Bangla Academy of Dhaka made her a Fellow, and after her death Dhaka University and the Bangladesh Women Writers' Association announced several awards and scholarships in her memory.

Very few writers have received as much recognition and as many awards for their work in their lifetime. In retrospect, it seems surprising that Nurunnesa wrote actively for only six years. Why did she stop? We do not get any answer to this question from her biography or from the introductions to her novels. Looking for an answer, or even a clue, to the problem in her work is also futile.

We asked Shama Qader as to what the reasons could be. Shama remembers only a homely grandmother, and not much of Nurunnesa the writer. Nurunnesa lived alone, Shama says. She would read the paper sitting in the sun, or scatter grains for the hens in the courtyard. Shama was then a girl of ten or twelve. 'When I think of Nanu I remember a tiny playhouse kitchen, little utensils, food for a single person being cooked in them. When we went to visit her we'd persuade her to cook a little more than she normally would. She lived in a state of contentment. She seemed happy.'

Did Nurunnesa regret the fact that she did not write anymore or could not continue writing? Shama does not think so. 'I can't say exactly, but maybe she came to a natural stop once her dream of becoming a writer was realized. She had succeeded after crossing many hurdles. Perhaps she couldn't embark on something new later in life. Perhaps she didn't want to.'

Nurunnesa and her husband had a large family: four daughters and two sons. They owned a house at Serampore, in West Bengal. During 1946-1947, when her children were growing up, they had to leave everything behind and move to a new country: East Pakistan. Shama knows about that phase in her mother and grandmother's lives: she can imagine what a terrible wrench it must have been. 'It was like leaving behind a whole life, a whole existence. Maybe Nanu couldn't ever adjust to this huge change of scene in her life. Maybe that's why she couldn't go back to writing.'

They came over to East Pakistan in 1947 and started living in

Kamalapur in Dhaka. They called the house 'Upakul' (On the Riverbank). After Nurunnesa's husband's death in 1963, she spent the rest of her life alone in that house.

The incident of Nurunnesa's family being attacked during the communal riots seems like a cruel joke played by history. Nurunnesa's writing indicates that she was quite conscious of the sensitive aspects of Hindu-Muslim relations. She had never wanted to write anything that might hurt the sentiments of people from other communities. She was aware that stories like *Janaki Bai* and *Bidhilipi* had the potential of being misunderstood. In the Introduction to *Janaki Bai*, Nurunnesa reminds her readers that 'during war it is common to have the commanders of both armies speak contemptuously of the enemy, in order to raise the morale of their own soldiers.' Therefore, 'I would expect discerning readers from all communities to accept this in the right spirit and not see it as communal or narrow-minded.'[9]

It seems, in fact, that Nurunnesa wished to avoid confrontation of all sorts. In her writing, therefore, we notice the influence of contemporary mainstream authors, rather than the incandescence that characterized women authors like Begum Rokeya or Mrs. M. Rahman. Again, Nurunnesa does not concentrate exclusively on homely matters, as do Akhtar Mahal Syeda Khatun and Fatema Khanam. Nurunnesa's stories deal with familiar things, told in a familiar style. Could this be the reason why Begum Rokeya and Mrs. M. Rahman did not want to admit Nurunnesa to their world? Was it because the rebellious streak in Nurunnesa was not strong enough?[10]

All this is a matter of conjecture. In the ultimate analysis, it would perhaps be more fitting to look at Nurunnesa Khatun Vidyavinodini as a woman who 'wished' to be a writer, and that her children would also write. Almost all of Nurunnesa's children did write. Two of her elder daughters, Kamrunnesa and Badrunnesa, published their detective novels in *Saugat*.[11] Her youngest daughter, Khaleda (Shama Qader's mother), writes regularly, even today. We had asked Shama if she, too, wrote. Shama smiled and said, 'A little bit, here and there. I do have a legacy, you know.'

M.B.

Destiny
(The author responds to society's comments)
Reiteration

The description given towards the end of 'Destiny', that of the interiors of the Puri Temple and the autumnal festival held there is not imaginary. Every word of it is true and drawn from my own experience.

I would like to state, however, that this portion of my story is not intended to hurt the sentiments of any particular community, or to ridicule its religious practices.

The Author

First Tide

Highly-educated young Bengali Hindus seem keen on propagating widow re-marriage these days, especially if they are from the city. The idea is to revive Ishwarchandra Vidyasagar's project which had since been forgotten. A certain judge here married off his widowed daughter and managed to retain his social standing. Lahiri, who lives in the periphery of Calcutta, married off his widowed niece and was ostracized from the Barendra society for sometime. But now these people are back where they belonged. These are the examples cited by young men who seem to be itching to have young widows married again.

The Rays of Bishghara were one of the oldest zamindar families of Bengal. Legend goes that Sadashib Guha, their ancestor, had made a lot of money working for the British East India Company during the time of Lord Warren Hastings. Sadashib had bought some property in town and established a huge zamindari in his native village. He had also earned the Company's gratitude and respect for his continued loyalty and received the highly-prestigious title of 'Ray'.

That was a long time ago. The Rays' property was subsequently split into three parts. The smallest shareholder was Ram Narayan Ray. The only son of his father, Ram Narayan did not have to share his portion of the zamindari with anyone, and consequently, his income was the largest among all the shareholders. Hari Narayan was his only son. He was the best looking among all the young Ray children, and undoubtedly possessed the fairest complexion. His unusually fair complexion had earned him the sobriquet of 'Saheb Babu', and that's what he was called since childhood, and so shall we call him.

Saheb went to study in Calcutta, and, as was inevitable, gathered around him a cluster of educated and enlightened friends. Soon, these young men established a society called the 'Arya Widow Re-Marriage Society'. All the members were unmarried, and their aim was to dedicate their lives to the noble cause of widow re-marriage. To begin with, they were determined to encourage young widows in their respective native villages to re-marry.

Very soon, however, Saheb's dream was rudely broken. One by one, his friends, persuaded by their guardians, got married and left the society unceremoniously. Nursing a huge sense of hurt, Saheb gave up his long-cherished endeavour.

Second Tide

Hari Narayan Guha Ray, alias Saheb Babu, had spent the first seventeen years of his life in his native village. He passed the Entrance Examination from Bishghara High School, once established by the Rays and supported by the income of their property. Then he left for Calcutta to pursue higher studies.

The village next to Bishghara was called Radhaballavpur. A poor kulin kayastha family lived in the eastern corner of this village. Harekrishna Ghosh, the head of the family, lived with his wife, Bimala, their daughter, Ashalata, and an elderly widowed aunt, Shibani Dasi.

Shibani's parents-in-law were from the same village as Saheb's mother. The two families were, in fact, distantly related: Saheb's mother happened to be Shibani's niece. Shibani had seen the boy Hari Narayan a number of times when he visited his grandfather. He was so adorable and ever-smiling as a child that no one could resist giving him a hug and cuddle. Shibani, not having any child herself, was very fond of the boy and would often bring him home with her. It was, in fact, Shibani, who had given him the pet name of 'Saheb'.

As Saheb grew up, sudden changes occurred in Shibani's life. She lost her husband, and as living with her parents-in law became more and more difficult, she decided to leave their house and seek shelter with her distant relative Harekrishna Ghosh in Radhaballavpur. Shibani offered the money and jewellery she had saved to Harekrishna, and began living with the family as a dependent.

The Saraswati River ran close to Harekrishna's house in Radhaballavpur. The river was about a mile away from their house, but it was the perfect place for an evening stroll, and thirteen-year-old Hari Narayan, who appreciated the beauty of nature, would often come to the riverside for a walk, with a servant. One such evening, as he was strolling along the riverbank, followed closely by the old family servant, Amulya Sardar, Hari Narayan saw a woman coming up the steps from the river. A small fair-skinned girl skipped along beside the older woman, her curly hair dancing merrily around her face. The elderly woman reminded Saheb of the grandmother he had spent time with in childhood. Trying to get a closer look, the boy stepped forward and the two were overjoyed when they recognized each other.

It was Shibani who had recognized the boy first, calling him by the name she had given to him in his childhood. She asked after his mother and the rest of the family. Any perceptive man, if he had been around, would have noticed, however, that although Hari Narayan dutifully answered Shibani's queries his eyes, unwaveringly, hovered around the young girl's face, eager to find out all about her.

'Well, Saheb Babu,' said Shibani, half in jest, 'it seems you like Asha quite a lot. I could talk to your mother and arrange a match between you two. It wouldn't be a bad idea, would it, to have such a cute little wife? What do you say?'

The idea of being wedded to Ashalata entered Hari Narayan's ears, like a beautiful tune reverberating in his head. Not a bad idea at all, he thought.

A sudden gust of wind blew, bringing with it a few drops of rain. Saheb followed Shibani hastily to Harekrishna's house to take shelter from the rain. After much persuasion, Harekrishna's wife Bimala was only too glad when the boy tried a few homemade sweets.

When it was time for Hari Narayan to leave, Shibani, who walked him to the main road, said, 'Saheb, whenever you come for a stroll near the river, drop in at our house.' Old Amulya Sardar, followed him dutifully, still munching the last few batasas that were given to him with the muri, puffed rice, at Harekrishna's house, using the few teeth he had left.

From that day on, going on an evening walk became a regular habit with Hari Narayan. He would pass by Harekrishna's house everyday and keep looking back at it as he went, trying to catch a glimpse of the girl. On a couple of occasions he did meet her and asked after her grandmother.

As time passed, the dream of marrying young Ashalata kept growing in his mind.

Third Tide

Soon, Ashalata turned eleven. Hari Narayan was studying in the First Class in their village high school. His final tests were over; and the Entrance Examination was due in another couple of months. Everyone at home insisted that these two months were very important; and that Hari should work really hard. Hari

Narayan would often be seen sitting with an open book before him, but his mind was elsewhere. His mother was the first one to notice the son's abstracted look. She started to make discreet enquiries, and found out about her son's regular evening walks and frequent visits to the Ghosh household in Radhaballavpur.

Soon afterwards, the elderly Shibani Dasi paid a visit to the Ray house. Mrs. Ray welcomed the relative from her father's village, and varied subject were talked about for a while. Then Shibani, who was looking for an opportune moment, said, 'I've come to see you with a request. Your husband knows my nephew Hare-krishna Ghosh rather well. Harekrishna is not too well off and he is not getting any younger. He has a daughter from his second wife. The daughter's just turned eleven. She's a lovely girl, looks like a goddess. By the grace of Goddess Lakshmi, you have enough. You would be doing a huge service to the poor man if you could make your husband agree to a match between Hari and Ashalata. Ghosh's wife is very keen to have Saheb as her son-in-law. Hari often goes for a stroll along the river and has seen Asha with me at the bathing ghat a few times. I could bring the girl over to see you, if you like.'

Hari Narayan's mother, the daughter of a rich zamindar and now married to one, made a face at the suggestion of a marriage between her only son and the daughter of a poor man.

'This proposal is not entirely unexpected, Kakima,' she said, careful to keep her voice expressionless. 'I've come to know my son has seen the girl a number of times. I know he's got into the habit of dropping in at Harekrishna Ghosh's house every other day. This is causing a lot of distraction, and I've decided to ask my husband to have him sent over to our house in Calcutta so that he can concentrate on his studies before his final exams.

'Let me be quite frank with you, Kakima,' continued the mistress of the house. 'My husband has already fixed up Hari's marriage with the beautiful daughter of a very wealthy gentleman in Calcutta. And, come to think of it, isn't it only proper that we negotiate with a family that is equal to us?'

Shibani had never felt so insulted in her life. She had always prided herself on her family's high social standing and the respect it commanded among all. She realized being poor was as good as being dead. Harekrishna was a high-caste kulin kayastha, and in no way inferior to the cash-rich and smug zamindar's wife. How could that rich family from Calcutta, who probably did not even know the names of their forefathers beyond three generations, be a better prospect for marriage negotiations?

'I think I should be leaving now,' Shibani said, and stood up.

'How can you go away from my house without having something to eat?' said Hari's mother, holding Shibani's hands and stopping her. She arranged some fruits, sweets and hot luchis on a plate for Shibani and asked her maid to get a glass of water. Shibani sat quietly and reluctantly, fingering the food.

'Well, Kakima,' Hari's mother said sympathetically, 'I shall talk to Hari's father and try to fix up a good match for Harekrishna Ghosh's daughter as soon as possible. We can help with some money as well, if necessary,' she added.

Ever since she had heard of her son frequenting Harekrishna Ghosh's house, Hari's mother had been apprehensive that the boy's affections might veer towards the young girl. Her anxiety became even more deep-rooted when she heard that the girl was extremely beautiful. She was keen to have the girl married off elsewhere as quickly as possible. Hari's father, Rama Narayan Ray, had never indicated that he wanted their future daughter-in-law to be chosen from a rich family; nor had any match been fixed for him in Calcutta. This was, in fact, Hari's mother's wishful thinking.

Fourth Tide

Towards the beginning of Baisakh, before Hari Narayan's Entrance Examination results were out, Harekrishna Ghosh's daughter, Ashalata, was married off to a wealthy middle-aged man. The groom was from an established family and quite well off. There was an absurd age gap between the bride and the groom. Indeed, when one saw them together, they did not look like a couple at all. It was more like a grandfather come to fetch granddaughter from her in-laws'. This was a second marriage for the groom, and he already had two grown-up sons from his first wife.

After her marriage, a heavily bejewelled Ashalata went to live with her husband, the bespectacled Gopijana Ballavpadarenu Palit, more commonly known as Pada Palit. But God, it seemed, had turned away from poor Ashalata, and happiness deluded her. She seemed destined for widowhood, and there was no way her fate could be altered. Within eight months of her marriage an epidemic of small pox visited their village. And once it had claimed its first few victims, ignoring the blessings of relatives and friends who wished that she was spared widowhood, the killer disease struck a blow at the root of Asha's hopes and dragged her husband away. Since his death, the abusive sons and daughters-in-law of Pada Palit would chide Asha day in and day out, till she could not bear it any more. Within a year of her marriage, she was back in her father's home, wearing a widow's garb. Before she left, some gentlemen of the village made sure that the sons allowed the helpless widow to take her jewellery and a lump sum in cash that would take care of her everyday needs.

Returning home, Asha found her father Harekrishna Ghosh suffering from chronic cough and fever. Seeing his beloved daughter dressed as a widow augmented his suffering. The fever was cured in two months, but the constant cough remained to torment him. The doctors assumed this was a symptom of tuberculosis and medicines were prescribed. Finally, he was diagnosed as suffering from an untreatable form of whooping cough. For the next two years Harekrishna suffered terribly, bore the pain of chronic breathing trouble and ultimately passed away, leaving his grieving family behind.

One day after Harekrishna's death, on her way to the Saraswati River for a bath, the zamindar's wife decided on an impulse to pay the Ghoshes a visit. As she sat talking to the older women of the household, Asha came out and bowed her head at her feet. The sight of the young innocent girl in a widow's white sari melted the heart of the zamindar's wife. She kissed Asha's forehead affectionately and held her close. As Asha sat next to her and talked, the lady suddenly felt that perhaps she had not done the right thing by stopping her son from marrying this girl. Asha was a good-hearted well-behaved girl and very beautiful indeed. She would be a good wife to anyone, thought Hari's mother, a little wistfully. It also occurred to her that maybe the reason why Hari was resisting all attempts to negotiate a marriage for him was that he was still in love with Asha.

The zamindar's wife left a little later, but could not resist going back to the Ghoshes' house after taking a dip in the river. Shibani was delighted and insisted that Hari's mother spent some time with them and had something to eat. Asha brought out some mohanbhog in a small platter. Hari's mother was moved by the sincere affection of the Ghoshes. When she left that day her heart had softened towards the women, particularly towards the young girl.

'Kakima,' she said to Shibani before leaving, 'do come over and see me now and then. I shall send my palanquin for you. And bring Ashalata over with you,' she added. 'I've seldom seen such a nice and quiet girl.'

Fifth Tide

Since then, the Ghoshes started to pay regular visits to the zamindar's house, and cordial relations between the two families were re-established in no time. Meanwhile, Ram Narayan Ray passed away quite suddenly as a result of an attack of high fever. Hari Narayan received the news of his father's illness and returned from Calcutta immediately, but he was there for only a few hours before everything was over. Before he breathed his last, the ailing

Ram Narayan held his son's hands and addressed him for the last time.

'Get married, son,' he whispered. 'Make sure that our ancient line lives through the next generation.'

Hearing of the zamindar's illness, Shibani arrived there with Ashalata. At first glance, Hari Narayan did not recognize Asha, who was sixteen years old now and breathtakingly beautiful. She was dressed in white, and that for a second had confused Hari Narayan. However, as soon as he spotted the familiar tiny dimple in the cleft of her chin, he realized with a slight sense of shock that this was none other than Asha.

In a flash all the old memories rushed into Hari's mind . . . the innocent moments he had snatched with Asha when both of them were young, Asha's marriage and widowhood, the 'Arya Widow Re-marriage Society' he had established with such a lot of hope and expectation and its ultimate failure . . . Hari Narayan's mind was in a whirl as he looked at the widow who, but for destiny, could have been his wife. Hari controlled his wayward thoughts with an effort as his mind tried to grapple with the tragic scene of his father's impending death. He stood looking helplessly at his father, knowing fully well that in a few moments the old man would pass beyond all worldly happiness and grief. As his father's eyes closed in his last sleep, Hari Narayan realized again how futile and absurd it was to erect barriers among people, for in death everyone—the rich and the poor, the big and the small, the wise and the foolish—was the same.

The last rites of the zamindar were performed by his son before dark. Saheb spent the next month shuttling between home and Calcutta, trying to sort out his father's affairs. When everything was arranged satisfactorily, he took leave of his mother and left for Calcutta.

Hari Narayan's mother started to feel terribly lonely. Trying to come to terms with her recent loss and loneliness, she would often send the palanquin to Asha's house to fetch Shibani and Asha so that they could spend some time with her. Hari's mother found Asha's company very soothing and restful at this time. Asha was naturally affectionate, respectful and caring, and it was not long before Hari's mother became very attached to the young girl.

A few months later, Hari's mother, who felt restless and wished to travel for a while, expressed a wish that her son should return home and accompany her on a pilgrimage to Puri. She also invited Shibani and Asha to come with them. The time was convenient for Hari Narayan since the puja holidays were to start soon. He returned home, and very soon they started for Puri. A cook, two maids, and their old servant Amulya Sardar accompanied them.

Hari Narayan rented a small two-storey house on the beach near Swargadwar in Puri. His mother had come to Puri once before. That was a long time ago, before rail service started. Saheb was very small then, and although he had come with his parents, he could not recall that visit. This was the first time Shibani and Asha saw the ocean. They could hear the roar of the waves at first, like the incessant firing of a thousand cannons in the distance. Then they turned a corner, and suddenly before them was a vast expanse of blue-green, that looked like a huge undulating meadow. They turned on the road to Swargadwar, the ocean accompanying them all the way. Asha got goose pimples, the sea was overwhelming. White-crested waves followed each other in an endless dance, crashing on the shore with a mighty roar. She looked at Hari Narayan. The look of utter amazement and delight on his face told her that he shared the same excitement.

Saheb could not wait to have a dip in the sea. Dropping their luggage in the house, he proceeded to the beach, followed by his mother, Shibani and Asha. Hari was brave enough to wade into the sea, but the women were too frightened. Asha took a few hesitant steps into the water, and immediately ran back when she saw the waves raging towards her. It was a new game, exciting because it challenged and tantalized her. The older women did not venture into the sea at all; they sprinkled some water on their heads and returned home content.

In the evening they made their way to the famous Jagannath Temple. Up the winding path, leaving the Garur Pillar behind, they climbed up the wide steps. On their right was Ananda Bazaar: the place where the mahaprasad of the deity was sold. Only Hindus were allowed to touch the offering. Or, rather, only those who looked like Hindus. If one was not attired in a hat, coat or sherwani and Turkish cap, one could pass off easily as a Hindu. One could just walk in, clad in a dhoti or sari, and pick up a handful of rice, dal or curry from the big pots, taste it, and put the rest back in the pot for the next person. The offering to the greatest deity was so sacred that to think the practice unhygienic was a sacrilege.

For Hari Narayan, however, it was quite an eye-opener. As soon as they entered Ananda Bazaar, Hari saw a man scooping out mahaprasad from the pot. The man was as dark as hell. His face was unnaturally red, his eyebrows half gone, the tips of his fingers and toes swollen. With a sudden shock, Hari realized that the man was suffering from a blood-related disease or some virulent form of leprosy. When he saw the man pick up the mahaprasad from the pot, eat parts of it, and keep the rest back, Hari made a resolve never to let his mother touch the puja offerings. If that meant a sin, it would be Hari's, not his mother's; but he could never let his mother eat the leftovers of a leper.[12]

Sixth Tide

Hari Narayan's mother went ahead with Asha towards the main temple. Hari followed them closely, looking around and taking in the sights and sounds of the place. As soon as he looked up to see the sculptures on the walls of the temple, he was shocked. Halfway up the temple tower, there was a series of sculptures depicting nude men and women in bizarre postures.[13] He stared in disbelief as Asha suddenly looked back. Her eyes followed Hari's automatically, and she immediately turned away, horribly embarrassed. Hari's mother, noticing the whole thing, immediately pulled the young girl towards her and led the way into the main temple. She did not stop until they were standing in front of the wooden idols of Jagannath, Balaram and Subhadra.

Hari Narayan stood outside the temple, his eyes rivetted to the horrible figures on the temple face. He felt anger burning up his insides, and the desire to go in and offer puja to the deities had vanished. He had been dissatisfied with Hinduism. He had never been able to accept the rationale of Sri Krishna's Ras Lila: there seemed to be no possible way one could morally justify the way the God was said to be dallying with numerous women. Now he found himself wondering again. Families visited the temple every day, father and mother walked beside sons and daughters to visit the deities and take their blessings. How could they expect people to feel pious when the temple face was decked with such obscene sculptures? Didn't the scriptures say that the reason for idol worship was that the human mind was too imperfect and tiny to contemplate the vastness of the abstraction called God? If that was so, then why couldn't we try to keep that imperfect and tiny mind free from all unnecessary complications and distractions by exposing it to such art?

Once not so long ago, Saheb had had an argument with a Muslim friend of his about the hoors in Islam.[14] He suddenly felt ashamed of himself as he thought about that. If we can condone such behaviour in our 'Gods', and moreover, worship them despite that, why should we object to the abstractions called hoors who are, after all, stationed in the Muslim heaven?

Hari's mother came out with Asha and Shibani. She decided to buy a pot of mahaprasad before returning home, but made sure that the pot was new and sealed. The next day was Bijaya Dashami. In the afternoon, Hari Narayan hired a carriage and took Asha and his mother for a stroll near the temple, to a huge bazaar. Hari, his mother and Asha walked around, exploring the shops, looking at tiny idols and clay models. Suddenly, there was a commotion. A few small platforms had been erected in front of the temple. People picked up little idols from the shops and danced to the beating of drums and cymbals, making their way to the platforms. They placed the idols reverentially there and bowed their heads before them. What surprised Hari was that most of the idols were of a completely secular nature. They were in very bad taste: there was one of a dog pissing on a drunken man's face, another, of a man pulling at a scantily-clad whore. There were also models of Englishmen and women, clad in perfect European clothes and holding hands. Among all these were scattered a few images of Goddess Durga. People were worshipping the Englishmen, the drunk, the dog and the Goddess with equal piety.

Saheb felt himself cringing away from traditional religion. Poor God, who had to be divided thus into thirty-three millions of His creations and worshipped like this! Standing before one of the most famous temples in India and watching his fellow creatures worship the idols of dogs and whores and Englishmen, Saheb saw clearly how idol worship blinds human beings to the true nature and nobility of God.

Seventh Tide

Living in the same house as Asha for days together had its predictable effect on Saheb. He could not help responding to her beauty and her gracious nature. After losing Asha, he had made a vow never to marry. His mother had tried very hard to change his mind but Hari remained steadfast. After all this time, however, he found his resolve weakening. Nowadays, he caught himself stealing a glance at Asha every few minutes; and if anyone else, even Asha herself, caught him at it, he looked guiltily away.

Love, in its purest form, is a heavenly gift. Love begets love, even animals respond if love is given freely. Like invisible waves, love travels from one heart to another and creates ripples there. Saheb's love for Asha was the purest, and so it was not long before it was returned. Asha started to return his looks and smiles. Inevitably, Saheb's thoughts reverted to his Arya Widow Remarriage Society. He made a resolve to resurrect the society and marry Ashalata.

It was as if a new world had opened up in front of Asha. Like a dutiful wife, she had tried to offer her devotion and respect to her husband for the brief time that she was married to him, and since his death she had never thought of any other man. From her childhood she had been fond of Saheb, but only as a younger sister. Now, suddenly, she found herself responding to him in a much more intimate way. This surprised and alarmed her, she saw a new woman in herself whom she did not recognize. The urge to hide her love from Saheb, indeed, from the outside world, was instinctive, and yet Asha did not know how to conceal something that was so transparent, so true. She suffered in silence, oscillating between extremes of happiness and an overwhelming grief, and her heart found its only relief in hot, secret tears.

After his unsavoury experience, Saheb had virtually stopped visiting the temple. His mother and Shibani still went there with Asha, from time to time. One evening, they left for their usual visit, but Asha, feeling a little unwell, stayed back. Just before evening Hari Narayan entered the room where Asha was resting.

'How are you, Asha?' asked Hari.

'I—I'm not feeling very well,' Asha stammered, sitting up hastily. 'I have a headache, and all my limbs are stiff with pain,' she added.

'Would you like to come for a stroll with me on the beach?' Hari asked.

They spent the next couple of hours strolling on the beach. A crescent moon rose slowly in the sky still alight with the last rays of the sun, and, smiling mischievously, threw a handful of light on the darkening sky. Evening gathered her sari around herself like an old fastidious woman and tiptoed away. With the twilight vanishing and darkness descending on the world, the moon became the undisputed king of the night, and began sporting with the ocean. Asha, tired after her long walk, sat down on the beach with Hari at her side. They sat there quietly for a long time, watching the moonlight playing with the sea.

It was very quiet on the beach. The only sound was the regular drumming of the waves on the beach, mingling with the susurration of them ebbing away. Hari and Asha were intensely aware of each other, their senses suddenly alert and alive. Each could hear the faint sighs emerging from the other and getting carried away by the sea breeze.

Hari Narayan turned to face Asha. 'Asha!' he breathed her name softly and held her hand. 'How long . . . this torment . . .' his voice choked and the broken words trailed away into silence. He touched her hand, feeling each and every little groove, brushing his fingers over every tiny little line. Caressing it still, he slowly raised the hand to his lips. Then, stealing a glance at her, he planted a soft kiss on her palm.

Asha started to tremble. Her tiny palm, sweaty and suddenly alive, slipped out of Hari's. She moved away a little and adjusted her sari over her head.

'Saheb-da, let's go home. It's getting late,' she whispered.

They did not say another word to each other on their way back home.

Hari's mother and Shibani were not back yet.

'I think they're waiting to watch the evening worship with lamps at the temple,' Asha managed to say in a relatively normal voice. She was determined to keep her riotous emotions under control. Saheb did not answer.

From that evening, Asha started to feel worse. She spent a sleepless night, tossing and turning on her bed with a splitting headache. Her temperature rose steadily and the headache showed no sign of abating. Shibani, who had stayed up the night beside Asha's bed, started to grow anxious and called Saheb early next morning. Hari Narayan had earned some name as a self-taught homoeopath doctor. He examined Asha and prescribed aconite. There was, however, no visible improvement. Asha continued to suffer from the headache, and now her whole body was wracked with pain. Hari Narayan prescribed some painkillers, but noticing all the symptoms, particularly Asha's bloodshot eyes, he suspected that it could be a case of chicken pox. He was proved right when, on the third day, the familiar little eruptions showed plainly on Asha's skin. It was not a very severe attack, however, and Asha started to get better within a week.

That one week turned the tide.

'Don't come near me, Saheb-da.' Asha would implore. 'This is infectious. I shall never be able to forgive myself if you get it from me.'

Hari would listen to her and not utter a word in reply. He would not stop coming to see her either. And whenever he was alone with her, he would say the same thing over and over again.

'I have come to think of you as a part of myself, Asha. I can't bear to be away from you. Don't say you will not be mine.'

Epilogue

Soon afterwards, Hari Narayan Ray returned to his house in Calcutta with his mother, Asha and Shibani. He contacted his old friends and the Arya Widow-Remarriage Society was revived. This time the work of the Society showed real progress, with all the members working sincerely for the common cause. A number of marriages were arranged between young widows and eligible young men, and the man who led from the front was the new zamindar babu Hari Narayan Guha Ray, marrying Ashalata Dasi in the presence of distinguished guests according to Vedic rites.

The Bengal Muslim Women's Association
President's Speech

Respected President of the Reception Committee and my sisters, I am sincerely grateful to you for bestowing this honour upon me. I am a very humble woman, and no one knows better than myself that I do not deserve it. You have, perhaps, formed an idea of the limitations of my knowledge and accomplishments from the introduction to my book *Swapnadrishta* (The Dream Vision). Yet I was given the chance to address you today. It is impossible not to accept and honour such warmth and trust. I cannot possibly express how much this means to me.

We are Muslim women in purdah. Even the men from our community had to struggle to make a space for themselves in the world of literature. Anything that a woman attempts, therefore, is bound to be doubly difficult. However, the distant horizon does not remain so forever. Striving towards a goal can bring it closer to us with every passing day. I'm here to tell you today that it is time we started to reach out towards light and freedom. We women have been crippled for ages—now we need to forge our own destiny, to force our way through all obstructions. Our freedom will not come from begging. We need to discover strength within ourselves. We need to improve our minds, acquire wisdom through our own efforts, and move forward. It is time we stopped merely breathing and started to live.

Some of you might think I'm trying to say that the only use of education is to spend our time rioting on the roads. Or maybe, excited by the idea of women's franchise, we might, like men, start knocking on the doors of offices for jobs! Let me assure you that nothing is further from my mind. I firmly believe that education should never be commercialized; that it is not to be used merely as a means of earning money. If we follow a path that facilitates our activities, we shall, no doubt, succeed in our mission.

I must declare that I consider women's education an absolute necessity. I am disappointed and grieved by the near-total lack of any effort in this direction in our society. I cannot see anything but an all-round degeneration in our national life today. As we proceed in time, we force our women perversely back into the darkness of ignorance, without realizing that this darkness will ultimately envelope society, entirely. We're putting our future at risk and we are blissfully unaware of it.

How is women's education going to help society at large? My answer to this is that an educated mother's child cannot remain unlettered. Even if just one girl in a household learns to read and write, the quality of life for the family improves. Moreover, education catches on. It spreads from one girl to another, from one household to another, and in no time at all, women of the entire neighbourhood become educated.

I should perhaps give you an illustration from my own life. When I was expecting my youngest son (who is now fifteen months old), I felt an irresistible urge to put pen to paper, to create something original out of my imagination. I started to write my book entitled *Destiny* at that time, and I am convinced that it is precisely because of this that my son, even at this tender age, prefers books and pencils to all kinds of toys. I've no doubt that at the time of pregnancy, the mother unconsciously transmits her own desires and aspirations to the child in her womb. My son, for instance, now sits quietly with a book and turns the pages on his own, perfectly happy in muttered communication with himself. I'm amazed to see that even if one tries to tempt him with a colourful toy, he ignores it and turns instinctively to the unattractive inkpot and the broken pen.

I'm not being so radical as to advise my fellow Muslim women to go ahead chasing degrees regardless of circumstances. What I want to impress upon you is that Muslim women should not be totally unlettered. Even as they remain within the purdah and fulfil household duties, they can make an effort to acquire basic education. The ultimate aim is to educate the next generation, and this, at the moment, should be our goal. Sowing quality seeds is good, even if you sow only a handful.

A look at history tells us that the achievement of our ancestors did not lie only in conquering lands and preaching religion, but also in acquiring and spreading education. Today Europe stands at the apex of civilization because of this. I feel ashamed to think that we, the descendants of such illustrious people, are wasting our potential. Ridden by laziness and other vices, we lack education, purpose and direction; and thus have become easy targets for exploitation and subjugation. Is it enough to stare enviously at the accomplishments of the races that have attained fame and glory? Sadly, it seems to me that all we have learnt from history is to calculate how much we have lost in this wide world and to lament.

Basic education, therefore, is an absolute necessity. Those who can afford it might wish to provide higher education for their girls. Nothing could be better than that. Besides, if these girls have the chance to travel from time to time with their fathers, brothers or husbands, it would prove to be beneficial. Travelling is very good entertainment and, thus, brings happiness to the mind, which in turn helps improve a person's health, considerably. Besides, seeing the beauty and diversity in the myriad creations of the Almighty Allah makes one wonder about the immensity of His power. Such thoughts always enlighten and elevate the mind. I would request my sisters, however, to preserve the purdah when they engage in such pursuits. Heady with modern thoughts, we should never ignore or slight the conventions of the purdah.

In my opinion, we women have to take an active step in order to eradicate the follies of our society. Men need to be aware of this need, and we can start by setting up a women's educational organization. Today we are gathered here to hold a meeting of the Bengal Muslim Women's Association. I propose we hold similar meetings in different parts of Bengal every six months. With time and sustained effort, our society is bound to reflect the changes taking place.

I'm aware that ours is a poor nation. But is that a reason to lose all hope and stop all efforts? We cannot wait for miracles to happen. We have to rely on ourselves to gather funds for our work. We have to toil with our blood and sweat. It is only been about three decades since education is being seen as a means to making money in our society. But the time has come for us to compete with other nations of the world. Why do educated young men today give up hope from the very outset, fearing inevitable defeat? Isn't there any way to earn money other than slaving for someone else? It is difficult having to send one's child to school, when one knows that a career in slavery awaits him in the future.

We had in the past sneered at certain professions like tailoring, thinking they were not respectable enough. Today Hindu young men have adopted the very same and are doing extremely well, showing us how modern technology can be used to prosper in life. A retail shop selling lengths of cloth, for instance, can do very good business. This is not surprising, because to cover the body is one of the basic human necessities—after all, we are not living in prehistoric times any more. Nowadays, however, people who are doing well in the garments' business are not Muslims but Hindus. Educated Hindus do not hesitate to take up any profession, whereas young men from our community feel ashamed to be shopkeepers. They are still sitting at home idle, hoping to land a paid job in some vague future, without realizing that they have a long and futile wait in front of them.

On the subject of namaz, I would like to say that I do not wish to offer any religious advice; indeed, I'm not qualified to do so. I would just like to say that offering namaz five times a day, as we have been taught to do, is not merely a good religious practice but good for one's health as well. A Muslim man or woman does not need to be told how refreshing it is to splash water on one's hands, feet and face, five times a day. One feels cleansed, in body and soul, as one performs the *oju*. Then, the physical exercise done while performing namaz helps blood circulation, making the body more flexible and agile. This perhaps explains why we invariably feel refreshed after performing namaz. Indeed, it will not be an exaggeration to say that we are given a new lease of life five times a day. Similarly, every other religious practice benefits our health and general well-being.

We are Bengali Muslim women. I have mentioned earlier—most recently, in my essay entitled 'The Muslim in Bengali

Literature' read out last year at the Munshigunj convention of Bengali literature—that we should be proud of our heritage. A Bengali Muslim is born with a natural advantage: a flexible tongue. Sadly, I've often noticed that our next generation is unable to pronounce words clearly. I hold the parents responsible for this. It is the duty of the parents to teach their children, and if the children grow up without proper schooling in their own language, it is a disgrace to their parents.

Arabic does not have the sounds of *ch, t,* the hard *d,* the hard *r,* or *p.* The Iranians cannot pronounce the *t,* the hard *d* and the hard *r* sounds. The English are unable to utter the soft *t* or the soft *d;* just as the French cannot pronounce the hard *d* or the hard *t.* Within our own country, people who speak Urdu, Marathi or Telugu languages, will never be able to speak Bengali as fluently as the native speakers.

On the other hand, prompted by nationalistic feelings, if the Bengali Muslim takes the trouble to learn Arabic and Persian, he is able to speak those tongues like a native speaker, in no time at all. With a little bit of effort and practice, even proper English pronunciations should not be too difficult.

No one but a Muslim will be able to pronounce letters like *zim, zal, ze, yod, yoy* properly; or to differentiate between *gayen* and *gab.* It would not be possible for a non-Muslim to distinguish between sounds like *zal* and *ze, alef* and *ayen.* Equally difficult are the sounds of *hutti* and *auaz* that emanate respectively from the pit of the stomach and the mouth cavity. The difference between the long '*kap koreshat*', uttered from under the palate and the short '*aap kaleman*', uttered by the teeth and the tongue, is very subtle. The corresponding English letters of *H* and *K* are much easier to pronounce; the origin of these sounds does not go beyond the root of the tongue.

Bengali is our mother tongue; and our children should learn this language automatically. If a Hindu boy were asked to pronounce the Arabic name of his Muslim neighbour, he would probably stumble after the first 'Abdul'. The proper pronunciations of the Arabic words *kahhaar* with *tashdid* or *ohhaab* would most certainly defeat him. A young Muslim student, on the other hand, would not find it too difficult to utter Sanskrit names like Krishna Dvaipayan Vedavyas or Dhrishtadyumna. Even after being born with this natural advantage, Muslim children, most often because of the ignorance of their mothers, mispronounce their mother tongue. Isn't this a matter of great shame and regret?

Perhaps it will not be inappropriate to say a few words here on the subject of our national unity. The Koran Mujid says: *Innamal momenuna ekhwatun*, that is, all momen are brothers to each other. The main purpose of the holy saying is to unite all of us, Muslims, in a brotherly bondage. But, sadly, we have strayed very far from such a lofty ideal. No other race in the world is subject to envy, malice and intra-racial squabbles as much as Muslims. We are singularly intolerant of success in others, and take a perverse pleasure in maligning honourable people. One simply has to look around oneself: in a cluster of ten homes in the neighbourhood, at least four are sure to be infected with this malaise.

Once, in the past, our most important asset was a feeling of unity. Islam wrought many miracles on this strength, and earned the world's applause. But down the ages we've lost that holy feeling of unity and today we're standing on the brink of disaster.

I should end my speech with something I should have mentioned earlier. I've already spoken on the subject of female education. I would like to impress upon the parents that while educating children, they should stress particularly the value of truthfulness. Children should learn to hate untruth from the bottom of their hearts; they should know that all the evil in the world have their source in lies and deceit. The importance of leading a truthful life should be imprinted on their young minds right from childhood.

Saugat, Magh 1925
Translated by Adrita Mukherjee

Notes

[1] Dedication, *Swapnadrishta* (The Dream Vision), *Nurunnesa Khatun Granthabali* (Collected Works of Nurunnesa Khatun) (Dhaka: Bangla Academy edition, 1970).

[2] Rashid Al Farooqi, *Nurunnesa Khatun Vidyavinodini* (Dhaka: Bangla Academy, 1987).

[3] Dedication, *Bhagyachakra* (*The Wheel of Fortune*), *Nurunnesa Khatun Granthabali.*

[4] Introduction, *Swapnadrishta.*

[5] Ibid.

[6] Ibid.

[7] The novel *Swapnadrishta* was first published by *Noorkutir*, Serampore, mid-September to mid-October 1922 (Ashwin 1330).

[8] Acknowledgement, *Janaki Bai, Nooronnesa Khatun Granthabali.*

[9] Ibid, *Anunoy* (A Plea)

[10] In Bhadra 1925 *Saugat* magazine published an article called *Banga Sahitye Musalman Mahila* (Muslim Women in Bengali Literature), written by Mohammad Abdul Hakim Bikrampuri. The article generated a debate, which was recorded in the next few numbers of the magazine. Begum Rokeya and Mrs. M. Rahman participated in this debate. What they had written in reply to Bikrampuri could be summed up in the words, please do not club with us. (*Saugaat*, Bhadra – Kartik, 1927).

[11] The detective novel *Ganguly Moshaier Songsar* (The Household of Mr Ganguly) by Kamrunnesa Khatun (Panna Begum) was included in the *Collected Works of Nurunnesa Khatun*. Rashid Al Farooqi writes in the biography of Nurunnesa, 'Her second daughter Badrunnisa Khatun, too, earned some fame as a writer. One of her stories called *Rekha* was published in *Saugat*.' (Al Farooqi: 22). We have found a story called *Rekha* in Bhadra 1928 *Saugat* and the writer's name is Kamrunnesa Khatun. A photograph of the author was also printed with the story.

[12] There is some amount of exaggeration here. Nurunnesa is probably writing about something she herself has not experienced, only heard of, describing the communal partaking of food blessed by the gods as a disgustingly unhygienic process. She might also be representing the point of view of the

protagonist Saheb who is a rationalist.

For more on Mahaprasad see Dr Hariharan Kanungo in http://orissagov.nic.in.e-magazine/Orissareview/June_July-2007

[13] The author has confused the temple sculptures in Konark, well-known for their depiction of erotic themes, with that of the Jagannath temple in Puri, bereft of any erotic content.

[14] Hoor, more commonly referred to as hoori, are the women of paradise whom none can touch before death. They are offered to men as rewards at the end of a 'good' life and are part of the ambience of paradise.

6

Akhtar Mahal Syeda Khatun (1901-1928): The Inner Quarters

Translated by Sipra Bhattacharya

In the Paush 1969 issue of the magazine *Prabasi*, an article by Jyotirmoyee Devi entitled 'Muslim Authors and Authoresses' was published. She noted with disappointment that though she enjoyed reading works by many Muslim authors like Mir Mosharraf Hossain, Reza-ul-Kamal, Kazi Abdul Wadud, Begum Rokeya, Shamsunnahar Mahmud, Sufia Kamal, Syed Mujtaba Ali, Muhammad Shahidullah, Mansuruddin, Kazi Nazrul Islam and the poet Jasimuddin, their writings hardly reflected 'a picture of the inner quarters of Muslim society, its history and the unique character of their lifestyle derived from the Pathans and Mughals, the small vignettes of their households, tales of joy and woe and the stories of day-to-day tensions and conflicts'.

It is, however, not entirely true that nobody was around to paint pictures of the inner quarters of Bengali Muslim society. The clarity with which such portraits were drawn by women was usually lacking in men's writings. This is true of all authors—Hindu and Muslim, Bengali and non-Bengali. In the Muslim world there surely were a couple of such female authors in the first half of the twentieth century, but they remained hidden from the eyes of a large section of society. Probably this is why even a writer of the stature of Jyotirmoyee Devi—who was far more well-read than an ordinary person—had not heard about Akhtar Mahal Syeda Khatun or the slightly later writer Umartul Fazl (b.1922), and others like them.

That it is possible to discuss the works of Akhtar Mahal Syeda Khatun today, though briefly, is because of an extraordinary coincidence. Born into an aristocratic educated family of Faridpur, Akhtar Mahal was educated at home. The atmosphere at home was truly conducive to literary and artistic pursuits, though there was no question of sending the girls to school or college in the early years of the twentieth century.

In 1913, at the age of fourteen, Akhtar Mahal was shifted from her familiar surroundings to distant Noakhali, when she got married to Maqbul-ul Khan, the eldest son of Khan Sahib Alhaj Sirajul Haq, the manager of the Saber Khan estate of Noakhali District. For Akhtar Mahal, this marriage was as good as being sent to exile. The feudal environment in her in-laws' house was completely different from the enlightened background and the interest in music and the arts that prevailed in her paternal home. Women keen on education or music were not appreciated in her marital home.

Akhtar Mahal continued to write despite the adversities. Her eldest son, F. M. Khan, still remembers how she would come to their room at night to read and write as she lay on the mat. She would preserve these writings carefully, away from prying eyes. Sometime between 1924 and 1925, the poet Nazrul Islam visited Noakhali and was invited to the house of the zamindar. As the young wife of the family dabbled in writing, she was asked to compose a laudatory piece for the poet. Akhtar Mahal wrote:

Bengal's garden's Bulbul,
Our dear Nazrul,
The son of our land,
Our brother dear,
In this vast country
You have no peer.
We bring you our silent tears,
Our respect and esteem too,
Take them, O hero of ours,
With love we great you.
Sons of the same mother,
Hindu and Muslim brother,
Come all, come and meet,
Let us touch his lotus feet.'

The poem amazed Nazrul. He wanted to know if the lady who composed the poem had written anything else. That was when other writings by Akhtar Mahal were made public.

Encouraged by Nazrul Islam who pushed her work, two novels by Akhtar Mahal Syeda Khatun, *Niyantrita* (The Woman Bound by Destiny) and *Maran Baran* (Welcome, Death) were published in *Nauroz* and *Saugat* respectively.[1] Yet, ironically, it was because of Nazrul's lack of responsibility that many of her works were lost.[2]

What did Akhtar Mahal write about? How well did she write? Commenting on *Niyantrita* (the piece follows), the writer-critic Abul Fazl said, 'The environment created by the author—the house and the courtyard surrounded by walls—is familiar to the Muslim reader. The heroes and heroines are men and women they know intimately.'[3] That Akhtar Mahal had the potential to be a successful writer is evident from her two novels—or perhaps they should be called novellas. What more can be said about an author who died at the age of twenty-eight?

Her art did not have the time to mature. Abul Fazl wrote, 'The work [*Niyantrita*] is not a piece of fiction—at least, it doesn't read like one. It is, from beginning to end, the chronicle of an excruciatingly sad life, described in a poignant, mournful style.'[4]

Did Akhtar Mahal Syeda Khatun base her stories and characters on her own life and world? The women of her stories—Ayesha of *Niyantrita* and Hasenara of *Maran Baran*, for instance—are very unhappy. Was Akhtar Mahal herself unhappy too? Raising such questions after such a long time is perhaps immaterial. But the reader remains curious, nevertheless.

Akhtar Mahal was the aunt of the late Rokeya Rahman Kabir, formerly professor of Dhaka's Eden College, and later the director of the NGO, Saptagram. In an interview given to us in 1997, Rokeya said she did not remember her chhoto phuphu, but stories about her were alive in her memory. She remembered what her mother used to say about her aunt. 'Amma used to say,' said Rokeya, 'You all are just like your chhoto phuphu, Kutti—or was it Kochi—spending all your time devouring novels and plays!'

Akhtar Mahal's brother Mujibar Rahman, two years her senior, was outstanding among the first batch of Bengali Muslim I.C.S. officers. The two shared strong emotional ties. Her brother's house, naturally, was Akhtar Mahal's refuge. The one who bore the brunt of this relationship was Mujibar Rahman's wife—that is, Rokeya Rahman Kabir's mother. Leaving the children in the care of her 'Bhabi-Saheba', Akhtar Mahal would read 'plays and novels' to her heart's content and fill numerous pages with her writing. Talking of 'Kutti', Rokeya Rahman's mother would say, 'She filled reams of paper with her writing. Nobody knew who was going to publish it . . . ' Sometimes she would tell her children, 'At least Kutti wrote something, you don't even do that!'

Taking a cue from Abul Fazl's comment, I had asked Rokeya Rahman Kabir, 'Was there a secret sorrow in her heart? Have you heard of any such thing?'

'Yes, indeed, she was very unhappy. Our house in Faridpur was unusual—my father and all his brothers read books and played the flute and sang. My grandfather played the flute rather well too. He was a scholar of Persian. There were many books in our house. Chhoto Phuphu was Abba's favourite sister. Born into an enlightened family, she was married into one in Noakhali, so far away. She had been promised in marriage to that boy a long time ago by someone in the family! Can you imagine? A hidebound feudal household, no environment for studies, and yet they sent her there. As far as I know, she was not on very good terms with her husband. Not surprising, considering that ours was a family of professionals.' Many male characters in Akhtar Mahal's stories are professionals, as she had seen in her father's house. Her women characters read books, write, listen to songs. Naturally, they are frequently told off for these activities.

Quoting from songs and rhymes are characteristic of Akhtar Mahal's style. Lyrics appear in the middle of common conversation, 'Touch me not, touch me not, O dark one, my body will darken,[5] or 'In the limitless blue sky/ the moon spreads out its light.'[6] Her women talk in riddles, using the language of the women's quarters. 'The soil, like black kajal/For it, I walk six months/White dhutra flowers/ Are not worth a penny.'[7] Rokeya Rahman Kabir had reminisced, 'Abba used to sing the songs of Rabindranath, D. L. Roy and Nazrul. On moonlit nights he would play the harmonium and sing. There were many records in our house. My younger chacha [paternal uncle] used to play the flute really well. He died very young. Abba did too. Perhaps it was in our family to die young.'

But this does not really explain a death at twenty-eight. Akhtar Mahal's eldest son remembered his mother being afflicted by kalazar. Rokeya Rahman Kabir had remarked, 'How unfortunate! Only a short while after her death the medicine for that disease was invented by a Doctor Brahmachari.' Akhtar Mahal's novel, *Maran Baran,* was published posthumously in *Saugat*. The editor, Mohammad Nasiruddin, wrote about the novel, 'I did not know that such a lovely novel could be written in such limited space.'[8]

In both the novels, *Niyantrita* and *Maran Baran*, love unfolds with great ease, and in a surprisingly uninhibited style. Often, desire finds expression in sensuous descriptions. A hero or a heroine may have 'blue eyes' or 'a dark body'. Sometimes the writer ponders, 'The wave that rises in the breast when the full moon rises in the sky—is it more or less intense than the secret tumult of hopes and fears in a young girl's heart, let loose by the first touch of her beloved?'[9] Akhtar Mahal was no more than a child when she got married. Ayesha, Layeli and Hasenara in her stories are also young girls. Love awakens in these young hearts, and sometimes remains unrequited. The girl may already be married. But despite the strictures imposed by society, the characters in Akhtar Mahal's works are repeatedly seen to surrender themselves to love. Had any such incident taken place in the novelist's life too?

Rokeya Rahman Kabir said, 'I have no knowledge of any such incident. Had there been anything like it, Amma would surely have known. She'd never told us anything. But, you never know . . . '

Akhtar Mahal Syeda Khatun was not just a writer of romantic novels, she wrote with acute social awareness, as her essays published in *Saugat* suggest. One of her remarkable observations on society was, 'Marriage and rejection *(talaq)* are oft-repeated children's games in unenlightened Muslim society.'

M. B.

The Woman Bound by Destiny

1

'Asha!'

'Yes, Maru.'

'You're so quiet!'

Ayesha did not reply. Mariam was silent for a short while, and then said once more, 'Well! Such poetic reverie doesn't suit me at all, my dear. It's a lovely evening . . . to be spent laughing, swapping stories and having good fun. Instead you silently stare at the moon! What sort of fun is this, dear!'

She immediately broke into a song: 'In the limitless blue sky/ the moon spreads out its light.'

Ayesha remained silent. Annoyed, Maru flounced off.

The young girl sat in the luminous moonlight, her heart bright with the same pure luminous joy, staring enchantedly at that joyous world. There was no sorrow, anxiety or despair—the whole world was full of hope, happiness and laughter. The holy smile of the full moon of Ramzan spilled across the earth and sky. Diamonds seemed to twinkle in the leafy crowns of the coconut palms. In the silent moonlight the distant villages looked like a dream world. In the pond in front, a thousand white lotuses formed a stairway, for the moon to descend and bathe in its water. The wistful song of the blackbird and the perfume of the flowers blooming at night filled Ayesha's heart with a tremulous enchantment. The swooning Earth wore such a dream-smile!

What did she want? What remained incomplete in that perfect beauty? Was there anything lacking in her young heart? The dim picture of an almost-forgotten pair of black eyes emerged in her heart, spreading itself across the sky. She could not remember where or when she had seen it. She could not even make out if she had really seen it, or if this was merely her imagination.

That picture was as dim, as indistinct, as those faraway villages.

'You wicked girl! I'll put an end to your enjoying the breeze, you useless creature, and not even married yet! The older she grows, the more shameless she becomes. Here we are, tired of searching the whole house, thinking where could the girl have disappeared so late at night! O Allah! She's been happily sitting on the terrace!'

'Oho! Let her be, Bhabi. Don't say anything to her! She is a very talented poet. She sits up till three in the morning, writing poetry, forgetting meals and sleep. Ha! Ha! Ha!'

'A fig for her poetry! And as for you, Maru, how could you leave her alone on the terrace and go off to bed?'

Mariam replied apprehensively, 'How could I know that she would stay here so long? I thought she'd come to bed after some time.'

'Come along, get going, you saucy girl! Have you no shame? What kind of a girl are you?'

Ayesha seemed to sink with embarrassment. It was true—what kind of a girl was she, after all? Where had she been lost all this time? Now that she had gathered her wits, she found that her elder sister, Amena, Amena's sister-in-law, her own friend Mariam and Amena's younger brother-in-law, Shaheed, had all come up to the terrace in search of her.

When Amena got up before dawn to eat the *sehri*, the pre-dawn meal taken during the month of fasting, she found Ayesha was missing from the room. She was flabbergasted. O disaster! A girl of marriageable age missing from home! Where could she have gone? When she found Ayesha on the terrace, the anxiety that was eating into her abated, but the relief made her lose her temper. What a terrible worry the wretched girl had put them through!

Ayesha's visits to the terrace were stopped from that day on.

2

The dak bungalow at Pangsha resounded with noise. The place came alive with the laughter of children and the scurrying about of servants and maids. Rafiq-al-Haque, the sub-deputy, was on his way to Jessore with his family. He had stopped by at Pangsha, invited specially by a close friend. He took leave of his friend and reached the station to find he had missed the connecting train to Jessore. The friend's house was quite far away from the station, so instead of returning he decided to stop at the dak bungalow.

A young girl of thirteen sat quietly next to the window, completely aloof from the noise. The sky brimmed over with the parting-rays of the sun. Its final kiss touched the world gently, making it magical and golden. As Ayesha remained seated next to the window, suddenly, a pair of arms wound themselves affectionately round her neck. 'Why, now, darling sister! Why are you crying, Ayesha?' Ayesha was startled to find Amena's voice was choked with emotion. She had not even noticed her elder sister come in. What a shame! What would Apa[10] think!

The dam had burst. Hearing Amena's loving tone, the tears that Ayesha had suppressed all this while were released, like a tidal wave, flooding her breasts. The two sisters sat arm in arm for a long time, weeping together.

After dusk, when there was nobody in the vicinity of the dak bungalow, husband and wife came out to sit in the verandah. The world was bathed in the light of the moon, halfway to its fullness. In the pond facing them, plenty of water lilies bloomed, gazing up at the sky. A mild breeze made them flutter, like a new bride at the first touch of her husband. Amena's fair face, with the moonlight falling on it, would put a rose to shame. Her eyes, dark as two bumblebees, were moist with tears, like the deep clouds of the monsoon.

'What is it, Amen? What is the matter, my dearest?'

As her husband took her in his arms, a tremulous smile touched Amena's lips. Rafiq asked again, 'Why such dark clouds on this lovely face?' Amena did not reply. She blushed—the pink hue of the rose slowly turned the deeper shade of a red hibiscus. Rafiq repeated, 'Won't you tell me what you are thinking?'

Amena said softly, 'What should I be thinking of?'

'Really? Aren't you?'

'I'm thinking about Ayesha.'

'Oh! But tell me, is there any use thinking about her?'

'Is this what destiny has in store for her?'

'Maybe! Otherwise why should her father—who had so lovingly brought up this motherless child—have such a strange fancy! What good will our thinking about it do?'

'Are you asking me to not say a word and watch Ayesha die?'

'Of course, we'll try to do our best. But if we can't do anything, we'll have to bear it.'

'Oh, my dear, please don't say that! I've brought her up with my blood and sweat. When our mother died, Ayesha was just a year old. Won't it break my heart to send her into exile?'

'I've already said, Amen, we'll try with all our might to save her. But what if we fail? It's Allah's wish.'

The person for whom they felt such anxiety and shed so many tears was sleepless too. The unfortunate young girl lay on a mat next to the window in the adjoining room. She, too, was thinking of the letter from her brother she had read on the sly—it contained the news of her impending marriage. She could not work out what her crime was to have deserved such a punishment. She could not think of a single evil deed she had done in her life. 'Why then? Why, O Allah! Please save me, O Allah, protect me, O Rahim!' Thus the girl prayed for a long time. At last, the load on her breast seemed lighter. Her simple, innocent mind was convinced that Allah must have heard her prayers. She watched the little stars returning home westwards across the dark blue expanse of the sky. Ultimately, only one star remained. Was it, perhaps, the night watchman?

3

Abdul Latif, the reputable lawyer of Jessore, was a well-known man. On the day his beautiful, virtuous wife departed for her heavenly abode, leaving behind three sons and two daughters, the highly-educated lawyer, who had cleared M.A. and B.L., clutched his baby daughter against his breast and wept like a child.

After the funeral was over, relatives and friends returned to their own homes. As the days went by, Latif, in order to forget his grief, began exploring the roads to all kinds of pleasure, including dubious ones.

His fourteen-year-old daughter Amena was married, as was Shafiq-al-Alam, the eldest of his children. Nurul Alam and Jaan-e-Alam were nine and five respectively. Ayesha was only a year old.

When well-meaning friends and fathers of nubile daughters got busy prodding the lawyer to get married again, he, rather reluctantly, tied the knot all over again. This happened two years after his first wife's death.

Ayesha grew up happily, in the loving care of her aunt—her father's brother's wife. Nine years passed by in happiness and sorrow, tears and laughter. Flowers bloomed and withered away; many a bud dried up before flowering. Women kissed the faces of their newborn sons; and children were snatched away from their mothers by destiny. Nine summers scorched the earth to ashes, to be decked again with the verdant beauty of nine springs.

Rafiq-al-Haque found a job and took his wife with him. Amena now had a son and daughter of her own. Shafiq-al-Alam went with his family to Allahabad, where he was posted as the deputy magistrate. Nurul Alam passed his F.A. and was studying for his B.A. degree. Jaan-e-Alam would take his Entrance Exam this year.

Ten-year-old Ayesha now lived with her stepmother, as the aunt who had been like her mother was also in Heaven to be united with her husband.

Often it is as difficult to get a stepmother's love, as it is to pluck the flowers of Heaven. Ayesha's case was no different. There was no one in the household to comfort the motherless child, who would be bombarded by the stepmother's acerbic barbs. Endless tears and the ragged textbook she had managed to retrieve were her sole companions. She would be taunted by all and sundry for her excessive attachment to that little book—a rarity among village folk.

Even when she was deeply hurt by the biting scorn directed at her, she would remain silent. Seeing her unbroken resolve, the critics finally conceded that one who showed such eagerness to learn Bengali could not but turn out to be utterly 'dishonest'.

But the shameless, obstinate girl continued to study with the same diligence. She visited Sultan on a regular basis, beseeching him, 'Please Brother, I beg of you, do tell me the meaning of this couplet!'

4

Rafiq was the sub-deputy of Rajshahi district. His home was in Shahjadpur, where his mother stayed with his two sisters and a brother. One of the sisters was married when their father was still alive. Rafiq was home with six months' leave, to get his younger sister Mariam married. Mariam Banu was married with customary fanfare, to the young lawyer Haidar Ali. Amena had sent for Ayesha well before the ceremony began. Her father and brothers also came for the wedding. At the time of leaving, Latif wanted to take Ayesha back with him. Amena requested her father, 'Let Ashu be with me now, Father. When I go to Rajshahi, I'll go via Jessore and reach her home.' Latif therefore went back with his sons.

A month went by. One day the two sisters were talking in

Amena's bedroom. Amena said, 'Ashu, you are missing home, aren't you?'

Smiling, Ayesha replied, 'No, Apa, I don't miss home at all. See how I play about all day—no work, no chores, and you never scold me either!'

'Does Ma scold you a lot?'

'I don't feel too sad when Ma scolds me. But I really feel miserable when she doesn't allow me to study. Just because I study a little Bengali, they say such ugly things!' Ayesha's voice became heavy as she said those last words.

'What does Father say?'

'Father does not know about this, he encourages me to read. And Rangabhai has sent me such lovely books, Apa! You could have had a look if I brought them along! Such beautiful stories!' Ayesha's eyes sparkled.

Gazing at her sister's happy face, Amena said, 'Well, you may read here without fear! Asha, do you remember Rangabhai?'

'Not really. Where is he now?'

'In Calcutta.'

Suddenly, they heard footsteps approaching and the two sisters drew the veil over their heads. Rafiq came in, three letters in hand. He gave two to Amena and said, 'Read them!'

Ayesha, who was about to leave the room, stopped on seeing the letters, asking, 'Where did the letters come from, Apa?'

Amena opened a letter and read it silently.

9th of Jaishtha
Jessore.

Dear Amena,

My blessings to you. The zamindar of Nabipur had invited me to meet him. He wants Ayesha as his daughter-in-law. They are very rich and have a huge house. It is surrounded by a large garden and fruit orchards. They also have a house in Calcutta. It is a very large estate. The zamindar has a son and a daughter. The son will inherit most of the property after his father's death. The zamindar's wife came out in my presence, to talk about

Ayesha. 'Oh, the poor motherless child!' she said. She showed me all the jewellery inlaid with precious stones that she has got made for her son's bride. I have given my consent after due consideration. Since they were in a hurry, I have fixed the date on the coming 5th of Asharh—I didn't have time to let all of you know. You all must come here by the end of this week. Asha will live in great happiness, dear. You needn't worry.

Yours affectionately,
Abdul Latif.

The other letter was from Nurul Alam.

'Apa,

Father is not giving Ashu in marriage, but sacrificing her! I beg you, Apa, don't throw her alive in the flames! I know the groom. Despite trying his utmost, his father was able to get him to study only up to the Third Standard. Now wine and harlots are his constant companions. He has some kind of a persistent ailment and his brain is slightly affected too. So far his parents haven't been able to marry him off though they tried very hard. They have taken advantage of the fact that our father's a simple soul, and duped him. Seeing their house and property, the jewellery etc,, Father thinks Ashu would live like a queen. I tried to stop him, but he didn't listen to me. I beseech you, please save Ashu. You and your husband must not give your consent to this marriage. If you are absolutely unable to stop Father, poison the poor girl's food without trepidation.

Yours,
Nuru

Amena glanced at Ayesha with a pale face. Ayesha repeated, 'What is it, Apa? Is everything all right in Jessore?'

'Yes. Now off you go to Amma.'

Ayesha departed, her thoughts anxious.

Amena looked at her husband. 'What do we do now?'

'Allah will show the way! I have an invitation to attend Hossain's wedding in Pangsha. Let's go to Jessore via Pangsha.'

'Why should I go to Pangsha?'

'Why, you've also been invited! No, it's true! He's asked me to bring you along. He'll be angry if I went without you. Let's leave tomorrow.'

'Will you save my Ashu?'

'Of course we'll try!'

'It'll be enough if you try. There's nothing you can't do.'

'Who do you think your husband is? The emperor of Delhi? Or some great pir or saint?'

'Someone even greater.'

They set out the next day.

5

Reaching Jessore, Amena and her family found that not many of the relatives had arrived. Shafiq had written to his father, expressing his disapproval of the match. Nur did the same. The lawyer was very annoyed. He just couldn't understand why these crazy, stupid wretches were opposing his dream of a happy future for his daughter.

Seeing her father's anger, Amena too did not have the courage to say anything. The wan-faced Ayesha sat alone, pondering over her future, which appeared too terrible to contemplate. Suddenly, Amena called her, 'Ashu, come here and see who has arrived!' Ayesha entered the next room and stood dumb-founded.

A young man who looked familiar sat in the room. What bright, cheerful eyes he had! Their glance, as dazzling as lightning, seemed to penetrate the innermost recesses of the heart. A wide forehead indicated how intelligent the young man must be. His full lips were forever smiling. The dark curved eyebrows seemed to put even Cupid's flower-bedecked bow to shame!

As Ayesha stood motionless, like a statue, and stared at the young man, he smiled gently and said, 'I hope you're well, Ashu?'

At the sound of his melodious voice, Ayesha was startled. She looked downwards. Amena smiled and said, 'Don't you recognize

Rangabhai, Ashu?'

Rangabhai! Anwar Hossain! Such a handsome man!

Ayesha bent low to salute him. The youth asked once more, 'Are you well?'

'I am,' replied Ayesha indistinctly, and sat down beside him. She did not even realize it when her eyes rose slowly and fastened themselves on the young man's face. When the two pairs of eyes met, she started and quickly lowered her own. A sudden smile glowed on Anwar Hossain's handsome face. Embarrassed, Ayesha quietly left the room.

Amena said, 'Father has fixed the wedding date on fifth Asharh. He is not listening to appeals from anyone. Allah alone knows what fate has in store for her!'

'I cannot understand why Uncle had this fancy,' commented Anwar Hossain.

'Well, he must be thinking that Ashu will be a zamindar's wife; wear gold jewellery all over her body. What else can it be?'

'Can a person be happy with landholdings and jewellery?'

'Who will explain that to Father?'

'Doesn't Aunt say anything? She is the one who should protest!' said the young man.

Amena heaved a deep sigh. A little later, Anwar Hossain went to see Amena's stepmother. She greeted him affectionately, asked him how he was, requested him to take a seat and served some refreshments. After talking to her for a while, Anwar Hossain left the inner quarters to go sit in the drawing room.

Amena called Ayesha, 'Ashu, go, check the time on Father's watch. Better still, fetch it if you can.' Ayesha was hesitating on the verandah of her stepmother's room. What if the young man who had wrought magic on her was still in there!

Her stepmother called out, 'What is it, Ayesha? What do you want? Come in!'

Ayesha walked inside and said, 'Apa wants the watch.' The elder lady picked up the watch, gave it to her sister-in-law who sat in front of her and said, 'Go and give it to Raushan's mother.'

Ayesha remained in her stepmother's room. Noticing a couple of biscuits and a piece of cake on a platter, she asked, 'Who are these for, Ma?'

'I had served them to Anwar. He picked up a few and left the rest. Why don't you have them?'

Ayesha hid a desire to laugh aloud. She thought, 'Food blessed by the Lord! And I am being asked to have it!' She thought it was a sign of God's grace that the suggestion should come from her stepmother. After all, these were hers by right. She picked them up almost reverentially.

6

Ayesha sat fanning her father. Suddenly, the sound of footsteps startled her. Her eyes, eager as those of a doe bewitched by flute music, turned towards the door. Whose footsteps were these? Anwar Hossain entered with a telegram in his hand. Opening it, Latif asked, 'Anwar, I hear you are leaving today.'

'Yes, Uncle,' he replied.

'Won't you come to Ashu's wedding?'

'I probably won't be able to make it, Uncle.'

The young man went away, each footstep ripping through the heartstrings of the fourteen-year-old girl.

Ayesha sat next to the window, staring at the dense darkness outside. Her heart too was filled with darkness, rid of a single beam of light. Anwar would go home tonight. Well, let him go! He was married. If he knew about Ayesha's feelings, he might spit at her out of hatred. Father, meanwhile, continued to be adamant. Doomsday—fifth of Asharh—was approaching fast! Only fifteen days were left!

'Save me, save me, O All-Powerful One! Can you not save this ordinary girl? Mother—O dear Mother! Why did you leave this unfortunate girl behind? There is no one here today to protect her, Mother, no one at all! She will sink deep! Allah, why then did you give her a glimpse of Heaven when she was destined to stay forever in Hell? Was the dazzle of lightning meant to highlight the nature of darkness, to show the tortures of Hell?'

'Anwar Hossain! What a honeyed name! No, I will not give up these thoughts. I cannot give them up! Let him hate me! I will find my happiness by loving him secretly, in my heart. I will never marry anyone else, never!'

The innocent, ignorant girl fetched the Koran Sharif, placed it on her head and said, 'O Allah, be my witness! O limitless sky! O limitless creation! You are my witnesses! I will never call anyone my husband except Anwar Hossain. Never!'

Alas! Unwise woman! Would you ever manage to atone for the wrong you committed today?

In the morning, Ayesha's brother and sister came into her room. Nur called, 'Hey, Ashu! Still in bed?'

Ayesha lay with her eyes shut. She opened her eyes now and sat up, hearing her brother's call. Looking at her face, Amena's grave face became even more so.

Nur said, 'Why is your face swollen? And your eyes – why are they all red?'

Ayesha replied nervously, 'I've slept a lot, that's why!'

Nur turned to Amena and said, 'Listen, Apa, I had quite an argument with Rangabhai last night! He said, girls should receive an education and I said, absolutely not. What do you say, Apa?'

Amena didn't reply. She was lost in thought.

Ayesha asked hesitantly, 'Has he left, Brother?'

'Sure. He must have reached home by now! Probably sitting and chatting with his wife.'

Ayesha lay down and closed her eyes again. When Nur called her later, she did not reply. Amena said, 'She's not feeling well. Leave her alone.'

7

On D-day, Ayesha was married off, and nobody could prevent the act. Amena's tears and Nurul Alam's pitiful appeals were dismissed as childish. Amena, already reprimanded, used her last argument, saying, 'Father, Ayesha will kill herself crying! She doesn't agree to this marriage!' The answer she got was, 'All girls cry at their wedding, my dear daughter! After marriage it will be impossible to persuade Ayesha the Queen to visit this home!' These words were accompanied by a loud fit of laughter.

Rafiq Sahib and Nur Alam made a final effort in the wedding-assembly itself. The groom's father told them, 'We hear that the girl doesn't agree to the marriage, that she is crazy about your brother? Well, is this the place to bring up such matters? You've forced us to talk! I accepted the girl in spite of the talk because my son has his drawbacks, but one should not condone a sin!' Rafiq and Alam felt such shame, humiliation and hatred that they wanted to take off their shoes and give the nasty, foul-mouthed boor a proper lesson. They, however, left the wedding-assembly quietly, praying for Ayesha's death. Incidentally, since Latif was not present there, he did not hear the comment.

Ayesha had believed till the last minute that Allah Himself would save her. And perhaps, if the marriage went through despite everything, she at least hoped to be dead. But Allah had already wrought her fate, and He did not revoke His own injunction. As for the child, though a storm of emotions exploded in her heart, it did not break and nor did the earth split beneath her feet! Her last hope was that she would not answer when they asked for her consent at the wedding ceremony. But her broken 'nays' could not stop the marriage. Her weak outcry was drowned in the clamour of pipes, drums and kettledrums. Even their mother in Heaven must have been moved by Amena's laments.

When the swooning Ayesha was lifted by others the whole world seemed to revolve around her like a haze of twirling smoke.

Dressed as a bride, Ayesha sat on a side of the bed. Her husband Omar Ali commanded, 'Come here.' The bride did not move. Not getting a response even after he had called her two or three times, the husband's pride in his proprietary rights was hurt. It became difficult for him to remain calm. Hurling obscene abuses at his wife, he roared, 'Oh, has your . . . forbidden you to speak to me?' Still, no attempt was made by the disobedient wife to respect his commands. Omar strode up to his bride and flung her veil aside. She was trying unsuccessfully to stop her tears by holding her lips between her teeth. But the unceasing stream of tears drenched the clothes on her breast.

'O you fallen woman! You wicked girl! Are you sorry because you're married to me?'

A violent kick by the husband flung the bride off the bed. Those who surreptitiously had their ears glued to the door, spying upon the newly-weds as was customary, were shocked. Someone ran to inform Amena and Latif. Amena went away, trying hard to control herself. An outraged Latif had begun to growl, but his wife caught hold of his hand. 'Shame on you, are you going to hit your son-in-law? How people will laugh! You have given your daughter in marriage—let her husband hit her or cut her up, do whatever he pleases! What right do you have to interfere? They didn't beg to marry your daughter!' And Latif Sahib sank down like a lion, trapped unawares.

Nevertheless, the matter was taken up with Ayesha's father-in-law the next day. He said, 'Omar is still immature. He will never repeat the wrong he did. I will take the responsibility for your daughter's well-being.'

After dusk, zamindar Abdus Sattar left for Nabipur with his son and daughter-in-law. Ayesha, who was like grief personified, touched her father's feet as she said farewell.

'May you live like a queen, my child,' the father said, with his blessings.

Amena clasped her sister to her breast and shed bitter tears. Her bosom pressed tight against her sister's in a close embrace, Ayesha wept with deep anguish. Staring at the head of his sister, who had bent down to touch his feet, Nur said, choking, 'I pray that I never see your face again, Ayesha!'

Drenched in tears, and making everyone around her cry as well, Ayesha went away. By then, the golden glow of evening had faded and the darkness of night had, mercifully, covered the world.

8

The palatial house of the zamindars of Nabipur was decked up, waiting to welcome the bride. Karima Bibi, the sister of the zamindar, called her son aside and said, 'You're working too hard, son. Eat something, please.' She served him some food and went out, her face drawn and anxious. She was the only one in the house today to feel a strange sorrow in her heart. The portrait of a helpless, motherless girl floated before her eyes—the unfortunate one who would see the end of happiness today. A drunken fool for a husband! An ogress for a mother-in-law! For the last thirteen years Karima Bibi had done nothing but serve her sister-in-law. She had slaved beyond human endurance; her strong, healthy body had become little more than skin and bones, and yet she had not been able to win her sister-in-law over. It was only the thought of her son that kept her going. Alas! Another unfortunate girl was coming to the house to die.

'Here comes the palanquin, here it comes!'

All at once, there was a huge noise outside. 'Ma, the bride is here! What are you doing, sitting inside?' Karima's son stopped, suddenly. Looking at the tear-filled eyes of his compassionate mother, he said, 'Shame on you, Mother! Does it hurt you more than those who have given their daughter in marriage to the son of this house? What will Aunt think? Shame! Go, greet the bride.'

'Alas, my son, she doesn't have a mother! Had her mother been alive, she would never have abandoned her like this. Her brothers and sister didn't want it. But they only saw the groom; they still don't know what the mother-in-law is like!'

'Let such matters be! Let them be, Mother. Go now.'

Karima went slowly to the spot where the ritual of blessing

the new bride was in progress.

'Aunt, dear Aunt! How pretty the bride is! Come and see, Cousin!' Sufia, the groom's sister, screamed in delight.

Her mother scolded her, 'Stop, you needn't shout any more. I know very well what's going on in your aunt's mind. I've never seen anyone as jealous as her. She could pretend she was pleased—at least in front of the others! Look at her, isn't she looking perfectly murderous!'

Karima never responded to such remarks, nor did she reply today. She went across silently to the bride and lifted her veil. She thought she would call her son to show the bride to him. When she looked up, Karima's eyes fell on the bride and it seemed to her as if the sorrows of the whole wide world had gathered in the bride's eyes. She also noticed that her son Abdul Kader was staring at the bride with an unblinking gaze.

9

'Maru! Dear Maru! O Maru mine, Desert Queen!'

Glancing at her husband with a weak smile, the wife said, 'What is it?'

'What are you thinking of?'

'I'm thinking that instead of giving up my life to make your path free from thorns, I have turned your life into a desert!'

'You'd better give up these riddles and talk in plain language.'

'I brought darkness to your life, which was so full of hope.'

'How?'

'With the shadowy clouds of my dark complexion!'

'Is that so? And what do you want to do now?'

'I wish only to die, so that you can marry Hasina.'

'Why must you die? Can't the two of you live together as co-wives?'

'Yes, indeed, I can. I can give up my life for you, dearest. But they won't marry her to a man with another wife!'

'And so, you must die. But if I tell you that I am enchanted by the soft glow of your dark complexion! Well, let it pass. Tell me, how long has it been since you received a letter from your friend?'

'A long time ago, alas! Unfortunate Ayesha!'

'Yes, Ayesha is unfortunate indeed. Not only is she saddled with a brute of a husband, she has also earned the hatred of her mother-in-law and sister-in-law.'

'How do you know about this?'

'That's what my friend Abdul Kader has written. He's just sat for his M.A. examination. He's Ayesha's brother-in-law. From what he writes, it appears that your friend's mother-in-law is a demoness. The husband has quarrelled with his father and gone looking for a job. He's got one too, as a clerk in a mercantile office in Mymensingh. He'll probably bring his wife over soon. Look, it's almost time for me to leave for my office. I'm going to take a bath. I'll try and find out where the fellow lives.'

Mariam was married two months before Ayesha. She was Amena's sister-in-law. At the outset, Haidar, her husband, was not pleased with his bride as she was dark. But very soon the glow in the dark girl's heart removed that shadow. Now he could not do without this darkness even for a day! This lover-nurse-wife rolled into one was his exquisite treasure. Mariam was dark, she gave birth to two daughters in two successive years, and both her parents-in-law died within a year of her marriage. The relatives naturally didn't see her as a harbinger of good fortune. Maru thought that were she to die, her husband would marry a beautiful girl who would bring him good luck, and he would be happier than he was at present. So she used to pray for death. But sometimes, looking at the faces of her daughters, she was afraid to die.

Hasina was the daughter of Haidar's uncle. She was beautiful and educated. Haidar was very generous in her praise. When she came to visit their house and chatted with Haidar, it looked as if he were intoxicated by her presence. Maru thought wistfully how fortunate Hasnu was. Perhaps her husband was in love with

Hasnu! He must be unhappy, only because of her!

She resolved to go ahead and meet death.

10

For two long years, Ayesha had been slaving in the house of her in-laws, yet she had not managed to endear herself in the eyes of any of the family members. Her husband was mentally unbalanced. Sometimes he would caress her and sometimes he would beat her up. Her mother-in-law was angry with her for a different reason. The bride had not brought a desirable amount in dowry, and that was mainly the reason she was dissatisfied with her. Besides, it is easy to find fault with someone we loathe. So, very soon, the young wife gained notoriety for being a loose woman.

The son was uncontrollable—he drank and visited prostitutes. If his father reprimanded him, the son was not averse to telling him off, quite rudely. The zamindar and his wife had hoped that the new bride would bring about a total change in the son. But no such change was visible since the bride's arrival. After a three-year-long wait, when the family's hopes were decisively lost, the new wife became an unnecessary burden to them.

The zamindar's household was somewhat strange. It was as if they walked backwards. The gentleman himself was quite soft hearted, but his wife was extremely tough. He was generous, while his wife parsimonious. It had to be admitted, however, that the lady, though niggardly, was an excellent housewife. All the others of the family had been ruined, the zamindar alone survived because of the stern watchfulness of his wife. Paribanu, the zamindar's wife, personally managed the affairs of the enormous household. They did not need to buy rice or vegetables: these came from their own fields. Two maids were hired to take care of the paddy, peas, lentils and other cereals.

The new wife did her share of the work silently. She felt no fatigue doing it. Her mother-in-law would have regular gossip-sessions with the neighbours to discuss her daughter-in-law's character. She'd say, 'I have brought home a girl from a low-class family! She didn't bring a penny with her. Her parents could not keep her anymore so they got rid of her quickly. What am I to do? She eats both her meals, doesn't she? One can't just keep feeding such a big girl who's sitting idle. So I make her do some work!' The neighbours thought, 'Why would anyone give his daughter to a young man like that if there wasn't a good reason?'

Ayesha would work on her own as if she were an automaton. From six in the morning to ten at night, there was no rest for her. She felt better that way. She could, at least, take her mind off the hardship. It was only when her husband was near her, his wine-clouded breath stinking, foul language on his tongue—only then would her rebellious woman's heart want to hide in the boundless darkness of hell. Her body and mind would burn with shame and humiliation, but she sat still like a dormant volcano. Thus Ayesha learned to turn herself into stone.

Even the impossible can be achieved with effort. She tried with all her heart to respect and love her husband. Despite whatever lay hidden in her rebellious heart, she always obeyed her husband's commands. Since it is not easy to win the love of a mad man, there was no end to the indignity she faced. There was not a place in the world where she could go for a respite; to seek solace for her burning wounds. Her mind and body would be aflame by the mere mention of her father's home. It was her father who had immersed her in this sea of fire! The company of her mother-in-law, sister-in-law, and husband were like poison to her. She was absolutely alone, bearing the lightning lashes of her world all by herself.

11

One afternoon, Ayesha was resting, book in hand, but her eyes wandered far away, towards the fields. Her thoughts were cast back, in search of a faraway past when life was not exhausting. It was full of hope, and light. How beautiful, how verdant life had been! Whichever way she looked, the world was lit up brightly with the iridescent light of young hope! And then, touched by the glowing rays of young love, earth and breeze made her experience a set of new feelings. She was intoxicated by a world full of rosy delirium. The birds sang a fresh tune. The sighing of the woods and the waves of the river seemed to her like a spiritual song, the emotional outpouring of some lovelorn fairy. All of these things were illusory—a cruel game played on her by the world of illusions! Today all her hopes, her sense of calm and happiness were burnt to cinders, like fields reeling under the unbearable heat of the midday sun. It was like an arid zone, as if it were the desert of Sahara.

Who had reduced her to this state! Who lived in her heart and painted dreams there? Who crushed them into smithereens? Who had opened the door of heaven, revealing its beauteous image to one who must spend her life in hell? Who had stepped forth to give a garland made of the flowers of Paradise to a mortal woman only to snatch it afterwards? Who had played this cruel game! Satan? Or was it Satan's creator?

Sighing deeply, Ayesha glanced at the book in her hands. The heroine of the book, Rahima Bibi, who carried her leprosy-inflicted husband on her back, was shooed away by all and sundry. Finally, they stopped in an empty field. Rahima went to beg for food, while the ailing Ayub Nabi, bewitched by Satan, swore to cane Rahima a hundred times once he got better! Clutching the book to her breast, Ayesha lay inert for a long time.

Suddenly, the sound of footsteps could be heard, and Ayesha sat up. Omar Ali entered with Abdul Kader. Seeing the book in Ayesha's hands, Kader laughed. 'I see my sister-in-law is really a modern girl. I hope nobody's telling you off for this.'

'It happens all the time!' replied Ayesha, getting up to fetch two chairs. 'Let it be!' exclaimed Kader as he sat down on the bed, pulling Omar beside him.

'Let me have a look at the book.'

Omar said, 'She is often punished for this habit of reading, but she just won't give it up!'

Glancing at her husband, Ayesha pleaded, 'Please forgive me! When I feel very lonely, I can't stop myself from reading. What else can I do?'

Kader, who did not quite get the meaning of her last words, said in a pained voice, 'Oh, do let her read, Bhai. Reading does not make a person bad! Rather, reading stories about the joys and sorrows in other people's lives could give one the strength to lead one's own.'

'But Mother says that a woman's work is at home—that too much reading makes one's mind wander out in the open!'

'But that is wrong, Bhai. Rather, it's the uneducated mind without a sense of purpose that is snared by petty temptations. It wants to rush out, thinking there is happiness outside. But a mind that is educated and trained to consider cause and effect isn't tempted so easily. 'The idle mind is the Devil's workshop!' It's not wrong to read books in one's spare time. In fact, it is good. By spending one's time reading, there's none left for evil thoughts. What do you say, Bhabi Saheba?' While speaking, Kader suddenly noticed that Ayesha's aimless gaze had drifted far away, along with her thoughts, to the distant ends of that sunburnt field.

Kader called her gently, 'Bhabi!'

Startled, Ayesha turned her eyes towards him and said, 'Sorry, did you say anything to me?'

'I did. I hear you are going to Calcutta.'

'We are.'

'Why?'

Ayesha was annoyed. For a long time, there had been talk of her sister-in-law, Sufia, getting married to Kader—indeed, it had begun since the time they were born. Since he took his B.A. examinations, Kader announced, however, that he would not marry. Everybody was shocked. The zamindar and his wife were outraged. The zamindar said he would give his sister her share of the patrimony and have nothing more to do with either herself or her son. But his sister flung herself at his feet, weeping. 'I have no one but you, Bhaijan!' she wept. The zamindar's wife twisted her lips with scorn. 'Why, dear, your son is now a very important man!' Weeping, Karima Bibi absolved herself from all blame. She would consider herself highly fortunate if the beautiful, accomplished Sufia became her daughter-in-law. But she was eternally unfortunate—otherwise, why should the son, who had never in his life disobeyed his mother's commands, now become impervious to his mother's tears, and refuse to marry not just Sufia, but any woman? This happened two years ago. The sixteen-year-old Sufia was now eighteen.

Ayesha felt insulted that she should have to discuss with Kader the necessity of visiting Calcutta, for she was going there in order to settle Sufia's marriage.

'Yes, we are going there, but why are you interested?'

Having understood Ayesha's sentiments, Kader smiled. 'If all of you are upset to find someone expressing his feelings openly, then I am helpless. Is it right to force a person to do what he does not want? Going against one's nature never leads to anything good, Bhabi. I pray with my heart and soul that the Lord grants Sufia happiness. But I won't be happy marrying her. Is it not inhuman to trample two lives under one's foot and destroy them?'

A faint smile of despair barely touched Ayesha's lips before it vanished. Ah, a man of conscience! Where do you leave your conscience when to satisfy your base instincts, you sprout a hundred arms to oppress a woman? When you grind the poor girl's hopes and desires to dust, where is your sense of justice?

Ayesha was silent. Kader asked, 'What are you thinking about?'

'Nothing, really. But Sufia is quite beautiful; I can't understand the reason why she might make you unhappy!'

'Is it possible to understand everything in this world? To me, the beauty of Sufia might be dim—how would you know?'

'Well, because I do! Some beauteous woman must have enchanted your mind. That's why you're finding a beautiful, educated girl unattractive. I am really keen to find out who that extraordinary beauty might be!'

'Ayesha—although she is extraordinarily beautiful, she is the Mother of all creations. It's not fitting for a child to discuss the beauty of the mother.'

'Let it be, I have no wish to argue with a scholar.'

'May it please you to step into this poor man's humble abode tomorrow. I'm going now to invite my aunt.'

'Well, yours is not a humble abode at all, but a palace. You people are not any worse off than us! It was one house after all, before the wall in between came up. You might have spared us the modesty. Well, let's hear what occasioned this visit.'

After all this time, Omar spoke. 'Don't you know? He's found a job.'

'Is that so? When did this happen? Where would you be posted?'

Omar said, 'In Mymensingh. He'll report on the first of June.'

'Good, that's fine. Both brothers can stay together. But now that you've come to your brother's house, how can you go without having something to eat? Please have some sweets, at least.'

Ayesha brought a glass of sherbet and a plate of fruits preserved in syrup. Kader stretched out his hand to take the glass of sherbet from her. Immediately, Ayesha stepped aside and placed the glass on a table in front of him. Noting her reaction, Kader laughed. 'Touch me not, touch me not, O dark one, my body will darken,' he hummed.

12

The full moon gleamed in the spotless sky, its ethereal light transforming the earth into a paradise. The exhausted Kader, having looked after his guests all day—greeting them, supervising the meals and finally bidding them a courteous farewell—at last heaved a deep sigh. He had not had a moment to breathe.

Only Sufia's mother attended the function from next door. In spite of his repeated entreaties, Ayesha had sent word that she would not be able to come. Her excuse was that Sufia would be left alone. It was not as if their house was far away—only a fence separated the two. And would it have mattered if Sufia too had come?

Kader's whole heart was on fire with humiliation. Ayesha had not come . . . well, all right! Surely, that was not going to add to her distress.

What was Ayesha to him? Was she just his cousin's wife? A glance at the innermost recesses of his heart made Kader turn his eyes away in fear. Who was that enchantress, the demoness who had entered his unguarded heart, trampling over its immaculate purity and innocence, and now sat enthroned in full glory, like an empress? Five years ago, an unknown young girl's sorrow had aroused a wave of compassion in his soft-hearted mother—it also touched his own heart. He had gone to see the new bride with sadness, and once he saw the sad, beautiful face, he fled the scene. Thereafter, for days, the image of that pale, mortified face had brought tears to his eyes, unaccountably. That tide of tears had washed away all hope of a successful career. But a strict sense of duty had prevented him from descending to the level of a beast. Looking at Ayesha's ever-sad face, he often felt as if he was losing sanity. At such times, he would have to exert all his strength to control himself. He never went to the other side of the house unless he simply had to.

He would never marry. He would devote his life to the cause of the uplift of women. This was his desire.

Was Ayesha—for whose sake he had sacrificed all his happiness—displeased with him too for not marrying Sufia? What should he do now? Should he marry Sufia? Impossible! To whom should he go for advice? Should he tell Ayesha? Kader trembled. She would despise him if she knew!

Kader climbed to the terrace with a tired body and an equally tired mind. The clear moonlight poured itself, smiling over the world. Kader stopped, startled. Who was that, sitting on one side of the terrace, washed by the moonlight? Her tumultuous emotions spread out over wind and sky in the form of a song. Kader heard clearly:

> 'Thou who art illuminated, embodied, Thou Light of all Light, O!
> Thou who art beautiful, fragrant, Thou, the Lord of the World, O!
> Thou art the Sun, the Moon, the smile of the bloom, the Heart's ardour and love, O!
> This Solar System ever chants the Song of your Praise, Lord, O!'

It seemed as if Nature herself, bewitched by the moonlight, sang in tune with the song, 'Thou who art beautiful and fragrant, Thou, the Lord of the World, O!'

Kader treaded softly.

'Who is it? Is it . . . are you . . . Ayesha?' His voice was half-choked with happiness.

The song stopped. The singer turned her face and asked, 'Who is it?'

'It's me, Bhabi Saheba. I'm so happy to see you! When did you come?'

'I came in the evening. Aunt came to call me. Please sit down, I'm leaving anyway.'

'Why don't you too sit for a while, we can talk a little.'

'No, no, Ma will perhaps look for me.'

Kader said, rather hesitatingly, 'I have something to say to you—I'll make it very brief. Could you wait for five minutes?'

Ayesha spoke, embarrassed, 'Can't you come to our house tomorrow and tell me?'

Kader heaved a deep sigh. 'That won't happen easily,' he said.

Ayesha sat down. Kader's gaze was lost in the limitless moonlit distance. Both sat in silence for almost a quarter of an hour. Suddenly Kader asked, 'Is it a sin to love someone?' Surprised,

Ayesha asked, 'Is that a question or are you talking to yourself?' He didn't reply, just turned his gaze and looked at Ayesha. Then he repeated, 'Is it a sin to love?'

'Are you asking me?'

'Yes!'

Smiling, Ayesha said, 'I knew it. An enchantress has bewitched this highly-educated brother-in-law of mine! That's good. Why don't you bring that perfect woman home? Is she unattainable?'

Raising two pain-filled eyes, Kader said, 'O please keep your pleasantries aside! I will not marry! But do please answer my question—is it a sin to love?'

Kader's tortured voice made Ayesha forget her smiles; somewhere in her innermost heart, she had suddenly received a blow. 'I don't know whether it's a sin,' she said, 'but it's certainly a terrible mistake. It messes up one's whole life!

'Committing an error is a sin, is it not? A mistake that makes one's life futile—that mistake—that great error—is certainly a terrible sin!'

Ayesha said firmly, 'Yes, certainly it's a great sin.'

Kader noticed that her two eyes were fixed aimlessly on the distant sky. Every word seemed to be wrung out of the deepest recesses of her heart. He remained silent. Ayesha said quietly, 'Why don't you marry the one you love? Otherwise, Aunt will be so unhappy in her old age.'

In a calm, controlled voice, Kader said, 'The one I love is already married.'

'Already married! And yet you hope to be with her!'

'I have no hope of being with her, but why should I give up the happiness of thinking about her!'

'Shame on you! Such words from an educated man! Shame, Bhai! I never expected to hear such words from you.'

'What did you expect to hear?'

'I expected you'd say, "I want this particular pretty girl"—and I'd run and pluck the rose for you!'

'How many human expectations are ever met, tell me! How

many desires have been fulfilled in your own life?'

'Neither would this desire of yours be fulfilled! Do give up such insane thoughts, you have an elderly mother—she's suffered a lot in life. You are her sole source of happiness and peace. Do you wish to make her unhappy? You must marry, even if it's only for her sake!'

'What after that?'

'After that the days life has allotted you will pass.'

'But I am not a woman!'

Kader's scornful smile wounded Ayesha. She softened her harsh tones as far as possible and said, 'Yes, I know, you're not a woman at the mercy of other people, trampled under male feet. You are not one of the humiliated women of Bengal, unable to protest even when her peace and happiness, her dreams and desires are being trampled over! You are but a self-centred, mean male, strong like a beast, looking only for your own pleasure! I know you people well! Your hands won't tremble as you prepare to sacrifice a hundred human beings for your own interest! You do not hesitate to suck the blood from the breast of another, simply to fortify your own demonic power! Nor do you flinch from laughing aloud, and clapping, to see the agony of a tortured soul! But let that pass, I said you should marry for the sake of Aunt, who is miserable.'

Kader listened in silence to Ayesha's emotional outburst, and said, 'You are exaggerating—perhaps someone has tortured you. Not all men are like that. One comes across both good and bad people everywhere. The world has both light and darkness. Nowhere is there only light or darkness. The world is not the playground of Satan alone—it is also the birthplace of Prophet Mohammad. And while it's true that you women are so dependent because men are not just, it's equally true that you are also at fault. The place of women is very high in Islam. The Prophet's own life was fulfilled by the love of his Ayesha and Fatema. How dear was his wife to him, how close his daughter! He even gave them a share of his property. In Islamic law, a girl cannot be married without her own consent. If one loses the devotion of one's mother, the affection of the sister, the love of the wife or the respect of the daughter, life can become a desert. So, in order to preserve the gentleness in women, to protect them from the harshness of the material world, the purity of the inner quarters is reserved for them. They—mothers and daughters—are the goddesses of a man's household.'

'Then, dear brother, why don't you wear this jewel round your neck? Is it because you have sinned by loving?'

'No! It is because I have done a good deed by loving. Truly, love is not a sin—it's a virtue, it doesn't bring despair to a man, it gives meaning to his life. Are you surprised? But it's true! I am not fit to wear this jewel round my neck. But my goddess—whom I worship—I will continue to do so, and that's how I will learn to worship the entire female race. Through that worship I will worship the universe, for the universe is her home. And I am the creator of this worship. The aim of love is eternal union, eternal heaven! Not hell! Do not destroy my purpose. Do not hate . . .'

Kader's voice was choked. Ayesha's unseeing eyes had wandered afar. With a suppressed sigh, she said, 'That same love which raises the free man to great heights, drowns the vulnerable woman's present and future into depthless despair. Suppose Sufia loves you, would she be able to live the kind of life you have spoken about? Her parents will marry her off by force and the unfortunate girl will spend her whole life wearing a false smile on her lips, even when her heart overflows with poison! Never mind, you didn't tell me the name of your beloved! But I can't wait any more, Perhaps Ma is looking for me.'

'Do you really want to hear her name?'

'I do, only if you don't have reservations about telling me.'

Fastening his calm eyes upon her face, Kader said, 'Her name is Ayesha Begum.'

13

Ayesha arrived in Jessore after many years. The family was on its way to Calcutta for Sufia's wedding, but Ayesha came to Jessore with her husband. Omar had escorted her to Jessore and left. Nuru would take her to Calcutta at the end of the week. Ayesha was pregnant. Her usual wan face had become even more drawn. Seated, she was feeding rice to Nuru's son. Her father and mother sat nearby, talking. A soft sound made Ayesha raise her eyes. Who was that standing at the door? Who was it?

Was it a dream? After a glance or two, Ayesha looked down. 'Who is that?' The sound made Latif turn in the direction it came from.

'It is I, Anwar,' answered a soft, shy voice.

'Oh! How are you? Where are you coming from?'

'From Comilla.'

'That's fine! Are you going home? Do sit down! Do you know when Id is due? Is it tomorrow or the day after?'

'Yes, indeed, I am going home. I think Id will be observed the day after tomorrow.'

Ayesha's fascinated eyes rose again. What did she see? The young man sat in front, as perfect as the full moon. Did his two gentle eyes wish to search her heart? What did his thin face indicate? When Ayesha raised her drooping eyelids once more, she found that the doorway was empty. The verandah was empty. No one was there! Her heart in a tumult, Ayesha thought since he was here, surely I'll meet him again? Gradually, the day was spent, evening descended. But no lightning flashed a smile across Ayesha's clouded heart. Anwar Hossain did not appear. Ayesha asked a servant, 'Hadn't Rangabhai come?'

'He did, but went away immediately afterwards,' the servant replied.

No words came to the lips of the stunned Ayesha. Why did

he come? And why did he run away, like the wayfarer who had glimpsed a snake in his path? Was it because he had seen her? 'Has he realized that I am an ogre?' thought Ayesha. 'Of course! Surely he has understood. Perhaps the flames of the terrible satanic pyre burning in my breast were visible in my eyes. That's why when he came to this house and caught a glimpse of this spirit risen from the depths of hell, he too fled, the way a wayfarer flees on catching sight of a snake.

'Alas, merciless one! Loving you, I have turned my heart into a cremation ground! Is this what you pay me with? Indeed, this was a punishment that an ogre deserved! I was not happy with Allah's gift. Despite trying my best, I couldn't lay myself at the feet of my husband. I was mad to have treated the Holy Koran Sharif like a toy! I wanted to fight my fate. I called Allah, the keeper of justice, unjust and heartless! O you favourite child of Allah! You who are His devotee and servant! Today you've given me the sentence I deserved for my sin by striking my breast with this dagger of hatred! But O my beloved! O my dearest! Could you not have desisted from awarding me the punishment yourself! O my deity, if only you had shown pity instead of hatred to me, you would be worshipped even in heaven!'

The intense darkness of a moonless night had hidden the earth and sky. A web of deep black clouds covered the planets and stars. Stormy winds appeared, desperate to overturn the created universe in a cosmic dance of annihilation and hide it beneath the limitless darkness of the mighty oceans. The pipes of destruction rang out in rumbling, cloud-like tones in the boundless sky. It was as if some unseen force wished to drown the world in a lonely woman's cascade of tears. The earth trembled with her heart-broken sighs. And in the midst of that revolution, threatening to undo and recreate the world, Ayesha stood on the verandah, stunned, gazing out over the pathway, her heart full of rebellious darkness.

14

A woman sat stitching a frock in a small, single-storied house in Mymensingh. A four-year-old girl, as exquisitely beautiful as a rosebud, sat near her mother, studying the Bengali alphabet. The tiny, silky black locks of hair on her small head danced in the breeze and fell on her face, and she moved them away impatiently with a hand as tender as a flower. The mother gave her a blow or two and from the clear-blue eyes of that face like a champak-bud's, fell large pearl-like dewdrops. Nearby, a champak tree was in full bloom and its flowers gazed at their champak-complexioned companion. Alas, unfortunate mother! Does your heart not break into a hundred pieces to strike that rose fallen from heaven?

Soon it was four o'clock. The woman put her stitching aside. She read the namaz of the hour, and went to prepare a snack for her husband. The four-year-old girl helped her mother, like an experienced housewife.

Sufia was now married to an inspector. Kader had not married anyone else, but the clever Sufia understood why Kader had rejected her hand. She wanted to sting Ayesha's chest like a vicious viper.

Zamindar Abdus Sattar had been very displeased with his frivolous son. He had brought a bride into the house to mend his son's ways, but that task was beyond the unfortunate wife. Therefore, the wife came to be deeply hated by the parents-in-law. Abdus Sattar thought that after his death, this household, managed carefully so far, would be reduced to cinders. He loved his daughter—the intelligent Sufia—more than his life. He would think had Sufia been a son, his family name would have continued to command respect. He had some affection for Kader as well. It was his wish to have Sufia married to Kader and treat him like a son. But when Kader's decision remained unchanged in spite of the promise of monetary gains, he found a desirable groom after an extensive search. The family returned to Nabipur, having accomplished Sufia's wedding ceremony. As for Sufia, the sorrow of not being married to one who was her childhood playmate, the object of desire in her youth—Kader was not only desired, but also assumed to have belonged to her—made her heart burn with rage. When Sufia realized that Ayesha was the cause of her sorrow, she became mad with rage. Though her sorrow was greatly mitigated by being married to an educated, loving husband, the fact that Kader had insulted her for the sake of Ayesha was something which neither she nor her mother forgot.

At this time, a daughter was born to Ayesha. What a lovely child! It was as if a rose from heaven had fallen on the earth! Sufia also bore a daughter, but everybody would praise Ayesha's daughter. Who was this princess who had come down to take refuge in the small house of a mad man—in Ayesha's arid breast. Would this blossom not wither in the intense desert-heat? Strange! The praise showered on the infant hurt Sufia and her mother like spears digging in their hearts.

Now with her daughter in her arms, Ayesha seemed to feel blessed. This was heaven! The ultimate happiness in the world! What more could she want? Nothing else! 'I am blessed,' she thought. 'I am content! I want nothing more.'

She had never been able to care for her husband with all her heart, but now she bowed down body and soul before the father of her child. All the faults of Omar Ali—the hatred, the oppression he had heaped upon her, appeared as honey in the ethereal glow of the child's sweet smile. The husband she had loathed as he was a tyrant, a drunkard and a slave of prostitutes, now appeared godlike to her, being the father of her child. She felt exalted, gratefully thinking of her husband as one she ought to worship. Her burdensome, painful life became full of sweetness in the heavenly glow of motherly love. But Sufia and her mother found Ayesha's happiness unbearable. They said things like: 'The madman has a daughter. What will happen to her? Never mind that she's beautiful, what value does her beauty have? Indeed, she has beauty. She will also learn the art of witchcraft from her mother. Yes, yes, that's what she will be. What else could she be? It's a curse!'

Ayesha looked back on her own life. True, wasn't it! What else was a woman's life but a curse! The luckless mother wept a torrent of tears and said, 'O Allah! Pray shield my small rose from the blows of the world, O Merciful One!' She made a strong resolve to educate her child well, and from being a loving mother turned into a dutiful teacher. As a result, the four-year-old Rahima Begum became everyone's pet, which made her aunt and her grandmother hate her even more.

Inspector Abdul Gafur—Sufia's husband—realized this was a supreme opportunity. If he could somehow get rid of his brother-in-law, he would become the sole owner of the property. The brother-in-law, after all, was of unsound mind and therefore should not take long to dispose of. He began to do everything in his power to humour his father-in-law, and thanks to Sufia's confrontations, Ayesha's position as the mistress of the house became shakier.

Though the son-in-law deferred to his father-in-law, he made his brother-in-law's life miserable, with barbs and jibes, rude behaviour, insults and insolence. The arrogant young man found no reprieve by complaining to his father. That's when he told his wife, 'Come, let us go away from here.'

Ayesha said, 'Where to?'

'You go off to Jessore. I'll go to test my fate.'

'I won't go to Jessore.'

Surprised, Omar said, 'Why not?'

'I don't want to.'

'What do you want to do then?'

'I'll stay here.'

'Here! If you stay here, your Rahima will die.'

Trembling with horror, Ayesha said, 'I'll go, I will. But don't ask me to go to Jessore.'

'Where do you want to go?'

'Wherever you are going!'

'Then stay here. Let me see if I can find work.'

Omar went away in search of work. In such a trying time, Ayesha gave birth to a boy. The laments of the unfortunate woman made the earth and sky tremble. Be it because of Ayesha's anguish, or the sorry state that the infant had been thrust into, Destiny was moved. Thanks to the untiring efforts of Kader and Haidar, Omar found work in a mercantile office in Mymensingh, for a monthly pay of Rs. 25. He had worked in the same office before, for a salary of Rs. 12 per month, but quit after a spat with a superior. The boss in question had left so Omar found employment in the same office. That salary was too little to pay house rent. Mariam offered her two spare rooms to the family. Very soon, Ayesha came with her son and daughter to live in Mymensingh.

15

Fateha-duaz-daham was being celebrated. There would be feasting at night, and Mariam was getting ready for the event. Suddenly, hearing the screams of a child, she came out. 'What is it, Ruhu? Why are you crying, child?' Weeping, Rahima said, 'Baba has killed Ma!' Mariam ran towards Ayesha's home. Haidar was at home. He followed her too. Ayesha was lying on the floor, blood splattered all over her body. There were two or three gashes in her head. Omar was not in the room. Maru and Haidar got busy nursing her. After a long time, there was a faint sound, 'O Ma!'

Looking up, Ayesha found that she was stretched out on the bed. Ruhu sat beside her, weeping. Mariam was fanning her, Haidar stood nearby, telling her what to do.

'Maru! My friend!'

'What is it, dear?'

'Where's my Alamgir?'

'He's asleep in his cradle.'

'Maru, has Ruhu's father had anything to eat?'

'You stupid woman! What is it to you whether he eats or not?

You were on your way to hell!'

Smiling, Ayesha closed her eyes. At this time, Kader came into the room and said, 'What's happened, Haidar?'

'Here Bhai! See for yourself. We don't know for sure what happened. But Ruhu says her father's the one who's done this. Who told you about it?'

'I thought you had asked me to come. Your servant told me that there was an accident and that you two have come here, that's why I came too.'

Since she had got to know of Kader's feelings, Ayesha never came out in front of him. Kader did not try to meet her either, not even when she came to stay in Mymensingh. Today, seeing Kader as a witness of her humiliation, Ayesha was incensed. She forced herself to get up and covered her head. Kader asked Haidar, 'What does she say about the incident?'

Ayesha said firmly, 'I'm saying nothing has happened to me. Please don't disturb me. Maru, go away.'

'Are you all right now?'

'Yes. Please, do go!'

'Well, you're quite heroic, aren't you? Come, let us be off. You'll come to our place at night, won't you, Ayesha?'

'I'll try.'

When they left, Ayesha clutched Rahima to her breast and threw herself on the floor, weeping. The eight-month-old child, Alamgir, slept contentedly in his cradle.

On the day of Fateha-duaz-daham, the excitement over the celebrations rose in each house. A gathering was due in lawyer Haidar Ali's house as well. Many gentlemen were invited. Poor beggars received rice and money. The moon was eleven nights old. The celebrations would begin at night. This was the birth and death anniversary of the Prophet Mohammad. On this day his arrival on earth was celebrated, and exactly sixty-three years later people bade him farewell, in a flood of tears. As usual, the function took place, and at its end the guests left one by one.

Putting her arms around Ayesha, Maru said, 'You'll stay here tonight, won't you?' Smiling, Ayesha replied, 'No, dear, perhaps he'll be angry if I did.'

'How can you smile? What do you think would have happened had we all not been around?'

'Why, nothing at all. You created a problem by being there.'

'Die, you wretched girl! You were off to hell, lying there in a pool of blood!'

With an uncaring smile, Ayesha said, 'Dear Maru, people jump into the sea quite often—but I haven't found the way to hell so far!'

'Is that so? In that case, we have to thank you a thousand times!' saying this, Haidar entered the room with Kader. Ayesha got up to leave but Maru held her hand. 'Why are you getting up?' she said. 'It's not as if an unknown man has entered the room, is it?'

Ayesha sat down. Haidar asked her, 'Do you want to go to Jessore?'

Raising her face, Ayesha said, 'Why?'

'I'm saying, if you have any problem living here, we can escort you to Jessore, if you so wish. Will you go?'

'No, I have no problems.'

The morning's scene floated in front of Ayesha's eyes. She seemed to burn with humiliation. In which limitless darkness could she hide her face? Shame on this hateful life! Ayesha raised her eyes to discover that Kader was gazing at her face with calm eyes. She turned her eyes away. She was burning with extreme mortification, her ire fell upon Maru: why did she come to look her up? She was furious with herself—why had she fainted? Her anger fell upon the Almighty. For which sin of hers was she facing such a terrible punishment? Only her mad husband and child Rahima were exempt from her anger.

'Are you telling the truth? Do you really have no difficulties? Say it again! I cannot believe that I am hearing these words from your lips.'

Raising her eyes, Ayesha said in a firm voice, 'Yes, I'm telling the truth—I have no sorrows! Please bless me so that I can die keeping this happiness intact, and be survived by my husband and children, Ruhu and Ali. This is my last prayer in Allah's court.'

Pointing to Kader, Haidar said, 'Look at him, Bhabi Saheba! This wretched one won't marry. O unfortunate fellow! Just see—what exquisite earthly treasure you are deprived of, you luckless man!'

Ayesha said to Kader, 'We are indeed very unhappy to find you not married yet. Maru! Why don't you find a bride for him? We'll tie his hands and feet, if we must, and get him married. They say a scheme hatched by ten people can turn a saint into a demon. How would he avoid marriage if we all plotted to get him married!'

'Pardon me! Any other command that you make, I'll accept with my head bent, Bhabi sahiba, but please don't make this one! If you are happy with a madman, believe me, I am very happy in my unmarried state.'

Ayesha stood up, folded her hands and said, 'I've never asked for anything from you in my life and I never will in the future, but please don't make my miserable life even more unbearable! I pray to you, and to Allah! Please marry! Unless the tears of my aunt dry up, my sorrows won't be any less. I am your senior in this relationship. Today I stand with folded hands before you. Please take a wife. This is the first and last prayer of my life, to you!' With those words, Ayesha removed herself quickly from the astounded gaze of three pairs of eyes.

16

It was three years ago that lacerated by the injustice of the elders and the oppression of the world, miserable Ayesha took her incapable and unstable husband's weak hand like a frail, parasitic creeper and jumped into the unknown sea of the material world, even as there was trepidation in her heart and her footsteps failed. Many things, great and small, happened to her during this long time. Who has the time to keep an account of the sin, good deeds, sunshine and rain to which her small head was exposed?

After three long years, at the insistence of her parents-in-law, she returned again to Nabipur. Black clouds came crowding to shape her destiny. This time, it seemed she was heading towards eternal rest! For the first few days she interacted freely with the mistress of the house, Sufia; and Sufia, too, said nothing much to her. But this early friendship did not last long. Ayesha's mother-in-law was unable to stop being partial to her son, but found no affection for his wife. The hope that had bloomed in Ayesha's mind withered without taking a form.

Omar Ali had a weak constitution and he could not withstand extra toil. He was bedridden for a prolonged period of six months, and hence lost his job. Neither did Ayesha, a mother of three, have a strong constitution. Her health too broke down. Knowing it was useless to hope for medical attention, she began to wait silently for death.

Ayesha would think she was the eternally unfortunate one, cursed the day she was born. She was like a comet—ill-luck personified! Perhaps, like a female Rahu,[11] she was responsible for shrouding the good fortune of her children. Else why did these innocent children, beautiful flowers—sinless blooms of heaven—suffer? They were paying for the sins committed by their mother! 'But O Lord, forever invisible!' prayed Ayesha. 'Show yourself just once. Listen to just one entreaty of mine! Let me have the answer to just one question. Whose sin was it that these children came into my womb? Alas, Allah! You who reside in the hearts of all! Which sinful act of mine has landed me in this state? Once, just for a moment, I had gazed with admiration at the most perfect object of beauty in all of Creation! I had a mad hope of plucking the beauteous and fragrant rose of this universe for myself! Was that a great sin? Tell me—do please tell me! Oh, You Creator of Sun and Moon! Lord of the universe! Endless

Beauty! Am I in this state because of that sin?'

Ayesha waited for death, but it did not come to her. What did happen was more terrible than death—beyond one's imagination and beyond description!

God too seemed repentant at having allowed the cursed, miserable woman a glimpse of happiness. So by the hard-hearted wish of the Wishful One, Rahima was afflicted by a dreadful disease. That incomparably beautiful, happy rosebud from Mohammad's garden in heaven began to grow weak day by day. Who knows whether it was due to the heat of the sun, or the impure touch of her cursed mother! The blind mother did not notice it. Or, even if she did, being helpless she was incapable of finding a remedy. Perhaps it was God's harsh wish that had made her blind! Not paying any attention to the child's present condition, the mother, thinking about her daughter's future, began to supervise her studies and her work in the house rather strictly. The quiet and soft-natured five-year-old child, raised in constant sorrow, had borne life's grief silently. She was never loved by anyone else in her family, except a few tender loving words from her mother.

However, she had received a great deal of love from others. When they were at Mymensingh, the young Hindu wife from next door would come to take the child Ruhu home. She would bathe, dress and feed her and even scold Ayesha, 'Well, sister! Why did foolish fate give this little fairy to a good-for-nothing like Ayesha! Had she been ours, we would have always dressed her up like a fairy!' Maru would laugh and joke, 'Do you believe that Rahima was born to someone like Ayesha? We've picked her up from fairy land, haven't we, Ruhu?' The mother's breasts would swell with pride. Was there greater happiness in life than this?

The day Rahima's ever-serene face, so like the moon in beauty, was distorted with pain, and the little child was confined to her sick bed, the helpless mother found her world go pitch dark. When she borrowed some money and went looking for a doctor, she discovered that it was almost impossible to find a doctor in the village. After a lot of effort, she managed to have a doctor come on call. Her father-in-law said, 'Child! You've brought a doctor all right, but the fellow's no good.' The doctor said carelessly, 'It's nothing much. She will get well soon.' Ayesha measured out the medicine with trembling hands, and the child drank it with unshaken faith. Can a mother give her child anything else but nectar!

All night the child cried for water. Ayesha's mother-in-law said, 'Don't give her water—her chest is full of phlegm.' The mother's heart was torn apart. Her child was pitifully crying for water! 'My breast is burning, Ma! Water!' She touched a drop of water to the child's lips, unnoticed by the others. Ah, what comfort! And seeing those calm eyes, the mother's torn heart was healed.

Very slowly, a soft, worn hand touched Ayesha's face. The startled mother cried, 'What does my little girl want?' In a weak, dying voice coming from far away, someone said, 'Ma! Kiss me!'

The mother's tears washed the daughter's hand. What happened next would have unbearable to a stranger, let alone the mother. Ayesha dropped down to the floor to pray. From the innermost core of her being, one word rose upwards, 'Allah!'

The child's father, then in the city, was extremely disturbed. Why was he feeling so upset, he wondered? Anxious thoughts rose in his mind. Was everything all right at home? Surely it was, else he would have got wind of it! But, no! 'Who is it pulling me? I don't know why, but I feel I must go back home!

'Why does the train move so slowly today? Is there any way I could get home faster? What shall I see there? Faster, drive the train faster!' Inside the train, Omar Ali moved about restlessly.

'Give her back to me, Allah! Give me back my sole treasure! Give Ruhu back in exchange for my life, my hereafter. Take my remaining years and give this beggar the gift of Ruhu's life! Let me lie on my deathbed and see my two children laughing and playing! This is my final prayer, O Almighty!'

As soon as Omar entered the house, Ayesha flung herself at

his feet. 'Pray forgive me! Please bless Ruhu. That's the only way Ruhu will live.'

'Ma! Ma! My little one!' At this wild call of the father, the answer came in the faintest possible voice, as if it were a heavenly song heard in a dream. 'Baba!' Then the bulbul of heaven flew towards the heavenly garden. The light went out from the house, immersing the world in boundless darkness. Tumultuous laments rent through the earth and sky. The zamindar flung his body against the ground and wept like a child. The earth-shaking wails of his wife, Paribanu Begum, made the leaves fall from the trees. The repentant Sufia, wild with grief, clasped Alamgir tightly to her chest. The mad father seemed to have finally gone completely mad. And the mother, who had lost all, clasped the lifeless body of Ruhu to her breast, covering it with kisses, trying to bring Ruhu back. From each speck of dust in the world, from the heart of every human being in the world, the same cry seemed to rise! 'Come back! O unloved one, come back! I'll love you with all my heart, come back! Come back, O you, who were hungry for love!'

But the unbending Judge, sitting on his high seat with a stern heart, watched with unmoved eyes as the terrible sentence was awarded to the sinner Ayesha for her act of great crime. Once she had played like a child with the Koran. That is why, today, her reading the Koran was no use.

17

Days passed. Nur Alam received a telegram one day and brought it home. He was now a deputy magistrate in Calcutta. His wife, Shiri Begum, put her book aside and asked, 'Why do you look so pale?' Her husband replied, 'Ayesha is very ill. I've just received a telegram.' Her eyes brimming with tears, Shiri said, 'That's been going on for many months, now. She lost everything when she lost Rahima! Isn't her family consulting doctors?'

'Yes, certainly. Her repentant father-in-law is making amends now, but to no effect. The doctor says she needs to travel to a healthier place. Our eldest brother has asked her to go to Allahabad. He is now in Jessore, on leave and has asked me to take Ashu to Jessore. I had written to Ashu's husband to bring her here. In that case, you and I can't start out tomorrow. If they arrive tomorrow, we can start for Jessore the day after.'

'O the ever-unfortunate one! None of you have ever taken the trouble to find out how she is doing! How heartless you men are!'

'You're saying we didn't keep in touch with her, Shiri! What do you know of all this! She was our beloved treasure! But look at what Father did to her! He just trampled on our pleas. In our eyes, she is as good as dead. It is so terrible, I can't keep myself calm! Well, probably they'll come tomorrow and we'll go the very next day.' Tears dropped down the deputy's eyes, unrestrained. Resting her head on her husband's breast, Shiri too wept. She too had lost a son a few days back. Kissing that face washed with tears, like a rose drenched in dew, Nur Alam went out.

The next day Ayesha arrived with her husband. They set off for Jessore together. Shafiq-al Alam was also there with his wife.

18 *In Her Father's House*

It was three days since Ayesha came to her father's house. Her father and brothers treated her with unlimited affection to make her forget everything. But the show of affection was like a thorn pricking Ayesha's heart. Alas! Ruhu never got an iota of such love! Ruhu—whose name meant 'soul'—had indeed left Ayesha with a soulless body. Why did she need to take care of herself now? The care she received when she was now no more than a corpse felt like a mockery! Ruhu had not been cared for, that is why she had to leave. Now her repentant mother-in-law and sister-in-law took great care of Ayesha. But her broken heart had not mended. There was a time when the slightest sign of love from her mother-in-law would have made her feel blessed; and

Sufia's presence would make her feel good about the day. Now without Ruhu she was unable to respond to her mother-in-law's solicitous behaviour or Sufia's genuinely friendliness. It was as if Ruhu had never belonged to her. Ayesha was now truly without a life.

In their grandfather's house, Selima and Alamgir found many playmates. Ayesha too tried to be cheerful. She became quite close to her two sisters-in-law, Shiri and Raushana. But somehow it seemed there was no life in what she did.

Ayesha sat in the verandah, watching the children at play. Suddenly, the postman called, 'Letter for you!' Alamgir ran out and entered holding a postcard. It was a letter for Latif. Ayesha read the two lines, rather reluctantly,

> '*Adaab*! I have to inform you that I could not come due to some work. With Allah's blessings, I will surely be at your service on Thursday.'
>
> Anwar Hossain.

There was no change in Ayesha's expression after she had finished reading the letter. Her heart did not stir either. This was the same Anwar whose approaching footsteps had sounded like the melodious pitter-patter of rain to her ears, once upon a time. Youth, indeed, was illusory, and imagination an enchantress!

On Thursday Anwar Hossain arrived. Since he was an elder brother-in-law, the wives of Nuru and Shafiq would not appear in front of him. So he remained in the outer quarters.

After a long time, Latif's house looked cheerful, dotted by the smiling faces of his sons and their wives. The noise made by the grandchildren filled the air. Both Latif and his wife were now bed-ridden. Latif had wanted to have all his sons and daughters together with him. Tomorrow Amena would arrive too. The children were supposed to leave in two days. Ayesha quickly took charge of caring for her parents. Shiri and Raushana set about getting their mother-in-law's disordered household back on track.

19 *In the Twilight of Life*

Amena was to arrive the next day, and the family sat on the verandah, discussing her impending visit. Ayesha said, 'Mejobhai, I didn't see Rangabhai!'

Indeed, Ayesha had not seen Anwar in the last few days since he was staying in the outer quarters. He had come to do Latif a service. Although Ayesha was past caring, she still had a desire to see him. If this was God giving her a chance to see Anwar once before her death, what was the harm in that? One would only see him, nothing more! In the dawn of her life, the world appeared golden in the light of those eyes. Her world became like the Sahara desert when she lost him. And in this premature dusk, before she got plucked from the branch of life by turbulent storms, there was no harm if she could see him once, in the glow of a rainbow. She had wanted to see him unnoticed by the others, and that was what made her say, 'I haven't seen him, Mejobhai!'

At Shafiq's request, Anwar took a seat in the verandah. The men started talking. Ayesha raised her eyes and looked at him. Their eyes met. Anwar looked away. Ayesha's breast rose and fell, her eyes, forever thirsting like the Sahara desert, fell on that desired face, but Anwar didn't look at her again. Ayesha went away quietly, looking for Alamgir and the others, to quieten the storm in her breast, but could not find them. The children were out with their father.

Anwar, responding to an earlier comment, told Shafiq, 'They say that in certain circumstances men fall from a height, meditating on a certain face. I'm sure that's what has happened to you.'

Ever since they came here, Shafiq hadn't been able to talk to his wife properly as it was difficult to do so within the joint family. Perhaps that is why Anwar made the remark. Everyone laughed. From a hidden spot, Ayesha continued to stare with unblinking eyes at that incomparably handsome face. A little later, Anwar Hossain went outside.

The next day, a little before dusk, Ayesha played with the children. She felt ashamed about herself. Who was Anwar Hossain to her? He was the husband of Rahimunnisa. She was the woman he loved. He was the father of Rabeya, while Ayesha was the mother of Rahima and her siblings. Rahima's father meant everything to her! Her husband was her beloved; even though he was a tyrant and a weak man, he was Rahima's father. If she saw Anwar again, she would behave like a sister. She would bow her head in a salaam to him, for wasn't he a brother to her? She would ask after his wife and children without the slightest trepidation in her heart. After all, what was the point when her fantasy had melted in thin air?

Seeing her cousin Hashem, Ayesha called him. He was as old as she was, and they had been close friends since childhood.

'Hashem!'

'What is it?'

'Where is he?'

'Who, Rangabhai? He's gone to Wahid's house. Should I call him? He'll be leaving soon.'

Ayesha raised her head, startled. 'When is he leaving? Is it to Dacca, or back home?'

'Probably Dacca. Shall I call him?'

'Yes, but will he come?'

'Why shouldn't he?'

'He hates me. I remember a time, four years ago. He came to Jessore on some work. Seeing me, he ran away.'

'Rubbish, silly girl. But I say, why go on like this? You are now the daughter-in-law of a zamindar. Can't you see how much everyone in this house respects you? Everyone is dazzled by the gold jewellery that covers you from head to toe. If anyone has the slightest suspicion about your feelings, do you suppose they would still treat you with respect?'

Tears rained down, soaking Ayesha's breasts. She said in deep distress, 'How would you know, Hashem! Had I been the queen of the world, and if, in exchange of that royal position, I could become the slave of Anwar Hossain's wife, I would accept smilingly. If I had the right to serve his wife, I would, at least, get to see him once, at the end of the day That would be a blessing for me, making my life worthwhile! But let that pass! Just tell him, "Ashu wants to pay her respects to you for the last time." He will come if he wants to!'

That evening, Omar Ali was visibly annoyed, demanding an explanation as to why he wasn't called into the inner quarters the whole day. Ayesha tried to explain that she had been busy. After a long altercation, when Omar finally flung his wife away with a kick and walked away, for a moment, Ayesha's whole soul rose in rebellion, but only for a moment! The next moment the picture of the dying Rahima appeared in her mind's eye. Omar was Rahima's father! Alamgir and Selima were still around, held close to her bosom! They were his too. Ayesha quickly got up, clasped Alamgir to her breast and catching her husband's hand, said, 'Indeed, I was with Father and didn't find time to see you. Do forgive me.'

At that moment, Shafiq called from the gate, 'Ashu, Rangabhai is leaving now, should he come to see you?' 'Yes, ask him to come,' replied Ayesha. Standing up, she arranged her sari properly, pulling the end over her head. The young man entered the room, the glow of his brilliance as dazzling as the midday sun. But today, the sound of his footsteps could awaken no sigh in Ayesha's dead heart. She bent low, doing a salaam and said, 'Please be seated.' Turning to her husband, she requested him to sit down as well. Anwar too said, Please sit, Dulha Miya.' But Omar's anger had not abated. He walked out of the house in a huff. Ayesha did not say a thing, fearing Omar might insult her in front of Anwar. Sitting down, Anwar said, 'I am meeting you after almost twelve years! That's more than a decade, isn't it?'

Ayesha said to herself, 'Only a decade? It seems like a thousand years to me!' She said aloud, 'Yes, but you did come once, before Ruhu was born, right?'

'I did, but didn't stay for long—only a moment or two.'

Why only a moment or two, Ayesha thought. What prevented you from staying longer? Was it really for two minutes? Does anyone really do that? Why did you run away like a traveller frightened by a snake? Was it because you had seen a snake in me? A storm rose in a tumult in Ayesha's breast, as if it was a night of destruction, but she remained silent, not allowing a single word to escape from her lips. She only asked, 'How many children does Riziya Apa have?'

'Four.'

'And your . . . how many siblings does Rabeya have?'

'How do you know of Rabeya?'

It's not difficult when one's interested to find out, thought Ayesha. 'I heard from Hafez,' she said.

'From Hafez?'

'Yes. How many are they?'

'Two girls,' said Anwar.

'What is the name of Rabeya's sister?'

'Rokeya,' replied Anwar in a soft voice.

Smiling a little, Ayesha said hesitantly, 'One hears you are going to marry again?'

'No, nothing of that sort.' Fixing his large eyes calmly on Ayesha's face, Anwar said, 'Are you upset about my marriage?'

Blood raced through Ayesha's veins. Why did he ask this question? Was he omniscient? She suddenly felt like saying, how does my opinion matter, but instead, said shyly, 'I am not entitled to having an opinion.'

Anwar only smiled. What a sweet smile it was!

Ayesha and her family were supposed to go out today. Habib came from the other house with the car and began hurrying them up. Ayesha was irritated. Was it necessary to go out today? This was the most precious moment in her life, eternally longed-for! The moment had not happened in her life so far and would not ever again. But there were too many hurdles! Roushana came up and urged, 'Where are you, Chhoto Bibi! Hurry!' Anwar Hossain stood up as Ayesha bade him farewell. She felt like asking him to stay the night, and once again felt she did not have the right to do that. Anwar might be offended! But Anwar Hossain's departure did get postponed that day because he still had some work left.

Ayesha stepped in the courtyard after Anwar, into the bright moonlight. It was her wish that she would fill her heart with his image, bathed in moonlight. In the clear blue sky, the winter moon smiled brightly. It was the end of the month of Magh. The bright moonlight had merged with the mist to create a dream world, and Ayesha stood in that magical light, her eyes and mind dreaming. In that flood of moonlight stood young Anwar Hossain, himself like a moonlit sculpture. His eyes, blue as the sea, were fixed calmly upon Ayesha's face. Ayesha wanted to drown in that blue ocean. How beautiful that dream was! The blue sky was beautiful. So was the magical smile of the sea, the early breeze and the world, bathed in moonlight. And most beautiful of all were those two blue eyes.

What remained at the bottom of that depthless blue? What was its mystery? Why did she wish to drown and die in them, and feel blessed? O turn them away, those blue firearms, O Magician! What was the point in killing the shrivelled tree that had dried up, the burnt forest or the traveller on the road to death?

'Death! Come! Do come! Come friend, today in this hour of complete fulfilment. Don't show me any sights after this. O my dearest, my eternal friend! Come to me at this very moment. Let all my yearnings end even as I gaze at those two eyes. Let this be the final moment of my life! Come, friend. Come, soulmate!'

A dream is a dream, as beautiful, as false! And as short-lived! The beauty of Ayesha's reverie was shattered by the harsh blow of reality. Habib said, 'The car is ready. How much longer will you take?'

Ayesha went with them for an evening out, but everybody noticed she was preoccupied, and clever Shiri smiled knowingly.

20

Amena arrived the next day. Ayesha had no time to herself all day. Anwar Hossain was leaving in the evening. She shook off her embarrassment with some effort and told Hashem, 'Rangabhai should meet me before he goes.' A naughty smile blossomed on Shiri's blood-red lips. 'Take care, dear! Yesterday, you fainted; today you'll have a heart attack.' Ayesha did not reply. Anwar Hossain came and stood in the verandah. Nuru said, 'Say whatever you have to quickly, there's no time.' Ayesha stepped out and stood before him. She was unwell. Anwar asked after her health. After talking to him for a minute or two, Ayesha knelt down to bid farewell, and said, 'I bid farewell to all, for ever.'

Nuru said, 'Don't listen to the crazy words of this crazy girl, Rangabhai.' Ayesha raised her streaming eyes a moment or two and lowered them. With a wan smile, Anwar said, 'When people go to Mecca, they take leave for ever.' His soft sigh betrayed him and made a mockery of his smile. Though others heard nothing, it did not escape Ayesha's ears, or her heart. Anwar went away.

Ayesha called after him, 'Please ask Bhabi Saheba to write.' From the gate Anwar's comprehending though warm smile hit Ayesha's heart like a blow and rose to the sky.

'Farewell, O Motherland! Farewell, Mother! I have no wish to come here again. I had come to your bosom, with a cry, today I take leave, with more tears. I don't have the good fortune to smile as I leave! This body was sustained on your water and air, nurtured by the grain growing on your fields, the water in your rivers. Today here I stand, Ayesha. This life began in your fields covered with young grass, Mother! Today it's turned into a grassless arid patch, burnt by the midday sun. This life which had laughed aloud in harmony with the hearty laughter of the pink rays of your early morning sun has turned into a desert. That river flowing past the village—I remember it now, I played happily on its banks, running around, rousing laughter, for no reason, and tears, for no cause! Perhaps the echoes of all my activities here still linger in your sky, Mother! And the rosy longings tinted with the ray of hope, which had spread their incomparable beauty over this heart, covering them forever with the deep darkness of unseasonal clouds—what about them? Who transformed your shy, rosy dawn into the cloud with thunder in its heart? The ardours of this tiny heart, like the tumultuous ocean, may be fused with the smile of the full moon. Yet again much tears from a broken heart are merged with your showers of rain. O Mother mine! Motherland! Will none of these remain in your memory? Man or animal, will no one ever call out by mistake, bring this unfortunate one's name to their lips?

'Grant me farewell! O blue sky, soft with affection! O you breeze, whose loving touch soothes all hurt! O friend Dawn, rosy with the shyness of love! The boundlessly beautiful full moon of my motherland! The morning sun! Trees and shrubs! The murmur of the forest! O cuckoo bird, Queen of my Motherland! Bid me farewell today!

'O Mother Earth! So many Ayeshas have come to your breast and gone! So many more will come and go. You are, O Mother, all-enduring! Then why does this heart, nurtured upon your breast, wish to break?

'And Mother, you who gave birth to me! I wept like a child, flooding my breasts with tears, trying to see your grave, but could not do so. I am a dependent, miserable woman of Bengal. Pray accept my obeisance, Mother! Did you bear me, the taint of your womb, only so that I could carry the sting of poison in my heart forever? And was it because you won't be able to see me suffer a fate worse than death that you gave in to an untimely death yourself, Mother mine? I failed to merge my body in the holy soil in which your blessed form is merged. My Ruhu is not here, you see! My body must rest where Ruhu's is, Mother! Pray grant me this blessing, Mother! Farewell, my green, bounteous

Motherland! My loving Mother, farewell!'

The next morning, Ayesha left for Allahabad with her sister-in-law, Roushanara.

Nauroz, Asharh - Agrahayan 1926

'Niyantrita'
By Abul Fazl, B.A.

When I first read this piece in the now-defunct *Nauroz*, there was a strong suspicion in my mind that the name under which the piece was being published must be the pen-name of a powerful author. Later I came to know that the name of the writer was Selima Begum, alias, Akhtar Mahal Syeda Khatun, a lady from a well-established family, and I was shocked to hear that she was no more.

Niyantrita is a short novel—it may also be called a novella. There are very few such writings in modern fiction written by Muslims. On reading it I felt, man's feeling of grief is eternal, it is constantly renewed. I comprehended afresh the words of the Western poet, himself a traveller on the path of light—'Our sweetest songs are those that tell of saddest thoughts.' *Niyantrita* is a tragic chronicle, from beginning to end. The pictures of the grief-stricken hearts of a number of people which we find here, are indeed exquisite. This mournful chronicle does not amaze the reader, it breaks his heart, and that broken heart does not mend when the book comes to an end: it takes a long time to set it right. The environment created by the author—the house and the courtyard surrounded by walls—is familiar to the Muslim reader. The heroes and heroines are men and women they know intimately. The author cannot be separated from the picture of sorrow she has painted with tearful eyes. That the pain of another can take such acute shape within oneself seems impossible, yet it is even more painful to think of the writer as the unhappy 'woman bound by destiny.' However, women like Ayesha are countless in Muslim society. Their humiliated lives of pain and sorrow have been spoken for in the novel, expressed not as a wayward or individual sorrow but as the universal sorrow of human life. This is literature's gain.

The language of this novella is powerful. I do not remember noticing such powerful language in any other Muslim woman writer—the descriptive style is excellent and fast-paced. The sequence of events is well arranged and progresses smoothly. The reader is forced to read from the beginning right to the end without stopping to draw a breath. There is a superb intensity throughout. The author's sensibility and imagination are moderate and refined, nowhere is there anything unnatural. Above all, a deep sincerity is evident in the entire writing. Sketches of men and women from middle-class Muslim families are life-like. There are no deviations from reality in terms of incidents or characters. And there are no errors in the analysis of a character's psychology.

There are many difficulties in the way of writing Muslim fiction. The main among these is the custom of seclusion. While it exists, it is doubtful whether any major creative work in fiction by Muslim authors is possible. The lives of men and women is the foundation of literature—there is no way for Muslim writers of either sex to find out about each other's lives. Their vision bounces off from the high walls surrounding them. That is why unnatural characters have been created in Muslim literature and are being created even now. It is the customs prevalent in society rather than the writer who should take the blame. When it comes to aristocratic Muslims, love or courtship is limited within the families. Thus love or infatuation is possible only between cousins. In many families, seclusion of women is so strictly enforced that even love between cousins is quite impossible, and love at first sight a very rare occurrence. Therefore, when authors make girls of aristocratic Muslim families fall in love with men outside their known sphere, it is simply being reckless! The author of *Niyantrita* has not shown such recklessness, her plot is limited to the members of the same family, and so, no event or character is unnatural . . .

The work is not a piece of fiction—at least, it doesn't read like one—it is, from beginning to end, the chronicle of an excruciatingly life, described in a poignant, mournful style.

The writer is now no more. This insignificant reader of literature remembers her with deep respect in this article.

(extract)

Notes

1 *Niyantrita* was first published under the pseudonym of 'Selima Begum' in 1926 in the monthly magazine *Nauroz*, thanks to the poet Kazi Nazrul Islam's efforts. *Maran Baran* was published posthumously in 1928 in *Saugat*. This second novel, however, was published under Akhtar Mahal's own name.

2 Afsarunnesa, *Lekhika Parichiti* (About the author), *Niyantrita* (Dhaka: Rahman Begum, 1979), p 6.

3 Abul Fazl, 'Niyantrita' (*Saugat*, Chaitra 1928); an excerpt is included at the end of this piece.

4 Ibid.

5 See *Niyantrita*, paragraph 11.

6 Ibid, paragraph 1.

7 'Maran Baran', *Niyantrita*, pp.62-63.

8 Mohammad Nasiruddin, *Bangla Sahitye Saugat Yug* (Dhaka: Noorjahan Begum, 1985), p.604.

9 'Maran Baran', *Niyantrita*, ibid, p.68.

10 Akhtar Mahal's own footnote: A Turkish word, meaning elder sister, in certain parts of East Bengal, used instead of 'bubu' or 'didi'.

11 Allusion to the Hindu myth of Rahu—a star that is believed to bring ill luck to people.

7

Fazilatunnesa, M.A. (1905-1975)

Translated by Nandini Guha

Readers would be justified in wondering why an entire chapter is being dedicated to a writer on the basis of just two essays published in the magazine *Saugat* in 1924 and 1926,[1] and whether this minuscule body of published writing justifies her being called a writer in the first place. Fazilatunnesa was not an essayist or a poet, nor a storyteller who made a sustained effort to continue writing.

The subject of her essays was exactly what would be expected of an open-minded, newly educated woman like her—the need for education among Muslim women, the importance of nurturing Bengali as a language, and so on. In those days, many Bengali Muslims felt it was necessary to talk about women's education and their identity as Bengalis. 'Just as the influence of educated mothers helps to take society forward on the path of progress, so does an uneducated mother's influence pull a society backwards.' (Her essay, 'The Need for Education Among Muslim Women' follows on p212.) These words written by Fazilatunnesa resonate in the writings of many of her contemporaries. Or, '[Muslim children] must clearly understand their motherland is not Arabia, Persia, Turkey or Egypt . . . they are Indians. Nationalism is not founded upon a common religion, but upon [sharing a] common homeland' (ibid). The writing was acerbic but, considering the times they were being written in, not surprising.

The surprise lay elsewhere. Fazilatunnesa, a Bengali Muslim woman, charted her own path in the beginning of the twentieth century. The courage with which she took the first step in that direction was awe-inspiring. Fazilatunnesa was the first Bengali Muslim woman to earn a postgraduate degree. In 1928, when she came to the office of the editor of *Saugat*, Mohammad Nasiruddin, and said she wanted to go abroad for higher studies, the latter had seen 'an indomitable resolve' in her eyes. Fazilatunnesa said, 'You may have heard of the humiliation I had to suffer to be able to complete my M.A. degree . . . [I] have no capital but my resolve.'[2]

It was probably her father who sowed the seeds of this strong resolve in Fazilatunnesa. Abdul Wajid Khan held a minor job in the Karotiya zamindari estate in Tangail district. Fazilatunnesa was born in a village called Kamalli, about two miles from the estate, in 1905. This is where she spent her childhood and the early years of her education. Her father was aware of her sharp intelligence and took her to Dhaka. On the strength of her steely resolve, Fazilatunnesa moved from small to large towns, from her homeland to foreign shores. She fared excellently at school, college and university examinations. After her return from England she joined Bethune College, Kolkata, as a teacher of mathematics and ultimately became the institute's vice-principal. Hers is the story of a woman crossing all the hurdles in her way to arrive at success. After the Partition of Bengal, 1947, by the time Fazilatunnesa became principal of Eden College in Dhaka, Muslim society had already begun to comprehend the 'need for education among Muslim women'. And in her personal life, Fazilatunnesa had tasted freedom.

'I wonder if it would be a good idea to inflict this prison—in which women are locked up and prevented from enjoying the beauty of the world and which prevents the rays of knowledge from entering the minds of Muslim women—on men! Nobody would suggest that women were responsible for the wrong and evil deeds done in the world. Why then should women be held prisoners?' (ibid).

Fazilatunnesa decided that she would never be imprisoned. In 1923, she was admitted to Bethune College to pursue her graduation. She was the first Muslim student of the college and the only Muslim boarder. She was also the first woman student of the M.A. class in Dhaka University. Mohammad Nasiruddin wrote, 'In those days, the attitude of Muslim society towards women was extremely old-fashioned.

They could not imagine a Muslim girl sitting with boys in a classroom. When Fazilatunnesa went to attend classes in a sari, without wearing the burqa, occasionally stones would be thrown at her. But she remained undaunted. She earned a scholarship and through sheer hard work and grit fulfilled her ambition of receiving higher education.'[3]

Viewed against the backdrop of the first four decades of the twentieth century, Fazilatunnesa may be seen as a nonconformist. She tried to set a precedent vis-à-vis female education and purdah—two highly-controversial issues dogging Bengali Muslim society through her personal life and choices.

She was not one to be easily dismayed. She was intelligent, hardworking, perhaps a little too practical and unemotional in certain situations. Hence, even the single-minded devotion of Nazrul could not move her. Hurt, Nazrul sang, 'First you stole my heart, then you plunged a dagger into it!'[4] Neither did she encourage the excessive affection shown to her by Kazi Motahar Hossain. In 1927-1928, she had just one firm goal: she would go abroad to pursue higher studies. She made it, thanks to the devoted efforts of Mohammad Nasiruddin. In 1928, Nasiruddin organized a special felicitation ceremony, where Nazrul, broken-hearted, sang dolefully, 'Stay not in Heaven, forgetting these mortal shores/ Return in your golden boat to this river-bank.'[5]

Fazilatunnesa did return from 'Heaven', but by then, she was Mrs. Fazilatunnesa Zoha, the daughter-in-law of the then director of education, Khan Bahadur Ahsanullah. Her husband, Shams-us Zoha, had gone to England to study law. The two met there and fell in love. Fazilatunnesa set an example by marrying someone she had chosen. But was there a difference between the firm and resolute Miss Fazilatunnesa before she went to England and the Mrs. Fazilatunnesa Zoha who returned from abroad?

In Dhaka, the capital of the newly-independent East Pakistan, Fazilatunnesa Zoha became the principal of Eden Girls' College. As one who wore sleeveless blouses, drank and smoked in public, her image was not that of the regular college teacher. Her westernized lifestyle was found unacceptable by many in society. She herself found it difficult to adjust to the semi-rural conditions of Dhaka. When the anti-Pakistan movement began, it was not quite certain if she was in favour of or against the 'Bhasha Andolan', the Language movement of 1952. Shortly afterwards, Mrs. Zoha was charged with corruption and lost her job. It is difficult to say whether she was really corrupt, or only a victim of the times.

More than thirty years have passed since her death. Even today some people berate her while others glorify her. A former colleague of hers, Akhtar Imam, commented, 'Nothing is given to a person free of cost. One earns what one deserves. In this respect, Fazilatunnesa is a shining example worthy of emulation.'[6]

Fazilatunnesa is the only writer featured in this book to whom the rules and prohibitions imposed by society were meaningless. She conducted her life her own way, according to her own views. It is difficult to judge her in terms of the commonly accepted standards of good and bad. We wanted to present the portrait of a pathfinder—an unconventional, supremely intelligent, modern woman of the 1920s. A society is always proud of its pathfinders; a society-in-the-making creates its image through its pathfinders. Perhaps that is why, when in the 1980s Nasiruddin wrote *Bangla Sahitye Saugat Yug* (The *Saugat* Era in Bengali Literature), he went beyond all controversy by describing the lady as, 'Fazilatunnesa, M.A', which surely was sufficient in itself.

M. B.

The Need for Education among Muslim Women

I was invited by the president of Al-Mamun Club to read an essay here today. There is nothing perhaps as beneficial as the enthusiasm for societal progress jointly inspired by the thought-processes of men and women. To unite these two streams of thought, it is necessary that men and women get to understand each other. Therefore, I am truly grateful for the opportunity you have provided for creating an acquaintance between your thought-processes and ours. But I have no suitable material for you: I must therefore beg your pardon for my unworthiness.

If you expect me to read out an essay, you will, no doubt, be disappointed. I came here today to speak about a few drawbacks for which Indian Muslim society is regarded as backward. But first let me point out that perhaps I will be forced to speak certain unpalatable truths. I hope your educated minds will be able to accept them in the right spirit. In every age, country and society young people welcome new ideas, since they are the ones who have the courage and directness to break away from tradition and habit and set out on a new untrodden path. When they feel the need for progress and look around freely, then and only then is something worthwhile achieved. Therefore, in spite of my unworthiness, I will gather together all my strength to point out our drawbacks and needs. Until these problems are addressed, they will have to be pointed out again and again, no matter how repetitious it might seem.

All educated people are aware of how far behind our country is compared to others in the field of education. The state of women's education is even less satisfactory, and the condition of our community, even worse! So today I wish to highlight the need for women's education among Muslims before the young men of the community. I have had the chance to step out of purdah and be acquainted with the world and, therefore, I think of the girls who have not had this opportunity. I would like to tell you about all the things missing from their world. Moreover, I want to stress that this incomplete state not only spoils their lives but has a destructive influence on society itself, threatening constantly to pull it down.

For enriching one's life and equipping one to work for society, two things are of prime importance: education and freedom. I am, of course, talking about social freedom. The primary need is education, because true education inflames the desire for social freedom by creating freedom of thought. Those who have been brought up in an atmosphere of freethinking and diverse viewpoints easily to break the walls of blind tradition, let their personalities develop and live with their heads held high.

The foremost intellectuals of the world like Romain Rolland and Bertrand Russell propagate the truth that what a human being most desires is personal freedom. So far, society has always sacrificed the individual at the altar of the group, but that age is over. The mantra of the new age is, 'It is wrong to sacrifice the individual for the good of society'. Societies that gave individuals the greatest opportunities to blossom have progressed the most. In most societies today this individualism is apparent.

What do we find when we look at our own society? Far from giving individuals any freedom, half of society has been suppressed in such a way that perhaps no one remembers that they exist! Each and every limb and organ of the human body is equally useful—and the same is true of society. Men and women are two parts of society's body. The needs of both are practically equal. But our society tries to progress even as it ignores half of itself. Can anything be sadder or more disappointing than this? Women are made to stay hidden behind the purdah; nothing from the outer world is allowed to touch them. Time goes by, but no effort is made to remove this weakness and restore a measure of health to society. Now that you are making an effort, I found the courage to say these words here.

I would like to express the noblest desire of my sisters in the words of Rabindranath Tagore:

> I am no goddess, no small
> Insignificant women!
> Not one to be worshipped
> Or neglected and to be cast off.
> That is not for me.
> If you keep me by your side,
> Amongst your fears and worries,
> Make me part of your path,
> A friend in your sorrows and your joys,
> Then you would know me!

Now, in order to fulfil this demand, get involved and throw themselves heart and soul in the service of country and society, what women need is education. By education I do not refer only to the degrees one earns from colleges and universities. We need education that removes the prejudices from men's minds and widens them; the sort that teaches us to sacrifice selfish desires and make strangers a part of the family; the kind that gives us a sence of judgment to know right from wrong. In short, what we need is, 'The harmonious development of all our faculties—mental, physical and moral.'

Generally speaking, we can say that every human being requires such an education in keeping with the special needs of his/her field. Therefore, since the demand is justified, I complain on behalf of women: why are Muslim women denied the benefits of education? I wish to say that they are the ones more in need of education. It is not difficult to find the reason. The adage, 'The hand that rocks the cradle rules the world' is an old and time-honoured truth, but the Muslim community stands in urgent need of being reminded of it! It is known by all that a mother's influence is felt by society through each child. Just as the influence of educated mothers helps take society forward on the path of progress, the influence of uneducated mothers draws a society backwards. This truth could be better comprehended if we discussed the present condition of our country.

There is perhaps no need for me to remind you how the conflict between the Hindu and Muslim communities is on the rise. Efforts are being made to bring the two communities together, though none has been successful so far. The true reason probably is that the right way of resolving this conflict has not been discovered as yet. I feel a major reason for keeping this conflict alive is the lack of education among women. Since I must speak on female education among Muslims, I shall point out how far the ignorance of Muslim women is responsible for keeping this conflict alive.

Firstly, I would like to cite an example of the extent to which blind orthodox beliefs influence human behaviour. A weeping child of five or six years called out to his mother, 'Ma, Ma!' At first the mother did not reply. Then she snapped at him in Urdu, 'Why are you calling me "Ma", you stupid brat? Can't you say "Amma"?' Even in the matter of a child addressing his mother, there is so much prejudice! The boy who learns his life's lessons from this mother will create all kinds of conflicts in society. The values he grows up with will surely let loose a tide that would lead society towards decline. Who should be blamed? Is it the boy or his mother? Or is it the people who, by blocking the path of female education, have wrecked all hopes for the future?

We all know that the ideas about man, society and the world implanted in our minds during the early years of our lives usually remain with us till the very end. Often in our lives we unconsciously act on the beliefs acquired during childhood. The education of a child usually begins on the lap of his mother. Therefore, the responsibility of the mother who is also the first teacher is inestimable. The ideas that take deep roots in a child's mind will, in the future, influence his views and course of action. Therefore, it is desirable to base a child's early education on freedom and liberal ideas. A child ought to be guided, single-mindedly, so that he devotes himself to the service of his downtrodden motherland in the future. These are the major things a Muslim child must be taught.

They must be made to understand that their homeland is not the Arab countries, Persia, Turkey or Egypt. India is their birthplace and they are Indians! Nationalism is not based on a common religion, but on sharing a common homeland. The English, French, German and other European nations as well as Americans are all Christians. But no Christian of France will try and introduce himself as a German or an Englishman! The Christians of France will remain French, just as the Christians of England will remain English. Religion is never of greater importance than nationality. In the same way, Muslims of India are also Indians, and they ought not to take pride in any other identity. It is shameful.

Further, children must also be told that their mother-tongue is the language of the Indian state in which they were born, the dress of that state is their national dress, and in joys and sorrows, in times of prosperity and poverty, Indians alone are their true kin! It is absolutely necessary that they receive this training. They must realize that even though religion is an important aspect of one's personal life, it is not the most important aspect of national life. To be able to explain this, one requires tolerance of others' views, which is not easy to achieve without a liberal education. In the words of Maulvi Mujibar Rahman, this is the kind of education Muslims require: 'You will not bear ill-will towards the members of other communities, I hope, you will never do that. That would be un-Islamic. That you have no untouchability amongst you, that your very religion teaches you universal brotherhood, goes to show that it is not at all the desire of Allah that one human being should entertain hatred towards another.'

The seeds of these ideas must be sown in the child's mind so that they may bloom when he becomes an adult. Communal conflicts could be resolved very easily, if only people of different communities felt this truth in their hearts and expressed it well.

To make this idea work, the community needs mothers who are educated up to the desired level. The renowned French hero Napoleon said, 'The hope of France is in her mothers.' I want to say the same words with a slight difference, 'The hope of India is in her mothers.' But Indians still have not learnt to give these words, and even more so the Muslim community, their due. While it is the mother's job to mould the child into a complete human being, her own human qualities remain incomplete, not progressing beyond the very basic level. There is no attempt to impart any sort of education to her, be it intellectual, moral or spiritual. She is exposed only to the fanaticism of blind faith!

These are some reflections on the need for educating women, as mothers are entrusted with the responsibility of bringing up children. How important education is in playing the roles of a daughter or a sister becomes clear if we think about it.

Whenever a change needs to be brought about in society—no matter how noble the improvement being sought—a conflict with that very society is bound to occur. Again, as long as a society flourishes, it must go through change, because any living entity cannot remain inert and static. Therefore every society has an eternal need of those who will stand in the forefront, face the conflict and destroy the obstacles in the path of change. When men return home, exhausted, listless and enervated, they would collapse unless there was someone to lessen their load and inspire fresh enthusiasm in them. Therefore, what they desire is sincere sympathy and unstinted inspiration. They want an exchange of ideas and feelings. Who will fulfil this deep-rooted desire, renew hope in their despondent hearts, or infuse their tired minds with fresh vigour? Whether as a wife, daughter or sister, only an educated woman can fulfil this role. Society is bereft of activity and achievement because it lacks such a woman.

If we analyse the problems dogging the country or society, we will find that in most cases men have wanted to progress alone by suppressing women. As a result an enfeebled society faces fresh problems every day.

Therefore, I appeal to the youth of the country to help destroy the enormous barriers in the path of women's progress, created by their lack of education. They will need little more than courage and enthusiasm—and these are not lacking among the youth!

There is much more to be said about the need for women's education. But if I proceed further you may not have the patience to listen. Therefore, I will take your leave by ending with the words of the poet Tennyson:

'The Woman's cause is Man's; they rise or sink
Together; dwarfed or God-like, bound or free;
If she be small, slight-natured, miserable,
How shall Man grow?'

Saugat, Agrahayan 1927

Freedom for Muslim Women

Perceptive people will have understood that the Muslim community is faced with many extraordinary difficulties in the twentieth century. The only way to solve these problems is by using one's own intellectual and moral judgment. Therefore, I will say what I feel on the basis of my own knowledge and understanding. Please forgive me if my words hurt anyone, for I don't intend to hurt anybody.

'Freedom for Muslim Women'—the word 'freedom' here implies freedom of the spirit. And freedom of the spirit implies using one's independent, individual thought to serve society and the nation and let one's intellectual and moral judgment guide one's actions. I believe religious texts and words of wisdom help enhance our sense of intellectual and moral judgment. Instead, if our intellect and conscience are warped or dimmed by religious texts, they become worthless.

The world is transient. In the twentieth century, therefore, tumultuous winds have managed to raise a flutter in the hearts of Muslim women who have been asleep for ages. Now they are looking at the world outside, at other women in the world. Realizing their own physical, intellectual and social degradation when compared to the others, they feel utterly ashamed of their situation. Women will no longer put up with being mere objects of pleasure, forsaking their womanhood and individual identity. So far women have deluded themselves and lived in an unreal world, deprived of enjoying the unique beauty of this earth. But now, full of regret, these women wish to stop living a life of leisure and be acquainted with the wider world.

Women have become rebellious. But they are not armed with the chief weapons of war—education and knowledge. All they have is a terrible feeling of self-loathing, self-reproach and, above all, an indomitable desire for freedom. Just as a the feeling of regret nullifies the errors a sinner has committed, making him pure, self-criticism will make every woman a true human being.

The first thing needed to achieve this is education. By education I do not mean acquiring a few degrees, but acquiring a power that makes one's mind noble, liberal and honest, guiding one's intellect and sense of moral judgment. It is a power that gives one the strength necessary for keeping one's personality and self-respect intact.

Muslim women these days are able to read a couple of Bengali books, write a few letters and read Arabic like a parrot, without understanding what the words mean. I am not against the study of Arabic. But I feel that if any language, including that in which holy texts are written, is read without comprehension, it is pointless.

More Muslims than non-Muslims among girl students attend primary school, whereas, at the university level, Muslim girls are hard to come by. Perhaps certain people feel it is not necessary for girls to aim at higher studies. But I believe—going by certain instances I have observed—that a little knowledge is a dangerous thing. It may cause great unhappiness within the family. Some women are quite proud to have received a little education. I want to stress that primary education is not enough. In fact, often it has adverse effects. But once education is more widespread, this misplaced pride ceases. Nowadays, just one or two girls are educated; hence they tend to be arrogant. When all are educated, this arrogance will disappear automatically.

Unless Muslim women are suitably educated, this society can never progress. Therefore women cannot sit back, complacent, having given men the charge. We must take the issue of women's education in our own hands. We must be able to introduce ourselves as mature human beings in a civilized society. Instead of crying like beggars, falling at the feet of men, and bearing the burden of rejection and humiliation, we must wrest our rightful inheritance and free ourselves from this bondage of womanhood. We lack education, hence we have no courage—but we must earn that by ourselves.

Muslim women must break the chains that bind them, making

them look like hapless, lowly beings in the eyes of the women of the civilized world. They might end up with bruises on their feet. But if the struggle frees them from humiliation and shame, they would have won the battle. These chains not only deprive Muslim women from gaining what is lawfully theirs, they pull the entire society down, to the path of destruction.

Many people probably realize how much a society's progress depends on its women. But there are people who wilfully refuse to appreciate this, not acknowledging their debts to women. Women should reject with loathing any empty words of praise or honour coming from them. Such people are incapable of showing true respect, they are merely play-acting.

I wonder if it would be a good idea to inflict this prison in which women have been locked up and prevented from enjoying the beauty of the world—which prevents the light of learning from entering the minds of Muslim women—on men! Nobody would suggest that women are responsible for all the wrong and evil deeds being done in the world. Then why should women be held prisoners? If imprisonment is necessary, both men and women ought to share the same fate. Else both have the right to be equally acquainted with the outside world.

All will agree that marital fidelity is an invaluable quality in a woman. But if a woman is locked up behind closed doors and windows, not allowed a glimpse of the sun's light, and only then her virtuous nature is made much of, does it matter? The woman who meets and overcomes various obstacles and difficulties and defeats temptation when faced with it is the truly virtuous one. Muslim religious texts do not sanction men keeping women in a cage; rather women are promised their lawful rights. It is also said that women must pay for their own actions. If it is so, women should get educated, be aware of their own rights and be free to lead their lives in line with their own convictions.

The education that one gets in schools and colleges today cannot be called perfect. But rather than sit at home and be guided blindly by another, it is better to take what is on offer. It is the lesser of the two evils. The problem of education is an enormous and complex one. People have many different opinions about what the ideal system of education should be. Without going into that, I will put forward what I, with my limited understanding, consider suitable for Muslim girls.

Compared to other women, we are really far behind. The pioneers who take the first step might have to forsake the dream of having a ticket to an imaginary heaven while moving ahead. While we are on this earth, it is better not to live like inert objects but gain some awareness and match our footsteps with those of the others. To ennoble and civilize our society, primarily we need women's education. I feel nothing will be achieved by writing countless books and reading out endless pages in the form of a speech. Real work has to be done. Muslim girls have to be educated.

Higher education is not suitable for all, especially the poor. Girls, whose fathers are somewhat well-off, might easily do something for society and particularly for women, if they put in a little effort. Thus, after a small group is set up, a huge amount of work can be done. Neither Eden School nor Bethune School was built in a day. What began with a handful of dedicated teachers has today grown into enormous educational institutions. Some of the Muslim girls, if they equipped themselves the same way, might well set up a few schools and colleges to help educate girls in keeping with the ideals of their own religion. Not only that, following Bethune School, they too might declare, to get their own back, 'Non-Muslim girls will not be admitted'. If they begin working this way, perhaps, in the future, Muslim women might be emancipated. Otherwise we shall forever be shackled, forever stumble in the dark.

Thus, my sole prayer to my young Muslim brothers is that if they encourage their sisters to follow this path, there is hope for freedom yet. Otherwise, not only will their sisters be destroyed, humanity itself will be endangered. Therefore I beg them to support the cause of freedom for Muslim women with enthusiasm and effort.

Saugat, Bhadra 1929

NOTES

[1] We have, however, discovered another piece of writing by Fazilatunnesa. In 1928 she wrote an essay for the Annual Session of the Dacca Muslim Literary Association, entitled *'Nari Jibaney Adhunik Sikshar Aswad'* (A Taste of Modern Education in a Woman's Life'). Later, the essay was published in the magazine of the Literary Association, *Shikha*; see Siddiqua Mahmuda, *Fatema Khanam* (Dhaka, Bangla Akademi, 1989, pp.28, 107, note 21).

[2] Mohammad Nasiruddin, 'Miss Fazilatunnesa, M.A.', *Bangla Sahitye Saugat Yug* (Dhaka, Noorjahan Begum, 1985: 585)

[3] Nasiruddin, 'Miss Fazilatunessa, M.A.': p.583

[4] Akhtar Imam, 'Fazilatunnesa, Higher Education and Progress of the Women of Bangladesh' (Begum Rokeya Memorial Foundation Lecture, Dhaka: Rokeya Hall, Dhaka University, 1994: p 7)

[5] Nasiruddin, 'Miss Fazilatunessa, M.A.': pp 590, 786.

[6] Akhtar Imam, 'Fazilatunnesa and Higher Education': p 29.

8

Mahmuda Khatun Siddiqua (1906-1977): A Single Woman outside Purdah

Translated by Nandini Guha

The poet Mahmuda Khatun Siddiqua was born on 16 December 1906 at Kushtia. Her father, Khan Bahadur Mohammad Solaiman Siddiq, was a divisional school inspector, well known as an educationist and a pioneer of the women's literacy movement. Her mother, Syeda Rahatunessa, was well educated. Her nani, or maternal grandmother, was an expert in Arabic, Persian, Urdu, and Bengali and could also write the Nagari script.[1] Evidently, there was a tradition of educating women in Mahmuda Khatun Siddiqua's family. The purdah system was followed too. Her mother and grandmother had learnt to read and write at home. In keeping with the tradition of the times, child marriage, too, was prevalent in this family. Mahmuda Khatun Siddiqua defied both purdah and child marriage. Like her sisters, she too was married as a child. But she walked out of this marriage and lived life independently. Her nani tried putting her in purdah when Mahmuda Khatun Siddiqua was twelve, but failed.

The literary and musical atmosphere in Khan Bahadur Mohammad Solaiman's family was unique. As a child Mahmuda Khatun Siddiqua was tutored at home by the author of the novel *Anwara*, Najibar Rahman.[2] She studied in a missionary school, where she came in contact with teachers who were foreigners. Mahmuda Khatun Siddiqua studied till Class VIII in school, after which her family did not let this continue. But she was not the sort who could be held in house arrest. Her literary pursuits and writing poetry—a hobby begun in childhood—continued in full swing.

Mahmuda Khatun Siddiqua's first poem was published when she was about twelve, in a magazine called *Al-Islam*, published from Calcutta. She wrote in all the publications of her time, irrespective of whether they had a Hindu or a Muslim character. Besides, she attended various meetings of literary societies in Pabna and Calcutta. In those days, when the women of Pabna sat behind bamboo screens to witness such meetings and gatherings, Mahmuda Khatun Siddiqua had set the unique example of sitting on the dais, in full public view, beside the male literary luminaries.

Invariably, once or twice a year, she made trips between Pabna and Calcutta. She lived in Calcutta for a few years so that her father could be treated by local doctors. He was a devotee of a pir in Taltolla, whom he would visit often. In Calcutta Mahmuda Khatun Siddiqua met the litterateurs Rabindranath Tagore, Saratchandra Chattopadhyay and Kazi Nazrul Islam. At that time, one needed a 'pass' to meet Saratchandra, but Mahmuda Khatun Siddiqua did not need one. She had discussions with editors literary magazine, litterateurs and other talented people of the time. Needless to say, she did not wear a burqa when she went out.

When the *Saugat* editor, Mohammad Nasiruddin, saw her without a burqa in public for the first time, he was quite taken aback. In the book *Bangla Sahitye Saugat Yug*, he wrote: 'In 1339 [1932], she suddenly arrived one day at *Saugat's* no. 11 Wellesley Street office. 'In that dark period, riddled by superstitions, when Muslim women were strictly confined to the fortress of the purdah, I saw this young lady, dressed in modern clothes and moving around freely. Even more surprising was that she had bobbed her hair.'[3] As Syeda Khanam, Mahmuda Khatun Siddiqua's niece, says, 'Maybe because one aspect of her life remained incomplete, Nana never prevented this daughter of his from doing whatever she pleased.'

Syeda Khanam, an international award-winning photographer, is also a writer. She lived with her aunt from the time she was a child until Mahmuda Khatun Siddiqua passed away. In an interview with us regarding her khala's married life and poetry writing, she said: 'My khala had another sister who had a talent for writing. Her name was

Saleha Khatun. Before Partition, a poem of hers was included in one of the prescribed Matriculation texts. Yet, thanks to the burden of domestic responsibilities, Saleha Khatun was never again able to write poetry. This is what usually took place—domestic stress, the atmosphere at one's parents-in-law's place and other such external pressures prevented women from pursuing their goals. Saleha Khatun too had been married as a child. My nana had got her married by the time she was eleven or twelve. Mahmuda Khala was the one to rebel and came out of her marriage. I do not accept this marriage, she said.

'If the marriage had lasted, her life, too, may have been similar to her five sisters. My nana had worked for the cause of female education, yet he got his own daughters married at a very young age, which was indeed quite odd. Perhaps because Nani had died, Nana felt insecure. He must have been worried about his daughters. So when a good match was proposed, he quickly married off his daughters. What else could he do?'

Mahmuda Khatun Siddiqua did not lead a married life, and nor was she involved in work that would help her make money. This is probably the reason why she had unlimited time for writing poetry and engage in multifarious social welfare activities. She evolved into a social activist and worker purely through her own efforts. She worked mainly out of her house. The activities included running a free clinic for homeopathy treatment to getting involved in the Swadeshi movement. Even as she wrote poetry, she contributed enormously towards human welfare, till the end of her life, quietly and away from public glare.

From the time she had been a young woman, Mahmuda Khatun Siddiqua lived in the ancestral home in Pabna with her father and elder sister. Earlier, she had lived in various district towns of undivided Bengal, places where her father was posted. She visited Darjeeling once, on holiday. Later, she accompanied her ailing father to Waltair, Ranchi and Giridih. After the Partition of India, she came to Dhaka and started living with her elder sister's family. Here too she was busy writing poetry and doing welfare work. In 1968, she had a sudden heart attack. Gradually she had to cut down on outdoor activities.

This was the time when Syeda Khanam would carry the details of literary conferences she attended back home to her khala. Mahmuda Khatun Siddiqua died on 2 May 1977.

Mahmuda Khatun Siddiqua was awarded the Bangla Akademi Award in 1969 and the *Ekushe Padak* in 1977. Her books of poems include *Pasarini* (The Seller of Trinkets) (1931), *Man-o-Mrittika* (The Mind and the Earth) (1960), and *Aranyer Sur* (The Music of the Woods) (1963). She wrote more than a hundred poems that were not published in book form. Quite a few of her uncollected stories and essays may be found in various journals, newspapers and in manuscript form.

S.A.

The Dream

At midnight today,
When wide-eyed I lay,
A dream quietly came
To take my pain away.
The emptiness was gone
I felt you were with me.
Hopes began to rise
In life's endless sea.
With the beauty of the world,
Tenderness and care
You stood, O my love,
Your sweetest smile so fair.
With soft words you touched
My heart at its core.
'I came because you called,
Do not weep any more.'
As I fell at his feet
In utter ecstasy,
With cruel blow my dream

Was taken away from me.
Through the open door came
Floods of morning light
Where did you go, O love,
Away from my sight?
I cried out in pain
Knowing what was true:
Dreams are only dreams
In sleep they come to you.[4]

Annwesha, Magh 1922

Song of Unity

Sons of the same mother, Hindu and Mussalman
Destined to be brothers we are, destined to be one.
Cradled by this dark earth,
Tied to this land by birth,
We drink in the same water, play in the same sun,
Speaking in the same tongue
Songs of love that we have sung.
In deep forests, in our blood, streams of poetry run.
Sons of the same mother we are, Hindu and Mussalman.
From our flowers to our skies
A spring of love will rise,
Silently, within our souls, its presence we must learn.
Hatred, anger, bitterness
Will cast us to a wilderness.
End of love in a land of death from where we can't return,
Sons of the same mother we are, Hindu and Mussalman.[5]

Gulistan, Sravan 1933

The Last Hour of the Night

The last hour of night touches with her brush
On sleepless eyes, rest them now.
Night departs at whose sweet call.
Golden streaks are etched on this blue.
All night long you have strung these flowers
Now it is but a garland of tears.
Step for a moment in this land of dreams,
Surrounded by gems, silent and alone.

Birds are singing in the blossoms of the trees,
Fairies sing and dance while plucking flowers.
Listen to the flute sounds that fill the air.
Come here, Sorrowful, and lose yourself.

Mysterious Night, she touches those eyes,
A calm, soft touch that cools the fire.
Lifts the pain as sleep descends,
A beautiful light begins to glow.

The stars have dimmed in the nuptial sky,
Drunken and dreamy, the dark night smiles.
All is asleep, silence all around,
Night fans the Earth with her silken brush.

Gulistan, Bhadra 1933

Literature and Art

There seems to be a lot of confusion regarding art and morality in literary matters. Some people believe art and morality are not related, others think they are. From the corner of my quiet home I would like to say a thing or two on this issue.

It would be a mistake to suppose that the presence of art in literature is meant only to create beauty and add flavour. If we do not take morality into account in whatever we do, there is a chance that something harmful will come of it. By abusing ethics, beauty itself may get damaged. Beauty, in fact, exists within the ambit of morality. Beauty, by itself, is not complete. It needs to be propped up by the ethics of aestheticism in order to grow. Only through morality can the world be kept in order. In fact, ethical principles were created to keep the world disciplined and orderly. The proof of this is in the fact that moral edicts are what have kept society in order. This can be understood if we take into account the fact that the foundation of peace is laid on orderliness. Hence, we cannot create art by ignoring morality.

I am not saying that literature should comprise lessons in morality. That will not and cannot happen. That is because literature does not belong to one or two people; it belongs to the whole world. It reflects the thoughts of the entire universe, all its happiness and sorrow. By leaving out any one of these, literature loses its strength. It cannot attract readers completely. And if a book fails to attract the reader totally, none of its qualities will endure the test of time. A certain group of authors have recreated man's daily joys and sorrows so powerfully in their books that they have touched the deepest chords in humanity, helping us to arrive on the path of truth. We look for reflections of our hearts in literature. We desire self-satisfaction. We are attracted to the source when we receive it. Yet taste is not the same in everyone. People look for books according to individual taste. Therefore, to keep the entire country devoted to reading, all kinds of books are required. But even within this variety, ideals have to be maintained.

I would say art is what keeps our ideals intact, takes us to the road of progress and yet manages to impress with its beauty. Sometimes, writers create horrible characters to clearly delineate a beautiful one, but a book could be written all the same, without having to do so. This is evident in Sita Devi's Bengali translation of George Eliot's memoirs. In this book there is no place for a morally corrupt male or female character. Writing such a book is very difficult, but by putting in a dedicated effort, one might even find a jewel in a dark cave. Nowadays, often we read about a woman leaving her husband to serve the country, or a mother sacrificing her morality for the sake of her child's welfare. These I cannot accept as ideals. For when women do such things, overwhelmed by idealism, such 'ideals' can only be called disruptive and negative. The above examples are life's exceptions. However, exceptions in life cannot constitute literature that represents mankind in general.

Sometimes people write that women belong to the world, that chastity is not related to a woman's body. How can they make such a frightening statement? If women belong to the world and being faithful has nothing to do with her body, the foundation of the whole world will turn to dust in a day. If you see someone you love surrender to another, will your heart not feel the pain? Those who consider this as art will see, if they cared to note, that given no one has any right over a woman's body, all kinds of atrocities do happen. Those who do this play with hearts, fooling themselves. Nothing sacred remains in their hearts, which are totally spent.

It is not easy to imagine the mind taking a definite shape. Like water, the mind too will change according to the shape of the vessel in which it is kept. If we live in a particular country for long, our tastes and morals become mostly like those of that country. Every book too, in the same way, constantly influences our minds. As a result even if the influence is not always evident, it shows in various ways and various works. Whether a worshipper of beauty or the teacher of morals, authors must remember that whatever they write does not remain limited within themselves alone.

Masik Mohammadi, Agrahayan 1928

A Woman's Responsibility Towards the Village Community

'If you want to satisfy me, then satisfy the poor and deprived people.' - Koran Sharif

Women think that the area of their work is confined only to their home and their city. But one's duties do not end at home. There is a lot to do outside as well. The thought does not occur to them because of a lack of education.

The rural areas in a country form its core. A third of Hindus and Muslims live in the villages. Amongst them Muslims are more in number. It is this class of people who produce the food for the country's consumption. The learned men of the country do not spare a second glance at those who suffer from malaria during the month of Paush and are pushed to the brink of death by their labour in growing rice. Festering ditches and ponds filled with water—breeding sites of mosquitoes—proliferate around their homes. The cultivators are not negligible in number, and people cannot progress by ignoring them. If a huge section of the human race does not progress, the progress of humanity is foredoomed to failure. The time has come to think about these things very seriously. Muslim society is unable to progress because the villages are lagging behind. The light of four fireflies is not good enough to remove dense darkness. Today we cannot afford to sit back any more. Why men alone? Women too must think towards the welfare of people living in villages, and ought to do for the village the little that they are capable of, and this way society will be able to develop much faster.

In order to prevent malaria in the villages, ponds and ditches need to be filled and jungles and forests cleared. These, no doubt, are difficult for women to do. But whoever can manage to work from home should do so by starting Muslim primary schools and educating a few girls. Surely, this should not be very difficult. Some light will have spread through this process. The effort may, at least, remove superstitions. In the villages, Muslims of the farmer class are only Muslims in name. Many do not even know who the founder of Islam is. They only know about the last Prophet and little else. They are unaware of the principles of generosity, friendliness, equality, democracy inherent in Islam. One who can make them understand that these issues would not just educate but would have done a pious deed as well. Of course, there may be an objection, that is, it does not look good if a Muslim girl goes to a different house to study. However, if one could make the guardians understand that stepping out of purdah was not wrong but necessary to develop as a human being, then the girl would not be denied permission.

From the village woman's point of view, it is enough to have one's basic needs of food and clothing fulfilled. It is beyond them to think that procuring food and clothes is not the only reason for living, that one does not gain success in life by these alone, and that there are other important duties and responsibilities in life. That the Muslim woman is lagging so far behind in education is really sad. One of the important reasons for this is the unjustified and unreasonable purdah system. This unfortunate practice is sabotaging the very foundation of women's education and is also the main reason for men's apathetic attitude towards women. Men are particularly responsible for the harm it is doing us.

(extract) *Gulistan*, Agrahayan 1933

The First Cup of Tea

The setting was a backward village, the venue a corner of a huge thatch-roofed verandah. The mistress of the house, seated on a wooden stool close to a stove, was happily putting firewood into it. Water was heating in a large saucepan on the stove. The lady's middle-aged husband sat close by, on a wicker stool. Just back from Calcutta, he shared a story with his wife, waiting for the water to boil for tea.

He had been to Calcutta for the first time and having tasted the lovely flavour of tea, also for the first time, he was trying to teach his wife how to prepare it. He was eager to have his wife taste this wonderful drink. The wife stared wide-eyed at her husband's face as she listened to the stories of Calcutta—in fact, 'devoured' would be a more appropriate word to use. The daughters-in-law and daughters sat around him—some of them rolling out rotis, some kneading flour into dough and yet others halting their work to look at the master's face and listen to his stories. A variety of pithas [sweet made of rice flour, coconut, milk, sugar], rolled by expert hands, were piled up inside a wooden frame. Children looked longingly towards the heap. In between, everyone looked with anticipation at the saucepan. Had the water boiled yet? Each one waited impatiently to get a taste of this drink, so far unknown to them.

The master of the house stepped forward, removed the lid slightly and declared, 'Just a little while longer.' The mistress beamed with joy. Her earrings and the tassel hanging from the jewellery on her arm swung as she turned. The dangling earrings worn by the girls and young wives of the house swayed. The mistress realized it was getting late. The rays of the sun touched the bride's green sari anchal making it shimmer. The anchals of the jamdani saris worn by the girls trailed in the dust, unawares. What a day it was! The master too looked at the sun and said, 'It is late.' Then he said grandly, 'Do you know, dear, it was such a big row in the zoo when the lion roared! At first I really felt scared. Then there was the hippopotamus in the water—unless you see it there is no way you can describe its appearance! How many different coloured birds—one cannot stop talking about them! I feel like showing them all to you.' The mistress turned her face, thrilled, and said—'Oh no! I feel scared.'

With those words, her nose-ring swung with pride. At that moment the tea water started to boil. Before anyone else could notice, the master himself did. He almost screamed—'Remove it from the stove, remove it now, the water is boiling!' The mistress, panicked by the master's shout, quickly held the pan with the end of her sari, although a piece of cloth meant for the purpose lay close by. The master stepped up proudly and dropped tea leaves into the water. The audience looked with awestruck eyes. Everybody was anxious to find out what next. After a little while, the master strained the tea, mixed milk and sugar in it. Immediately, there was shouting amongst the children—'Me first, me first.' Laughter, talk and cries raised quite a din. With great difficulty the master began to pour one cup of tea at a time. The children, wives and maids were already happy with anticipation.

The youngest daughter-in-law stood beside the door shyly. Spotting her, the mistress said, 'O dear! What are you doing there? Come here immediately.' As soon as she came forward, the mistress poured a little extra to please her. Today the mistress was overflowing with joy and pride. Her husband was the first person in the village to visit Calcutta, and this new phenomenon, tea, was being tasted for the first time in her house! The joy and pride was evident in all her actions. In fact, when the young cowherd employed in the house asked for a sip, she filled his bowl up to the brim. In the end, the master and mistress began to drink their tea, exchanging happy glances as they did. Finally, when the tea drinking ritual was over, the master, casting a meaningful look at his wife's face, said, 'Tomorrow is Id. When our new son-in-law comes, remember to call me when the tea is prepared.'

Golden-hued mustard fields lined the road on either side. Through the narrow path in between, the bearers carried the new son-in-law's palanquin. Cold winds blew the mustard stalks this way and that. The wind blew through the jungle in the distance, raising a rustling sound. The flowers of spring were yet to bloom, but blossoms of red, pink, yellow and other colours bloomed in the young man's heart. The bearers, happy to be carrying the new son-in-law, sang merrily, 'On the banks of the river cranes graze/ Picking up emerald-green grains.'

Finally, when the palanquin halted at the gate of the house, the son-in-law covered his mouth quickly with a handkerchief to hide his smiling face. All his brothers-in-law, sisters-in-law, and grandma-in-law, came forward smiling. Grandma-in-law, who came close to the palanquin said, 'Hey, young man! Have you come to see me, or your bride?' The new jamai laughed and retorted, 'You, of course.' 'That's for sure,' said Grandma and went towards the room where the young man would be entertained. All the brothers and sisters-in-law collected behind him. Grandma served the food. The groom sat down to eat after he had washed, but did not seem to have an appetite. His eyes were looking for someone in all possible directions.

Noticing this, Grandma said, 'Aha, I know whom you're looking for. You shall not eat alone.' She looked at the children and the young crowd assembled there and said, 'Go away, otherwise my granddaughter will feel too shy to eat with our jamai.' She went looking for her granddaughter. The young crowd, amused, had been staring fixedly at the young man. They went away now, disappointed.

Grandma knew how to get things done. She returned soon, dragging her granddaughter along, and made her sit next to her husband. The old woman said, 'Well, young man, now you have to eat everything.' She went away to return after a little while with two steaming cups of tea. Placing them in front of the two, she said, 'Now this old busybody is leaving, so eat together happily.' Walking out of the room, she fastened a chain to lock the door from the outside.

The groom had not had an opportunity to see his bride properly. He pulled off her veil surreptitiously from the back. Looking at her, enchanted, he said, 'Turn around.' The bride shyly tried to pull the veil back on. But the groom tightly held both her hands. She was as beautiful as an angel come down from heaven. He pleaded with her, 'Say something.' Feeling even more shy, the bride hid her face. Trying desperately to raise her face with his two hands and failing, the young man gave up and let her go. The bride pulled her veil to cover her face and sat with her back to him.

The young man began to wonder how he was going to get to hear her speak a word. How was he going to converse with her? After much thought, he finally raised a cup of tea to her lips. The mischievous wife laughed and pushed. The cup clattered to the ground and the tea splashed all over. Now looking at her stunned husband's face, the wife began to laugh. Although the joke was at his expense, the groom couldn't help laughing himself. At that moment Grandma unlocked the chains on the door, to remind them about lunch. Entering the room, she guessed what had happened and laughed out loud. And then, for the benefit of the people in the family who were entitled to tease the couple, she called out, 'Hey, come, all of you, see the new son-in-law's antics.'

Hearing her call, the others rushed in from wherever they were, and filled up the room. Soon, the room was filled with sounds of laughter. The couple too felt a heavenly loveliness in their hearts.

Gulistan, Paush 1933

Women's Responsibilities Today

Women have to suffer many inhuman tortures, because of widespread illiteracy. There is no limit to the number of unbearable things we women have to suffer in every sphere of our daily lives. Marriage is a particularly difficult proposition. Following society's whimsical decree, every girl is to be married off—regardless of whether she agrees to it or is ready for it; without thought of the possible result of such a marriage.

Needless to say, women's own stupidity and ignorance are to be blamed for this. What a terrible life a woman leads, as a result! She lives in great fear in her husband's home, where she should enjoy full rights. A woman seems to accept that this is all she is. In sadness and joy, she will have to spend her whole life with her mouth shut, like a mechanical toy—not a single desire or wish of hers will ever be expressed. She will have to live and die this way. In case she is widowed, the shame and insults she will have to take to be able to earn a little food and clothing will make her pray every moment for death. In the life of a human being what can be more pathetic than this? What is the use of such a life? How can we, human beings, possibly bear the burden of such a life?

To save herself from this horrible existence, a woman must be capable of earning a living—so that she never feels completely helpless and weak, so that a man never thinks 'a woman cannot survive without me'. Thinking of oneself as weak and helpless makes one weak indeed, which is as good as being dead. Weakness can never help anyone in this world. The confidence that comes from one's ability to earn helps keep one's soul alive. Weakness is a sin. Women must be free of this weakness.

(abriged) *Moazzin*, Asharh–Chaitra 1931-32

NOTES

1 The Nagari script is an ancient form of Devanagari that is used today: it appeared in AD eighth century.

2 Najibar Rahman (1860-1923) had written two novels with social themes: *Anwara* (first published Calcutta: 1980; second edition Dhaka: Ananda Prakashan, 1988) and *Gariber Meye* (The Poor Man's Daughter, first published Calcutta: 1924, second edition Dhaka: Ananda Prakashan, 1988). These two novels became extremely popular.

Najibar Rahman lived in Pabna town, where he taught and wrote. The women in his stories were mostly examples of ideal wives or mothers, moulded by their husbands, somewhat educated and religious. The husbands too were newly educated, besides attending the madrassa, they received some English education. Syed Mustafa Siraj has spoken of Najibar Rahman in his interview, see this volume, pp 370-84.

3 See interview with Mohammad Nasiruddin, this volume, pp 335-41.

4 Mahmuda Khatun's poetry reminds the reader of the charasmatic Nazrul Islam's songs and poems; here it points to his song *'Mor ghumoghore ele manohar'*.

5 This poem reminds us of Nazrul Islam's *'Mora eki brinte du'ti kusum Hindu Musalman'*.

9

Razia Khatun Chowdhurani (1907-1934): An Artist Who Died Too Young

Translated by Nandini Guha

Razia Khatun Chowdhurani was born in 1907 at Noakhali. Her father was Abdur Rashid Khan and mother, Hajera Khanam. Abdur Rashid Khan was a close associate of Deshbandhu Chittaranjan Das, the mayor of the Kolkata Corporation at that time, who had appointed him as the deputy executive officer. Therefore, most of Razia Khatun's childhood days were spent in Kolkata. Razia Khatun's education began by taking lessons from the imam of the mosque in their house at Noakhali. Later, her mother's brother, her Boro Mama, Mohammad Abdul Quddus (artist Qayyum Chowdhury's father) taught her Bengali, Urdu, Arabic and some English. In Kolkata a private tutor came to teach Razia Khatun and a few other children.

Razia Khatun Chowdhurani began writing poems rather early, while she was still a child. Initially her work was published under the name 'Razia Khatun'. In 1924, the title of Chowdhurani was added to her name after her marriage.[1] Razia Khatun was married to Ashrafuddin Ahmad Chowdhury, who belonged to the Shuagazi zamindar family of Comilla. Ashrafuddin was about thirty years old and had taken part in the Indian nationalist movement. After passing B.L., Ashrafuddin had completed all formalities for going to England. But instead he chose to join the Congress, responding to Mahatma Gandhi's call for satyagraha. He went to jail many times. Even after India's Partition, he spent the remaining years of his life wearing only khadi and a Gandhi cap.[2]

Razia Khatun Chowdhurani developed a friendly relationship with her much older and idealistic husband. Letters to her husband (some are compiled here) bear proof of this friendship. In Razia Khatun's essays and stories, a hint of his influence can be found, although nothing very distinctive is evident. In fact, the influence of Rokeya is evident in comments such as: 'Between a blindfolded bullock pushing the wheel in an oil mill and a Bengali Muslim woman, there is no particular difference'[3] Rather, the few political poems and songs composed at the request of her husband clearly show more originality.[4] It is in her letters that Razia Khatun Chowdhurani's artistic mind is revealed at its best.

Two of her books were published while she was alive. The first was a collection of poems called *Upahar* (The Gift), the second a collection of stories called *Pather Kahini* (Stories of the Road).[5] Her essays, stories and poems were published in journals like *Saugat*, *Nauroz*, *Naya Bangla* and *Mohammadi*. In 1982 Comilla's Abdul Quddus Saheb collected her writings and edited a book named *Razia Khatun Chowdhuranir Rachana Sankalan* (The Collected Works of Razia Khatun Chowdhurani).[6] The book was published by Rabeya Khatun, Razia's second child. Razia died when Rabeya was barely three years old.

Like her father, Rabeya Khatun too belongs to the world of politics. She lives in Comilla town, and each day is a busy one. Even so, Rabeya took out a little time to talk about her mother, whom she barely remembered. She took a special interest in showing her mother's picture and letters. The daughter, now over seventy, constructed the image of her long-lost mother through stories she had heard, newly-discovered writings, torn letters and whatever she could remember. Truth and imagination, memories, remembered and forgotten, were mixed in creating the image. On that morning in February 1997, Razia Khatun Chowdhurani took shape in front of our eyes, in the image of an artist who did not have the scope to complete her work.

'I was three and a half years old when my mother died. My elder sister, named Saleha, was five years old then. Amma died just five months after our youngest sister was born.

'My father was always in jail. My mother was so sensitive that she felt my father's absence very deeply. Although she wholeheartedly supported his involvement in politics, his going to jail would make her very unhappy. Later in life, my mother suffered from mental illness. For quite some months before her death, she had lost her mental balance completely. However, just before her death, she was also diagnosed with tuberculosis, and was treated by Dr. Bidhan Roy [the distinguished doctor who was also a Congress politician]. Later, a kaviraj named Shyamdas Bachaspati examined her. That kaviraj was a very orthodox brahmin. Once out of mischief, she upturned a bowl of chicken soup on the kaviraj's head!

'I heard these things from my nani and khalas. They brought us up in our nana's home. After my mother passed away, we lived for a long time in Calcutta at Nana's house, 4, Suhrawardy Avenue. When my father went to jail, Amma would come to Calcutta from Comilla. Father was mostly interned at Dumdum Central Jail, and she was allowed to meet him once or twice a month.

'We were quite small then, and do not remember much. Only one last impression remains in my mind. Amma had passed away and her hair was hanging over the side of the bed. My mother had very long hair. After she died her hair was possibly washed. And, as is normally done, incense sticks were lit. It is as if even today that smell wafts back to me.

'Amma was married at sixteen. She had eight brothers and sisters, of whom she was the eldest. When my mother got married, Nani was barely thirty-one or thirty-two. The purdah system was prevalent in those days, especially in aristocratic families. Girls from our family circle were not allowed to study in schools and colleges. That is why my mother was unable to go to school and she studied at home. After marriage, my father was very encouraging about Amma's studies. She had already begun a little writing here and there, much before that. A small book of poems called *Upahar* was printed and the poem 'Manush' (Man) was in it. These poems were written by Mother between the ages of nine and twelve.

Amma's sister who was next to her in age, my khala, Saifura Hossain Chowdhury, had passed Matriculation before marriage, and later studied till her M.A. Her husband was a judge and it was because of his wishes that Khala could to study so far. My Mejo Khala sang very well. Not on radio, just at home. Till the end of her life she would sing songs. The purdah system was followed at home and my nani and khalas all followed the system. There was purdah at my father's house as well. We wore burqas until a few years ago.

'When we were very small, we studied in a school called "Shishu Vidyapith" in Calcutta, run by Nirupama Devi. Later Nana admitted us to Kolkata's Victoria Institution. When I was studying in the Eighth or Ninth class, my father brought us to the Shuagazi village home. I took the Matriculation Examination as a private candidate, not attached to any institution, and passed it. During the Kolkata riots, Lila Ray (Nag) of the famous *Jayashree* magazine used to visit our house.[7] We called her Pishima and she took great care of us. She would say, "If you can't go to school and college, then study at home." Also, a lady called Malabika Mitra came to teach us.

'Amma knew English, Bengali, Persian—all three languages. After marriage when Amma came to the Shuagazi village home, she spent most of her time in studies. She was not very good at cooking. Almost thirty to forty women worked in the house. Amma used to teach the village girls and had set up a kind of school in the house. Amma would help the girls with their studies, stitching and embroidery and such like. I mean the village girls were quite dependent on her, they sought Amma's advice on any matter. This was something very unusual in a zamindar's home. Amma had completely changed the tradition of a zamindar's house, especially, the class divide that existed in such a household. She had brought up two maids as if they were her own daughters, and married them off.

'However, all this did not cause any problems in her in-laws' home. My Dada was no more, but two Dadis (paternal grandmothers/great aunts) were there. None of them stopped Amma from doing her work. Being educated, she commanded a special respect. In the mornings after quickly making some suji or semolina and luchis or something similar for breakfast, tidying the house a little, combing and tying the hair of her mother and aunts-in-law, she would go to her room and sit with books. Books would be strewn all over the bed. At times my father would return to find Amma sitting like this. I have heard these stories from my father who was greatly influenced by Amma. Father would tell us very often, "I was an uncultured man, unused to the ways of the world. Quite a savage. It is your Amma who turned me into a gentleman." Once in anger, Father had slapped a maid. Later he returned to his room and found Amma sitting quietly. Tears were ceaselessly flowing from her eyes. Amma had said, "Shame on you, you hit a girl!" Later, telling us the incident, Father said, "That day I really learnt a lesson!" Father called Amma by the name "Razu".

'I have heard from my phuphus that Amma had such a sweet nature that if one of them liked any of her saris, Amma would immediately give it away. Amma herself, of course, only wore khadi at all times. Even her wedding sari was made of khadi. It had zari work done on it. Amma had a lot of jewellery. She gave some of it to father to start a newspaper called *Naya Bangla*. Some were sold to pay for the treatment of her brother-in-law (he didn't survive though). After she went mad, Amma had taken to throwing down a lot of her jewellery from the fourth floor terrace of our Calcutta house.

'Amma had only one hobby. She would ask Nana to bring her all the papers published in those days, *Saugat, Mohammadi* . . . Ma sent her writings to all these journals, either by mail or by hand. The son of *Mohammadi's* editor, Akram Khan, would personally come to collect Amma's writings from her. Nasiruddin Sahib was the editor of *Saugat*. My Amma's essays were very good. So were her poems. Her stories had a Muslim flavour. I like the intellectual quality of her poetry. For my father, Amma had written a poem called *Chasha* (Farmer). And once, for one of father's meetings, she had written a poem which was set to tune by Monoranjan Bhattacharya of Comilla[8]:

Sitting by the sea of death we sing
The joyful song of life.
We who sit on the edge of death,
It's our adventure, it's our strife.

'Amma was slightly younger than Sufia Khalamma [in fact, Sufia Kamal was younger]. Khalamma had once told me, "If Razia had lived, she would have been a very great writer." Amma's pet name was Noni. As I grew up, how often I heard people talk about "Noni". It is our misfortune that we never got to enjoy Amma's care and protection.'

M. B.

Women's Place in Society and at Home

Whenever I begin to write about the tortured and oppressed woman, worn down by sorrow, my mind is overwhelmed with pain. In the past our society had Chand Sultana, Noor Jahan, Jahanara, Zebunnisa and others; is there any benefit in talking about them? Thinking about such great women gives us only a momentary self-satisfaction and happiness. It is not correct to be so fascinated by the past so as to lose one's sense of self, nor is it correct to forget the past altogether. The past needs to be remembered and discussed so that the future could be made to look brighter and more glowing in comparison.

For a long time Muslim women remained silent in spite of suffering all the injustices of society, because their world was confined to their homes. Now a few of them are being educated and getting acquainted with the outside world. Gradually their eyes are being opened, at which the old fashioned section of society is saying, 'No wonder! By learning how to read and write these women have come under an evil influence. Unless they are locked up in the strictly-disciplined ambience of the harem, they will not survive.' That we are alive after so long is surprising in itself. Societies for the prevention of cruelty to animals have been formed. Thanks to the generosity of the government, if a man commits murder he is hanged. But nobody seems to be bothered about the slow death of our souls—deprived of light and air, emptied of hope, joy and enthusiasm and confined to the inner quarters, the *zenana*? We do not want to go out in the streets exposed, free of the veil and heads uncovered, because by doing that women lose their dignity and grace. Without opposing the purdah system which is prescribed by the Shariyat, we want our freedom. Freedom does not mean dancing around on the streets. We want true freedom—that which helps the mind to be uplifted, pure, refreshing and strong; which, by acquainting us with our own faith and the truth, brings to our knowledge realities about the inside and outside world. Can society not grant us this little thing?

Men give us respect and honour, depending on our quality. Rather than valuing us for playing the roles of daughters, mothers, sisters and wives, they are concerned only with our being able to entertain them with our beauty, culinary skills and care. Usually these are the attributes that count. If women fail men in any of these departments, there is no limit to the ill treatment they have to suffer. Men do not stop to think whether they are good looking so that they may claim beautiful brides, and whether they are able, caring and noble to be worthy of efficient, devoted and chaste women! The word 'chaste' is an enigma. It can be used to describe women at any time or place, but there is no male equivalent of the word, neither in Bengali nor in the so-called refined English language. 'Chastity' and other words with similar meaning have been routinely coined for women. Isn't this indicative of man's moral inferiority? Of course, moral character does not indicate only one aspect; all qualities related to one's character are to be considered. From the word *sat* (honest) was born the word *satitva* (chastity). Would we use the word 'unchaste' to take the measure of a man the same way as we would call anyone—man or woman—'dishonest' without bias when they are lacking in basic human qualities?

It surprises us to find an immoral husband getting angry when his wife's veil falls, when an ebony-skinned husband is desirous of a beautiful nymph of paradise or a winged fairy, and when at the old age of sixty a man is keen to bring home a bride who is only sixteen! This reveals the worth society places on women.

In the rural communities, many men beat up their wives out

of habit. And I would not say this is a trait distinct only in village people. Many gentlemen in the cities may put the above-mentioned talent to good use in a drunken or normal state. But the trend cannot spread in the cities for fear of shame, the spiritedness of women and the fact that city-bred people are aware and educated. On the whole, however, an uneducated husband is preferable to an educated but cruel and uncaring one. While the former might find the wife's behaviour unforgivable and attack her, in the heat of the moment, an educated person's anger and neglect is frightening. Many women have been pushed to the brink as a consequence. I spoke to many village women who thought that the attack, spurred by sudden excitement, was an evidence of love's demands on the wife. However, there are unhappy women in the villages as well. And torture is not similar in all cases. Generally, in the village, men are not drunkards or immoral like the gentlemen in the city. Of course, I do not say that they are all very pious. There are good and bad in all societies. The solution is in the hands of women. They can save themselves from disgrace if they are strong and powerful; no cowardly man will have the guts to torture them in that case.

Evidently, we are loved only for our beauty and service—and not for the relationships we have with men. Often it is physical beauty that is more prized than one's qualities. The proof of this could be found in homes where there are two wives. Beauty and youth are what men find attractive in women. And the woman who can care most for her husband is the most valued. I hope no one thinks we want womankind to revolt against men. Indeed, we ask women to be good housewives in order to control and organize indisciplined men; to claim their rightful places and reign like empresses. In this world, man and woman share an unbreakable bond—one cannot live without the other. Man is action, woman strength; man represents the workplace, woman home; man is longing, woman satisfaction; man is desire, woman restraint; man anxiety, woman peace. Life is made sweeter by the meeting of these two and that forms the foundation of marriage.

Marriage that was oriented to mutual cooperation has now been relegated to a selling of the self. When a woman is forced to entertain her husband, that is what I call prostitution. We hate prostitutes, failing to notice the fact that prostitution takes place in a lot of households. Even when a husband does not love his wife, she must try to bind him by using her beauty, youthfulness, dress and jewellery. Even when a wife does not love her husband, she still makes it a point to try new ways every day to entice him. If you want to call this practice being 'faithful' in refined language, say so. In my opinion it is just the opposite. If a husband loves his wife, she will try to please him anyway—but why dress up like a prostitute? How many children are born out of pure feelings? Their minds, as a result, become like that of their fathers and mothers, indisciplined and lustful. This is what they call 'flirtation' in English. Many husbands care for their wives only till their infatuation with the novelty wears off. Soon afterwards, they are looking out for someone new. In such cases a wife should try to make use of her spiritedness, reason and love to make the husband return to her. If this does not work, she should leave—following the man around like a dog is definitely not the right thing to do.

Many say there is no love in marriage—because love is without desire. This is baseless. True love is the ability to find the fulfilment of all desires and hopes in one's object of love; finding beauty and perpetual novelty even in an ugly old man. Everyday intimacy tempers desire and quietens what may be an obsessive love. When the night jasmine blooms during day, it loses its fragrance. No love is without desire. A mother desires that her son will grow up and make his country and people proud; that he, by getting a beautiful and accomplished wife, will make her happy. Children want parents to love them, care for them, get them the finest gifts and higher education. Husband and wife want mutual care, love, devotion and sympathy.

Our love for Allah too is full of desire. We do not love Him selflessly. Even the ascetic Rabeya who did not want fulfilment of her desires either in this life or the next, did want mental happiness. In fact she wanted the love of Allah Himself. Union with one's beloved may not always be possible because of one's allegiance to social and family tradition. Unrequited love inspires a poet to write of selfless love. But infatuation is of no consequence whatsoever. Get two frustrated lovers to meet, and you will find that the passion and fascination raging in their hearts quelled soon enough. Soon the man would stop making distinctions between the much-desired paragon of beauty and any ordinary woman. A distinguished feature of marriage is that the spouses love each other, in spite of each other's faults and mistakes. What can be purer and sweeter than this? Instead of running behind an impossible dream—a mirage in the desert—if both men and women could be satisfied with the person Allah has Himself brought into their lives, it would do their homes a lot of good. A home or society will find it very difficult to progress if women are not given their due respect.

Saugat, Bhadra 1931

The Literary Endeavours of Muslim Women

A woman has to work so extensively at home that there is little scope left for her to work outside. Time, too, is short. But one must admit that God has vested nature with the specialities, wonders, treasures and indeed whatever the world has to offer. The closer one is to nature, the greater one's share of joy. Like fruits and flowers, the natural gifts of the creator, maybe literature too is God's gift to mankind. Although one can't quote an ideologue to support this claim, it seems very true. Women should also have the courage to accept such a deep-rooted truth. Looking around, one feels that women are not satisfied with simply their physical needs being met. They need food for thought as well. It is not a new trend; the desire was always there in women's minds—hence even in the far off countryside, in huts surrounded by dark shades, and in spite of unbearable purdah restrictions, the village maid hums sweet poems and songs:

> Her hair falls like a waterfall, champa decks her bun,
> Her glowing face touched by the full moon's rays.
> Sweets and scents spread on her plate, paan, *gua* and sandalpaste,
> For whom, girl, this magic trap she lays?

Women enjoy songs like these during the free afternoon hours. They also waft out of the bustling courtyard of a noisy house of ceremony. For example:

> If you thought a thousand gifts could win a heart,
> The one who's stayed aloof will always stay apart.

> Better to be fed on brooms and sticks
> Than feed from the co-wife's plate.

Women living in villages often recite rhymes like these. Most of these seem to be composed by the singer. The songs seem to bear witness to years of experience, pain and sorrow. Aren't these proofs of the fact that cutting across cultures, time and class, one needs food for thought and tries satisfying one's hunger? Food for the mind is also called literature. Newspapers came into being with a view to publicize and disseminate news to all. Therefore literature is not limited to a particular class or time. A thirst for knowledge causes it to spread among people, just as water flows everywhere.

Even when a part of an unnecessary burden is shed, childcare and running the household like clockwork remain the woman's heaviest responsibilities. If one is a little more efficient and a little less lazy, even after completing one's duties one might find time enough for pursuing literature. Many educated women also say that it is difficult to find time to study. If there really is no time, how do these women find time to embroider ridiculous figures of dogs and cats on thick cloth or weave carpets? Sewing is a very necessary skill, but a lot of time gets wasted on unimportant things as well. I do not understand why they do not realize that it pays more to write or read a good book than do piles of unimportant housework. Men have more opportunities. A mother, when she teaches her daughter to do the chores, should also teach her not to waste her spare time gossiping, but to spend it trying to understand what literature is all about. It is not necessary that by doing this every girl will turn into a veritable Goddess of Learning, but at least this will ensure that no one dries up prematurely because of a lack of opportunity. Even if one in a thousand girls attains the beauty of a creative and enlightened mind, it will be a matter of national pride.

Much more can be expected of women writers. An educated woman is a national treasure, as a mother is the child's first and best teacher. As far as character traits go, men and women represent two sides of it. A man can give his child food, clothing and bookish knowledge, while a woman can bestow her affection, care, love and for that matter, by sacrificing herself, can arouse and keep the finer perceptions of a child's mind alive. A man's disposition is action-oriented; while women, mainly, tend to be emotional. It is obvious that those who are used to studying human emotions so closely will understand human experiences of joy and sorrow far more easily and portray them most wonderfully. Women who are known for their ability to understand and respect other peoples' feelings are, nevertheless, subjected to untold mental trials and tribulations. Therefore, it is a woman's words of consolation that people want to hear in times of distress.

Saugat Women's Issue, Bhadra 1928

The Labourer

'Are you listening—will you wash my shirt?' Saying this a young man of about twenty-seven or twenty-eight came and stood in front of the kitchen. Inside the room a young woman of twenty-two or twenty-three was cooking. She washed her hands, came out of the kitchen and said, 'But I washed your shirt only yesterday! Do you need it washed again today? And I put the vegetables to cook on the stove only a little while ago, the rice and dal are done. If I leave it now it will burn. I mended an old shirt of yours and kept it inside the trunk, why don't you wear that? I will wash this one in the evening.'

The young man tweaked his wife's nose mischievously and said, 'Quickly cook the rice, it is 9:30 already. I won't be back home tonight. Can't say when I'll return tomorrow, either.' The wife laughed and moved away. The young man took his clothes and went to have a bath.

This young couple were quite well off in the past, but had to give up their earlier zamindari way of life. The young man's name was Taher Hussain. He had lost his mother as a child. As a result of which his father lost interest in material concerns. Taking advantage of his state, his employees looted him completely and left him penniless. The father educated the son till he took his Matriculation examination, with a lot of difficulty and at the age of twenty-one married him to a local gentleman's daughter. That was six years ago.

The father had passed away in the meantime. He saw the birth of a grandson before going. Now two more children were born to the couple. His father-in-law helped Taher Hussain get a guard's job in the Railways for a salary of Rs.30. The money would have been sufficient for a poor family, but this one was not a small one. There were six people in all—Taher himself, his wife, their three children aged five, three and six months, and an errand boy of about thirteen. They got a place to stay in the station quarters. The servant drew a salary of Rs.2 per month and had to be given food and clothing. Besides they needed money to support themselves too. The elder son was almost always ill. The daughter and the six-month-old baby were quite healthy. Although neither the beauty of Rahima, Taher's wife, nor her dress was much to write home about, she could still be called charming. She was not as glamorous as the heroine in a novel—not too ugly either. She was like any ordinary gentleman's daughter would be. She had soft skin and a lovely dark complexion, an oval face, two big black eyes and a proportionately built tall figure, all very fetching. At the time of marriage, though the father-in-law was unable to give much to the daughter-in-law, he had given bangles, earrings and one or two small pieces of jewellery. The pair of bangles had to be sold at the time of the old man's own sickness, but the earrings always remained on her ears. She wore glass bangles on her arms. In spite of a lack of ostentatious clothes or jewellery, she looked very pretty. The playful, self-absorbed look forever present on her face was enchanting and inspired respect. The daughter, like her mother, was dark but comely. However, the two sons, like their father, were fair complexioned and handsome.

The children had a meal of rice and dal. Rahima quickly returned to the room and brought out the rice and curries. She rolled two paans. Her husband had a bath before sitting down to eat. The food was very simple: rice, dal, tamarind chutney, and mourola fish with potatoes. But the touch of Rahima's hands made them taste like honey. At least that's what her husband's sentiments must have been.

Two days later, as evening approached, Rahima quickly finished her housework, and fed the children. Holding the baby to her breast, she began to read a book. She had retained the habit of reading. She knew Bengali and Urdu fairly well. Her husband never stopped her from enjoying the little free time she had after the day's hard work. In fact, he would take great pains to save a couple of rupees from the monthly expenses and buy her a magazine or a novel or two. Hence Rahima's literary pursuits continued. Secretly, she wrote a little too.

Even as she read, her ears were alert, waiting to catch the sound of her husband's return. Suddenly she could hear her husband call in a hoarse voice, 'Romu!' Rahima ran to open the door. As soon as her gaze fell on the husband's pale and worried face, she reeled back in fear. How terribly the handsome youth had changed in two days! He looked as though he was guilty of murder, and seemed old beyond his age. Taher put his hands on Rahima's shoulder and said, 'Let's go in, Romu.' Inside the room, Rahima silently began to fan him. Both were silent. A little later, Taher said in a totally dejected voice, 'Hard times are ahead, Rahima. The way the railway strikes are carrying on, my job may be on the line. How will five people survive? A lone dog might manage to survive, but who will feed five? Moreover, the Congress leaders and volunteers have started insulting us everywhere. Tell me, what should I do? They say, if I leave the job, they will give me a job in a local company paying Rs.60 a month. But I know all about that. There's no telling how many more people they have won over in this way. The Hindus are merrily working. It's we who seem to be at fault. They cite the Swadeshi movement at every step! It seems we do nothing at all for the country. Our older boy is ill. The other day Nilmani the doctor asked me to pay for the medicine. How much do you have?' Rahima said in a low voice, 'How long can Rs.30 last? The boy is continuously ill. Apart from the doctor we owe the grocery shop and the milk woman – Rs.8 to 10 in total. I have saved Rs.20 with great difficulty.' Drawing a deep breath, Taher said, 'Last year during our little boy's dysentery and my pneumonia, I sold the country house for Rs.500, out of which Rs.200 to 300 were spent on the treatment itself. Whatever was left was spent because I had to take four months of unpaid leave. Having served for four years, this is what I am left with. We don't even have a place to stay.' That night neither husband nor wife could eat anything.

The next day as soon as Taher woke up, a volunteer came to take him to the Congress office. Babu Bishwa-Vijay Mitra, Maulvi Abu Naser Saheb and other well-known workers were there. A discussion was on. As soon as he saw Taher, Mitra Saheb spoke up, 'Hey! So you have come to see us at last. We were talking about you, brother. Now see, you are a sensible boy. And yet you don't seem to listen to anything I tell you. I am giving you fifteen days' time. If you do not leave your job by then, we will stop the washer man, barber and even the grocery storekeeper from having any business with you.'

Taher went pale. He said, 'If you say so, I can somehow manage to donate one or two rupees to the Congress Fund. If I leave my job what will the five of us eat?'

Mockingly Mr. Mitra said, 'The nation wants lives, not money. Money helps to a certain extent, of course.' Taher courageously asked, 'What will be gained by taking my life? Why don't you ask Naresh Mitra to leave his job?' Mr. Mitra's face lost its brightness. Naresh was his nephew. He said arrogantly, 'Go away, you cheeky boy, his case will be dealt with when we call him. You mind your own business.'

Out on the road Taher saw a group of volunteers carrying the flag, and singing the national song. Seeing him, one of them said in a hushed voice, 'Traitor! Anti-Swadeshi!' The roots of Taher's ears and fair cheeks turned red with shame. He came home and wrote a resignation letter.

The Station Master said, 'Look, you haven't thought this out properly. You simply danced to their tune. Given the way you are leaving us in the lurch, you will have difficulty getting a government job after this.' Taher left without saying anything.

Back home, Rahima said anxiously, 'The older boy has a high fever. The doctor will have to be called in the evening. We need a bottle of quinine, two pomegranates and barley for him.' Taher said in a broken voice, 'I left my job.' Rahima stared at him vacantly.

The next day a uniformed messenger came and hung a notice—'Vacate the house in fifteen days.' The elder son's illness got worse. The Rs.20 Rahima had was spent repaying the loans of the grocer and the doctor. Now they did not know where to get any more money to pay for the food and medicines. Rahima's pair of earrings and worn out gold-plated conch shell bangles, and their daughter's pair of silver anklets had to be sold. Selling things do not get you their actual value, how much can one make, after all, by selling old jewellery? The jewellery fetched only Rs.16, all of which was spent on food and treatment.

Today was the fifteenth night since the boy was taken ill. The state of the ailing boy's health was like the last bright flicker of a dying lamp. For the past fifteen days Rahima gave one meal a day to her husband and son. The last two days they only drank the rice water. Today even that was finished. There was a fistful of rice that she fried and fed her daughter twice a day. Today even Taher was fasting. The ailing boy, who was half-dead, had only barley for a meal. Rahima's father had just passed away. Taher had written to her brother for help and his reply was, 'You know our state. This year the crops failed. I was unable to feed my wife and son, so I sent them to my in-laws'. Therefore bringing my sister here, I don't think, will be a good idea.'

It was the second hour of the night. Fatigued by starvation, Rahima had fallen asleep, next to her son. The baby, finding no succour from his mother's breast, sucked his thumbs. He had not been able to feed for three days. The lamplight falling on his curly hair and puffy pink cheeks made him look like an angel.

Taher gazed unblinkingly at the vast unlimited star-studded sky. It was a dark night. The stars and the blue sky were so beautiful! What happened to people after death? he thought. After ages he remembered his lost mother. In the midst of sorrow and poverty, his mind brimmed over with emotion at the thought. He began to cry quietly. Gradually a pale yellow moon rose in the sky. In the eastern sky, the polestar began twinkling.

All of a sudden the ailing boy called, 'Baba, water'. Taher got up and put a little water in his mouth. The tiny child said, 'Baba, sing that lovely song—the one which has the name of Hazrat in it!' Taher began to sing the ghazal. 'Come, Habib my beloved, the light of God's eyes, give us peace and comfort.' Taher's doleful voice and the silent language of the night became one in solemnity and sorrow. When the song finished he saw that the tender life of the child had ebbed away while listening to the holy name of Rasul.

The tears in his eyes dried up. Covering the dead body with a white cloth he returned to sit down at the same spot. He did not disturb anyone's peace. What he would eat tomorrow, where he would live—nothing was known. In this huge wide world, they did not even have a place to stay. His half-starving ailing son had found peace in the lap of the Almighty. Tomorrow his small baby might die of starvation. The girl, not getting any rice from her mother, would look up at her—what answer would she give? If he had hung on to his ancestral land and laboured in the fields, then they would not have been in such a bad state. The rice and vegetables grown in the fields would have sufficed for them. The fascination for the respectability of a white collar job had ruined him. If he had not felt ashamed to farm his land, he would not be in such a terrible state now.

A well-known courtesan from Calcutta was visiting a neighbouring zamindar's house on the occasion of his son's wedding. For three nights of song and dance she charged Rs 10,000. Taher's wide eyes blazed. He whispered, 'There is no food in my house, my son dies of starvation—and this man, is spending so much money just for the sake of entertainment! Allah, is this what you call justice? Am I to understand that you too are cruel, unjust and whimsical like human beings? Have you no kindness or sympathy? Are you there only to rain painful curses on the heads of human beings?' The next moment he fell on the ground and in a pleading voice cried, 'Of course, you are present, O Allah? In a mother's love, a father's compassion, children's affection, courtesy and sympathy of neighbours, in the coolness of water, in the worthiness of life—you are present everywhere. How can I be so impertinent as to dare deny your existence?'

The next day the earth was lit by the sunrays. The child's burial was complete by nine. After burying his son, Taher returned home with sunken eyes and dishevelled hair. His eyes were dry, and his body fatigued due to starvation. There were no tears in Rahima's eyes. She lay on the ground, as if in a swoon. The baby boy too was about to faint because of hunger.

At this time the government messenger arrived and said, 'Saheb! Go elsewhere, the new babu has come.' A drizzle had begun. A few clothes and household utensils had already been sold. Rahima's last resource, the nose ring and earrings were sold off. They went out in the rain, headed for Rahima's paternal home. Nobody had a clue as to how they would be spending their days in that house without food, replete with poverty. They reached their destination in the evening to find that straws were missing from the thatched roof and rainwater had flooded the room. Rahima's brother had left for his parents-in-law's place that morning. A young servant was left to guard the house. Rahima sat down, tired. The boy went home and got some rice to feed the girl.

In the evening the party workers gathered at a local leader's house. One of them, raising a cup of tea to his mouth said, 'Hey, did you know that Taher Chacha ran away?' Another, banging loudly on the table, said, 'Is that so? We had to take great pains to tame him.' A new worker said, 'His elder son died this morning. Only Allah knows what the poor chap will eat. Couldn't we give something from the Congress Fund?'

Mr. Mitra wagged a finger and said, 'Don't try to act smart. He had sufficient land in the country, just liked to lick the boots of the white-skinned sahibs. How can we give him any money? So many have left their jobs that we do not have enough to pay them even Rs.2 each.'

Cup after cup of tea was drunk and numerous cigarettes were smoked at the office. The labourer's blood went up in smoke.

Saugat, Ashwin 1927

Letters[9]

Azizpur
22/1/25

My Beloved!

You remembered me after two days! Not bad, I had thought may be—no, I am not going to tell you, it will make you angry.

Today Chhoto Mama gave me a torn exercise book. I was so happy to get it. I wrote my first ever piece in it on 22 Jaishtha 1327. It felt like getting a call from a long-forgotten friend. The jottings [I had made] seemed so sweet. Perhaps these have no literary merit. But seeing these I remember the games, laughter and tears I experienced as a twelve-year-old. A human being can go through tremendous changes overnight. I must acknowledge Chhoto Mama's role in preserving the exercise book. Else it would have turned to dust. I am indeed very disorderly. I don't think there's another one so peculiar as me in this world. It's just that I look like a human being, otherwise I am not much different from an animal. It is not that I am proud of this, but what to do? How will I account for this to my creator? I will say, 'I have remained exactly the way you made me, I have not had the good fortune of becoming anything else.' That will be really wonderful, won't it?

Hope you are keeping well. Since you don't write, I don't have the right to know anything I assume? Anyway, let it be, your staying well is more than enough for me. What could one do, if you didn't write? Hoping you are fine-

Yours,
Razia.

Azizpur
26/3/25
10 o'clock

My Beloved!

I have received your letter of the 23rd today. Since the morning, in spite of all efforts, I have been unable to take in anything of what I read. Seeing your letter, I thought perhaps now something would begin to register at last. But just as I am—so is my reward. My heart belongs so completely to you that it is too preoccupied to think about anything else.

Do I ever deny that I am bad? I am bad, what I write is bad, my mind is not very happy. Everything about me is bad. Can one write letters to such a person? All this time you didn't understand this—so you wrote. Now have you suddenly become intelligent? That too after so long! You have been stupid for more than just a day or two. This is not a wrong statement, is it? Compared to one's life, eight-nine months or eight-nine years is not much. In fact, eight-nine years is less than five minutes on such a scale. Perhaps our acquaintance of a few days—no, I won't write anymore, I don't want to hurt you. What I have written is enough. Please, do not be angry. Why did you write what you did?—Don't I feel hurt too?

I do not want to be a straightforward person like you. You do not have the right to deny me my due. Do not I have the right to receive news of your welfare? If you say I 'don't', I would have nothing more to say. But to say that you will have to, at least, write me a letter. Just say it once. I will see what I can do.

Yours,
Razia.

Shuagazi
1/4/30

I have got your letter and understood it well. We have a problem here, though. Your child is ill. He has a fever every night. Please pray for Allah's blessings.

The Hindus say the world is false, transient, an illusion and that this life is temporal and the next is the real truth. What do you say? I think Islam does not support all this. If this was true, one wouldn't have the scope of doing good deeds and collecting sustenance for the world in general and for one's future—sustenance that would see one through on the Day of Judgment. The blessed memory of the pious, the Hadith's eternal message, the stream of nectar from the Koran, give this world and its people their life and strength. Man could gain proximity to Allah in this mortal world itself, by working towards it. This world, therefore, cannot be false.

I really want to see you. But I do know that only my wishing it is not good enough to see it fulfilled.

Yours,
Razia.

P 304
P.O. Circus
15/6/32

I received your letter long ago. Why haven't you written since…

Yesterday I sent the spirit, kerosene, a stove's needle, soap, biscuits and the Asharh issue of *Bharatbarsha*—all that you had asked for. You must have received them. Boro Bhai Sahib wrote that he sent Rs.15 to you. Let me know if you have received it, else I will send it. He sent me Rs.10 at the beginning of April to buy Mafiz's food etc. He didn't send anything after that, but has written to say that he will soon. It seems Sharifa has reached Muradnagar with Bajlu from the Qazi's house. Boro Bhai Sahib had her fetched from there to stay with Ma. That's a good thing. I suggested that she be married off. She is quite incorrigible. At the moment I do not need anyone else. If I do so later, we will think about it then.

Here Amma and Bacchu have upset stomachs. Saleha, Rabu and others are well, thank God. At home Ma is okay. Boro Bhai Sahib, has written to say he cannot see very well since he had fever. I am all right now, but the weakness does not seem to go away. I'm still having the medicines. I feel scared for the future. Staying alive doesn't appear to be very attractive. This world, which is God's creation, is so beautiful! But jealousy and hatred—the black shadow of man's dirty mind—is so ugly. I am tired of having to see these things at all times. I wish I could run away.

I will most probably not go to meet you. I do not feel like pleading with people for what is my God-given right.

Grandfather is yet to arrive. Maybe he will, in a month or two, with his daughter-in-law. Kalu, too, might come towards the end of the month. This house is almost complete. The roof of the fourth floor will be ready day after tomorrow. The work on the veranda too will start soon.

Hope you are keeping well. Has your cold gone? Write and tell me if there is anything you need. *Bichitra* hasn't been published yet. I will send it later. You have never written whether you got the two tablecloths I sent you earlier. I am stitching two more. Should I send them? Do you need pillowcases? Do try to write and tell me how you are keeping at all times.

It seems they do not allow more than twelve mangoes at your place. Yesterday quite a few were sent back.

Razia
Janab Moulvi Ashrafuddin Ahmad
Chowdhury Saheb
"A" Class Prisoner.

P 304
P.O. Circus
8/3/33

I have not received any letters from you in the last two weeks. Hope you are well. My throat ache has healed, but now Amma and Binu have aching throats and Binu's tonsils are badly inflamed too. My coughing is a little better. The baby is suffering from a small boil on its cheek. Boro Baba [Grandpa] is the same as before. I have received Boro Bhai Sahib's letter the day before. Everyone is reasonably well at home. He has written to say he will be coming to take us home soon. Who knows when that will happen. Amma tells me not to go before you are here. She tells me the children will have a difficult time. I will decide when Boro Bhai Sahib comes. At the moment I have not decided whether to go or not.

I sent *Saugat* to you day before yesterday. The stories published there are rubbish. A lot of trash is written nowadays—it's the new writers' shortcut to fame. This is what art has come to. In the beginning the disrespect shown to women in such pieces would anger me. Now I think these writers are less than human. It is not that there aren't a few ignorant and irresponsible individuals among women. But is it necessary to give them a permanent place in literature?

Sharifa was married for the fifth time on Friday, to a kebabwala. Anyway the trouble is over now. Let's hope she manages to stick it out. I have better things to do than keep such a maid. Seeing her antics I was reminded of Kamal in *Shesh Prashna.*[10] Do too much education and illiteracy yield the same result? I read in the papers today that a university founded last January in America will offer courses on 'The purpose of marriage and purity', 'The tradition of marriage in the eyes of faith', etc. whereas in this country novels on themes like 'Greater than Marriage' are being written. In fact, people in those cultures are fed up with such things [i.e. licentiousness], the reason why old ideals now appear new in their eyes. In this country there's room for social revolution yet. The process will end only when it has reached an extreme point. That's when we will rediscover the old morality and endorse them again, shan't we? Do not laugh at my limited intelligence.

I am told the eggs broke last time, while putting them down. You must have received ghee, toothpaste, and the English book. You made me read the first poem in it while we were in Azizpur. I have given it to Saleha to read, she's always up to mischief.

Reply soon. What if I too were silent, like you? Can I be free when you are imprisoned? My three bodyguards have their weapons drawn at all times. I am subjected to all sorts of beatings—boxing, slapping, biting. Now even the baby has learnt to hit and pull one's hair. It is as if they want to eat me up, if I make a slight mistake. No surprise there, given their wide-eyed father is so quiet! I had written to Boro Bhai Sahib for money, did he send it?

Razia.

To Ashrafuddin Ahmad Chowdhury Saheb

"A" Class Prisoner

P 304
P.O. Circus

Received your letter dated 18th. It is easy to preach but difficult to practise. Even if unimportant details hurt me I easily brush them off. But Allah has begun testing me in another way, which is neither easy to bear nor to speak of.

An anonymous letter arrived about ten to fifteen days back. Baba collected it from the postman. The writer's main point is that since I write poetry, have literary and musical interests, I am capable of doing maximum mischief. Never in so many years of my life did I imagine that such awful things would be said about me in foul language. I threw the letter away, having read just a little bit. Baba and Amma have read the letter, which is now with them. I feel like laughing, and crying as well. Given the vastness of the unlimited storehouse of knowledge, I have barely managed to recognize the alphabet. Shattered as I am, in spirit and mind, I have been living all by myself, far away from the wide world. Is this what I, a mother of four, deserved in the time of crisis? A question to Allah arises from my heart, 'Why did such a terrible opinion even come into the mind of someone created by you?' Am I to be ridiculed by the Almighty God as well? Well—just like I had no control over my being born, I have no control over my fate either. He is making the world look black in my eyes. But I will try to be positive and shining—bless me. Even a piece of coal glows when burnt in fire. I am, after all, only a human being.

I had thought I wouldn't tell you about all this, so as to not make you anxious. But as you know I am unable to hide my joys and sorrows from you. And you tell me to write more!

Doubtless, dreams are more beautiful than reality. But I am scared that the people who get your … in these ugly present times may not be around in the beautiful future. Two have already gone. Salahuddin, Ala, and your most important treasure 'Ma'—God's greatest gift to human beings—I don't suppose she will live for very long. And what's the use of her living anyway? You think it's a weak mind babbling away, but it is not so. Ma herself thinks this way, and says so too. Maybe some day you will realize the truth in this.

Yesterday I sent a cigar. Why did you start smoking this rubbish after such a long time? I simply can't tolerate this. I have got the soap, but who took the watch? If the tablecloth disappears, I will call you the thief. Losing things is an old habit of yours and I am no better. I keep losing so many things. If you are so scared of losing things, give me back those two, and I will send two new ones.

I have received Boro Bhai Sahib's letter. He is forever troubled by minor illnesses. Ma is the same as before. You think my daughters have got their mischievous streak from me? I have heard from Amma that I wasn't so naughty as a child. On the contrary, I have heard about your fine reputation from Ma!

When you were at home, I rarely allowed the maids to do your work. Now what is it that I do once in seven days for which you are going to scold me? Your daughters really make me struggle. They have become so demanding. Day and night I have to keep them happy. Rabu has an infection in her tummy. They went to Dumdum yesterday. I have written so many things, don't get angry. Do reply. Boro Bhai Sahib has sent me Rs.15.

Razia

Notes

1 Mohammad Mafuzzulla, *Kabi o Katha Shilpi Razia Khatun Chowdhurani* (Dhaka: *Dainik Ittefak*, 9 Phalgun 1383).

2 A detailed description of Ashrafuddin Ahmad Chowdhury's role in pre-Partition politics may be found in Abul Mansur Ahmed's *Amar Dekha Rajnitir 50 Bochhor,* 3 vols (Dhaka: Srijan Prakashani, 1988-89) and in Abul Hayat's *Mussalmans of Bengal* (Calcutta: Jahed Ali, 1966). His daughter Rabeya Khatun Chowdhuri informs us that he was a leader of the Nizam-e-Islam Party in the Pakistan days, and became a minister as well.

3 '*Bangiyo Muslim Mohilagoner Shikshar Dhara*', *Razia Khatun Chowdhuranir Rachana Sankalan,* ed. Abdul Quddus (Comilla: Rabeya Khatun Chowdhury, 1982), p 4.

[4] The poem '*Chasha*' was published in Journal *Nauroz* in Asharh 1338. For her husband's *Naya Bangla* paper, Razia Khatun Chowdhurani had even written a message:

> Every heart must be touched
> With the fire of Truth.
> Death's shadow will recede,
> Life will yield its fruit

[5] On the poetry collection *Upahar* Abdul Quddus has written: 'The collection was published before her marriage from Dumdum, Calcutta, on 5 Magh 1924. Of the five poems, the first two were written on 19 September 1924 and the last in June 1919.' (Introduction, *Razia Khatun Chowdhuranir Rachana Sankalan.*). However, Rabeya Khatun has written in the same *Rachana Sankalan* that her mother was married in May 1923 (p. b). Mohammad Mahfuzzullah wrote that *Pather Kahini* was published by Mohammadi Book Agency, Calcutta, by Mohammad Khairun Alam Khan (*Dainik Ittefak*). The book is now impossible to procure, hence no date of publication is given.

[6] *Razia Khatun Chowdhuranir Rachana Sankalan.*

[7] An account of Lila Nag's (Ray after marriage) contribution in the field of women's education can be found in the history of Deepali Sangha, established by Nag. Between 1920 and 1928 the members of this organization established four girls' schools in Dhaka. Around 1924 the first school, known today as Kamrunnesa Girls School, was founded, followed by Bartaman Bangla Bazar Girls' School, Nari Shiksha Mandir, currently Shere Bangla School, and Purana Paltan Girls' School. For more on the subject one may consult Sonia Nishat Amin's *The World of Muslim Women in Colonial Bengal* 1876-1939 (Cologne: E.J.Brill, 1996): pp. 161-68.

[8] In 1936, under the chairmanship of A. K. Fazlul Haque, the Comilla District Farmers' Conference was organized. This was its inaugural song.

[9] Most of the un-addressed letters were written by Razia Khatun to her husband in prison. We were unable to get additional information on the minor domestic matters taken up in the letters.

[10] Reference to the novel *Shesh Prashna* by Saratchandra Chattopadhyay.

10

Shamsunnahar Mahmud (1908-1964): Biographer and Leader of the Women's Movement

Translated by Nandini Guha

Shamsunnahar Mahmud was born in Noakhali district of undivided Bengal in 1908, at a time when the male members of her family had been given the opportunity to educate themselves. Her paternal grandfather and his brothers were highly educated, which in those days meant they were graduates. Hence, the wife of Shamsunnahar's great grandfather, Munshi Tamijuddin, was awarded the title of *Ratnagarbha* (Mother of Gems) by the British government and also given a gold medal. Yet there is no knowing if any of the women on her father's side was educated.

It is interesting, though, that the Dacca Mussalman Suhrid Sammelani (Dacca Muslim Friends Society) was founded under the leadership of Shamsunnahar's maternal grandfather, Abdul Aziz, paternal grandfather, Fazlul Karim and some others in 1883, to educate the women in the zenana. Thanks to the cooperation of the Sammelani's enthusiastic members, girls sitting at home could study school texts, clear examinations and get promoted to higher classes. In this way Shamsunnahar's maternal grandmother studied up to Class Five. Her daughters too knew Bengali and Urdu well. It appears Shamsunnahar was the first girl in her family to be admitted in a school.

Incidentally, after the death of her husband, Nurullah Chowdhury, Shamsunnahar's mother, Ayesha Khatun, came back to live in her father's house at Chittagong with her children, six-month-old Shamsunnahar and three-year-old Habibullah Bahar. Shamsunnahar's grandfather, Khan Bahadur Abdul Aziz, was the Divisional School Inspector of Chittagong. After she passed the sixth standard in the Khastagir School of Chittagong, Shamsunnahar was not allowed to go to school, the reason being that the founder of the Dacca Mussalman Suhrid Sammelani, Abdul Aziz, however enthusiastic he was about female education, was not against the purdah system.

Young Shamsunnahar nursed a grudge for having to drop out of school. In the book *Nazrulke Jemon Dekhechhi* (As I Saw Nazrul) she wrote that at nine she was asked to leave school. 'Since then I sat at home, casually studying my books. Year after year passed. I saw my classmates—Hindu, Brahmo and Christian girls—move around freely, get promoted from one class to the next, go on to Bethune College or Diocessan College in Calcutta. Once in a while they wrote letters, containing glimpses of a new world. The Baidya girl next door, a senior in school, Jyotirmoyee Chowdhury, whom I called Didi [later the author of *Bilet Deshta Matir* (England, A Country on This Very Earth) and other books] studied in Chittagong,[1] Calcutta and Rangoon, before going to England for higher studies. I felt that we were creatures of the dark while they were citizens of a lighted world. The rebel in me groaned inside, for days together.'[2]

Unable to manage this rebellious granddaughter, her grandfather ultimately engaged an elderly Hindu teacher. What followed was a novel way of imparting education. A curtain was hung from the top, dividing the study table. The student and the teacher sat on either side. The student listened to what the teacher read out. The teacher set her tasks. The student, after completing them, pushed the copy across to the other side of the curtain. Despite the constraints, Shamsunnahar passed her Matriculation Examination and was placed in the first division. By that time, her book, *Punyamoyee*, about the lives of virtuous women, was already written.[3] After she had passed the examination, she went back to a life of unending confinement.

In 1926, Kazi Nazrul Islam visited their home from Calcutta with her elder brother Habibullah Bahar. On that occasion she did not get to meet him. She only heard him read and sing his poetry of protest from the inner chambers. Back in Calcutta, Nazrul wrote to

Shamsunnahar, 'The girls in our country are very unfortunate. I have seen many girls born with enormous talent, but their potential dried up under demands of society. They are imprisoned by domestic necessities. [It's a shame that] those who are so sought after by the wide world outside should be enclosed in rooms measuring twelve feet by eight feet. External attempts to tear those walls down are staved off, repeatedly. Unless the blows are dealt from within, I don't suppose the walls would give way. Therefore, I ask women to rebel. They should hold on to the doors from within and keep saying, "We are prisoners." Where is that daredevil woman who can open that door? She is the one that time demands.'[4]

At that time Shamsunnahar had begun her campaign for the higher education of women. It was as if Kazi Nazrul had added fuel to the flames of her rebellion. Her grandfather, Khan Bahadur Abdul Aziz, had passed away. Her mother and grandmother found a match for her in the educated and magnanimous Dr. Wahiduddin Mahmud, and assumed that Shamsunnahar's long-cherished desire for higher education would be fulfilled. For her the marriage opened the doors to higher education and ended her days of confinement. There was no looking back, only a steady climb up the ladder.

In 1932 Rokeya Sakhawat Hossain organized a function in Sakhawat Memorial Girls' High School to felicitate Shamsunnahar on her passing the BA exam.[5] Around this time Shamsunnahar became Rokeya's favourite protégé—a girl who could overcome all odds to receive higher education, and dedicate her life to the cause of women's liberation. Shamsunnahar did not fail Rokeya. She began her career at the Anjuman-e-Khawatin-e-Islam, established by Rokeya, and later joined the Nikhil Bharat Mahila Sammelan (All India Women's Association).

In 1935, when the British government passed the Government of India Act, Indian women did not have the right to vote. On behalf of Nikhil Bharat Mahila Sammelan, Shamsunnahar began agitating for women's enfranchisement. Finally, a law was passed, sanctioning Indian women's right to vote. In 1939, when Lady Brabourne College was established, Shamsunnahar was appointed head of the Bengali department, on condition that she would have to pass the MA examinations in three years. Ten years after she passed BA in 1942, Shamsunnahar received her MA.

In 1933, under the joint editorship of brother and sister, Habibullah Bahar and Shamsunnahar, the literary journal *Bulbul* was published from Calcutta. Regarding the anti-communal role of the journal *Bulbul*, Rabindranath Tagore had written, 'When winds of civil strife and animosity among brothers have poisoned the air of the country, in these extremely dangerous times if somewhere the words of protest can be voiced, I consider that to be an auspicious sign . . . Your journal expresses the agony that is spreading in this foolish and insensate country, after being hit by this unfortunate and cruel blow.'[6]

For many years, Habibullah Bahar and Shamsunnahar were partners in their literary endeavours. It is rare to find a lifelong friendship in work and writing between a brother and sister. Nazrul, in his dedication to the book of poetry entitled *Sindhu Hindol* (The Undulating Sea) had written:

> Who is the better of the two of you—
> 'Bahar' brings roses to the garden,
> 'Nahar' brings light.[7]

In the 1930s Shamsunnahar's work was creating innumerable waves. She joined many women's organizations and became active in the women's movement in undivided India. She was a tireless worker for the All India Women's Conference, National Council for Women in India, Bengal Women's Education League, Bengal Provincial Council of Women and other women's organizations and she got the opportunity to exchange views and discuss ideas with well-known women from India and abroad. In 1944, in recognition of her achievements in the fields of education and social welfare, the British government honoured her with the title of MBE. In 1945, she was suddenly taken ill and had to leave her post at Lady Brabourne College.

After the Partition of India, when Shamsunnahar returned to Dhaka, she went back to her work. She joined the government-run women's organization, APWA (All Pakistan Women's Association). As a representative of the Pakistan government she attended many seminars and conferences abroad. Ultimately, the guiding principle of her life was to get women involved in the work of moulding the new nation of Pakistan. She seemed to believe that only through government legislation in social development schemes could women's development be brought about. As a result in 1952, when the Bengali nationalists' agitation for the promulgation of Bengali in East Pakistan took the form of the Language movement and turned into a resolute battle against West Pakistan's domination over East Pakistan, Shamsunnahar turned her back on it. However, on the question of women's rights, her stand remained irrevocable and she was always extremely vocal. In the drawing up of Muslim Family Law, in 1961, her role was pioneering. She was the president of the 'Begum Club' in Dhaka, from its inception till the end of her life. She died on 14 April 1964.

Her two sons were Mamoon Mahmud and Moinuddin Mahmud. In 1929, the birth of Mamoon Mahmud was celebrated by Nazrul, then in Chittagong:

> 'Crossing many seas and many a river wild,
> On these shores you arrived, little magic child.'

On 26 March 1971, this little magic child, aged forty-three, attained martyrdom in the hands of the Pakistani armed forces. He was then the DIG of police at Rajshahi. Since 1966 Mamoon Mahmud had opposed the Pakistan military government's undemocratic and cruel role. After killing him, the Pakistan government, almost as if in mockery, named two roads in Dhaka after Shamsunnahar Mahmud and Habibullah Bahar.[8] After Partition, Habibullah Bahar became East Pakistan's minister for health and self-government. In 1952, the news that students had been massacred on the main road, in broad daylight, left him distraught. On 6 April 1953, while delivering a speech on World Health Day, he suffered a heart attack and lost consciousness, living for another decade without regaining his health.

S.A.

Rokeya: A Biography
Author's Concluding Chapters

When I first thought of writing Rokeya's biography, she was still alive. I had the opportunity to interact extremely closely with this gracious lady for a few years. She would talk about many interesting incidents from her own life whenever she had time to talk to me. This way I got to know many hidden facts about her amazingly unique life and even more unusual character, things unknown to a third person.

Talking of how I got involved in the job of writing Rokeya's biography, the person I remember before anyone else is my mother. She was the first one to realize the necessity of writing the unique life story of this exceptional woman and of publishing it for the reading public. I took up the task because Mother had asked me. My mother, indeed, was also largely responsible for collecting most of the resource material. Even after Rokeya's death, Mother seemed to enjoy collecting information on her from all kinds of people, whenever she got a chance. Today she too, like Rokeya, has passed away. It is my misfortune that *Rokeya: A Biography,* a book that she had so cherished, did not see the light of the day during her lifetime. I will not compound my shortcomings by saying that my lack of time was the only reason causing the delay. If I had not procrastinated, maybe this small book would have been blessed by the touch of not only my mother's but also of Rokeya's hallowed feet. May these two noble women bless the humble fruit of my labours from the other world!

My work will be incomplete if I did not mention the names of people like Mr. Iskander Ghazhnavi, respected Qazi Abdul Wadud, Mrs. H. T. Hossain, Mrs. F. Rashid, Mr. Saber and others among those who contributed to Rokeya's biography. Finally, I must acknowledge that my elder brother took a huge responsibility towards seeing this book published. It would be hard to say when Rokeya's biography would finally be published, if he had not constantly encouraged and inspired me.

Last year Rokeya's biography was published serially in the monthly *Bulbul*. At that time many of our sisters read it with great eagerness; and, I have been told, experienced within themselves the awakening of a new life.

If each of those for whom this small book was written read it lovingly, I will be honoured.

Bulbul House, Calcutta
Shamsunnahar

Women's Movement in Muslim Bengal

Any discussion on the social life of Muslim women in Bengal will show that it has gone through amazing changes in the last twenty years. Twenty years ago, those who considered stepping out of the four walls of their homes a grievous sin, are today canvassing for their political rights and even travelling up to London for the purpose. Wherever you look in society, Muslim women are showing signs of a new restlessness and enthusiasm in all respects. We are living in an age of development—all around us society is changing by the day. The nature of the needs and desires of the women of this country is changing rapidly.

A few days ago, women had even applied for the recently announced Das-Ray Memorial Scholarship for training as pilots. Today they are earning repute in responsible government jobs, as High Court advocates and in many other fields. In schools and colleges there is no dearth of Muslim girl students. Muslim women are setting up and managing schools, founding societies and showing great competence in social work. There are many schools, homes and organizations for women, not only in Calcutta but outside it as well, driven, primarily, by the dedication and hard work of Muslim women.

Government reports show that as far as primary education is concerned, Muslim girls have progressed much more than Hindus.

The first woman who competed with men, cutting across race

and colour, to be elected Municipal Commissioner was a Muslim.

In this new era of awakening, I remember before all else the lady who initiated the Bengali Muslim Women's movement and was a pioneer of women's education: Mrs. Rokeya Sakhawat Hossain. We know that during British rule the first attempts to lead Muslim women out of the world of ignorance and superstition into the path of enlightenment were made towards the end of the nineteenth century. The emissary of light, Begum Rokeya, was born in 1880.

Talking about the history of women's movement in our country, one finds a few young men, who in spite of hindrances, worked silently, with heartfelt dedication, for the cause of Muslim women's development. As students they founded the organization Suhrid Sammelani in Dacca in 1882 and began propagating liberal ideas on women's education and emancipation through it. Like a university regulating the education of thousands of students in schools and colleges all over the country, they introduced education for girls in different parts of Bangladesh, within the zenana of different homes.[9]

However, the response from within came only the day the messenger of light, Rokeya, was born. Our achievements have not peaked yet, but the woman who kept this flame of enlightenment burning and ignited other lives with it, will surely receive our respectful salute the day when we shall be seen marching ahead victoriously.

Rokeya lit the auspicious lamp of education in intense darkness. She took upon herself the responsibility of shaping the future role of women in society, besides which she felt the need to improve the social life of Muslim women. In 1916 she established the Anjuman-e-Khawatin-e-Islam or Muslim women's organization, which became one of her missions for life. The history of this organization is linked in every way with the story of Rokeya's twenty-year-long working life. A few days before she passed away, I had told her that the events of her unique life needed to be put together. In reply she had said, 'If you go through the papers and documents of Anjuman, you will find many details of my work and life.'

During the long years of its existence, Anjuman-e-Khawatin provided funds to a number of widows, helped poor girls of marriageable age to get married to suitable grooms and sponsored the education of many needy girls. But it would not be just to mention only these small charities and social services undertaken by the organization. If one considers the history of Muslim women's gradual development over the last twenty years, it is evident how hugely indebted Muslim society is to this organization that worked away from the public glare for long.

Initially, when Rokeya went from door to door, trying to establish the organization, how often in the eyes of society she must have appeared contemptible and a butt of ridicule! At that time, it was difficult to imagine Muslim women leaving the confines of their homes to join meetings and voluntary organizations. For days together, she would go from house to house, pull the veils off the women's faces, and hold their hands as they stepped out of their homes, one by one.

When a woman living in confinement inspired by Rokeya's example got desperate to come out of her home, she might, at once, be reminded of her guardian's eyes, red with anger. On the day of a meeting, Rokeya advised her to step out of the house, pretending she was going to visit a close relative's house, and carry clothes appropriate for attending the meeting in a bundle. In these ways Rokeya spent year after year trying to help unfortunate women to break out of their fetters.

A single comment of hers illustrates the extent of censure and slander she had to endure in her solitary journey through darkness, and the many obstacles she had to overcome. When I became active in the organization, towards the end of Rokeya's life, I was slightly upset to hear adverse criticism from outside. But Rokeya smiled and said, 'If you want to do social service, you have to be sufficiently thick-skinned so that no attacks of censure—disgrace, indifference or insult—can injure you. You have to toughen yourself to such an extent that loud storms, thunder, lightning are repulsed and sent back by you.' This statement reveals the profound secret of her life. Throughout her life she was attacked from all directions. It was her indomitable desire to do good work for others that always protected her from such attacks.

In many cases, Rokeya had to explain the concept of organizations and societies before she could even start her work. Once, after much effort and persuasion, a woman from an educated Muslim family was made to attend a meeting of 'Anjuman'. The meeting was over in due time and the women who had attended it were ready to go home. At that point the newly invited lady confronted Rokeya, saying, 'You got me out of the house with the excuse that I had to attend a meeting, but I can't see any meeting!' With great difficulty, Rokeya was able to make her understand that the just concluded activity went under the name of a meeting.

Rokeya used to say, 'The walls of a room are so reddened with betel juice after each meeting that we need to have them whitewashed.' None of the assembled ladies, including the chairperson herself, felt it was necessary to sit quietly while the meeting was on. Today, twenty years later, it is difficult for us to imagine the kind of meetings Rokeya conducted in her time.

Gradually a small group grew around Rokeya. Slowly, very slowly, they understood what meetings and societies meant. They saw to what critical depths their condition had deteriorated; learnt to think of solutions. In a word, the fruit of their daily labour for over twenty years was that the ladies of Anjuman were able to open the eyes of hundreds of Muslim women.

Today Rokeya is no more. But it is a matter of good fortune that the flag that she had held aloft for so long is not rolling in the dust. All those who were awakened by her clarion call will now have to carry the victory flag that was in her hands with care and move on. They must now complete the task that Rokeya had left half-finished.

It seems as though the influence of the Anjuman-e-Khawatin Islam is spreading in society. Having worked jointly with all the powerful women's organizations in the country, in the last few years its effectiveness in social welfare work for women has been pervasive. The movements to secure educational, social and legal rights for women led by this organization have not been futile efforts. In fact, the national government has accepted these matters and attached due importance to its opinions.

This organization has, on its own and with other women's groups, been active in matters of women's right to reform the Indian administrative system. Towards the last half of 1935, a committee was appointed under the leadership of Sir Laurie Hammond, the former governor of Bihar and Orissa, to make a final decision on administrative reforms. The organization had meetings with the committee, campaigning for women's rights. In the Calcutta Council House, the organization's representatives deposed in front of the committee and argued over the political rights of Bengali women.

Keeping in view the need for women's economic independence, the organization has laid the foundations of a handicrafts outfit, which might, in the future, help formulate a solution to one of the major problems faced by women of this country.

The session of the International Women's Conference held in Calcutta will be inscribed permanently in the history of this country's women's movement. In the interests of women's welfare, women workers from Ireland, Great Britain, Belgium, Romania, Switzerland, China and many other countries of the world converged in the metropolitan city of Calcutta in February 1936. By fittingly participating in this conference, the Anjuman-e-Khawatin-e-Islam, Bangla or Nikhil Banga Muslim Mahila Samiti (All Bengal Muslim Women's Association) proved Muslim women's dedication to work.

It is not that Rokeya's followers did not have to overcome obstacles at every step, but the credit for winning this war must go only to the person who expended herself little by little for such a long time to bring about an awakening in the woman's psyche.

The End

In the history of Bengali women, 9 December 1932 was a day of mourning. Rokeya, our dearly beloved, our great pride, and our very honourable Rokeya, left for her heavenly abode on that day. One who with such unstoppable courage, single-minded dedication and strong resolve worked for so long towards one goal, had only a second to prepare to follow the notes played on the flute of an invisible commander, leaving us all behind. What a wonderful resemblance Rokeya's life has to the life of a soldier!

The sun's rays had barely brightened the Calcutta sky after piercing through the darkness, when the fateful evening of Rokeya's life came to a close. The city of Calcutta, like any other day, was getting ready to plunge into work with fresh energy. At that moment, suddenly a thunderbolt had struck a major hub of activity in Muslim Bengal.

It did not take long for the sad news to spread through the lanes and by-lanes of Calcutta. Before long the news of Rokeya's death spread to Howrah and all other adjoining areas, like a forest fire. Countless Hindu, Muslim and Christian women collected in the compound of Sakhawat Memorial School to take a last look at her.

Rokeya always stayed up late at night, attending to school-related work. The night before she died, she was immersed in her file of papers and letters. Who would have known that it was the last night of her life? At daybreak, when she rose from her bed, there was no indication at all of any physical or mental fatigue. The sun smiled in the eastern sky. Rokeya too looked peaceful and happy. She entered the bathroom to wash her face and hands. The messenger of death, it appears, was waiting for her, amidst the shadows. With an excruciating pain in her chest,

Rokeya came back to her bed and collapsed, writhing in terrible agony. She was not fated to suffer for very long. Within a few hours, her heart stopped beating. Thus she died, silently and quickly, leaving her lamenting near and dear ones behind. On a life so charmingly beautiful, admirably great and memorable in terms of achievement, Time brought down its fateful curtain in a flash. For about half a century or even more, the lamp that shone brightly was extinguished by a mere whiff of fate.

Rokeya's health must have been gradually breaking down from within for some time. But there was no way of knowing from the outside. Whenever I went to her, she greeted me with that ever-familiar, bright and pleasant smile. Only once in a while during a conversation I would learn that she was undergoing medical treatment. Almost six months prior to her death, she gave up eating rice, as the doctor had prescribed. When the doctor advised that a change of diet and complete rest were absolutely necessary, the patient would answer, 'How can I rest, I do not even have the time to die!'

Her words would arouse fear in my mother's mind. Mother would say that perhaps it was really time for Rokeya to retire, in a more final sense. My mother was very keen to collect the entire history of Rokeya's life. Whenever she got the opportunity, she wanted to hear every little story from Rokeya's past and would tell me, 'On you lies the responsibility of recording this mysterious life history in the form of a book.'

Once in a while, I was called by Rokeya to discuss various school or Anjuman-related matters—sometimes to write the report of the Anjuman, sometimes to tidy the school papers in their files and sometimes, when there was a shortage of teachers, to help with teaching. In between work, sometimes she would sit in a private corner, with just me for company. These were occasions to raise different issues. A few days before she died, she suddenly said, 'I shall be off soon!' I was startled out of my wits, and said, 'Where?' She replied, 'Am I supposed to kill myself carrying the burden of this profitless venture forever? Now it's my turn to take leave. A "shack" is being prepared for me. I will stay there incognito for the rest of my days.' She did not reveal more.

Later I came to know that a new house for her was being built in Ghatshila. I could not believe, however, that she could leave the work she had spent her whole life, youth, strength, and wealth on, before it achieved complete success. I said, hesitantly, 'What will happen to the school then?' She smiled and said, 'You all are there to look after the school. Give me leave now.' I said, 'Will you really be able to stay away from the school? Rest might feel like a curse to you!' She did not reply verbally. Instead she got up and took out a letter from the drawer and put it in my hand. Reading it, I found the letter was written by an old friend and a well-wisher of hers, a senior official of the Education Department. The letter discussed, among many other things, the state of the school, society's behaviour towards it and Rokeya's endurance and fortitude. In each and every line society was criticized while sympathy and respect overflowed for Rokeya. Finally, the friend had written: 'What has this unfortunate society given you in return for your life-long sacrifice? At times I feel like telling you to give up your concern for this ungrateful society. What will you gain by destroying yourself for this school? What you have done so far is already beyond the capacity of a human being. Now turn around and look at your own personal peace and happiness. Cut your connections with the school and in the fag end of your life enjoy the pleasures of a restful life.

'Yet, having said that, a question comes to mind: Will this be possible? Will you be able to give up your association with the school? A fish cannot live out of water for a moment, so how will you survive unless you are ensconced within the school?

'Then there is the issue of society's criticisms, frowns and antipathy. This is what your life is all about! This is your reward; in this is your satisfaction. Without all this, after all, what would you live with?'

I felt this letter echoed Rokeya's innermost thoughts. I

understood that what she had suggested at first did not reflect her true feelings. Giving up her ties with the school was truly impossible for her. Yet, who would have thought that the casual remark she had made in the course of a conversation with me would come so remorselessly true so soon?

Rokeya passed away. Leaving mankind in the grip of a permanent debt, she disappeared into the world of celestial bodies. One who was inseparably linked to every particle of dust in the school building was separated from it forever. The day Rokeya died, it was as if a tempest of sorrow had swept through the city of Calcutta. Bengal's Muslim women and men were in a state of shock that day.

On the morning of 10 December, a poignant expression of a nation's grief could be seen in the pages of every daily newspaper in Calcutta. The well-known periodicals came out with special editions. Through the newspapers every small and big politician and literary personality expressed their respects for this noble lady. His Excellency, the Governor of Bengal, expressed his sorrow at this tremendous loss to the nation and mankind through a letter.

To honour Rokeya's memory, the people of the country, irrespective of caste and creed, collected at Calcutta's Albert Hall in a grand function. This meeting was organized by Bangiya Parishilan Samiti (Bengal Association for the Refinement of Culture), Bangiya Mussalman Chhatra Samiti (Bengal Muslim Students' Association), Anjuman-e-Khawatin-e-Islam and Bangla or Nikhil Banga Muslim Mahila Samiti (All Bengal Muslim Women's Association). On that day, there was not an inch of space in the huge hall. Many women seated on the stage at Albert Hall had never before in their lives come out of purdah. The meeting was chaired by the founder of the Calcutta Gokhale Memorial School, Mrs. P. K. Ray. People who have distinguished themselves in society gave speeches in English, Bengali and Urdu, about Rokeya's brilliance, single-minded devotion to social service, great sacrifice, quest for knowledge, literary pursuits, and so on.

Who would have known that secretly, deep within the very society which all along had always attacked her, there was so much respect, love and gratitude for her?

At the very end of the function, a young man full of deep respect towards Rokeya stood up. He said, 'At today's condolence meeting, everyone has gathered together, from very important people to the ordinary citizen. It is surprising that it is the death of a lady and not of any emperor or millionaire which has brought so many people together. This proves that mankind has awakened!

'At this meeting, people have said many things. Each of the qualities and heroic achievements of Rokeya's that were mentioned is true to the letter. But may I ask what mankind gave her in return? What did she get from society as a reward for her life-long sacrifice? Only vulgar criticism and unspeakable insults. No one in this huge gathering can oppose this fact. Let every individual stand up today at this meeting and ask honestly who were the people who had made her life unbearable for not just a day or two, but for twenty-five long years? Who were the people who had aimed blow after blow at her till the last day of her life? Can they tell us today what right they have to express their sorrow at Rokeya's death?

'Rokeya is no more. She is now far above our criticism and anger. She has earned the honour of martyrdom. I think in this meeting hall today her battle-weary soul is moving around unseen, complaining in unbearable pain against society's tortures and persecutions.'

From every wall of the vast hall reverberated the echo, . . . 'in unbearable pain . . . complaining.' No one could find the words with which to reply to this heart-rending allegation. The huge crowd could only shed tears in silence. The tears that flowed that day were in the form of penance for the sins of mankind against the woman who was like a mother to all her countrymen and women.

Although in her lifetime, pain and blows were her only rewards, at the function to commemorate her death she was crowned like an empress, drenched in a shower of respectful tears. Yet it seemed as though from the other world she pronounced with intense sorrow, 'It is too late.'

The young speaker spoke again, 'The grave sin that we have committed will not be wiped out by tears. There appears to be only one possible penance. In this meeting hall, even as Rokeya's memory is our witness, every one of us can pledge that in our homes we will try our level best to educate each and every girl. Our penance will be complete only the day not a single girl in Bengal remains illiterate.'

The chairperson in her moderately long speech expressed her great respect for the departed soul. She said, 'It is very difficult to believe that Rokeya is no more and that we have gathered here to express our grief on her death. Only the other day I met her and we discussed several matters relating to the school.

'Almost twenty-five years ago I met her for the first time. I have not forgotten that day. A diminutive, extremely beautiful woman—on seeing her I felt she had a distinctive quality in her. She appeared to be the living icon of enthusiasm, perseverance and strength.

'I was then busy with the administrative work of the Calcutta Brahmo Girls' School. The Sakhawat Memorial School had then only just been started. She wanted to be introduced to the internal work culture of our school. She herself had not had the opportunity to study in any school or college. She wanted to see for herself how a school was run, and having had a direct experience aimed to build her own school on the same lines.

'As days passed, I got to know more about her great mind and was fascinated by it. She knew that external customs and traditions should never be confused with true religion. The only religion that could raise human life to a higher level was true and undying faith.

'I esteemed her; because my hopes and desires were very similar to hers. She made no distinction between a Hindu and a Muslim, and neither did I.

'I respected her because what I had always cherished in my mind as the ideal of Indian womanhood, which sometimes I thought was exclusively Indian, was manifest in her life.'

Not content with attending the memorial meet at Albert Hall, the women of Calcutta organized a massive women's meeting at Sakhawat Memorial School. The meeting was chaired by Lady Abdur Rahim. Irrespective of colour or creed, hundreds of women's eyes overflowed with tears of sorrow. Standing up to speak, many were rendered speechless. Even those who never knew Rokeya in her lifetime were now enlightened about her. Written on every particle of dust of Sakhawat Memorial School on that day was a silent and unspoken lamentation.

Rokeya was buried in the outskirts of Calcutta, at Sodepur, in an old family cemetery. Under the care and supervision of her relatives, her dead body was taken to Sodepur.

However, a soft murmur of unhappiness and dissatisfaction was heard amongst the women of Calcutta regarding this arrangement. 'As long as the cuckoo stays in the crow's house, she belongs to the crow, but once she sings and learns to fly, she belongs to the world of nature, to spring, to the universe.' Rokeya's relatives' rights over her were claimed by the masses. If she were put to her final rest in an ordinary burial ground where hundreds of peoples' remains were mingled, her soul would certainly have been more satisfied. However, screened from the eyes of those with whom she spent the most important twenty-five years of her life, she slept eternally in the secluded corner of her village.

Even today, on 9 December every year, a memorial meeting for Rokeya is organized under the aegis of the Anjuman-e-Khawatin-e-Islam. The tears of sorrow may have dried up today, but the feelings of respect, love and gratitude towards her have not been exhausted—maybe it never will. Rokeya's sacrifices will remain alive in the memory of this country's Muslim women for ever, as an eternal source of strength and inspiration.

Having awakened the Bengali Muslim women, Rokeya went on her heavenly journey. Rokeya died, but since her death hundreds of Rokeyas have been born. Attending a memorial meeting for Rokeya, this is the first thought that comes to mind. On Rokeya's death anniversary hundreds of women feel deep in their hearts that Rokeya being dead is a big untruth.

A Dream Come True

I have already stated that the lamp of Rokeya's life was extinguished at the precise moment when the darkness of the night sky in Calcutta had only just been pierced by the rays of the sun. It seems to be an example of the state our society is in. Rokeya was like a morning star in the life of our nation. Her departure, too, was like bidding the morning star farewell. She came in the darkness of an inauspicious night and sang a welcome to the coming dawn. The night ended, the darkness cleared away. In the sunshine under the free and open sky gathered her followers, whose lives she had filled with light. Rokeya had shone in the night sky like a star, glowing like a lanp in the dark. In the light of day she was not required to shine anymore. Her work completed, she could now joyously take her leave.

Rokeya was not only a worker, but also a dreamer. The novel dream that she had of awakening womankind appeared before her eyes like a golden dawn. Her entire life was spent turning this dream into a reality. There is no end to man's hopes, desires and high expectations. Many colourful dreams of the future light up in front of a visionary's eyes. Many dedicated workers and kind-hearted people have sacrificed their lives to fulfil their dreams of social welfare. Often the dream remained only a dream during their lifetime, not taking wings in the realm of possibility.

But Rokeya's destiny was of a different kind. In these times we see Kamal Pasha, Mussolini and many other great people enjoying the fruits of their labours during their lifetimes. From this point of view their destinies are comparable to Rokeya's.

Like them Rokeya, too, turned her dreams into reality in her lifetime.

In the English novel named *Sultana's Dream*, Rokeya had described an imaginary journey by air and showed the possible outcomes of the advancement of science. What had been a vision has now turned into reality.

In this connection she had said, 'When I wrote *Sultana's Dream*, aeroplanes and zeppelins did not exist! In fact, at that time even the motor car had not come to India. Electric light and fans were impossible to imagine. At least, I had not seen any of those things then. Almost six years later (in the year 1911) after coming to Calcutta, I first saw an aeroplane from far down below, flying in the sky. That I would ever be able to board a flying plane was something I had never expected. I would only sigh longingly, and silently.'

However, how that strange dream of Sultana's was fulfilled in Rokeya's own life has been described in her own writing:

'On 2 December 1930, Tuesday, we began our journey at four o' clock. On reaching the Dumdum aerodrome, we saw an open field. There were only our three cars and ourselves. Thanking Allah, I went and sat in the plane. Bengal's pride, the first Muslim pilot, Murad, was our pilot. Flying in the sky, I found the whole earth was like one round bowl. Gradually, we scaled an altitude of 3000 feet. The view then was absolutely wonderful! To my south was the setting sun. The almost full moon of the twelfth day of the lunar cycle was on the other side. Both seemed to be looking at me and smiling. Looking down I saw the brick houses of Calcutta, the bungalows, multi-storied buildings, the edifices, all looking like tiny mounds of brick. The Howrah Bridge looked like a small toy! And the Hooghly River looked like a mere line of water. After circulating a fifty-mile radius, we came down again.

'I actually flew around in the aeroplane I had described in *Sultana's Dream* twenty-five years ago. The first lady who lived in seclusion and flew with Bengal's first Muslim pilot was none other than myself.'

The joy of experiencing the fulfilment of the dream she had seen through the eyes of her imagination way back in the past filled her heart on that day. But that was not all. Experiencing the powerful magic of modern scientific development was not the biggest dream of her life. Her greatest dream had to do with awakening womankind, a dream that informed her life from the beginning to the end. It is a matter of joy that her long wait was not in vain. Towards the evening of her life, her imagination took a form in front of her eyes, her dreams assumed a novel shape in reality.

If one analyses the last days of her life, a beautiful picture comes to mind—that of a society of women gradually awakening into a new life, and an altruistic widow dedicating her entire mind and soul in making this dream of awakening come true.

Just a few months before Rokeya passed away, I had organized a women's conference. She honoured us by chairing this meeting. Every line of her address that day was overflowing with pride and satisfaction at her success.

She said, 'Today I am gratified beyond belief at seeing you all. For almost twenty-five years now I have been trying to awaken Muslim women; but it was a difficult task. I would keep calling out to awaken them but they would only turn over and go to sleep again. Having run the Sakhawat Memorial School for the last twenty-two years, I have seen that whereas earlier they turned over and slept, later they sat up and dozed—but never shook themselves and stood up. It is therefore a matter of joy that since the last few years I am seeing they have actually rubbed their eyes and woken up. Today being able to see so many educated women as a result fills my heart with boundless satisfaction.'

A few years before this, at a women's conference, she had said, 'You all may be surprised to know that for the last twenty-five years I have been crying out for India's most inferior creature.

Do you know who that is? It is the Indian woman. For this creature no one's heart has ever cried. Even animals have people to think about them. That is why I see societies for the prevention of cruelty to animals everywhere. But no one in the wide world would cry for women like us, living in seclusion.'

However, at the conference I organized, while drawing the attention of women to the progress and stability of Sakhawat Memorial School, she said jokingly, 'When women in purdah like us are burnt, even ghosts do not eat us. Only those among us who have been able to courageously tear through the purdah will come forward in this work.' While speaking her eyes began to shine brightly with hope and trust. Today she did not have to search for people to be concerned for the lot of women. Who was more confident than her in the power of awakened women? In reality, being able to hand over the responsibility to those whose right it was to bear it, she appeared to heave a sigh of satisfaction.

Very often when I met Rokeya she would complain, 'How many more times must I tell you? Why have you left your BA exams incomplete?' It is a matter of joy that in the year she died her wish was fulfilled. The day the results were declared, there was possibly no one as happy as she was.

One day I was surprised to hear that to celebrate my success in the examinations she was organizing a women's gathering. I realized this was not so much due to my credit as an expression of her own joy.

At Rokeya's invitation, on that day irrespective of class and creed, many respected women of Calcutta gathered together. I will never forget the joy in her eyes, shining brightly as she addressed the meeting.

While delivering the welcome address she said, 'A thirty-two year old dream that I wrote about in *Motichur*—that of seeing a lady magistrate or barrister—is today about to be transformed into reality. Words are inadequate to express my overwhelming joy. Many are unable to see the fruition of tasks they undertake in their own lifetime. The emperor who began the construction of the Qutub Minar never lived to see its completion. But today I have been able to see with my own eyes the successful completion of my victory tower.'

It seemed there was nothing left incomplete in her life. She died at the age of fifty-three. Once in a while I heard her say, 'Not too long—if I can live for just another ten years, I will be able to make the foundation of Sakhawat Memorial School so strong that there will be no more cause for worry regarding its stability.'

That the school required its own premises was something she felt very deeply in her heart. It was not as if she had not collected enough funds for the building, although she had to literally beg at every door for it. She was hoping to see the school running in its own premises in a few years' time. But cruel fate did not grant her the time she had prayed for.

She is today in a world beyond death, but her beloved Sakhawat Memorial School has since developed into a leading educational institution. Recently the government took the responsibility of running it.

And it is not just that. In the midst of an all-pervading inertia and lack of enthusiasm, it is surprising to see the work begun by Rokeya being carried on, and, indeed, going from strength to strength. Her benevolent eyes seem to be awake and steadfastly watch Bengal's Muslim women, journeying on the path to freedom. It seems that even now Rokeya is incessantly showering blessings on them, from the world beyond this.

Character Sketch

The renowned poet Rabindranath Tagore had said about Shah Jahan, 'More than your achievements, more than your Taj Mahal, greater were you, O King.' When one talks about Rokeya's life, this is exactly what one wishes to say about her. In order to make education more easily accessible by Muslim girls, Rokeya established a school. Many years later, remembering this, people will bow their heads down respectfully. That her true identity is not restricted to being the founder of a school is evident when one considers the history of Bengali Muslim women over the last fifty years. In this past half century, society has been transformed completely and the credit for this amazing transformation goes to this gracious lady more than anyone else. This is an undeniable fact.

Rokeya bloomed like a lustrous lotus in darkness, like a mystery of nature! Realizing her dream after years of dedicated work makes a marvellous story. Yet discussing her life, it appears that the seeds of success were hidden in her own character.

The main reason for Rokeya's success lies in her sincerity towards her ideals. Her motto was: 'Whether the truth is liked or not, whether it is acceptable to all or against the prevalent opinion, I will understand the truth, search for it and accept it.' Her ideals were even higher. Mere acceptance of a truth did not satisfy her. The guiding principle of her life was to preach the truth, to bring each and every unfortunate woman in the country to the path of knowledge. Until the end of her life, no obstacle could deflect her attention for even a moment from her firm sense of determination. Many people do social service, but who has ever seen a completely selfless social worker like Rokeya? For the sake of humankind, how many individuals in this world have been able to give up home and hearth, relatives and friends, wealth and property, honour and prestige and become virtually a destitute like her?

In the political arena, many well-known leaders have been seen to change their opinions and embrace new paths and new ideals, but from the beginning to the end Rokeya had a single political agenda: female awakening. Till the very end she clung steadfastly to what she had realized as truth half a century ago, despite the innumerable obstacles in the way of freedom. It is difficult to believe that one who was so steadfast and single-minded would not achieve success ultimately.

Talking of Rokeya's life, one of her sterling qualities that is most evident to us is a wonderful balance between softness and firmness. Her heart was full of sweet love and kindness. Women's sorrows melted her heart, and she would be extremely distressed in trying to find ways to solve their problems. Yet, deep in the mind of this lady, there was much strength and determination! From where did this soft woman get her unshakable perseverance and an unimaginable strength and courage?

Rokeya had declared rebellion against the prevalent social system. She knew that this society had to be demolished completely and built anew; but this rebellion could not curb the deep sense of sympathy in her tender heart. More than the triumph of destruction, the agony of creation proved to be effective in her life. Her genius was oriented to creativity. Rather than the earnestness of rebellion what manifest itself in her life and work was the intense sense of pain in her compassionate heart. If the diversity and originality of her brilliance was to be found anywhere, that is where it lay.

Very early in her life she woke up to the dreadful state of society and shuddered to think of it. But she had diagnosed the treatment required for this disease as any expert doctor would. She knew with certainty that the worthless superstitions collected over several ages could only be removed through education. She understood very clearly that the day the light of education shines on us, superstition would melt away like mist.

She had realized that the system of seclusion for women within the zenana was the main obstacle in the way of Muslim women's progress. She used to say, 'Seclusion could be compared to the deadly carbonic acid gas. Since carbonic acid causes death painlessly, people do not bother to guard against it. In the zenana too hundreds of inmates are dying painlessly, little by little, killed by what can be called the gas of the seclusion system.'

To her observing purdah also represented strong individualism, not external vanity of any kind. Whoever knew her closely will say so. 'Purdah and seclusion are two different things: purdah is

Islamic but seclusion is un-Islamic,' is what a lot of people keep reiterating these days. Yet Rokeya made a rational distinction between the restraint and decency that comes of living in purdah and seclusion that is meaningless and life-destroying, way back in the past before anyone else. *Motichur* will bear testimony to the fact that she was the first to write about this.

In spite of this, it will have to be accepted that Rokeya's main rebellion was not against seclusion of women. She was not impatient. She knew that this system was going to disintegrate as more people were educated. That is why all her strength was devoted to spreading education. I cannot say how many reformers in the world have been able to display such control and alertness, patience and fortitude.

Rokeya, instead of becoming a slave to the words [in the scriptures], had wanted to reveal the essence of Islam. Her message, when it was published, managed to shake up society, which was otherwise blind. 'Who is this religious rebel who wants to take us to the path of sin?' they asked. But Rokeya was not perturbed. By tearing through the impenetrable screen of false traditions and rituals, she had been able to discover the true face of Islam and she knew it for sure. She did not cling to the external façade of religion, which is what makes her achievement so distinguished.

She hated the idea of memorizing the Koran like a parrot. Often I heard her say, 'From childhood we are all made to memorize the Koran, but ninety-nine people out of hundred do not know the meaning of a single word. Those who have learnt it are terribly deluded. They did not understand a single syllable of the essence of Islam. Can there be anything more unfortunate than that?' In this connection she used to give an apt example. She said, 'The sweetness of the coconut is enclosed inside its impenetrable shell; blind people, instead of trying to break the hard shell open, spend their lives licking it.'

Regarding women's education she would say: we are not asking for alms or charity; only our birthright. Our demand is not one jot more than the rights already given to women by Islam, 700 years ago.

She said, 'Some of our brothers think that by depending on Aligarh University and Islamia College they will cross the bridge to the next world, and at that time will stuff their wives and daughters in a handbag and take them across as well.' From the depths of this ironical and penetrating allegation a burning resentment bursts forth.

She also said, 'Whenever I ask for contributions for the girls' school, I hear that Muslims are very poor; they have no money. But is this statement believable? Could those who have ungrudgingly donated thousands of rupees to the Calcutta Islamia College be poor? If they obeyed the Shariat, each would have donated for the girls' school at least half of what they donated for the education of boys.' Society did not hesitate to call her a traitor to her religion. But she repeatedly tried to draw society's attention to the true teachings of religion. Instead of confining Islam's instructions to the pages of the Koran, she tried her best to apply them in real life.

Rokeya was born into a very aristocratic and honourable family. She had close relations with many families in Bengal who command the maximum respect, honour and wield a lot of influence. But I never saw her taking pride in this fact. Rather, in her view, aristocratic meant 'cursed'. When I passed the B.A., she had said in a speech, 'Lately, some other Muslim women have passed the B.A.; but Nahar's passing is special. The reason being that she is the daughter of a 'cursed', meaning, aristocratic, family of Bengal, where education is absolutely forbidden!' She would shudder at the mention of the words, 'aristocratic family', as it is in these families that illiteracy and superstition had a chance of accumulating, citing family honour and respect as an excuse.

She knew her work had more to do with the outside world than the domestic set-up. She knew the relationships one had at home were of body and blood; but what was forged in the wider world involved the heart, and people closest to one's heart.

I was first introduced to her through the monthly magazine. I can remember how her candid, witty, effortless yet sharp forceful writing overwhelmed my child's mind even then. Every line of her writing revealed a new message of life, and it was as though these imperceptibly knocked at one's heart and touched thousands of lives.

As I had to leave school at the age of ten and go into purdah, I had nursed an intense desire for higher education, which Rokeya saw as the most important goal. Once in a while I would blame this cruel society in the pages of the monthly magazine. Later I learnt that even these feeble efforts made in my childhood had not escaped the eyes of Rokeya.

Fifteen or sixteen years ago she had written to me, 'Sitting down to write to you, I remembered something way back in the past. Once at night we were travelling by boat across one of Bihar's waterways. Nothing could be seen in the darkness outside. Only from the dark forests on the riverbanks, a mild fragrance of the keora flower wafted towards us. Similarly, I have never seen you but I know your fragrance.' In this way, without a formal introduction, she bound me to her by love and affection. In some lonely Bengal village, if some young girl imprisoned behind purdah showed even an iota of enthusiasm for education, she would be considered Rokeya's closest friend, as if she was most closely linked to Rokeya in spirit.

I first met the mysterious lady of my childhood and youthful imagination in person in 1925 in the heart of Calcutta. I felt I was blessed, that I had been born again. Since then I had met her till the very last day of her life. It was as if new traits of her character were being revealed in front of our eyes every day.

Her sense of simple courtesy and sweet behaviour could very easily attract people to her. The trace of a beautiful and candid smile was always evident on her face, never dimmed despite the hundreds of blows and attacks she had had to face. At Anjuman

I often found women using shallow pretexts to attack her with distasteful language and discourtesy! Indeed, some uneducated women insulted her over the financial accounts of Anjuman and the school. But I never saw her agitated.

I went to see her a few days before her death. I thought she looked a little sad. It seemed that a small shadow of dejection fell on her ever-cheerful face. I realized today's blow had been exceptionally heavy. When I asked her, she said, 'In life I have endured many stings, but today's bite feels the most deadly.' While relating the incident in detail it seemed sparks were emitted from her eyes in anger and grief. Yet the smile at the corner of her lips had not disappeared.

Even when the talk was work-related, she could make it humorous and pleasant by giving comparisons and quoting apt verses. Her love of humour was an amazingly distinctive characteristic in her nature. Whether it was in discussions, lectures, or her writings, this speciality of hers shone through very brightly.

None of Rokeya's own children survived, but she had a different mission in life. In the long twenty-five years she was with Sakhawat Memorial School, she had brought up the children of countless others. The innumerable girls of the school discovered in her a mother figure. She showered on each and every girl her deep affection and each of them, in turn, looked upon her only with extreme respect! I shall try to give a few examples and thus end my deliberation on this exalted woman's amazing character. The words have been spoken by a former student of Sakhawat Memorial School, brought up with great care and devotion by Rokeya. This model girl is Roshan Ara.

> 'It was as though a deep sincerity was revealed in each word and act of the noble lady. This did not fail to arouse a similar response in the souls of those who came in contact with her.
>
> 'I remember, according to her instruction, we would stand in rows in the vast hall before the classes began. She would read out a prayer

and we joined her. From her reading it seemed as if she called Allah with all her heart, urging him to lead us to success on that very day. The depth of that sincere prayer can only be experienced in one's heart—it cannot be conveyed in words.

'She would, once in a while, take us for different exams to other schools—like the Bangiya Parishad exam, Britti (scholarship) exam, etc. On the specified day, before leaving, we examinees gathered together. Rokeya approached us, looking like a pure, immaculate ascetic. She would make a gesture, indicating that we join her and start reading the prayer. We would read along with her, and then follow her into the bus. Till the bus left the school compound we continued to read the prayer in exactly the same manner. Later, as the bus picked up speed she would stop, and so would we. Our minds by then seemed to have become free of fear, and in our souls a divine inspiration had entered.

'I didn't understand much then; but today I wonder, who were we to that woman who had no husband or son, that in her desire for our welfare her deeply fervent prayers shook even the throne of God? It was as if the only thing desirable in her life was the students' welfare. Parents want the well-being of their children. That is natural. But why did this noble lady spend all her life praying for girls to whom she was not related? The echo reverberates, who has the answer?'

NOTES

1 Jyotirmala Devi (1903 to 1981) came from Chittagong. In 1924 she passed BA exams and went to England to study commerce and journalism. There she came close to Dilip Kumar Ray, and through him to Sri Aurobindo as well. Towards the end of her life she had lost her equilibrium.

2 Shamsunnahar Mahmud, *Nazrulke Jemon Dekhechi* (Calcutta: Navyug Prakashani, 1958), p. 35.

3 *Punyamoyee* (Calcutta: Bulbul Publishing House, 1925), about which Shamsunnahar in her *Nazrulke Jemon Dekhechi* has written: 'In 1925 my

brother (Habibullah Bahar) went to study medicine in Calcutta . . . [and] because of my brother's eagerness and enterprise my childhood composition *Punyamoyee* was published. Through my brother, Nazrul sent me a message of blessings, citing this book. Nazrul's handwritten poem was printed on a block on the first page of *Punyamoyee.* Apart from this, Dr. Mohammed Shahidullah had written a eulogy, which was printed as a part of the book.'

4 *Nazrulke Jemon Dekhechi*, p. 34.

5 See *Rokeya-Jibani* (Calcutta: Bulbul Publishing House, 1938), pp 92-93.

6 Quoted from Anwara Bahar Chowdhury, *Shamsunnahar Mahmud* (Dhaka: Bangla Akademi, 1987) p. 59.

7 Quoted from *Nazrulke Jemon Dekhechi*, p. 25. *Sindhu Hindol* was published in 1927. In his dedication Nazrul wrote (31.7.26): 'These writings of mine I dedicate to my beloved brother and sister Bahar and Nahar'.

8 Selina Bahar Zaman, *Smriti Sudhay* (Sweet Memories) (Dhaka: Bulbul Publishing House, 1991), p. 53.

9 Shamsunnahar's note: Among these tireless workers and well-wishers of women, Maulvi Abdul Aziz, Maulvi Fazlul Karim, Maulvi Bazlur Rahim of Noakhali and Maulvi Hemayyat Uddin of Barisal. are noteworthy. These were a few of those pioneers who received Western education in Muslim Bengal.

11

Sufia Kamal (1911-1999): Poet and Social Worker

Translated by Adrita Mukherjee

'You write pretty poems, but even poets need to work for society,' Rokeya Sakhawat once told Sufia Kamal. Begum Rokeya's advice proved to be an oracle for Sufia Kamal: she found her vocation. Indeed, the era of enlightened women initiated by Rokeya Sakhawat towards the beginning of the century found its last living representative in Sufia Kamal.

Sufia Kamal—at that time Sufia N. Hossain—had the opportunity of interacting intimately with Begum Rokeya from 1927-28 to 1932. A letter written at that time to Mohammad Nasiruddin, the editor of *Saugat*, shows how deeply Sufia was inspired by Rokeya and how easy she must have found it to identify with her mentor's ideals. An eighteen-year-old Sufia writes in a letter dated 23 July 1929: 'For ages women have been made into mere puppets and thrust to the background. They have silently endured countless atrocities. Writing a few pages on the subject is not the way to avenge these wrongs. The real answer lies in bringing about a revolution. The obvious questions that arise are who is going to rebel and against whom? I would answer: It's women who will do so, against men . . . . The few women who emerged out of the darkness of our Muslim society, in search of light, are being led by Mrs. R. S. Hossain (Begum Rokeya). She has had to endure countless hardships for the courage she has shown. I have faith, however, that one day in the future society will recognize the value of her efforts, and scores of people will follow in her footsteps.'[1]

At that time Sufia Kamal was associated with the Muslim women's association called Anjuman-e-Khawatin-e-Islam established by Begum Rokeya in 1916. This provided the link between Begum Rokeya and Sufia that helped the latter to get to know Rokeya intimately and imbibe her ideals. Indeed, the four years proved to be crucial for Sufia who would not be exclusively a poet but surpass all her contemporaries in the field of social work.

In 1933, after the death of her husband Syed Nehal Hossain, Sufia came to live in Calcutta for the second time. The times were difficult for her. She had two dependents—a young daughter and a mother who had lived always in her own father's house. The future was completely uncertain, and Sufia did not have Begum Rokeya's support, something that she had learnt to rely on. It was Mohammad Nasiruddin, the editor of *Saugat*, who came forward to help the widowed Sufia. With Nasiruddin's help, Sufia managed to find a job. For the next nine years she taught at the Corporation School in Calcutta at a salary of Rs.50 a month. Her income was supplemented by writing in some journals. In 1937 and 1938 respectively were published a collection of short stories, *Keyar Kanta* (The Thorns of the Keya Bush) and her first collection of poetry, *Sanjher Maya* (Twilight Magic). After reading *Sanjher Maya*, Rabindranath Tagore wrote:

> 'My dear Sufia,
> Your poetry amazes me. There is no doubt that you have acquired a significant place in Bengali literature, and I feel that your fame is assured. May all my blessings rest with you.'

(Sufia was introduced to Tagore in 1927-28. She had attended a few informal functions at the Tagore house. On one of Tagore's birthdays, Sufia had written a long poem and sent it to him as a gift.)[2]

In the period 1933-39, Sufia Kamal is revealed to us as a creative personality, courageous and subversive in her personal life. She had taken the bold step of leaving her uncle's house in Shayestabad, which, incidentally, was her husband's house as well (her husband had been a cousin) and chosen the uncertainties of a life in Calcutta. She did not have any formal education and yet managed to find a teaching job and run a household on her own income. Possibly because of the rigours of such a life and the loneliness that she suffered from, Sufia fell seriously ill. In 1939, some friends arranged for her re-marriage, to Kamaluddin Khan of Chittagong.

The next few years saw Sufia Kamal taking part in the anti-British movement and anti-riot activities, and becoming the editor of *Begum* magazine. She became the mother of four children. The Language movement of 1952 gave Sufia Kamal's work focus and direction. Within four years of East Pakistan's coming into existence, many of her contemporaries found they could not decide which side to take. Some of them accepted government jobs and became directly involved in politics. This was the time when Suifia Kamal's path diverged from that of her long-time friend and co-worker, Shamsunnahar Mahmud. Sufia could not condone the government's opening fire on students. Nor could she accept Urdu as the national language. She said, 'Our mother tongue came under attack as soon as Pakistan was founded. Now we have Urdu as our national language. Although we spoke Urdu at home in Shayestabad, I cannot help thinking that the language that is in our blood is Bengali.'[3] Sufia Kamal wrote powerful poetry during this period. Indeed, she has not written as many poems on any other subject as she has on the Language movement. The volume *Ekusher Sankalan: Granthapanji* (The Collection of 21: A Bibliography), published in 1991 by Bangla Akademi, mentions sixty-five poems written by Sufia Kamal on this subject.

In 1961, the military government of Pakistan announced a ban on the celebrations of Tagore's birth centenary. Sufia Kamal led the protest of students, teachers, intellectuals and social workers against the ban and arranged for the centenary celebrations, flouting the government order. For a month meetings and functions were held in almost all big cities in East Pakistan. Sufia Kamal came into prominence during these protests. She, along with Shamsunnahar Mahmud, had already taken the lead in protesting against the fundamentalists' propaganda after the Muslim Family Law came into effect in 1961.[4]

For an entire year in 1971, Sufia Kamal provided active help to the freedom fighters from her house at number 32 Dhanmondi in Dhaka. She became a living legend for her contribution to the freedom movement. There are not too many instances of such sheer courage in the face of death. Indeed, she escaped certain death in the hands of Pakistani soldiers only because there was a lot of international pressure on the government. The native collaborators had refused to shoot at Sufia Kamal.

In the ice-cold days of military rule in post-independent Bangladesh, Sufia Kamal's voice continued to be heard on issues of politics and society. In 1990, defying the curfew, Sufia led the public protests on the roads of Dhaka. Till date, hers was one of the strongest voices in Bangladesh against atrocities on women. The fundamentalists had declared countless *fatwas* against her for her uncompromising attitude. All their journals and public platforms were loud in their recriminations of Sufia Kamal.

Sufia Kamal had been associated for a long time with the politics of Bangladesh, even as she remained outside the establishment. She had never been a member of any political party or a government organization. This was remarkable. The courage, determination and sacrifice that her life demonstrates could put to shame even renowned political leaders. The history of her life was one of incessant struggle against compromises. 'I do not have any 'philosophy'. I just talk about my conscience,' she said about herself. It is, indeed, a difficult task to measure the immense contribution of Sufia Kamal to the women's movement in Bangladesh. We would perhaps have to wait for a few more years to see objectively through the glory surrounding her.

Sufia Kamal published fifteen books and acted as president of sixteen associations. She received almost thirty-five awards from all over the world for her work in literature, women's movement and humanist movements.

S.A.

Evening Illusions

When eternal sunset comes at evening time,
Shaking the forlorn sky in the west,
With its southern breeze, colouring it strangely,
As if at this end of day it will give all it has,
Offering its joys, in great celebration.
In sweet attraction,
Slowly and slowly it comes,
The flaming sun to the end of light and
Sinks with grace,
Spreading its hues through the evening sky of Spring.
Tired, weary Sun! Your last festive song
Echoes through the leaves of the trees on this earth.
With the final rays your sad, parting kiss
You have sent. Light draws patterns on the head
Of the stately banyan,
So silent and mute, making restless its heart.
Even more troubled the eyes of the girl entrapped
As she gazes at the way of the setting sun,
Unable to move.
She pleads from afar,
Again and again she asks
To summon her unto your evening assembly, some day.
When the day's work is done and all is quiet and still
Let your call come into this unlit room and stir
The heart with its twilight touch. In silent song,
As the evening raga rings, let this prisoner soul
Be free—dreaming of beauty, preparing.
Let the last breath be breathed so the flower may bloom.[5]

Woman Unloved

Wordless pain lies stacked in the layers of my heart,
There is none in this world with whom to share.

Tears come streaming but the body does not die
Come and see how proudly I bear this pain.
Thus goes foolish man trampling on this soul
That has not known love nor any care.
What was asleep in the depths of the heart,
Sleeping and dormant for eternal time,
O you loveless careless fool,
You mocked and broke that silent dream.
The flower that bloomed and fell to the ground
What scent can it have? Why wander through this dark?

I remember, I do remember still
How he came to me from another land.
With clear, happy eyes he looked up and called,
Embracing me with his beautiful song,
'Dearest', he said. The words still ring,
I remember, O Love, I do.
The garland I gave you that twilight hour,
Your arms around me, the first sign of love
Brought blood to my cheeks, colouring me so.
With unquenched thirst you looked,
Said I was beautiful, you gave me all,
Awakening the poet within.
O Poet of my heart,
I cannot, I cannot forget.

Then your love,
Then it grew so deep.
Who knew like the sun that fades away at dusk
Your love would fade away too?
I knew not, I thought not, I saw not that you
Burnt with desire, loving as you did.
The flame rose and swelled
Slowly and slowly it went up high.
Love died then, but your fire

Burnt my woman's grass-like soul.
Then to redeem yourself you cast me aside.
In the twilight of life I stand all alone.

Now in pain and rage my heart cries out,
When will you come to douse the flames?
A speck of hope flickers,
That you will return.
If ever you come back, then I will light
The lamp of love in this temple of dark.

Nauroz, Asharh 1927

Offerings

If you ask me, then I will wait,
Holding in each hand,
Pure *aab-e-Hyat*[6] in one
With lute in the other I'll stand.
Let poets Hafez and Omar stay
At my door, while I take sips,
From this cup filled with eternal love
That I hold here to my lips.

Saugat, Baisakh 1928

The Winner

The autumn morning was touched with the scent of shiulis. Asmat Ali, the S.D.O. of the district, was out for his usual stroll near the bank of the Bhairab River.

He returned home late and breathless. 'Hajera!' he called out urgently as soon as he stepped into the house.

Hajera Khatun, Asmat Ali's wife, was serving her son breakfast. She came out at once, without pausing even to wash her hands.

It was unusual for her husband to call her at this hour. Something important must have come up.

'I met an old friend near the river,' said Asmat Ali. 'He's in a boat and he's seriously ill. In fact, he may not live.'

'O Allah!'

'Yes, I was shocked too. But I can't possibly leave him there with only a few servants. Sending him to the hospital seems too heartless. I'm going to send my palanquin to bring him over to our house. He's a childhood friend of mine, comes from a rich family. I've no idea how he's landed up like this . . .'

He stopped abruptly, aware that he was losing precious time.

'He'll be here soon,' said Asmat Ali briskly to his wife. 'Do you think you can look after him? Perhaps you should get Masuma to help you. Where is she?'

Masuma, who was standing close by, said, 'Of course. Which room do you think we should get ready for him?'

'The room where you have your afternoon meetings would be ideal,' Asmat Ali said to his wife. 'We just need a bed in there. Do you mind?'

'Not at all,' said Hajera. 'But who is this friend? Do I know him?'

'You've heard of him, at least. Abul Kasem Chowdhury, of Pabna.'

Neither Asmat Ali nor his wife noticed that Masuma had looked up with a start at the mention of the name. Asmat went downstairs to send the palanquin to fetch his friend.

'They'll be here soon,' Hajera said to Masuma. 'Give me a hand, Masu, will you? Let's bring in the extra bed from your room and move a small table into the room. We must make sure he's comfortable.'

The two women left to make arrangements.

It was late evening. The namaz was over at the mosque. Asmat Ali returned from office, had a quick cup of tea and went to see his friend. In the morning he had arranged for the doctor from the government hospital to examine Abul Kasem. Another specialist had been called in as a consultant. Both the doctors were noncommittal about the patient at this stage: his condition was too serious for them to be hopeful about his recovery.

Asmat had requested the consultant doctor to stay back that night. The doctor was to examine Abul Kasem every hour. Hajera and Masuma gave him medicines regularly and took turns in holding the ice bag to his head. There was a single candle burning in the room, its gentle light throwing soft shadows on the walls. The delicate fragrance of incense floated in the air. Abul Kasem lay on the bed inert, flushed and unconscious from high fever. Excessive strain and irregular meals had caused his blood pressure to shoot up abnormally.

Asmat sat at the head of the bed looking anxiously at his friend. Kasem wore clothes that were soiled and wrinkled; his salt-and-pepper hair was tangled and dry and the rough stubble of a few days rose on his unshaven cheeks. Asmat could not bear to look at his friend. He closed his eyes and prayed, 'Let him get well, Allah. Here he is, so far away from his family, poor and desperately ill. If he dies he wouldn't even know his friend had tried to help him in his last hours.'

Miraculously, almost like an answer to his prayers, Kasem's body twitched suddenly. He seemed to be trying to turn on his side. His bloodshot eyes opened for an instant, trying to focus on the unfamiliar room. Masuma was holding the ice bag to his head. 'I think you should call the doctor, Bhai,' she said softly.

'Kasem! Can you hear me? Do you know who I am?' asked Asmat urgently.

Kasem tried to lift a hand. 'Asmat!' he gasped.

'Here, Kasem, here I am,' Asmat said, tremendously relieved that his friend was not delirious anymore. 'Masuma, call the doctor,' he said.

Kasem started. 'Masuma?' he asked. 'Who's Masuma?'

Masuma had already left the room.

'She's my sister,' said Asmat. 'You were terribly ill and I brought you to my house. How are you feeling now?'

Kasem had not been able to calm himself yet. He remained quiet for a while and said, 'You are asking me how I am? I can die in peace now. Praise be to Allah that He brought a sinner like me to a friend at my last hour.'

'Don't say that ever again. You're going to be all right. Here's the doctor now.'

The doctor examined Kasem. He relaxed visibly once he was through. He even permitted himself a smile.

'Nothing to worry about,' the doctor told Asmat, drawing him aside. 'I expect the fever to go down by the morning. But on no account should he be excited. Anything can happen if he does. I have seen patients like him often getting agitated. Talk to him and keep him calm when he is awake. And make sure he gets some sleep. I have changed the medicine. Now should I go home or stay?'

Asmat did not let the doctor go home. Hajera soon came in with the medicine. Kasem, by this time fully conscious, raised his hand to his forehead in a salaam. Hajera returned the salaam and handed the ice bag to Asmat. 'Hold this to his head,' she said. 'I shall get him something to eat.'

Hajera was back soon with some soup. She fed Kasem with a spoon and wiped his mouth gently. 'Try to get some sleep,' she said. 'I'm sure you'll feel much better in the morning.'

Weak and exhausted, Kasem dropped off to sleep very soon. Asmat sat awake at the head of the bed, his friend's emaciated hand held firmly in his own.

It was eleven o'clock at night. Kasem was sleeping fretfully. He opened his eyes at the sound of the clock striking the hour. 'Asmat!' he called.

Masuma was sitting at the head of the bed, gently fanning Kasem's feverish forehead. She leant forward at the sound of his voice. Kasem's eyes rested for an instant on Masuma's face, half hidden in the shadows, and immediately his body tensed. There was a strange light in the eyes that stared almost fanatically at her. Masuma was alarmed. 'I'll call Bhai,' she murmured, and left the room quickly.

Asmat came in a moment later and touched his friend's forehead lightly. 'How're you feeling now?' he asked.

Kasem did not reply. His breathing had quickened and his eyes were unnaturally bright. Asmat hurried out of the room and woke up the servant who was sleeping outside the door. 'Call the doctor—quick!' he urged.

The servant rushed down the stairs. Asmat came back into the room and started to fan Kasem's forehead. Kasem reached up and held his friend's hand.

'I don't need the doctor,' he said. 'Just tell me something, Asmat. Who was sitting at the head of my bed?'

'It was my sister,' Asmat replied, surprised.

'Your sister? I never knew you had a sister of your own?'

'Why, what's wrong? Has Masuma said something to you?'

'Masuma! Yes, I thought I'd heard that very name.'

The doctor came in and checked Kasem's pulse. 'Why are you so excited?' he asked reprovingly. 'I told you it's not good for you. The fever is coming down, now all you need is rest.'

'Yes, I shall sleep, but I need to tell Asmat something first. My time is running out.'

'Kasem, I've told you once that I don't want to hear such things from you. You're being obstinate and childish.'

'Asmat, please ask the doctor to leave. I need to talk to you. It's very important. Please, Asmat.'

The doctor realized it was useless trying to stop Kasem. It was only making him more agitated. 'All right,' he said. 'I'm leaving. But don't talk too much. It's not good for you. Try to get some sleep.'

Kasem's lips parted in a half-smile. 'Yes, I'll sleep, maybe forever . . . But I'm glad you're here with me, Asmat, I'm really glad.'

'Stop, Kasem,' Asmat said. 'I shall listen to everything you have to say in the morning, I promise. But you should sleep now, my friend.'

'If I went to sleep I may not wake up again, Asmat. Don't try to stop me. I need to confess my sins. I can't bear this burden anymore.'

Asmat was startled, but the urgency in his friend's voice convinced him. 'All right,' he said. 'I'll listen.'

'I have disturbed your sleep,' Kasem said, 'why must you give me shelter and suffer for it?'

Hajera came in. 'Why don't you get some rest?' she suggested to her husband. 'I can sit with him for a while.'

'It's all right, tomorrow is Sunday,' Asmat said. 'You get some rest and ask Masuma to do the same.'

'She's already gone to sleep. She has a bad headache. All right then, but do call me if you need me.'

'Of course,' Asmat promised.

Hajera left the room.

Kasem said, 'Can I have some water please?'

Asmat helped his friend to drink some water and wiped his face gently. After a while Kasem began to speak.

'Your sister is called Masuma, isn't she? I knew someone called Masuma. "Knew" is perhaps not the right word, but . . . well, I like to think that I knew her. When I heard that name and saw that face it seemed so much like her . . . I'm not sure, but if you ever find my Masuma . . . you've got to look for her, my friend. This is my last request to you,' Kasem held his friend's hand in a tight grasp.

'Kasem, you're going to get well soon, and then you are going to find your Masuma yourself.'

'Mine? No, she's not mine. She was never mine. I just want to tell you my story so that if you find her you can tell her how sorry I am. You know I haven't been to Pabna since I was a child. When we shifted to our new house in Calcutta my father had a feast for the housewarming. Lots of people came from our native village. Among them was this girl called Masuma. Her father was a cousin of my father's. He was the gentle and quiet sort. Masuma was a child then—maybe seven or eight years old. I was about fifteen. The house was full of people, there was feasting and celebrations . . . we had great fun. I'd never had a sister and Masuma somehow filled the gap. Initially it was just that, affection, not love, but later . . . may I have some water?'

Asmat gave him some water.

'Why don't you stop now, Kasem? I'll listen to the rest of it tomorrow,' he said.

'I'm not sure I'll live to see tomorrow,' Kasem said, almost to himself. 'Besides, I may not feel like telling you any of this if I get well. This moment will have passed. No, I must tell you the whole story now.'

Asmat fell silent again.

'After the *moulud*—the housewarming feast—was over, I entered my room and found Masuma there. She'd brought heaps of books down from my table and was sitting on the floor, staring admiringly at them. She was a little embarrassed at first to see me, but very soon she became her normal self.

'"Are all these books yours? Do you read all of them?" she asked me.

'I smiled and nodded. She turned the pages excitedly and said, "I'll also read all these books when I grow up. I'm learning to read, you know."

'I stretched out on the bed.

'"Really?" I asked. "What have you learnt?"

'She immediately started to recite rhymes from her Bengali book *Hashi Khushi* and then went on to tell me what she'd learnt from her Urdu primer.

'"That's wonderful," I said. "I can't read half as well as you."

'"You're teasing me," she pouted. "You couldn't have so many difficult books if you couldn't read well. No, you said that because you don't really want to read out to me."

'Her father suddenly called her from outside and she ran out.

'The next day after returning from school I asked Ma for food and went out on the terrace to water the plants. Masuma was there, digging up the earth around the roots of one of the potted plants. I was annoyed.

'"Who asked you to touch the plants?" I asked sternly.

'She went on working. "Why, the soil was completely dry!" she said. "The roots need this."

'"That's enough," I snapped. "Move."

'She immediately moved away. I became busy with the plants. A little later I stole a glance at her. The sun was setting, and Masuma's little face reflected all the colours of the sunset. I thought I'd never seen anything so beautiful.

'"Are you angry with me, Masuma?" I asked, contrite.

'"No," Masuma said easily. She kept pulling her hair back with her muddy little hands.

'"We're leaving today. Once I go the plants will all die because you won't water them. Do you know I watered all the plants yesterday? If I didn't, they'd all be dead." She smiled.

'"Are you leaving today? When?"

'"By the night train. All the lights will be switched on in the train, and the fans will be running. Such fun!"

'I came up to her and took her hand.

'"Aren't you going to miss me?" I asked.

'"Not you, but Chachi. She loves me so much."

'I pulled her close and kissed her on her soft red cheeks.

'"I love you very much too, Masuma," I said.

'"Honestly?"

'"Honestly. I'll cry when you go away, I'll miss you most terribly. Nothing will be the same."

'"I'll love you too, then. Come over to our village during the vacations and we shall play a lot, shall we?"

'"All right. Give me a kiss, then."

'She put her arms around me and touched my cheeks with her lovely soft lips. You know something, Asmat? Those childish kisses were so innocent . . . there was nothing even remotely exciting about them, but I still remember them . . . they are the best memories I have. I kissed her again and again, and she kissed me back.

'Masuma was such a child that she never thought twice about it, but I was growing up. I had never experienced such a thrill, neither had I felt so guilty about anything I'd done in my life. I went downstairs and she did too. I had the snacks my mother served me, went out to play with friends—but all the while my mind was left back home, where Masuma was. I desperately wanted to return home; at the same time I was curiously reluctant to face her. Finally when I returned home it was quite late. Masuma and her father had already left.

'I went to my mother. She was chopping betel nuts. "If you returned a little earlier you'd have met Masuma. The poor girl was so upset. She was asking after you," she said.

'My heart lurched wildly. Had she told Mother more? Perhaps even the whole story? I hung around the kitchen a little longer but Mother didn't say anything else. I was so tense I couldn't eat anything. I merely picked at my dinner and ran upstairs as soon as I could. Sleep eluded me. I stared into the darkness, feeling utterly alone.

'After a long time, I heard my mother coming upstairs with my father. They were talking, assuming I was asleep. It was long past my bedtime.

'"Masuma is such a nice girl, and so beautiful," said Mother. "I wish we could get her married to Kasem."

'"Huh!" said my father. "What's the use of beauty in a daughter-in-law? Her father is only a schoolteacher. If he lost his job he'd be a pauper. We can't possibly negotiate with a family like theirs."

'"They might be poor, but they're our relatives after all, and it's a good family," Mother said. "Besides, Kasem is our only son. Why do we need to arrange his marriage with a rich girl? By

Allah's grace we have enough!"

'"Don't even think about it," Father said sternly. "It can't happen."

'My mother fell silent.

'I think that was the moment when I woke up to reality. It was as if someone had rudely torn my most tender dream apart. Perhaps I never really recovered from that pain.

'Time passed. I grew up, completed my education. Mother had passed away by that time. Perhaps I'd even forgotten Masuma. I'd heard that her father had died, and before that, had married her off to a teacher like himself. Meanwhile, I was all set to go to England for further studies when my father fell seriously ill. He told me that he wanted to see me settled before he died. I had never done anything to upset my father, and soon, I got married to please him. My wife came from one of the richest families in Calcutta. To tell you the truth I was not unhappy with my marriage. Perhaps I even fell a little in love with my wife, the beautiful and elegant Asema.

'Father passed away. He died happy. I, his only son, had money, respect, happiness, a beautiful wife. What more could he want for me?

'One morning soon after that Masuma's husband, Abu Ali, suddenly came over to my house to meet me. I learned that his father had borrowed heavily from my father and had lost everything in debt, even his house, before he died. Abu Ali, however, had not come to plead with me to return their house. He'd come to tell me that my father had annexed a portion of Masuma's father's property, which they wanted back.

'I promised him I'd ask my manager to look into the matter immediately. "What do you do?" I asked him.

'"I used to teach in our village school, but now I've got a job in Calcutta."

'"Have you brought Masuma over?" I asked eagerly.

'"Yes, and my brother too. There's no one else in my family."

'"Where are you staying?"

'"I've taken a house near Entally on rent. We arrived a couple of weeks ago."

'"And you never thought of visiting me! Let's go to your house right now."

'"We were thinking of inviting you once we'd settled down," Ali said, a little embarrassed. "Masuma said—"

'I stopped him. "Yes, I suppose Masuma has become quite the mistress of the house! Let's see what she says when I surprise her with a visit."

'It was eleven o'clock in the morning. I took my car out and drove to their house with Ali. When we knocked at the door a familiar voice rang out from inside, "I'm not going to open the door unless I hear your name!"

'Ali blushed and said quickly, "It's me, Ali. Open the door."

'The door opened. I entered first, followed by Ali.

'I was expecting to see her, but the first moment of eye contact was overwhelming. Her crushed sari was wet in patches; she must have been mopping the floor. Her face was flushed from exercise, sweat glistened in beads on her forehead. And yet how lovely she looked! She was startled to see me enter the house with Ali, and immediately pulled her sari over her shoulders and moved away a little.

'"Don't you recognize me, Masuma?" I said. "I'm Kasem."

'She smiled and raised her hand, doing a salaam.

'"If you wanted to salaam me you could've come to see me," I said. "It's been quite some time since you came to Calcutta."

'Ali brought out a chair on the verandah for me.

'"To go to a rich man's house unasked—" Masuma said, still smiling.

'". . . is scary, is it?" I finished for her.

'"Not at all," she said spiritedly. "I'm not scared of anyone. It was just that—"

'"Yes?"

'"Well, I wasn't sure the rich man would recognize me. But

now that you've come to see me, I'll perhaps go to meet Begum Saheba one of these days," she added with a smile.

'"You know what he says?" Masuma said, pointing to Ali. "He says I shouldn't go to your house because I don't have expensive saris and jewellery. Don't you think if someone is close to me, I'd be welcome even if I visit him in a torn sari?"

'Ali was fidgeting, clearly very embarrassed. I felt a rush of affection for the shy young man sitting before me. Masuma was obviously the stronger of the two, and I could see how much Ali depended on his wife. I'd caught the little glances and the intimate smiles passing between them, I'd noticed their eyes seeking each other out. I was happy for them, and a little envious too. This young man did not have wealth or material comfort, and yet in my eyes he was one of the luckiest people on earth.

'"You must stay back for lunch," Masuma said. "I'll get both of you some sherbet while I go and have a bath."

'I was very touched. "This is an awkward time," I said. "Why don't we make it another day, sometime soon?"

'"No way," Masuma said, offering a glass of sherbet to me. "I won't let you leave without having lunch. Oh, I know Bhabi's lunch will be delayed, but it's just for a day, after all. I have to go through this all the time. Why don't you ask him, he's right here. Previously he had many friends to offer him lunch while I was left starving at home. Let's see how many friend he can make in Calcutta!"

'Now Ali spoke for the first time, "She seems to have collected lots of friends quite fast. So be it, let her get her own back now, can't take her caustic comments any more."

'Ali and I sipped the cool sherbet and started to talk.

'"I studied up to B.A.," Ali said, a little hesitantly. "But then my father passed away and I had to drop out of college. Everything we had back in Pabna had to be sold to meet my father's debts. Masuma's father's house was still there, of course, but we had a tiff with the manager of your father's estate over it and Masuma said it would be better if we moved to Calcutta. So—"

'"What are you going to do here?"

'"I've taken a share in a business. Let's see how things work out."

'I gathered they were not too well off but I'd be blind not to see their contentment. I learnt from Ali that Masuma was expecting. They would hire a maid now, he said.

'Masuma came back after taking a bath and kept working and talking at the same time. Ali's brother Abu Emam returned home and Masuma introduced me to him. Her completely natural behaviour amazed and delighted me. To be absolutely honest, I was also a little atrracted.

'"When Bhabi hears why you were so late today she's going to be awfully angry with me," Masuma said, smiling, as she served us lunch.

'"She's not at home. Gone to see her mother."

'"But today is Sunday!"

'"Well, I don't work, so every day is Sunday for me."

'"That's true. But I'm feeling guilty now. I shouldn't have held you back. Poor you—instead of having sweet conversation with in-laws and pulao and korma served at Bhabi's father's mansion under a fan you get to eat only dal and rice in this little house, hot as hell. Not fair," she said, shaking her head.

'"Your Bhabi goes to her father's whenever she pleases," I said, shaking my head. "But I don't follow her every time. If you ask me, I'm enjoying your dal and rice much more than my father-in-law's pulao and korma. Trust me, Masuma, I can't possibly express how much this means to me."

'My voice choked slightly towards the end and I stopped abruptly. Masuma's smile faded and she suddenly fell silent.

'That day was magical for me. The more I noticed the easy intimate relationship between husband and wife, the more keenly I felt the absence of it in my life. I'd never stopped to think about it before, but it suddenly struck me how empty my life was. When we were newly married, I'd return home every other day to hear from the servants that Begum Saheba had gone to her father's house and left a message, asking me to follow. The first few times I went too, and it wasn't bad to spend some time chatting and laughing with my brothers-and-sisters-in-law. But then I started enjoying those visits less and less, and began to ignore my wife's messages. I'd eat lunch alone at my house, served carelessly by servants. Sometimes I'd return home early in the evening with a half-formed plan to go out with Asema to the movies or just for a stroll, but invariably I'd find Asema gone to her father's. At times she'd leave a note for me, at times just a cryptic message with the servants. Asema and I almost never talked about it, and even if the subject came up Asema would be so adamant and tearful that I'd have to relent. I had not really minded that, not even thought about it consciously, but now, looking at this happily married couple, I realized how much was missing from my own married life.

'One day soon after my first visit to Masuma's house I took out my car and brought her over to meet my wife. I watched them as they talked to each other. Do you know what I thought, Asmat? I felt Asema was a magnificently made cut-glass ornament whereas Masuma was an uncut diamond. Asema had polish and an acquired glitter, but she couldn't begin to compete with Masuma's natural radiance.

'Masuma came to visit Asema from time to time. The first few visits went well, but slowly and imperceptibly, the relationship between them began to sour. I was amazed to see Masuma's natural intelligence. She had already joined several associations in Calcutta and spoke surprisingly well on a wide range of subjects. Masuma, I realized, had effortlessly passed into a wider world. In worldly terms, Asema had everything Masuma didn't, but with every word and gesture, Masuma proved she was way ahead of Asema. Asema realized this instinctively, and she didn't like it.

'I knew Masuma was expecting a child. I asked Ali what arrangements he'd made for the delivery, and Ali replied that Masuma had decided to give birth to her child in the hospital.

Although it was none of my business, I was very angry. I tried to talk Masuma out of it and offer help, but she brushed aside my objections and offers of help smilingly. Soon she returned from the hospital with her son. I went to see them one day. Her eyes, her smile, every little gesture was glowing with the newfound happiness of motherhood. This proved to be the last straw for my wife. She now started to express her jealousy quite indecently. Masuma was intelligent enough to sense it and very unobtrusively, she made herself scarce. When her visits to my house became infrequent, it had a curious effect on me. The attraction I'd felt for her became stronger and I found I couldn't control myself any longer. I didn't want to.'

Kasem suddenly became agitated. 'And I insulted this woman. The woman I longed for so much and so completely. I can never forgive myself for that, Asmat,' he said. Asmat quietened his friend, wiping his feverish forehead. A little later Kasem resumed talking.

'A year passed. I visited them quite often. I found a kind of vicarious pleasure in watching their happiness. Their expenses had increased, but Ali's salary had gone up too, and they could now afford a nurse for the child. Masuma had also started earning some money by stitching clothes and doing some embroidery work. They left their house in Entally and took a small house on rent near Park Circus. It had only two rooms, but Masuma kept the house so neat and clean that it would make you feel good just to enter it. Ali and Masuma were not comfortably off, but they never borrowed a penny from anyone. The more I saw them, the more I learned to respect them.

'My wife fell ill and the doctor said a change of climate would do her good. We decided to go to Ceylon where Asema's brother lived. It felt bad to leave Masuma behind. Before leaving I asked Ali to write to me.

'There was no news from them for a month and a half and then suddenly I got to know that Ali had passed away. He had typhoid and within a week everything was over. I felt like dropping everything and running back to Masuma. But I could offer no ostensible reason for returning to Calcutta, and Asema insisted that we stay back for some more time. She was jealous and suspicious, and she wasn't far wrong. I felt guilty and didn't find the strength to defy my wife. As a result we returned to Calcutta after five more months. I went to see Masuma the first free moment I had. But I had a surprise waiting for me.

'I was expecting to see a grieving widow. I was prepared for tears and laments. Instead I found a woman almost removed from the mundane world by the radiance of her strength and dignity. Her little boy lisped a thousand questions and Masuma answered him patiently and quietly. Ali was dead, but his presence in the house was palpable. Even his pillows were arranged carefully on the bed, as if he'd just stepped out, and would return any moment. I had gone there prepared to offer my condolences, but was left speechless.

'Ali's brother was studying for his I.A. exams but he'd had to drop out of studies and was looking for a job. He was the one who spoke to me as I sat, dumb, in the familiar room. Masuma addressed only a few words to me. "I have a small plot of land in our village," she said. "If you help me construct a small house I'd rather go and live there." I promised I'd do whatever I could to help.

'My wife was incensed that I'd gone to Masuma's house. "Why did you go there?" she screamed. I felt something snap within me. "Because I wanted to," I replied. This started a terrible row. Asema hurled accusations at me, her words spewing jealousy and rage like venom. In a perverse way, this resistance from Asema brought my desire for Masuma out into the open. I was now determined to make Masuma my wife.

'Despite the trouble at home, I did not stop seeing Masuma. I was, however, increasingly frustrated and angry at her attitude. She seemed to have detached herself completely from me and withdrawn into a private world, the key to which was consistently denied to me. I tried stubbornly to help her with money, so that she became dependent on me in some concrete way, but Masuma refused politely every time. The only help she'd ask from me was with constructing the house at her village. I told her I'd go to the village in a month's time and would take her along, silently praying that she would give up the idea.

'The situation at home was getting worse every passing day. Asema had started to complain to her family about Masuma. My in-laws confronted me soon with the question about my relationship with Masuma. I was livid at this and in a heated moment told them that I wished to marry Masuma.

'It was as if they were holding their breath to hear me say this. As soon as I put into words what had been a vague apprehension in their minds, they were shocked into silence. One day very soon after that, I returned home to find Asema had left. She left a message that she'd gone to her father's house and would never return. I was relieved more than anything else. Instead of going to Asema's father's house and trying to persuade her to come back, I proceeded to Masuma's house.

'It was ten o'clock at night. Masuma's brother-in-law opened the door and looked very surprised to see me at such an odd hour. I didn't bother to explain anything to him and ran upstairs. Masuma had just put her child to bed and finished her namaz. Her dark thick eyelashes still held the droplets of the *aju* water. For a second the thought flashed across my mind that she had been crying.

'"Can you spare some time to listen to me?" I asked.

'"Yes, of course."

'I told her everything. She listened silently, attentively. Not a line on her face moved. I had no clue to what she was feeling.

'"What do you think I should do?" she asked once I'd stopped. "I could go to Bhabi's father's house and try to bring her back if that's what you wish."

'"I don't want her back. I want you."

'Masuma looked stricken. "Me? What are you going to do with me?" she cried out.

'"Do with you?" I cried frenziedly. "I've loved you from my childhood, Masuma. I'm going to love you for the rest of my life. I want you to bring happiness to my empty house."

'Masuma stared silently at me for a long time. "You're not yourself," she said finally, in a voice that was surprisingly steady. "I've always looked on you as an elder brother. A tiff between husband and wife is not unusual, I'm sure Bhabi will return home soon. And, if she doesn't like you to come here, I'd rather you didn't come."

'I was shocked. Masuma's voice softened. "Go home, it's very late. I'm sure you know this is sheer madness."

'Madness? The woman for whom I was ready to give up everything thought my love was madness! I'd never been so angry in my life. I'd never felt so completely helpless either. I spent the next hour or so arguing, cajoling, pleading, and finally crying, but she remained firm. All she'd say was, "Go back home. When you come back to your senses you'll understand what I'm saying is right. If Bhabi allows you to come and see me, it's fine, otherwise I wouldn't like you to see me again."

"Aren't you going home?" asked Masuma's brother-in-law, entering the room.

'Before I could answer Masuma told him, "Yes, of course, he is leaving. Why don't you see him off?"

'I returned home like an automaton. I was awake the whole night, making plans. My thoughts went round in circles, on and on . . . I was alternately miserable, furious and pathetic. Towards dawn, exhausted and desperate, I thought like a mutinous child, I'd go on seeing her every day, and I'd refuse to make any arrangement for her to go back to her village. It was as if I dared her to continue to thwart me.

'I went back to her house in the morning. She was not at home. She had apparently started teaching embroidery a month or so ago to a woman who sent her car to pick Masuma up and drop her back home. Ali's brother had resumed his studies and taught a few students privately in the evenings. I was incensed at these efforts of Masuma to get her life back in order. I realized how with every step she took she moved away beyond my reach.

'I went back to see Masuma that evening. She was on the terrace with her son. The little boy was in her arms, and she was showing him the beautiful moon.

'"Is Bhabi back yet?" she asked with a smile. "I'll go and see her."

'I felt bolder. "No, she isn't back, and I don't want to bring her back either. You come with me."

'Masuma's smile lost its brightness, but a trace of it still remained on her lips. "Isn't it typical of you men," she said sadly. "If you wish to get married again whom do you blame it on but your wives? Never ever do you look at your own weaknesses."

'"Think of another evening like this, Masuma, in the past," I said emotionally. "Why did you let me declare my love then? Do you think it was possible for me to forget you after that evening?"

'"If you loved me so much why didn't you marry me?" she asked, smiling again.

'"I didn't have the courage to go against my father's wishes. You can imagine how difficult things were for me. But now that I am my own master there's nothing to stop us from coming together. You mean the world to me, Masuma."

'"I know. But you don't necessarily have to possess the woman you love, do you? I care for you, too, but I think it's meaningless to say that you cannot live without me. You can live without me, as you have been living so far. Just go and bring Bhabi back."

'All her words but a phrase passed me by: "I care for you, too." Like a fool, I thought she was returning my love. I tried to hold her hand, but she stepped aside and started kissing her child.

'"Please, Masuma," I said, "please say you will marry me. I'll give you my all."

'"Really?" she asked, turning to face me. "What do you have to give me?"

'I don't remember what I told her in answer to that. A lot of theatrical nonsense, I suppose. She listened to everything smilingly, without saying a word. She made me feel ashamed, but I was still adamant. "I am going to make you mine," I repeated stubbornly, and climbed down the stairs.

'I went back after a couple of days to find that Masuma's son was ill. The doctor was not sure what it was, and everyone was very worried. Now I had a legitimate reason to see her. Masuma had to stay at home, and she did not have too much money saved. This time when I offered to pay for the medicines and treatment she could not object. She was a mother, after all, and nothing, not even her pride, was greater than her son's life. Her son had been diagnosed with typhoid, and Masuma spent a very anxious time, thinking perhaps that he would join his father. Like the creep that I was, I was elated because I'd discovered her single weakness.

'On the thirteenth day the child's temperature returned to normal. The doctor said he was on the way to recovery. For the first time in days, Masuma began to relax. She sent her brother-in-law to her student's house to talk to them so that she could resume her job. I did not like this at all. When I voiced my objection Masuma refused to listen to me. That started another spate of angry words, recriminations and tears. But Masuma remained firm.

'A few days later when I reached their house I found they were packing.

'"What's the matter?" I asked.

'"Bhabi doesn't want to live here anymore," said Ali's brother. "We've decided to go and live in our village."

'"Why didn't I hear of this before? And where do you think you're going to stay in the village?"

'"For the moment, we will put up with someone Bhabi knows. Later we can build our own house."

'I was so hurt and angry that I returned home immediately without even meeting Masuma. As I stepped on the road I looked up. Masuma was on the verandah, looking down. I looked away and went home.

'Never mind my anger, I was too obsessed with Masuma to stay away from her for long. That evening I went back to her. Ali's brother was playing with Masuma's child. He did not go to teach that day. When I entered through the door, I heard Masuma's voice.

'" . . . and you don't need to worry about my future. As long as you're there . . ."

'She was speaking to her brother-in-law.

'I felt as if I'd suddenly banged my head on the wall. Ali's brother was the same age as Masuma. Was there anything between them? Were they—I couldn't think anymore. I strode into the room and walked up to them.

'"Will you leave us alone, please?" I asked Ali's brother curtly. Even my own voice sounded harsh to me. He left the room, but I could feel his piercing eyes on me.

"This is the last time I'm telling you this, Masuma," I said. "If you want the best for yourself, listen to me. You'll live to regret it otherwise."

'"Don't talk nonsense," Masuma snapped.

'"Nonsense! Yes, of course. And I suppose whatever that fellow says makes perfect sense to you!" I was furious. I shouted at her. "I understand now why you don't want to marry me. That brother-in-law of yours is your 'future' now, is he?"

'Masuma's face was suffused with blood. Her eyes were burning. I was scared, but I was possessed by madness. I couldn't stop. "Well, I shall see how you can be happy with your precious brother-in-law. I'll teach you such a lesson . . ."

'Masuma's brother-in-law came running. "That's enough," he said angrily. "It was only because of Bhabi that I showed respect to you so far. But now that you've insulted her you've lost all right to be respected. Get out of here right now."

'"Emam!" Masuma said sharply to her brother-in-law. "Have you lost your senses as well? Why did you speak like that to him?"

'I'd reached the landing. I stopped and turned to throw my last barbed words at her. "Oh yes!" I spat out. "He's lost his senses all right. Over you."

'"Let me go!" yelled Emam. "I'll teach him a lesson he won't forget in his life."

'"No!" Masuma said. "When a dog bites you, you don't bite the dog back."

'I left their house feeling exactly like a caned dog. I was incapable of thinking straight. A black rage boiled inside me and a burning desire to get back at them somehow, to punish them, drove me around the dark streets of Calcutta for hours. When I returned home it was past midnight. My eldest brother-in-law was waiting for me. Apparently he'd been waiting since eight o'clock. He told me he knew where I'd been, but he didn't follow me there because it might have embarrassed me.

'How considerate! "Did you have anything to discuss?" I asked.

'He nodded. "Asema is miserable. I'm sure you're not too happy either. If you agree, we could try to arrange a good match for Masuma? After all, it's not right for a young girl like her to live alone . . ."

'I still don't know what came over me. I heard myself say, "You don't have to worry about that. She isn't going to marry anyone."

'"What do you mean?"

'"She's living with her brother-in-law."

'I said this about the woman to whom I had dedicated everything I had; I maligned the very embodiment of purity for whom my heart has cried out in longing in front of people who were already hostile to her.

'It breaks my heart now, Asmat. How could I do such a thing?

'My brother-in-law nodded sagely. "We knew about this," he said. "It's all over the city. In fact that's why I came to talk to you today. You shouldn't have got mixed up in this unsavoury business. Anyway, what's done is done. You're a man, after all. Now come with me and bring Asema back. She is sick with grief."

'Now that the words were out I suddenly felt utterly hollow within. I could not take back my words but at the same time at that moment I couldn't think of welcoming Asema back into my life and pretend to love her.

'"I am not coming with you now," I said. "In fact I'm not coming at all. Asema has left my house voluntarily. She could return if she wants and when she likes."

I went into a room and slammed the door shut on my brother-in-law.

'I woke up quite late the next day. I could hear a lot of voices in the house. I came out to find the whole house filled with Asema's relatives. Asema was standing near the door, her head bent low, as if in shame. I couldn't stand the sight of her. She reminded me of Masuma, of everything I'd lost. I ran into the bathroom and poured buckets of cold water on my head.

'Even the cold bath did not make me feel better. The whole day I lay in bed, pretending to be asleep, but I couldn't help hearing the comments that were tossed gleefully about Masuma and her immorality. I felt my skin burning; it was as if they were talking not about Masuma but me. I'd read in the *Ramayana* that Hanuman had burnt up the city of Lanka, but couldn't douse the fire on his own tail. I couldn't bear to hear their words because I knew I'd started it all.

'Towards the evening I escaped and walked to Masuma's house. It was locked. Masuma had left with her child and brother-in-law. I made enquiries, but they had not gone to the village, nor had they left any message with anyone. I searched each and every lane of Calcutta for them but they'd just vanished. I left home on the pretext that I was not well and needed a change of air, and travelled around to look for Masuma. Three years passed by but I couldn't trace them. I lost hope and returned to Calcutta.

'Shortly after that, I glimpsed a young man in College Street who looked suspiciously like Masuma's brother-in-law. I followed him and stopped my car in front of him. He was, indeed, Emam.

I was desperate to find out about Masuma. I clung to his hands and pleaded with him to tell me where she was. He turned away and pulled his hands free. I could see the hatred in his eyes.

'"She's alive and well," he said finally. "I'd come to Calcutta to look for a job and I'm going back now."

'He never revealed where they were staying.

'As I stood helpless in the crowded street of Calcutta and saw the young man turn his back and walk away from me, I seemed to wake up. It was as if in an instant all my futile rage, filthy desires, and black thoughts of revenge drained out of me. I was still determined to find Masuma, but I knew this time it would be to ask for her forgiveness.

'I'd heard vaguely that Masuma's uncle lived somewhere in East Bengal. I left home again, and have been searching for her since then. It's been almost a year but I haven't had a single clue about her whereabouts, until today, when I suddenly glimpsed a face that looked in the half light heart-stoppingly like her, and heard her name. But my Masuma was a widow. This woman is probably married; I thought I saw a few bangles on her wrist. Maybe she has married again. I don't mind at all. I only wish I could see her once again so that I could tell her how sorry I was. And I'd ask just one thing of her: to let me help with her son's education. I know there's no one she loves more in this world.'

Kasem's voice choked, his eyes filled with tears.

'Be quiet, Kasem,' Asmat said. 'You've spoken for far too long. Allah Himself accepts genuine penitence, how can a mere mortal refuse to do so? You get some rest, I'll be back soon.'

A few minutes later, Asmat was back with Masuma. He switched on the lights and called Kasem softly. Kasem opened his eyes and stared at the woman standing before him. His lips trembled, but no sound emerged.

'This is the same Masuma,' said Asmat. 'After leaving Calcutta she'd gone to live with her uncle. You were right. She is not my own sister. Her father was my teacher and I knew her since childhood. I met her at her uncle's house and brought her over to live with us. She's more than a sister to me now.'

Kasem was silent. Tears spilled over from his sunken eyes into the pillow.

'Ask for her forgiveness now. My sister has suffered a great deal, Kasem,' Asmat resumed. 'So have you. But money doesn't buy true love. You should've known that. I wouldn't be unhappy if you married Masuma. But now that I've come to know her well, I've realized that Allah meant her for greater things. All the needy and poor people of the world are her children now. She has found a new direction and meaning in her life.' he turned to face Masuma.

'Masuma, please forgive my friend,' he pleaded.

Masuma was wiping the tears in her eyes; now she rested a soft cool hand on Kasem's forehead. Kasem trembled at the touch and shut his eyes.

'Forgive me,' she said. 'I was young then, I didn't know how to reason with people. You've wasted so many years of your life, and I feel responsible for it.'

'Now that you've forgiven me I don't have anything left to wish for,' Kasem said, his eyes still shut. 'But your son . . .'

'He's fine,' Masuma said. 'He's in Calcutta, in a boarding school. Asmat Bhai has given Emam a job. I'd heard from him that you'd seen him and asked after me. I'd thought I'd go to Calcutta during the holidays and meet you. I was hoping to bring Bhabi back.'

Kasem was incapable of speech. Masuma wiped his tears away gently and continued, 'Don't torture yourself anymore. Because of you I learnt the ways of the world. I needed that lesson in pain. I've left all that behind me, and I wish you would forget everything too. Asmat Bhai has taught me that everyone has something to contribute to the world. Life is too precious for a single person to ruin it.'

Masuma paused. Her hand still rested on Kasem's forehead. Kasem lay still, eyes shut, as if he was sucking in the warmth and kindness of her touch through every pore.

'I haven't married again,' Masuma said. 'Bhabi—Asmat Bhai's wife—doesn't let me live like a widow, she finds it much too painful. That's why I wear bangles, eat hearty meals . . . surely you can see how much weight I've put on?' she laughed a little. 'No, but seriously, you get well, and we shall all go to Calcutta together. I can't wait to see Bhabi and you together.'

The clock struck three o'clock. Asmat switched off the light. The soft light of the single candle touched Kasem's face like a caressing hand.

'Try to get some sleep now,' Masuma urged. 'I'll sit here with you.'

Hajera came and stood at the door. 'It's only a few hours till morning,' she said to her husband. 'You get some sleep, your friend will be fine with the two of us to look after him.'

Masuma sat down at the head of the bed. Her hand slid in and out of Kasem's dry, knotted hair, untangling it gently; brushing away beads of perspiration from his forehead. Kasem's body relaxed, the lines on his face softened and dissolved the pattern of grief they had etched there for years. Kasem slept.

From 'Keyar Kanta', 1937.

Letter

14/1, Sareng Lane
Calcutta.
4th July, 1927

Respected Editor Saheb

I have fallen into the bad habit of running to you with every little problem I have, but will continue to do so till the day you remain the editor of *Saugat* by Allah's grace. I know this might have annoyed you sometimes, as it was bound to, but you are too good to express your impatience with me. This has actually made me bolder and more demanding. I never hesitated or felt any inhibition writing to you. What I feel today seems unreal, and yet . . .

I saw a report in the newspaper that some people had attacked him [Kazi Nazrul Islam] in Dacca; that he got beaten up. If he's actually done something to deserve this insult, don't you think that's all the more reason for us to protect him?

This is not an issue of an insult to an individual any more. The prestige of the entire Muslim society, particularly its intellectuals like you, is at stake. I am aware that some of the so-called intellectuals are too vain and self-important to care for anyone but themselves. There are very few, in fact, who care enough for others to come forward to work for society or in national interest. Otherwise, how can we possibly explain the utter neglect of Kazi, the single bright light in the Muslim literary world? There doesn't seem to be anyone left in the world today who is willing to acknowledge or accept him as a friend.

If Mrs. M. Rahman were alive today Kazi would be as safe as a child in his mother's arms. But poor man, he doesn't have a mother to look after him any longer, nor a sister. Couldn't someone among the scores of Bengali Muslim men recognize him as a brother today? I am pained and ashamed to think that almost everyone shrinks back if so much as Kazi's name is mentioned in their presence. Isn't this a shame we all share?

My husband is now busy with his examinations; otherwise I'd have asked him to find out Kazi's whereabouts and take care of him. You are the only other person I can dare to appeal to. Please look after him. Could you let me know where he and his family are right now? I heard that his mother has passed away. I'm certain that if she were alive she would write to you with the same request. Think of me as an anxious sister of the poor man—I implore you to bring my wretched brother back from the streets. He doesn't need punishment; he needs love and affection. If you can somehow bring him back to Calcutta he just might be saved. If you fail, it will be a shame for Kazi himself, and for each and every one of us, Muslim writers and thinkers. Some time in the future a second Rabindranath might come along, but there will never be another Kazi Nazrul Islam.

With regards,
Sufia N. Hossain.[7]

Notes

1 This letter was later published in Saugat.

2 Quoted in Selim Jahangir, *Sufia Kamal* (Dhaka: Nari Udyog Kendra, 1993), p. 182.

3 Sufia Kamal, *Ekaley Amader Kaal* (Our Time in This Age), (Dhaka: Gnan Prakashani, 1988), pp. 53-54.

4 See Introduction, this volume. Notes by the Editors, and introductory note, Chapter 10, 'Shamsunnahar Mahmud (1908-64)', this volume.

5 Sufia Kamal must have been deeply marked by the poetry of Rabindranath Tagore, as this poem shows. This was, of course, to be expected in any young poet of that time.

6 The Urdu term *aab-e-Hyat* signifies the water of life.

7 Sufia Kamal (then Sufia N. Hossain) wrote this letter to Mohammad Nasiruddin, the editor of *Saugat*, in July 1927, expressing her anxiety about the unfortunate condition of Kazi Nazrul Islam at that time. Nasiruddin writes about this letter: 'I was moved and not a little ashamed by Sufia's letter. It is true that no Muslim writer or, indeed, anyone else, had spoken so sincerely on behalf of Nazrul in his difficult times... Sufia wrote that we should bring the poor man back and give him all the love and affection he needed. I decided to try to do just that.' [*Bangla Sahitye* Saugat *Yug* (The Saugat Era in Bengali Literature), Dhaka: Noorjahan Begum, 1985, pp. 681-2].

Part II

Conversations

All the translations in Part II,
Conversations, are by Rukmini Sen

12

Mohammad Nasiruddin: A Pioneer of Women's Emancipation

Mohammad Nasiruddin (1888-1993) was one of the pioneers in the movement for Muslim women's emancipation. Many Bengali Muslim women started writing in his magazine *Saugat*, first published in 1918. It was because of Nasiruddin's inspiration and encouragement that many women could continue writing for *Saugat*. He lived through many decades like a sturdy old tree. A couple of years before his death, *Rupantar*, a feminist magazine published from Dhaka, carried an account of a conversation between him and Shaheen Akhtar. With *Rupantar's* consent, the piece is reprinted here with slight modifications.

'Right from my childhood, I was fond of reading books and magazines and liked reading books containing pictures. I noticed that these were written and edited by our Hindu brothers who were our neighbours. The Muslims did not have a magazine in the Bengali language. The paradox was that although Muslims were the majority in Bengal and their mother tongue was Bengali; they studied the Arabic, Persian and Urdu languages. This led to ignorance, superstition and a decadent thought process at the time. I realized this at a very young age—when I was in school.'

The childhood that Mohammad Nasiruddin spoke about covered the early years of the twentieth century. At that time there was a debate as to what the mother tongue of Bengali Muslims ought to be. One perspective was that Bengali was the language of the Hindus, and Bengali culture belonged to the Hindu community. Another group, while maintaining their distinct religious identity from the Hindu Bengalis, agreed that their mother tongue was Bengali and it was necessary to cultivate Bengali culture. Mohammad Nasiruddin belonged to the second group. Besides creating a congenial atmosphere for language and culture; he also lent a hand in support of an oppressed section of the society.

'One of the three main reasons for publishing *Saugat* was to facilitate the emancipation of Bengali Muslim women. I observed that women comprised half of society. If they are handicapped, society too would be disabled. This thought propelled me.'

Mohammad Nasiruddin remains one of the pioneers of Bengali Muslim women's emancipation. At 103, this omniscient man still enjoyed talking and reminiscing. He told us that the doctor had not discouraged him from talking, but asked him to talk about things he liked.

I took a chance. On two consecutive days (8 and 9 March 1991), for two hours, I listened to his reminiscences. I asked a few questions, here and there. The questions which might have offended him were not asked. Mohammad Nasiruddin was an exceedingly thoughtful human being. At the very outset he asked why I wanted to talk to him. For the next two hours what he said pertained to the subject we were addressing in some way or the other. This is an edited version of the conversation we had. At the outset, I would like to thank this wise and thoughtful man.

Saugat was first published in 1918. Fifteen years earlier the radical writings of Begum Rokeya Sakhawat Hossain had created a storm in the reading community. Fresh new life was expected to burgeon on the earth, made fertile by her writing. But that had not happened yet. Rather, for twelve years (1905-1917) Begum Rokeya too had stopped writing. Mohammad Nasiruddin said, 'For the first volume of *Saugat* in the first year, Rokeya contributed two pieces, one a poem named *Saugat* ('The Gift'), and another a sketch of society called *Sesame Phank* ('Open Sesame'). At that time I had not received any writing from any other Muslim woman.'

He spoke at length on Begum Rokeya on day one. 'When

Saugat was about to be published, I got in touch with Rokeya and impressed upon her that women's writing will receive a priority in this magazine. Just as her school had been the pioneer of modern education for Muslim women, *Saugat* too would make a similar contribution in the field of literature. She was very happy to know that *Saugat* would be published. Frequently she would call or send messengers to enquire about the date of publication. Rokeya was not a poet. But she was so overwhelmed by the publication of *Saugat,* she wrote a poem and sent it in with a letter. "I am not a poet," she wrote. "Since I could not contain my excitement, I wrote the poem. Maybe it has not made the cut as a proper poem, but if you accept it as my best wishes, I will be obliged".'

Welcoming all Muslim women, this poem, also called '*Saugat*', was published on the first page of the maiden volume of of *Saugat.* For the second issue of *Saugat* Nasiruddin received rather immature writings by two women. One of these, a poem, was published. During that time women started their literary careers by writing short poems.

At that time Mohammad Nasiruddin published pictures of women writers in *Saugat.* He created a section named 'Woman's World', which was illustrated. This angered the moulvis. Nasiruddin retorted, 'The more the moulvis get angry, the more I will publish writings by women with pictures.' Given the circumstances, he decided to bring out an illustrated *Women's Saugat.* He was influenced by English magazines. According to him, 'Women are now becoming pilots and scientists. These things strike me. I saw Hindu women stepping outside their homes and participating in conferences. All these accentuated my anger against the fundamentalists.'

But this was an uphill task. There was, on the one hand, a lack of women writers and on the other, pressure from the conservatives. I asked him how he was able to tide over this impossible problem.

'It was a dedication of sorts. Every problem is solved when

one is determined enough. It was a matter of pride to have the famous Ashapurna Devi write in *Saugat.* She visited my house. Rabindranath Tagore's elder sister Swarnakumari Devi would send her work to me. Even Sarala Devi Chowdhurani wrote for us. Sarojini Naidu sent English poems for *Women's Saugat.* I published their writings with their photographs and presented the magazine to Muslim women. At that time a newspaper named *Illustrated Weekly of India* was published. There was a foreign newspaper. I would gather information and photographs from them.

'Before publishing the women's issue, I advertised in the newspaper, asking for contributions. A couple of women started sending aritides. Through *Saugat* and *Saptahik Saugat* (the weekly issue), I could propagate the message of women's education and emancipation. We spread the word among certain people asking them to keep us informed about women writers.

'It took us a lot of effort to find Rokeya, who was busy with her school and many other things. I had discovered a few young women writers by then and started with them. Then I found Syeda Motahera Banu of Barishal who wrote extremely well. There were eight or ten of them, like Razia Khatun Chowdhurani and Mrs. M. Rahman.

'Many people were surprised at my fearlessness when in 1929 *Women's Saugat* was published. There was already quite a stir in society, and to top it now came a women's issue of *Saugat* with pictures. When the women's issue was released, I found that more than anyone else it was the mollahs who were enthusiastic about buying a copy from the hawkers.'

Saugat's editor did not intend only to print women's writings with photographs. He had attacked the practice of purdah, observed by Muslim women. Even Rokeya was behind the veil at that time.

In the interview Mohammad Nasiruddin described Sufia Kamal and Mahmuda Khatun Siddiqua's stories of breaking free from purdah. Nasiruddin could no longer see, but his voice rang passionately, narrating the achievements of a woman who fought her way. Very simply, what Mohammad Nasiruddin said was this:

'I got hold of the exercise book of Sufia [Sufia Kamal] containing poems through one of her relatives. At that time she wrote in secret. In her house, writing Bengali poems was banned. This was in 1927. The office of *Saugat* was to the north of Islamia College on Wellesley Street. One of Sufia's male relatives came to the *Saugat* office with her exercise book. Her handwriting was immature. Since she had not received formal school education, there were many spelling mistakes and none of the poems was titled.

'I had published one of Sufia's poems in *Saugat* the previous year. That poem too was untitled, and without any punctuation. She had written it at one go. I read it three or four times, inserted punctuation marks and read through it once again. I appreciated it. She had expressed her feelings very simply. Although she did not receive higher education, I could make out that poetry came naturally to her. I named this particular poem *Basanti* (Vernal). I still remember a part of it:

> Here my wooded path,
> Untrodden and alone,
> None came to tend the grass
> Nor make the flowers bloom.
> Then one dawn of Spring
> As the first light shone,
> From the south blew in
> An absent-minded breeze.

'Then one day, a young lady wearing a velvety veil arrived with the afore-mentioned male relative at the *Saugat* office. Lifting her veil, the lady said, "I am Sufia. You have created a havoc in my home by publishing my poem!"

'I said, "What does your husband say?"

"I have come to see you at his insistence. He asked me to

write more, and told me to do whatever you say. My husband says that he does not have any opinion about it."

'I said, "It is good that you have come. But I have an objection to something. Poets have a different style, they never wear a burqa. You are writing poems. You will become a poet. You will meet Rabindranath and Saratchandra. There are so many things that you have to do. Burqa does not suit you." She took off the burqa and gave it to her male relative. "What can I do, I have to abide by family norms. I, however, dislike burqas."

'After that she would frequently visit the *Saugat* office. She took off the burqa once she had reached the second floor. Gradually, Sufia completely discarded her burqa, when her husband gave the nod.'

Sufia was the first poet who could break the walls of the zenana and the burqa and come to the *Saugat* office.

'Then one day, the poet Mahmuda Khatun Siddiqua arrived at the *Saugat* office like a comet. I was startled. In those dark days of orthodoxy and superstition (1930), this young woman wore modern clothes and had her hair cut in a bob. On entering, she moved about restlessly. I asked her to sit down. She exclaimed, "Let me go to the terrace and see what the city of Calcutta looks like." She lived outside Calcutta. She was inspired by watching the women's movement take shape in *Saugat*. That is why she rushed to the *Saugat* office once she had reached Calcutta. Mahmuda Khatun Siddiqua wrote for the magazine for thirty years.

'They were here to break rules. *Saugat* gave them the encouragement and inspiration.'

My question: 'Do you see anybody in the present generation carrying your work ahead?'

'At that time we would work with immense commitment for the cause of women. Now it has become a business. I do not see any editor who is sensitive towards women's issues today.'

'Would you say your entire work has been a wasted effort? Did our country actually witness a women's movement?' My last question provoked him to make comments in the nature of a prophecy. This is something we are more or less aware of, but do not seem to comprehend. I am narrating verbatim the last section of Mohammad Nasiruddin's interview:

'Women's emancipation has definitely arrived. The lack of a progressive mentality among the social policymakers lead to women's suffering. Apparently, they speak differently. But they do not want the women to acquire the positions that men hold. When a conservative ruling class indulges in mumbo jumbo, women find it difficult to hold on to whatever [freedom] they have achieved. Until a progressive person or party starts governing the country, the situation cannot change. If the mollahs come to power the government will become something on the lines of Khomeini's reign. They would push the women indoors. The fear persists. But the situation in Bengal can never be similar to that of the Arab world. The women are moving ahead, they will move further ahead.'

First published in *Rupantar*, 1991

13

Sufia Kamal: The Legacy of Begum Rokeya

Sufia Kamal was born in 1911. At the time of this interview, eighty-seven-year-old Sufia was bogged down by ill-health, but her mind was alert. She had not only seen the '*Saugat* Age' of the 1930s, but had a role in it as well. She lived long and her twin pursuits—literature and social service—continued till almost the very end. She was 'Khalamma' to the present generation of Muslim women writers. The first time we visited her house, surrounded by greenery, we talked over tea and snacks, sitting on her verandah. She was not physically fit that day. Afterwards, Shaheen Akhtar went back to see her on 6 and 20 September 1996. On these two days, Sufia Kamal narrated many stories while talking about her journey as an author. Here is a first-person account. Sufia Kamal died in 1999.

I was born in an educated family. We were taught in Arabic or Persian. My uncles were well-known scholars. They knew many languages, from Sanskrit to Assamese. However, they were not interested in women's education—perhaps they did not like the idea very much. In our family, I learnt Bengali from my mother, who in turn had learnt it from my father. I remember even the watchmen in our house reading books at the time. There would be performances like jatra and milad mehfil,[1] which I would watch. When I started reading Bengali literature, I was a child—I used to spell out the letters and read.

I spent my childhood in my maternal uncle's house: the nawab's palace at Shayestabad in Barishal. There was a big library in it. People would say that among private libraries, this was second only to the one in the house of Khodabaksh of Patna.

Many scholars from within the country and abroad visited the library, but there was little scope for female education, especially in Bengali. I first read Rabindranath Tagore in this library, in the magazine *Prabasi*. At that time, I had no sense of rhyme in poetry. But how I enjoyed what I read! This was the first time I got a taste of literature.

At that time, a magazine named *Muslim Sahitya Patrika* (Muslim Literary Magazine) was published and edited possibly by Dr. Mohammad Shahidullah. Kazi Nazrul's novel *Hena* was published in that magazine serially. This was a time when I used to spell out the word while reading. I enjoyed both the poem by Rabindranath Tagore (I have forgotten the name) and the novel *Hena*. I was nine or ten. I would read Bengali in secret, not wishing to let anyone know about my love for the language. At that time Rokeya, Sara Tayfur, Syeda Motahera Banu were writing. I was inspired to follow their examples. I started writing. I do not remember what my early writings were about. I was excited about writing.

I used to read the works of Rabindranath Tagore and Nazrul Islam. Then I read Sita Devi, Shanta Devi, Badhurani (Jyotirmala Devi). Many Hindu women were writing at the time. Begum Rokeya, Nazrul Islam and Rabindranath Tagore were my favourites.

I was married at twelve. I had written quite a bit by then. Our house was in Barishal town. Saral Kumar Dutt, the nephew of Mahatma Ashwini Kumar Dutt, edited a weekly magazine called *Tarun* (Youth) in Barishal. My first piece appeared in *Tarun*, a story called '*Sainik Badhu*' (Wife of a Soldier), which upset my family members. Everybody in the house was angry that I had learnt Bengali, published a Bengali piece and my name was printed in Bengali! I had to face a great deal of resistance and endure many unsavoury remarks at the time.

At the same time the highly-placed officials in Barishal, such as judges, magistrates and the police, told my maternal uncle, 'We've heard a girl from your family is writing plays. This is a matter of great pride for us. Why do you discourage her?'

I published a number of poems in *Tarun*. I started with a short story which was lost while I was in Barishal. My writing was published in a magazine named *Dhakar Abhijan* (Dhaka on an Expedition). Reading it, an overwhelmed Kazi Nazrul wrote me a long letter: 'I cannot believe that a Muslim girl can write this. I heard that you will be coming to Calcutta. I will come and see you.'

But my pieces had not appeared in *Saugat* yet. After coming to Calcutta, I sent a piece to Nasiruddin Saheb [the editor of *Saugat*]. In a note I wrote that I was sending the article at Nazrul Islam's behest. My poems were published for the first time. Nasiruddin Saheb helped me carve a niche for myself by publishing my work on a regular basis. And my literary pursuits were possible because of Nazrul's encouragement. Rabindranath Tagore too had showered me with his blessings.

We began living in Calcutta. We, the women, still wore the veil at most times. Unexpectedly, one afternoon, when my husband [Syed Nehal Hossain, Sufia's first husband] was in college and my brother not at home, I heard Nazrul calling my name as he entered the house. My mother and I were the only people in the house at the time. Nazrul was by nature unrestrained, like a rushing tide. You never had the chance to see Nazrul in such a state. If you did you would have realized the kind of man he was. He entered the room without warning. Noticing me, he exclaimed, 'Are you the same Sufia! You are such a small creature! I had thought that Mrs S. N. Hossain would be a "big" writer. I do not have a younger sister, so you shall be one to me!' He said all this in one breath, and resumed talking. 'You will call me "Dadu", won't you? Where is Amma?' My mother was old-fashioned, unwilling to come out in front of him. Nazrul entered the bedroom, touched her feet to show his respect. Nowadays it's difficult to find such people. He would laugh loudly, as if he were opening his heart out. Suddenly he said, 'Get me some tea! Get me a paan!'

Had it not been for Nasiruddin Saheb, Nazrul would not have survived. Nazrul used to live at Krishnanagar. His novel *Mrityu-Khudha* (The Hunger of Death) was based largely on his experiences of this period of his life. At that time, he would commute from Krishnanagar to Calcutta. Khan Moinuddin was an intimate friend of Nazrul's. He told Nasiruddin Saheb that Nazrul was hard up. Nasiruddin allowed Nazrul to stay in the *Saugat* office premises and gave him a monthly salary. A number of Nazrul's works were penned sitting at the *Saugat* office.

Dhaka was not so huge at that time. Its boundaries extended till Wari. Nazrul had stayed in Dhaka for some time. He would give lessons in singing to students from Hindu families. Nowadays Hindus and Muslims interact easily. At that time young Hindu men were outraged to find a Muslim frequenting a Hindu household. Once the boys chased him on his way to the student's house. Nazrul managed to disarm and resist them single-handedly. When I heard of this incident in Dhaka, I wrote to Nasiruddin Saheb.

I never studied in Rokeya's school. After coming to Calcutta, I began working with Anjuman-e-Khawatin-e-Islam, a group founded by her. Begum Rokeya died after a while. It was as if she were our kin. I met her as a child, when we lived in Barishal. That's why I could not study in her school. Later, when I met Rokeya in Calcutta, I was already married.

I met Shamsunnahar Mahmud while working for Anjuman-e-Khawatin-e-Islam. Many Hindu and Muslim girls worked there. We, the Muslim women, visited the slums wearing a burqa. Begum Rokeya would say organizing meetings among a few women was not enough, women needed to work in the slums. I, too, had worked in the slums of Calcutta. She led us towards this path. That was the first time I witnessed the sufferings of people living in a slum. They lived in such terrible conditions! Often men did not allow us to enter the slums. They wanted to turn us out. There were many Urdu-speaking people in Calcutta's slums. They would say, 'They are Hindus, they are Bengalis.' It was disgusting. We tried educating the slum women. We taught them certain vocational skills like stitching, pottery and handicraft. I was with Anjuman-e-Khawatin-e-Islam for a long time. After Partition in 1947, I came to Dhaka.

After my husband's death [Syed Nehal Hossain died in 1932] I continued to write even as I was teaching in a corporation-run school and bringing up children. Nasiruddin Saheb was like an elder brother to me. Every Sunday I went to his residence. I was writing for *Saugat* as well as *Mohammadi*, besides working in a school. I made some money by writing in a few newspapers. I suffered a lot. But that is natural, you girls have been through it too. But the respect given to women in those days is missing now. Granted, boys made fun of the girls even in my time, but there were men writing under a girl's name to encourage the latter. My husband wrote under many females pseudonyms so that women would step forward and start writing. In our times, people would say, will women become judges or magistrates by learning to read and write? We would quote Begum Rokeya and say, surely they will. And that's precisely what happened. Women have become judges, magistrates, doctors and ruled nations.

While I was in Calcutta, I met Ashapurna Devi. Mahashweta Devi was younger than us. I also knew Radharani Devi. She was one of the first women writers to make a name as a poet. We used to call her Radhadi. I would run into her at meetings and conferences. Many Hindu women wrote in *Saugat*. They probably had to deal with family resistance. I will talk about my family here. I wrote despite a lot of resistance. Nobody in my family wanted me to write. Ultimately, I became detached from my family. Only my mother was with me. My mother and I became completely dissociated from our family [in the year 1933], because writing and speaking in Bengali, mingling with Bengalis and abandoning the purdah to do social service was considered demeaning to family honour. The family members, out of utter shame and disgust, did not want to see our faces ever again.

The first Muslim woman to write in Bengali was Nawab

Faizunnissa. I have heard that there were more women from earlier generations writing before we did. Actually we were ashamed of the fact that we wrote. Bengali Muslim women writing in Bengali was considered to be a shameful act. Even if they wrote, they did not publish their work. It is not known how many women writers have disappeared into oblivion. If a woman was writing in our times, it would be a talking point—why is she writing in Bengali?

The first person to have written for the benefit of society, the nation, and race was Begum Rokeya. Then it was somebody called Mrs. M. Rahman. I never met her, but knew about her writing. Mahmuda Khatun Siddiqua and Motahera Banu were the poets. Sara Tayfur wrote a biography of Hazrat Mohammad. Shamsunnahar wrote on politics and child welfare. M. Fatema Khanam, who wrote less, was good. She fell ill. As far as I remember, these were the few women writers of our time I knew. I was better acquainted with Mahmuda Khatun Siddiqua, Shamsunnahar Mahmud and Begum Rokeya. I was very close to Mahmuda Khatun Siddiqua. The two of us would attend meetings under cover. She lived in Pabna and came to Calcutta regularly.

Women did not get the opportunity to write. One needed to develop one's skills in the chosen area. Most women writing essays or poems at that time had social reform as their goal. This trend began with Begum Rokeya.

I feel we have been like porters and sweepers, cleaning up the road. Women can now walk freely on those roads. Their conduct has changed. This change is reflected in their writings. Look at the poems—how the content has changed! During our times faith would be the main theme, besides moving towards work and progress. Now all people want is to establish one's claims. You have to compete with others to survive. You are a woman. Life's experiences have made you realize that no man will want you to move up the social ladder, by giving up his own space for you. That is why I say women these days have to earn their places by being assertive. You have to be brave and ready to struggle. We were highly courageous. We were constrained by religion, family, social norms and prejudices. Women also had to take the responsibility of running a big family. In those days, families were joint and big. As a wife and daughter I had to abide by others' wishes. One got a chance to write only after performing the assigned tasks and pleasing the family members.

Mahmuda Khatun Siddiqua, however, was a lot more independent. She did not have to face the resistance that we did from our relatives. Her father was very supportive and cooperative. She did not live with her husband. It was her father who gave her shelter as well as financial assistance.

However, your problems are greater than ours were since in our times we received trust and respect. Now there is neither faith nor respect. This is the age of scepticism, no one trusts the other. Men encouraged us, and that is why we succeeded. Would I have become a writer if Kazi Nazrul did not give me strength, if Nasiruddin Saheb did not support me and if my husband had not encouraged me? There were exceptions, though. Now we only have competition. Nowadays you have to claim a space for yourself.

Today, women write so much and yet fail to get recognition or support. They have to make a great deal of effort to make a mark. These are big changes. Moreover, earlier, women's writings had considerable seriousness, depth and social consciousness compared to what is being written by women now. The main aim of those writings was social reform. Begum Rokeya had a commitment. Through our literary pursuits and other work we embraced that commitment. And that's how I still am.

Note

1 *Jatra* is a form of folk theatre. *Milad Mehfil* is a prayer ceremony with chants and singing.

14

Nurjahan Begum: Mohammad Nasiruddin's Daughter

Nurjahan Begum is the editor of a woman's weekly literary magazine, *Begum*. The magazine was launched by Nurjahan's father, Mohammad Nasiruddin, in Calcutta on 20 July 1947, and Nurjahan has been editing the magazine for the last six decades. After Partition, the magazine changed its address, from Wellesley Street in Calcutta to Patuakhali in Dhaka.

Nurjahan Begum spent the first twenty-five years of her life in Wellesley Street. Mohammad Nasiruddin was the editor of *Saugat* magazine and his residence doubled as the *Saugat* office. Literary discussions would be held every evening, and thus Nurjahan Begum got to see most of the famous litterateurs and poets of her time from up, close.

Mohammad Nasiruddin was of a liberal dispensation and a member of the progressive literary circles. At the same time, he had taken many bold steps towards the emancipation of Muslim women in Bengal (see Chapter 12, this volume). It was, as expected, her father who initiated Nurjahan Begum into the world of literature. Today, the octogenarian still follows in her father's footsteps.

The monthly *Saugat* magazine paved the way for many progressive writers to practise their craft for about half a century. At the same time, many women writers were first published in *Saugat*. In the post-Partition period, the opportunity for women widened. *Begum*, the magazine, created solely for women, and the Begum Club became a centre for Bengali Muslim women, social workers and cultural activists. Many foreign representatives were felicitated there. Until the creation of Bangladesh, *Begum* and the Begum Club made historic contributions to the women's movement. Subsequently, although a few women's magazines emerged, the wide enthusiasm surrounding *Begum* was not witnessed anywhere else.

Saugat is no longer printed from the historic Saugat Press at Patuatuli in Dhaka. Its publication stopped in 1969, at the height of the anti-Pakistan movement. *Begum*, however, continues to be published on weekends. The dust-covered, shabby auditorium of the Begum Club can still be seen in Dhaka; its glamour and glory merely memories of yesteryears. Nurjahan Begum visits the place every day to attend to the paper work of the magazine. Raushan, who used to be Mohammad Nasiruddin's press assistant, waiter and manager, all at the same time, is in attendance. Now he is the company's foreman.*

We took the following interview of Nurjahan Begum on 15 June as she reminisced about her life. It was 3 pm and she had not had lunch because of the workload at *Begum*, which she had to manage single-handedly. She got up to eat in the middle of the interview when we insisted. But she seemed more interested in serving food than eating. Mohammad Nasiruddin's hospitality at the literary events that took place at the *Saugat* office was legendary. The lady who bears his legacy made it a point to feed half a dozen cats roaming around in the seat of literature before serving herself.

* He has since passed away.

My Childhood

I was born on 4 June 1925 in a village named Paikardi in Chandpur. I spent my childhood there. I had nearly drowned twice but managed to save myself. My father brought my mother and me to Calcutta. It was our first visit to the city. We lived at 11 Wellesley Street. When we came to Calcutta, *Saugat* was booming. I saw many poets and writers like Kazi Nazrul Islam from very close quarters. Because I was a child, I was loved and petted by all. They called me Nuri. When someone came to drop off a manuscript while Father was away, he would say, 'Nuri, tell your father when he returns that I left these articles.' At night when I carried the articles to Father, I felt I was doing a great job.

I doubt if any girl in Bangladesh grew up in a similar environment as I did. This is because people like Kazi Nazrul Islam, Abul Kalam Azad, Abul Mansur Ahmad, Abul Fazl and other contemporary Muslim and Hindu authors came to attend the literary gatherings at *Saugat* every evening. Although I did not understand much, I used to hang around my mother, feeling that something grand was taking place. I had the task of carrying tea and snacks to the the meetings. I would go with the maid, and we carried paan and *zarda,* tobacco, especially for Kazi Nazrul. Seeing Kazi Sahib being driven in a private car decorated with roses to a felicitation was one of the happiest moments in my life. That was such a magnificent sight! I shall never forget it.

Just after the felicitation, Kazi Sahib came to the *Saugat* office and asked for 'Nuri'! He too used to call me Nuri. There is a story behind this. My father would lovingly call me Nuru and Kazi Nazrul's nickname too was Nuru. Then he said, 'No! I will call her Nuri!' He took out a pen and inkpot made of gold from his bag to show us what he had received. He was so overwhelmed with joy!

Women at the Literary Circles

I never saw any woman attending the literary meetings in those days. When I went to Calcutta, I saw only one—Sufia Kamal. At that time she was Sufia N. Hossain. From then on the poet Sufia Kamal became my aunt and remained so till her last day. Whenever I got into trouble, I would run to her for help.

You asked me whether women attended the literary meetings. During that time, Muslim women were barred from moving about outside the house, or going to office. But my father said, 'Let us do something. We will break the barriers if necessary. My wife will not wear the burqa from today. All those who are with me will also not wear the burqa. Those who come to the *Saugat* office will bring along family members. They will talk and discuss things with each other.'

That is when members began to bring their wives along. They would go to the inner quarters of the house to talk to Mother, and discuss politics, rather than cooking or embroidery. Ultimately my father said, 'It is not necessary to remain confined within the four walls of the house. Bring the women out!'

But how was that possible? 'Let us go out on a steamer,' said Father. Five or six of the men brought their wives along. There was not much of a reaction after the steamer-ride. This is because the women—my mother and the others—had their husbands' support. They did not bother about criticism.

Rokeya's School

After Kazi Nazrul Islam's felicitation was over, Rokeya said to my father: 'Nasiruddin Saheb, please send your daughter to my school!' My father said, 'My daughter is too young; how will she go to school?' Rokeya said, 'I have attendants—they will bring her in a car. There will be no problem.' My father asked my mother who said, 'No! I will not allow so young a girl to go to school.' Father said, 'Let her go. If she likes staying at school, she will do so; else we will bring her back.'

I liked school very much; there were many young children. I saw Begum Rokeya whom I can still visualize. Her work is discussed each year and her memories have not faded away. Rokeya Sakhawat Hossain was extremely beautiful. She was short, wore spectacles, a long-sleeved blouse at all times, a white sari and black shoes. She walked and spoke very softly. She visited every class in the morning, possibly to check whether all the students attended regularly. When she entered all of us stood up, and then she would smile a little and depart. She taught Classes Eight and Nine. The education system she followed was interesting. We were given small cots and pillows to lie down after lunch. We ate our tiffin, sitting in a row, and lay down. Some of the children fell asleep. Those of us who were naughty talked while lying down. When the bell rang, we went to attend class. But those who fell asleep were not awakened. It was only when school was over that the attendants or guardians took them home. This was a very student-friendly system.

My father observed that his daughter was being taught Arabic, Urdu, English and Bengali. He felt learning too many languages simultaneously was a huge burden and so he brought me home. A private tutor was employed to teach me. Begum Rokeya telephoned my father again and said, 'Your daughter has not attended school for a while! I have made some changes. Now the school has teachers from all religions groups: Christian, Hindu, Muslim. Please start sending her to the school.' My father sent me back to Sakhawat Memorial. But I did not see Rokeya again—she had died by then. I was enrolled in Class Five. I took the Matriculation examinations from Sakhawat Memorial.

The change in the school was wonderful. There was not a single subject I did not learn there. At Sakhawat Memorial we took lessons in musical instruments like the esraj, sitar and violin, picking up the basics. I liked playing the sitar and picked up the notations fast. I could not play the violin. The teacher who taught us harmonium also made us sing in chorus. We learnt embroidery. A competition was held every three months for the girls who were good at it. Art competitions were also held. Besides, there were theatre and sports. There were restrictions on practising these and not everybody was encouraging. What good will learning to sing and dance do to Muslim girls, they would say. They said these activities were against Islam. But my guardians did not listen to them. It is good to be involved in such pursuits, go ahead, they said. A young group of Muslims was trying to instil progressive thoughts into the minds of their wives and children.

About My Father

It amazes me to think that years ago my father had talked about the progressive ideas that we utter today. He was not concerned with looking back and never suggested reverting backwards. He advocated moving with the changing times. There can be no progress if you deny the spirit of the age, he said. He had planted the seeds of this idea in the minds of people close to him, like me. It is quite incredible that he held such liberal views so early in that age.

He began *Saugat* with Rokeya's writings in 1918, to give women writers their due respect. One of his major concerns was to collect and publish women's writings. He surprised everybody by publishing the women's issue of *Saugat* in 1930. The conservatives hit back at him, called him a 'kafir'.

How did he manage to send Fazilatunnesa abroad? She was the first Bengali Muslim woman to do so! He thought that even if one Muslim girl went abroad for higher studies, it would widen the way for Muslim women's education in general. As a result of facilitating Fazilatunnesa's studies, Father was harassed tremendously, and there was a possibility that he might get killed. But he did his job, unflinchingly. My point is that whatever work Nasiruddin Saheb did helped to widen the path towards progress. It is we who have not been able to complete the journey. We have not been able to achieve what Rokeya Sakhawat Hossain had envisaged vis-à-vis the woman's cause, emancipation and rights. We are still struggling. But we are hopeful that an educated woman will not take long to overcome the hurdles in the way.

Ashapurna Devi

I met Ashapurna Devi in 1946. When the last issue of women's *Saugat* was being readied, my father noticed all except three pieces had pictures to go with them. Those still without images were by Sufia Kamal, Ashapurna Devi and Jyotirmoyee Devi (a daughter-in-law of the estate of Gauripur). Anyway, he went to Ashapurna Devi to ask for a photograph. She said, 'I do not have a photograph of mine!' No magazine had printed her photograph till then. My father said, 'You will be taken to a photographer's studio for a shoot. Sufia will come with you.' He said the same to Jyotirmoyee Devi.

My father had a Skoda car, which he drove himself. I sat beside him. The ladies sat at the back. After the photographs were taken, he brought everyone back to our house, where refreshments were served. Ashapurna Devi said, 'I am not superstitious. I am quite liberal. But my mother-in-law does not like the idea of eating out. She will know if I ate here and that will displease her immensely. So I shall not eat.' She put her plate away. Everybody else ate the snacks. What I remember even today is that she had so much respect for her elders. After Ashapurna Devi passed away, I wrote about her in *Begum.* I referred to this anecdote in her obituary, remembering the lesson about respecting elders that I had picked up from her.

Poet Sufia Kamal and *Begum* Magazine

To Sufia Kamal my father was like an elder brother and my mother a younger sister. She visited us every Sunday. Her only daughter, Dulu, was my friend. We did not have much money then. We had good food only on Sundays. Khalamma [Sufia Kamal] cooked delicious food with whatever ingredients my father could afford.

My father was introduced to Khalamma through her writing. In *Bangla Sahitye Saugat Yug* (The *Saugat* Era in Bengali Literature), my father had written, 'I had not seen Sufia earlier. Suddenly, one day she came, clad in a burqa, and said, "I am Sufia."' By this time a few articles by her had already been published in *Saugat.*

Besides Khalamma, I met Mahmuda Khatun Siddiqua who was among the literary personalities of my childhood. She lived outside Calcutta, and whenever she came to Calcutta, she brought along a few articles for my father, and she would leave immediately after.

After my graduation, father said, 'It won't be possible to take women ahead by merely publishing *Saugat* for women. Women have to move fast.' He called upon Sufia Kamal and said, 'Your writing sundry articles in the women's special of *Saugat* is not helping the cause of woman's literature. Why don't you bring out an illustrated weekly magazine? Women will find the idea of a well-produced magazine with images exciting.' Khalamma was extremely enthusiastic. She agreed that this was a good idea. I had just graduated from Lady Brabourne College. Sufia Kamal became the editor of *Begum*. A large image of Rokeya Sakhawat Hossain's was used on the cover of *Begum*'s first issue. Khalamma collected a few articles by women. A few more arrived after an announcement soliciting articles. We had to translate in most cases. A lot of women were inhibited about visiting the magazine office. To let their writing go out of their homes was blasphemous. In spite of the obstacles, we published *Begum* in Calcutta for three years. The writers who would visit our office included Syeda Khanam, Mahmuda Khatun Siddiqua, Jahanara Arzoo, Sajeda Khatun, and Selina Khan Panni (Selina Doza). I ran *Begum* for three years in Calcutta. Pratibha Ganguly worked with me. She was shot dead later. There was also a young girl named Pratibha Basu. Many Hindu girls dropped by to submit articles. Our activities in Calcutta included organizing get-togethers. I invited many women to the foundation ceremony of *Begum*. Many Hindu women attended and spoke on the occasion. There were not too many organizations for Muslim women at that time. The Bengal Muslim Women's Association was one, and we sometimes took part in their activities and covered the events in *Begum*. After Partition, I would gather news on the events taking place this side of Bengal from daily newspapers and have these published in *Begum*.

I was the executive editor of *Begum* for the first five months. Sufia Kamal could not put in long hours at the office. After caring for family, children and her ailing mother, she did not have much time to sit in the office. That is when she said, 'Make Nurjahan the editor. I will continue to do my bit.' Since then I have been the editor of *Begum*.

When we arrived in Dhaka in 1950, we were considered outsiders who had arrived from Calcutta. The residents of Dhaka did not like us. They said girls from Calcutta would move around freely and that would have a bad influence on our girls who too would wish to go outdoors. They tortured their women, put barriers in front of the door, created trouble and tried hurting us to stop Dhaka's women from going outside the home. My current residence at 38 Sarat Gupta Road was made the *Begum* office, as my father wished. In Dhaka, my father organized a conference for *Begum* which was attended by Sufia Kamal, Mahmuda Khatun Siddiqua, Shamsunnahar Mahmud and many others. Thus we began *Begum*'s work with great flourish. It took us two to three years more to enter Patuatuli.

In the Company of Other Women Writers

Mahmuda Khatun Siddiqua was a natural poet who had a generous heart. I have met few women like her. She encouraged me tremendously. She would always tell me if she liked anything I wrote. More importantly, she would bring along women writers, whenever she found one. She went knocking at different publishers' doors, urging them to publish books by a lot of women writers. Most of them still remember her. I do not know much about Mahmuda Khatun Siddiqua, except that she did not live with her husband. She was extremely independent-minded. She could not tolerate anything being said against her family. She wanted to travel on her own, which was met with resistance. That's when she walked out on her husband and severed links with her parents-in-law. She was guided by her own, independent thought.

I met Syeda Motahera Banu in Calcutta. When we left Calcutta, I wept a lot. I do not know why but I could not help it. I was leaving behind my writer friends. Motahera Banu held me in her arms, trying to console me. 'Do not cry, dear! The country is being partitioned. We are leaving too.' She came to Dhaka after a long time. I met her. Later, she was in hospital, on her deathbed. She had such a clear voice. Seeing me, she said, 'Oh! You have come, I will get well now.' She died a few days later. Syeda Motahera Banu was a poet. She wrote only poems.

Fazilatunnesa wanted to see me during her last days. I had met her when I took a cousin of mine for admission to Eden College. I went to see her. Seeing me she asked after my mother and me. Before going abroad, she had stayed at our house in Calcutta. After the death of Fazilatunnesa her only daughter sold the property and went to London. There was no reason for her to stay back.

Nurunnesa Khatun Vidyavinodini stayed at Howrah [*sic*, Srirampur]. I had not seen her in Calcutta. I heard my father used to visit her in Howrah [*sic*, Srirampur] to collect her articles. She was an out-and-out family woman.

Many of the women writers faced a lot of difficulties. Majeda Khatun, for instance, had never been to school. Sufia Kamal was a wonderful writer. She would write stories. She said, 'When there was no domestic chore to attend to, I sat down to write. At once there would be abuse—"What rubbish does she write all day? Is there no other work?" The poisonous barbs unsettled my mind. Once I had finished writing, sending it to the journal office through a messenger was a major problem.' She had to overcome many hurdles in her life.

My Work, My Principles

I got married in 1952, at the time of the Language movement. I have had a happy life in every way. I had the blessings of Allah! Before marriage I was under the protection of my father, which I did not lose after my marriage. My husband is a journalist and he knew everything about my family before our marriage—he knew about me also. Therefore, I did not face any resistance once I was married. Now you find me sitting here. I will leave this place around seven or eight in the evening to go home. In the meantime my husband would have had his lunch, rested, and gone out to work. I might not see him when I go home. But he would not say a word about this. He knows that I am carrying a huge responsibility on my shoulders.

I am influenced by my father and Rokeya and trying to follow their path. I have two daughters. One has an MA in English, the other in sociology. I have fulfilled the responsibility of educating them. They were brought up in a literary environment. I have instilled in their minds basic ideas about society. But I was unable to make them write or attend the magazine office regularly. They say, 'Our lives would be wasted if we spent them the way you have, working in this office. Your life is wasted, as it is. You are in the office from morning till night. But we have lives to live, places to go to, social functions to attend.' I hope they will get over this once they got older and not so charged by the heat of youth.

I always fitted into my father's tight programme. Father never allowed me to roam around. I never went to attend programmes without his permission. Once my husband bought tickets to a six o'clock show. My father asked me to chuck the tickets and come with him to the *Begum* office instead. My husband did not say anything at that moment but grumbled later. I was made to cancel many programmes this way. But the fact that I have been able to keep *Begum* afloat three years after my father's death makes me happy. The magazine was supposed to have stopped immediately after his death, but that did not happen.

15

Hameeda Khanam: Higher Education, The First Forays

The search for the biography of Mahmuda Khatun Siddiqua brought us into contact with her niece Hameeda Khanam. At first we talked about Mahmuda Khatun Siddiqua, hoping to obtain information, hitherto unrecorded, of the writer's experience of life in the inner quarters. Because Hameeda Khanam was so articulate and her views of her life at Pabna in the 1920s, Bethune College in the 1930s, the Hindu-Muslim relationship, and the situation of Muslim women were so interesting, we decided to include her interview in the anthology. Initially she had refused to be interviewed formally, but subsequently she invited us to her house.

Hameeda Khanam was born in 1923 in Rajshahi and was brought up in Pabna at her maternal grandfather's residence. She went to Pabna High School and passed her secondary school examinations in 1936. She was in Calcutta till Partition as a student of Bethune College and Calcutta University and later as a lecturer of philosophy in Lady Brabourne College.

The first four decades of the twentieth century were significant for Muslim women. While Bethune College had only a handful of Muslim girls as students in the last years of the 1930s, the beginning of the 1940s saw a considerable number of Muslim girls being admitted. Hameeda Khanam was a witness to this epoch-making period.

Just as she belonged to the first generation of Muslim women who received higher education. her mother and aunt belonged to the first generation of Muslim women who got the chance to attend school. Hameeda, therefore, belonged to the second generation of school-educated Muslim women and thus she did not face any resistance from her family regarding her education. Her elder sister, Mohsina

Ali, was a student of the Calcutta Art College. From a very young age her elder brother, Abdul Ahad, had music lessons and also went to study at Santiniketan. Later he became famous as a musician. At the beginning of the 1920s, the ambience of education and culture in this house in a small town in Bengal was truly exceptional.

Hameeda Khanam and her elder sister were distanced from the Muslim community. Their friends and classmates were Hindus. Even their mother's friends were from Hindu families. The wealth and fame of her nana, Khan Bahadur Mohammad Sulaiman, helped support Hameeda Khanam's school education in Pabna and education and boarding charges in Calcutta.

Her mother also had a pivotal role: she was uncompromising and tenacious when it came to her daughters' higher education. Thanks to her descriptive skills, three decades of the twentieth century are recorded in this interview. Hameeda Khanam served as the principal of Dhaka Domestic Economics College for nearly twenty years, and is now retired. She remains actively involved in many social-work related activities.

When I joined school, I was just four years old. My mother and maternal aunt took my elder sister to a school for admission. Mother was so impressed with Pratibhadi [who ran the school] that she immediately decided to admit me as well. I was admitted instantly. I did not know the alphabet and had no idea about schools. Nevertheless, I was admitted and would regularly attend school with my elder sister. I remember the recitation class very well. A girl would recite, 'O my Mini, my little pigeon, coo for me,' and all of us who were smaller would pick up the refrain and chant, 'Coo, coo, little pigeon, coo for me.' I remember this very well. Maybe that was the children's section. Then I got a double promotion and became even with my elder sister. That is why I passed the secondary exams very early.

Most interestingly, I do not remember if there was any other Muslim girl studying with us till I was in Class Six. In other words, no one else was admitted. In Class Seven three Muslim girls were admitted in the same class, but got married soon afterwards. Once again it was just my elder sister and I. That is why we did not have any Muslim friends in our school life. Friendships are difficult to develop when two people are not in the same class. The school had 250 students—all Hindus. Pabna was full of members of the landed gentry. Girls from extremely rich families studied in the schools. Those from the middle and lower-middle classes would study too. When we were in Class Ten, the number of Muslim girls in the school was not more than six or seven.

In Class Two, I vaguely remember a zamindar's wife in a milk-white sari, quite fashionable, coming to visit our school. I was told that she had come to award a medal and I was the one to get it! On one side of the medal the words 'In memory of my beloved son, Gopal,' were inscribed, while the other side read 'Hameeda Banu (that is how I wrote my name then) for Superior Intelligence.' Later when I grew up I thought that the woman must have been extremely generous to give a medal to a Muslim girl in memory of her deceased son.

In Pabna the Hindu-Muslim relationship was amicable. There were neither problems nor riots. However, there was a difference in status between the two communities. Muslims were very poor. The number of educated Muslim families was no more than the digits on one's hand. An average Muslim would be a tailor, weaver, potter or a small-time shopkeeper. There was a community called 'Nale', living along the banks of the Padma. Once a year they would go towards Barishal to cut long bamboos called nal-khagra—hence their name and the neighbourhood was called nale-para. On the banks of Icchamati lived Saptatirtha Thakur. He ran a school from his house. Many students came from afar to learn Sanskrit. Right behind his house lived a Muslim milkman, and next to him was the house of a Christian carpenter. The fact that Christian, Muslim and Hindu brahmin houses were alongside each other never created a problem. Many Hindu officers resided in my neighbourhood, while the Muslim houses were right behind theirs. But there was no bitterness between the two communities. Clashes were yet to happen. Communal clashes happen only when there is a conflict of interest. The two communities were too dissimilar in status: one comprised zamindars and the other commoners. There were no clashes as a result. In spite of the difference in status, I would say that the relationship was good. We were yet to face the dangers of communalism.

I would say my maternal grandfather's efforts towards educating young boys and girls resulted in this harmony. People from both the Hindu and Muslim communities revered him. In recognition of his contribution to education, the British government gave him the title of Khan Bahadur. He established a high school with his own efforts. My grandfather's friend's daughter—a highly-educated Brahmo lady—was appointed as headmistress. There were three or four more female Brahmo teachers. They managed to bring about a change in the school's environment. Initially, we would wear shoes to school, but stopped later as the Hindu girls would not wear shoes made from cow hide. Since there were just two Muslims, in our class, we too had to stop wearing shoes to school. But as instructed by the Brahmo headmistress, we started wearing shoes again in Class Four. Our Brahmo headmistress wore leather shoes and covered her head with her sari. The end of the sari was wrapped around the head and fixed with a brooch. She was very dignified. Following her, everybody started wearing shoes.

In the beginning, we would walk to school. Later, to allow older Muslim girls to attend high school, my maternal grandfather imported a bus from Calcutta. The windows of the bus were covered with netting. Even so, the number of Muslim girls did not go up as Muslim society was yet to accept the idea of educating Muslim women. It was thought that a little bit of letter writing and the basic ability to read books were good enough.

My mother and aunts were married at a very early age. Maybe they suffered greatly, living a prisoner's life. My mother decided she was not going to marry any of her daughters off early. The girls would study as much as they could. People would say my mother married late. She was married at fourteen or fifteen, which was late by the standards followed in those days. At that time, girls got married at nine or ten. Since my maternal grandmother had passed away and mother had younger siblings to take care of, she was married later. My aunts were married earlier.

My mother went to school at a very young age. After growing up she was taught at home by missionaries. My aunts went to missionary schools. My mother knew Bengali very well and had a smattering of English.

For a few days I went to school in the bus that grandfather had imported from Calcutta. My mother asked me to drop out soon after as the bus took a longish route to school. We began walking to school. Kamini, a maidservant employed by the school, would stand in front of our house in the morning and call out, 'Hey Sisters!' We would be ready by the time she came and would go join the rest. She would escort us to school and back. The senior girls walked close to her and we juniors followed like a herd of cows. But nobody passed any comments on the street, which was rather unusual. Perhaps people treated school-going girls with respect.

Since my elder sister and I did not take the school bus and did not observe purdah; we avoided going to Muslim houses. We were afraid that they would be critical about grown-up girls like us not being married, and not observing purdah and that the bad name would harm our studies. So we never visited any Muslim household. In the evenings, sometimes we went to Hindu houses with our mother. Our mother and aunts did not observe purdah either. My great, great grandmother from my mother's side knew three languages: Urdu, Arabic and Persian.

We never went out during the day, except at the time of going to school. We went out with Mother only in the evenings. Because it was a small town, a young errand boy would accompany us. He used to carry a lamp and a stout stick. The stick was meant to ward off snakes. There were lots of snakes in Pabna. The boy led us, my mother walked behind him and we followed her. Most often we went to Saptatirtha Thakur's house. His wife was my mother's friend. Hindu girls probably went out during the day. We did not know for sure because we never did. However, the way girls freely move about these days was unimaginable. It was not common to let girls go to the cinema, and so on. Hindu girls were allowed to go out during religious festivals.

My mother wanted me to go to Bethune College. My father took me to the college for admission. I had visited Calcutta many times before. From Pabna one had to take a bus to Ishwardi. It was a wide tarred road, stretching for about of 18 to 19 miles. The journey from Ishwardi to Sealdah station took another four to five hours. We had been to Calcutta many times before to see doctors or simply travel with Mother.

I remember an incident when I had just started Class Six. I wore frocks then. The present Nilratan Sarkar Hosptial was earlier called Campbell Hospital. My maternal aunt (Mahmuda Khatun Siddiqua) and I had put up at a hotel opposite the hospital. The famous singer Abbasuddin came to meet my aunt. At the time aunt wrote regularly, attended literary meets and visited Calcutta on a regular basis. She told Abbasuddin Saheb, 'This niece of mine sings very well.' He listened to two songs by me—one originally sung by him, and another one. Having heard me, he decided to record my songs. He said, 'Practise well and regularly. We will record your song during the puja vacation.' Once we were back in Pabna, the news spread immediately. There was a tremendous negative reaction. It was thought if songs sung by Khan Bahadur Saheb's granddaughter were played in paan-shops and movie theatres, the family honour would take a blow. There were similar negative reactions everywhere. The scandalous talk was all over the place. My mother told me, 'Why not drop the idea of recording your songs?' I agreed. I was not too keen on the idea anyway. So there was no recording but I continued to sing. Ahadbhai gave me music lessons. I never recorded a song in my life. Actually, mother was worried that music might come in the way of my education. I agreed that studies were my priority at the time, and singing something to be done on the side.

At that time there were two girls' hostels in Bethune. I stayed in the new one. There were seventy-five boarders. There were only four Muslim girls in all the classes taken together. Among them was Rabeya Ali in the fourth year who later became Syed Mujtaba Ali's wife. Women were guarded very strictly in Bethune. My uncle reached me to the college gate on my first day there. I went inside and saw a boundary wall, the fencing on which was as high as the wall itself. The wire was covered with greenery, ivy shrubs and morning glory twined around it. Even people travelling on the upper deck of a bus would not be able to see the girls in the college campus. Stringent discipline was observed in Bethune. Girls could not leave the premises without permission and even with permission nobody was allowed out alone. Only a local guardian could take a girl out. Our superintendent was a Brahmo lady. The assistant was a Hindu. They would take us out at times. Once we went to see Tagore's dance drama *Chandalika,* staged in the presence of Rabindranath Tagore. This was the first time I watched a dance drama. Afterwards, by the time I went to Santiniketan, the poet had passed away.

All the Muslim girls studying in Bethune were from north Bengal. Akhtar Imam of East Bengal (former provost of Rokeya Hall, Dhaka University) was in the fourth year; Jahanara Haider who later took up social work, was there too. She was the only Muslim student to attend college in a burqa. Later I met a burqa-less Jahanara in Dhaka, where she was engaged in social work. She was from Comilla. None of the other girls bothered about her wearing a burqa. Jahanara lived in the hostel. Going by personal experience, the relation between Hindu and Muslim girls was amicable. At that time a Brahmo lady named Tatini Das was the college principal, and many of our teachers were Brahmos. There was a Brahmo influence on the Hindus, when it came to education. The Brahmos were more liberal than the

Hindus. In our hostel, the ayahs were Christians, and the cook a Hindu. We did not enter the kitchen, and did not bother about this. But all of us would have our meals together. Even if somebody had reservations, it was never made public, as a negative attitude was not encouraged. This was hugely commendable.

Begum Mariam Rashid was my mother's cousin sister. She was also Begum Rokeya's cousin. Aunt Mariam was extremely orthodox. She had two daughters—Janu and Ranu. Both were married after completing Class Eight. Whenever Aunt Mariam met my mother she exclaimed, 'Would you be able to marry your daughters off? You are making them study so much! That's very brave.'

In those days, Muslim women from respected families did not use public transport. That is why Aunt Mariam did not like our going to her house in Park Circus in trams or buses. When I was in the first year I visited her house only once with Aunt Mahmuda Khatun Siddiqua. We travelled by tram from Cornwallis Street to Park Circus, and boarded a phaeton car from Park Circus. Colourful phaeton cars with beautiful pictures pasted on them would be available for hire. All the drivers were Muslims. Once we boarded and mentioned our destination, they immediately drew the curtains on the window. Muslim girls were supposed to practise purdah—that was the rule.

A different tradition was followed in Bethune College. The women who had a role in India's freedom struggle were mostly from Bethune. The new political environment had an effect on Hindu society and Hindu women nurtured progressive sentiments. Despite the strict discipline followed in college, most girls were politically conscious. However, there was no political activity inside the college. I was the sole Muslim student in the MA class. Mary Hameeda from Assam was studying economics. Meher Taimur (later Kabir) studied science. Altogether there were three Muslim girls in Calcutta University.

There were a few married women studying in Bethune. Fatema Sadem was married. There were very few married Hindu women.

A couple of them studied till graduation. Male professors taught in Bethune. We were taught Bengali by Chintaharan Chakraborty. He would always keep his eyes lowered while teaching. Everybody sat silently in his class. At that time, Fazilatunnesa taught mathematics in Bethune. It was difficult to tell when she walked in and out of college. She was the only Muslim professor in Bethune at the time.

While studying for my M.A., I lived in a hostel in Harrison Road. A part of a private house was rented out to serve as a hostel for the girls studying in Calcutta University. There were nearly ten of us living there. I was the only Muslim. Everybody else, including the cook and matron, was Hindu. Nobody was bothered about my being a Muslim. This was something special, it cannot be generalized. When I was in school, I remember, we were never allowed entry into a Hindu family's bedroom. This was easily acceptable and therefore did not hurt us.

In 1942, I completed M.A. in philosophy and started research under Suresh Dasgupta, a professor of philosophy. Calcutta University granted me a fellowship to research 'Religion and Human Personality'. I joined Lady Brabourne College in 1945. There were a few Muslim professors teaching Arabic and Persian. Bengali was taught by Khadeja Khatun, and Shamsunnahar Mahmud before her. The latter had fallen ill and could not rejoin. I was the only one teaching a non-specialized subject.

In the 1940s, the number of Muslim girls who went to college had increased since our times. Those who stayed in the hostel were not just Muslims from Calcutta, but from all over Bengal. Fazlul Haq [the then chief minister of Bengal] had established Lady Brabourne College to help Muslim women get educated.

I went to England right after Partition and returned in July 1949. I had received an Honours degree in philosophy from London University. Having opted for Pakistan, I went back to Dhaka and joined Eden College after completing education.

I wrote a letter to my father before going back to Dhaka, 'Baba, since we do not have a close relative in Dhaka, we might stay in a hotel.' My father answered every query of mine except the one about the hotel. Reaching Dhaka, we found Dhaka Boarding was the only hotel around. There was no hotel fit for a respectable woman to stay at.

On the way to Dhaka, I felt sad when we reached Ishwardi station. Ishwardi is a junction station. In those days, the Assam Mail, the Darjeeling Mail—all mail trains would go through Ishwardi Junction to arrive at Sealdah station. The junction would be extremely crowded at all times. But this time Ishwardi seemed deserted—there was nobody except a man sleeping on a bench on the platform. It felt really strange. My father and I were passengers of the upper class. I pushed open the waiting room door to see the tables and chairs lying in darkness.

We reached Dhaka station the next morning. I had never seen so many horse-drawn carriages. It was a strange sight. We boarded a carriage. The moment we entered the vehicle, the coachman shut the two windows. Since I was a woman, I had to be kept behind the purdah.

16

Syed Mustafa Siraj: Views on Society

Syed Mustafa Siraj, one of the major writers of short stories and novels of these times, was born in Khosbashpur village, Murshidabad district, West Bengal, in 1929. His father, Abdur Rahman Firdausi, was a Congress worker and a follower of Mahatma Gandhi. His paternal grandfather was a preacher of the Farazi sect. Anwara Begum, Siraj's mother, wrote poems, stories and ghazals. When M. Anwara Begum died, Siraj was only nine. In most of his writings, the influence of Siraj's mother is apparent.

The fun-filled and exciting ambience at Mustafa Siraj's family residence was marked by learning, creative writing, music and politics. There was also a rare collection of pre-Independence magazines. Abdur Rahman Firdausi was in charge of their safe keeping, till he reached a ripe ninety. Unfortunately, most of the magazines borrowed by aspiring researchers were not returned.

Syed Mustafa Siraj has been through very interesting life experiences. He became part of a group of roving musicians as a young boy and toured across many villages of Bengal. Later he joined the editorial team of *Ananda Bazar Patrika*. He has won many awards and laurels. Now retired from his job, Siraj spends his time in relentless literary pursuits.

On 16 September 1997, Moushumi Bhowmik met Syed Mustafa Siraj. The interview took place in the afternoon, in a small third floor flat in Beniapukur, Calcutta. It started with reminiscences of Siraj's mother and then drifted from one subject to another. In the evening, standing in front of his door, Siraj exclaimed, 'It feels good to have spoken my heart out.' Here is an edited version of the interview.

'Please share something about your mother.'

'My mother died when I was nine. That must have been around 1938 . . .'

'How old was your mother when she died?'

'Mother was not very old, around twenty-six, at the most. It was an acute case of pneumonia. The local doctor could not diagnose the nature of illness at first. Mistakenly, he treated her for malaria. The ailment spread across her chest. Finally, a civil surgeon came from Berhampore who said nothing could be done. Both lungs were destroyed. Mother died. As a child I would look at the handwriting of my mother. It was beautiful, written using a pen made from reeds. She wrote about me too, referring to me as Bharatpakhi (the little bird),—writing down whatever her Bharatpakhi did in the form of a diary.'

'Were you the first child?'

'Yes, I was the first. I vividly remember things from when I was five. I remember my mother reading and writing. She would read in the afternoon. In those days villages would be extremely quiet in the afternoon. We had many books in our house. My father had a huge collection of Bengali books. My mother had read them all. I remember an afternoon when she was reading Saratchandra's novel, *Shesh Prashna.* On the first page there was a word, *"ojuhat"*. I am trying to remember a time when I was very young. I asked her what is an *"ojuhat"* was? She told me off. "Why are you disturbing me? Why don't you study?" she asked. But I would quietly lie down beside her and listen.'

'Did she read aloud?'

'Yes . . . No . . . I mean she read in her mind, but while reading she would sometimes utter a few words. I heard the word *"ojuhat"* from Mother for the first time. I remember there was a library in the next village, Gokarna. It was just across the road. The library was named Sraddhananda Smritimandir. I would fetch Mother books from that library. I would do it for both my own mother, as well as the lady who later became my mother—my mother's sister. My father had a brother and my mother a sister. Incidentally, my paternal uncle [who was married to my mother's sister] died immediately after my mother's death. My aunt became a widow. We were quite young at the time. I was nine, my younger brother seven and another five. We were four brothers, each born at an interval of two years. My father had to marry my aunt so that we could be taken care of. Our new mother brought us up with love and care. She is still alive—aged around eighty. She too, like her sister, is into reading books borrowed from the library.'

'Did she also write?'

'No she did not write much. However, the language used in her letters was very modern. Just like that of my mother.'

'In Comilla, we found a lady named Razia Khatun Chowdhurani, wife of Ashrafuddin Ahmed Chowdhury. She also died at a very young age. The prose of her essays and stories sounds slightly stiff. But the letters she wrote to her imprisoned husband were beautiful and very modern.'

'My mother was also unusual in other ways. In 1930 I was about a year old. My father was in jail, in connection with the Civil Disobedience movement of the Congress. My father was sent to jail immediately after I was born. I was extremely ill and could have died. In those days it was difficult to get hold of a doctor. My father wrote to my mother, 'I would sign an undertaking and come to see my dying son, if you want.' My mother replied firmly that it was unnecessary. 'Even if my son died,' she wrote, 'I would never be able to accept a husband who comes back from prison by signing an undertaking.' I know the letter's contents by heart. My father still has it. On that occasion, father stayed back in jail and I eventually recovered.

'In those days, purdah was observed in our village rather stringently. Now the idea of seclusion is rejected. The women of Muslim households get educated. The year I got married, I would take my wife out to various places. But the time we are talking about was different.

'I was about four or five. One night I was woken up suddenly. It was possibly 1934, the year of the earthquake. I must have been five. There was an earthquake in Bihar's Muzzaffarpur. I woke up to find Mother was not there. Bubuji was lying with me. I called my paternal grandmother Bubuji. When my mother returned late in the night, I woke up. My mother told me stories of what she had seen. She had been to a film with my father in Berhampore town. They took the night bus back home. Mother started narrating the story. They had watched an English film. Assuming that the wall was the cinema screen, she made figures on it using her hands as she narrated the story. That was our first film. In those days cinema was called "talkies". That was the first time I heard the word "talkies".'

'In that case, the relationship between your parents was rather tender, wasn't it?'

'My mother was very brave. Once when we four brothers were young, and one of us was small enough to be carried along, we tried picking lotus flowers from a pond. We had taken off our pants. Father caught us in that state. He was involved in the peasant movement at that time, a colleague of Binoy Chowdhury's. One afternoon he came back home to be told that we were picking lotus flowers from a pond. He shooed the three of us back into the house and made us stand naked, holding our ears. The youngest still did not know how to walk. There was a carpenter called Kinkar. He had a son who was blind since birth. Kinkar would bring him along when he came to work. Kinkar was laughing at us, intermittently. The blind son asked why the father laughed. Kinkar did not say anything, just kept laughing. My mother had been watching this whole episode for a long time from the kitchen verandah. After a while, she came and took us inside. Quickly, she made us put on clothes. She was very angry with my father and said, "This is how you are spoiling our sons."

'These are the kind of memories I have about my mother. The most recurrent memory is about returning from school to find a study circle. Most of the farmers in our village were Muslims. We were the only outsiders. My paternal grandfather was a spiritual guide who settled among his followers in the village. The character of the holy man in my novel *Alik Manush* (*The Unreal Man*) was based on my grandfather to an extent. Many incidents recorded in that novel are real.

'Subasini, a gypsy girl staying in the neighbouring village of Gokarna, would visit us in the afternoon, with a copy of *Bidyasundar*. She had a bit of reading and writing skills. She would hand the book over to my mother and chant the verses. Although we were very small kids, Subasini would drive us away if we happened to be around. She would say that boys ought not to stay there and listen to what was being read. She wanted my mother to explain the stories to her. These are the memories I have.

'It would be quite impossible to imagine how backward the way of life in that village was. Even as we lived in such a milieu, my mother took the responsibility of teaching us from a very young age till I was about nine. My father would be away from home most of the time. I remember borrowing a lot of books from the library for my mother.'

'Did she request for specific titles?'

'Yes, she would name an author and ask me to get a book by him. Banaphool's novel *Dwairath* had probably just been published at the time. She used to keep track of advertisements in magazines and asked us to get new books.'

'Did you get magazines at home?'

'Yes, magazines would be delivered to our house. Magazines like *Saugat*, *Mohammadi*, *Nauroz* and *Bulbul* were being published. My father subscribed to all of them.'

'How did your mother learn to read and write?'

'My mother's natal home was in a village called Nagar, 10 miles west of Gokarna. Mother's education began at a school adjoining the mosque. My parents were married by a quirk of fate. My maternal grandfather was a Farazi Muslim. He was the odd man out in Nagar, since the rest were Hanafi Muslims. It was very difficult being a Farazi those days as they would be harassed greatly by the Hanafis. I have referred to this in *Alik Manush*. The Hanafis would say, "Farazis move their heads like a husking pedal while chanting namaz."

'One day my dadaji (paternal grandfather) was returning from the house of a disciple. At Gokarna, weekly markets would be held on Sundays and Wednesdays. On such a day, grandfather travelled in a bullock cart on the road running across the market. On his way he realized that it was time for his afternoon namaz. Before entering the village, around half a mile earlier, he stopped his bullock cart and sat under a banyan tree to offer namaz. At that time my nanaji also arrived there. They did not have a market at his village, so he walked across a 10-mile stretch to reach the market at Gokarna. He too was returning from the market. He suddenly saw an old man in a cap and long robe-like garment, wearing long hair and beard and a gentle countenance, standing under the tree and offering namaz. The Farazis have a different manner of offering namaz. My nanaji went and stood beside him and began offering namaz as well. When my dadaji said, "Amin", nanaji repeated it. They shared a glance at this moment, each feeling that the other was, after all, from the same community.

'The Farazis were extremely strict. They considered wearing gold or listening to music a sin. Things like superstition, pirs dominating others, making prophecies and even mysticism were denigrated as well. The Prophet Mohammad was, after all, a human being. My two grandfathers embraced each other after the namaz. They exchanged notes and found out that one had two daughters and the other two sons. After finding out how old they were, matches were made on the spot. My nanaji asked my dadaji to send his two sons over, on the following Friday. Everything was settled. In those days, keeping one's word was extremely important. The following Friday my father and my uncle, who were eighteen and twelve respectively, went to my Nanaji's house. My mother was around fourteen then. The weddings took place.

'Although the school in Nagar was right next to a Hanifa mosque, my mother and aunt went there to learn basic Bengali with Arabic.'

'Was there any resistance about learning Bengali?'

'Not at all. In any madrasa or *maqtab*,[1] learning Bengali was compulsory, as was mathematics and geography. I cleared the primary-level exams at nine in 1939. I still have the certificate which says 'Private Maqtab'. Many students of the maqtab took the exam with me. Many among those who passed joined school. Maqtabs for Muslim boys and girls could be found in villages that did not have a school. After passing out of the maqtab, students would join English-medium high schools, in the upper-primary section. They would get admitted to Class Five or Six. Many students were admitted with me. Bengali is compulsory in maqtabs, even now. My mother learnt Bengali at one of these, but learnt to write only after her marriage. My father taught her how to write.'

'How far did your father study?'

'My father dropped out after the secondary school-leaving examination to join the Non-Cooperation movement. He never returned to studies.'

'While your father supported your mother's interest in reading and writing, was there any resistance from other women at home?'

'No, never. My dadi-ma (paternal grandmother) never objected. In fact, she could also read and write a bit; and always encouraged studying. My dadaji was a strange man, an orthodox "Ahle Hadis", would ask his disciples to observe purdah. He tried to undermine the supremacy of pirs and in fact had destroyed shrines dedicated to them in a lot of places. On the other hand, he would argue with Hindu landlords, making a case for a Muslim's right to animal sacrifice.

'Grandfather relaxed some of the rules for us. He was highly liberal about us studying; women, including my mother, studying in purdah. He did not mind these things. His disciples sometimes demanded explanations from him. He would quote a paragraph from Hadis and explain.

'Anyway, I was talking about how my mother spent her afternoons. I remember that my mother would lie down and read. She would get books that were essentially meant for children, like the ones written by Kuladaranjan Roy, and the *Shishusathi* magazine. She subscribed to these for me. I was in Class Two or Three. She would read out and explain the stories to us. Mother taught me the basics. Father was away from home most of the time.'

'Didn't your father write?'

'Yes, he used to. But he had very little time for writing because of his role in the movement.'

'The women in your stories are unusual. They are especially strong, like in the novel *Alik Manush*. Were there women like these around you?'

'My mother was feisty. A lot of my female characters are on the lines of my mother. The feisty spiritedness was transferred from my subconscious.'

'Did that happen because of watching your mother from close quarters?'

'Yes. Once the earthen wall of our house collapsed. The house lost its privacy. One day, a few men who had been working in the fields came and sat beneath the mango tree in our orchard, talking among themselves. Mother sent Zulekha, the housemaid, to ask those men to leave. I created a character in the mould of Zulekha in a story of mine. My grandmother asked these men to leave as well, but they did not bother. That's when mother went out and talked to the men. The men left quietly, and never returned. The police had come to our house too. This is how it happened. Once he was released from prison after his arrest following the Non-Cooperation movement, Father travelled across the districts in connection with his political activities. At that time he was associated with the banned Communist Party. The police watched our house very closely. One day I found a red paper and tried deciphering the words written on it. Mother snatched the paper from me and burnt it. After a few days, the police visited our house in the afternoon. They turned over every article, but did not find anything suspicious. I remember my mother arguing with the police inspector. The sari end covering her head had fallen off. Finally the inspector apologized and departed. Mother lifted me on her lap and said, "Thank God, my boy had found the paper."'

'Was your aunt also like your mother?'

'Not so much. She studied a lot. I have hand-written letters from her. Her language was very lucid. It's difficult to come by that kind of prose—'

'Isn't there a lot of controversy about the language of the Bengali Muslims?'

'The problem is, before the eighteenth century, Arabic and Persian words would be freely used in the Bengali in vogue at the time of the nawabs—the sort we would hear in villages in our childhood. It's colloquial, regional Bengali—including different dialects. You might find this in Tekchand Thakur.[2] For instance, I have often heard Hindu boys in our theatre club using words like 'barkat' in normal everyday conversation. I am talking of the recent past—the 1950s. Nowadays, we don't hear that kind of usage. The Hindu, Sanskritized version of Bengali came into use at the time of Mrityunjay Tarkalankar and Ishwar Chandra Vidyasagar, when the East India Company began propagating Sanskritized Bengali. As a result, the Bengali used by the Muslims also showed a marked Sanskrit influence. All countries have a natural inclination towards adopting the language in which their religious texts are written. It is that language which gradually becomes colloquial. For this reason Muslims have a passion for Arabic and Persian, while the Hindus have the same towards Sanskrit. As a result, the use of words with Sanskrit roots increased, even while talking about routine matters.

'Talking to our grandparents or relatives, we would, naturally, use Arabic and Persian terms. One such word used very frequently in regular conversation by us was *khana* (food). The word came from Persia. However, as education spreads, this is becoming infrequent. The minorities of this country are influenced by the culture of the majority. Both men and women are using the language of the majority. Even the stress, accent and manner of speaking—the differences between the two styles—are disappearing. Till a few years back, in the 1960s, I could tell a Muslim from a Hindu by just looking at the person. There would be a difference in the choice of words, stress and accent.

'The nawabs, badshahs, and upper-class Ashraf Muslims who came from Persia, Middle Asia and Turkey brought along their language and elements of their culture. In Burdwan, Birbhum and Murshidabad districts, their descendants are called *mian*. I have written about them in my novel *Swarnachampar Upakhyan* (*The Tale of Swarnachampa*). At least in West Bengal, most of the educated Muslims were *mians*. In contrast, the low class converted Muslims, called *atrafs,* were very close to Hindu culture. As part of an *alkap*[3] team of roving musicians, I realized that such groups were a combined platform of low class Hindus and Muslims. Therefore the difference in language remained. It has reduced over time. Upper class Muslims still tend to use a few Arabic and Persian words. There is something different about their families and talk. Therefore when one writes a character, whether the writer is my mother or me, there seems to be extensive use of Arabic and Persian words.'

'I feel when it comes to our women writers, the problem lies elsewhere. Working on this book, I found a lot of them write in a language that is not quite developed and somewhat confused. There are influences of Rabindranath Tagore and Nazrul Islam. Formal and colloquial styles have been mixed up. It seems there was an influence of the sort of Bengali that appeared in the magazines in those days. However, Rokeya is very different, she has her own pure style.

'Yes, Rokeya Sakhawat Hussain is different. Rahimunnisa, who wrote in the era of handwritten books, would use words with

Sanskrit roots. The writers from Chittagong in the eighteenth and nineteenth centuries also used similar words. There were two traditions. As far as I understand, there still are two of them. One adopted words with Sanskrit roots completely and Hinduized the language. Since the Hindus of this land were ahead in the race, words used by them were incorporated, like Mir Mosharraf Hossain did. He would add the honorific *Shri* to his name, and addressed the lady to whom he dedicated his book as *Arye* (The respected lady). Another trend ran parallel to the first, to use Muslim vocabulary while depicting Muslim lifestyle or writing essays. I read an article on Eid by Mother a long time back. The language was slightly different.'

'Your mother's writings were published in *Gulistan*, Rokeya's in *Nabanoor*, Mahmuda Khatun Siddiqua and Razia Khatun Chowdhurani's in *Saugat*. Besides these Muslim-edited Bengali journals, weren't *Prabasi*, *Bharatbarsha* and similar journals read in houses with a cultural ambience? The Muslim-edited newspapers probably were not circulated in non-Muslim households.'

'Not many besides *Saugat*. Premendra Mitra and others wrote as well as worked in *Saugat*. Nazrul was accepted as a part of the *Saugat* family by Nasiruddin Saheb. *Mohammadi* and other journals did not have similar reach or effect. Many magazine editors tried to source articles by both Hindus and Muslims. Advaita Mallabarman's novel *Titas Ekti Nadir Naam* (*Titas, the Name of a River*), was serialized in *Mohammadi*. The Hindus were not so keen on the idea. A cold indifference was palpable. I have no fear or hesitation to say now that there is indeed a cold indifference towards Muslim writers. One is not interested to find out about Muslim society in detail. There can be many reasons for this. There is a kind of conservatism embedded in society.

'I will give you a very simple example. In my childhood, I was hugely fond of *Abar Jokher Dhon* (*The Treasure Hunt Again*) by Hemen Roy. My youngest uncle read me the story on a summer afternoon. A mysterious and wonderful world was created in my mind ever since I heard the story. My uncle named me "Manikbabu", a younger brother "Bimal", and the others "Kumar", "Ramhari" and "Gatule Sardar"—all after characters in that adventure story. I read *Pather Panchali* while I was in school. After reading it I felt my life and Apu's were quite similar. I too liked spending time roaming around in natural surroundings. I had internalized these characters. I am not sure if a Hindu would be able to do the reverse. Now if somebody argues that there are foreign elements in Muslim society and culture, I would say 700 to 800 years is enough time to internalize these.

'It happened amongst the lower classes. Hindus and Muslims mingled with each other. I realized this when I was travelling with the *alkap* singers. I saw it at a *kabigaan*[4] contest. The competitors were Sheikh Gomani and Lambodar Chakrabarty. At a fair in Mehrul village, Lambodar Chakrabarty acted as a Muslim and Sheikh Gomani a brahmin. Gomani, as a brahmin, was trying to run down the Muslims in his songs; and Lambador Chakrabarty representing Muslims, argued in favour of monotheism, the unity of his community and their status as human beings. He had Muslim religious texts and Sufism at his fingertips.

'I have seen many Hindus living in villages who knew the basic tenets of Sufism. I have seen many bauls,[5] including Hindu ones. They knew the Persian words for *Panchabhoot*.[6] Brahmos followed a similar trend. Their Girish Chandra Sen translated the Koran. Did any Muslim object? Instead, he was being called Maulavi Girish Sen. A group of Brahmos was interested in knowing Muslim society. However, there was no general interest in finding out about the Muslim way of life, whatever be the reason. This was, surely, a very sad development. One reason for this could be that Hinduism tried to hijack every religion that arrived in India from outside. They may well have hijacked Islam through Sufism, but the power and resistance built in the religion did not allow them to do so. In turn, Islam too has been unable to gobble up the Hindu religion. The evidence of this may be found in an essay by Julius Germanus from Santiniketan.[7] There may be economic, socio-economic reasons for this. It is a matter of research. Both Hindus and Muslims go to the shrines of fakirs and pirs, but not out of love. The reverence comes from fear. Again Muslims attend narrations from the *Ramayana* and plays based on the life of Lord Krishna, because of the dearth of festivals in Islam. Islam is too plain. There is not much of culturization of religion. or using culture to project a religion, in Islam. The Sufis had tried doing it through *qawwali* songs, etc., but sadly it did not happen that way. Muslim festivals are only about eating and offering namaz. On the other hand the Hindus have many festivals. This could be a reason for the lack of interest and distance between the two communities.'

'We felt the lack of interest lots of times while working on this book. For example, how many people read the journals your mother and women like her wrote in? How many knew about them?'

'Indeed, very few people. Only a small number of people subscribed to *Gulistan* and *Mohammadi*. Only the upper class, educated Muslims who wanted their children to be educated subscribed to these papers. This can be traced back to Syed Ahmed's school, i.e., the Aligarh trend. As children we would visit my aunt's joint family in Burdwan's Mangalkot. The family was spread over an entire neighbourhood. There were many books in the house, most written by Muslims. The poet Kader Nawaz's house was in Mangalkot and he wrote like Kumudranjan Mallik. He used to write folk-poems. He wrote a poem named *Maral* (The Swan). I knew three to four brothers, with a surname 'Kazi', from Murshidabad's Keshdanga Mahmudpur. Theirs was a prosperous family. My maternal grandfather once took me to their house. I saw many journals there. Later, during the *alkap* phase of my life, I saw people engaged in a literary culture. I do not know whether a popular book like *Anwara* has been written in any other language. So many editions have been published and are being published even now.'

'We bought it off the pavement.'

'Yes, Najibar Rahman was given the title of "Sahityaratna"—I read the book in my childhood.'

'Najibar Rahman tutored one of the authors, Mahmuda Khatun Siddiqua, featured in our book. Just as the novel *Anwara* became very popular, certain writers also became very special from time to time, I suppose, like Nazrul—'

'Yes, he was called the Rabindranath of Muslim Bengal.'

'Maybe it was thought that Nazrul would establish a Bengali Muslim society.'

'Nazrul, oh yes. The historical tragedy of the Hindu-Muslim relationship is reflected in Nazrul's life. Nazrul had to be cautious and row two boats simultaneously. On the one hand he had to write that Islam was sinking, to please the Muslims. He was forced to write this, else the Muslims would call him a kafir. On the other hand, he had internalized the culture of West Bengal, where he belonged. Very naturally many mythical examples featured in his writing. But the Muslims were unable to accept the spontaneity that was a part of Nazrul's writing. He was compelled to write in a different manner for the Muslims. He used Arabic and Persian words very frequently. That was a tragedy. There was significant progress in the Bengali language during Turkish rule in the thirteenth century. However, during the Renaissance in the nineteenth century everybody—Bankimchandra, even Rabindranth—looked to the West. The tradition inherent in Bengal was neglected. Muslim history became one of destroying temples. Everybody—the British, Hindus, Muslims—has misread Muslim history, leading to a grave loss.

A song by M. Anwara Begum, Syed Mustafa Siraj's mother.

Ghazal

Day in and day out
        My eyes rain tears,
Stormy winds wail in my heart

But there's none to hear.
Who can hear this cry,
Who can feel this pain –
In this arid desert
Alone, I cry in vain.
The bud that withers away
Before it has bloomed,
Is like my life that fades,
Darkness comes, the light goes out.

Gulistan, Chaitra, 1934

Notes

1 Madrasa and maqtab are Muslim primary schools.

2 Tekchand Thakur—Pseudonym of Pyari Chand Mitra. Popular author of social satire in nineteenth-century Bengal.

3 Alkap: a troupe of folk singers, wandering from village to village, performing in open gatherings.

4 Kabigaan: a form of folk entertainment in rural Bengal, where two *kabis* (poets) have a contest. The contest is largely improvised, with the two contestants replying to each other in songs, made up according to the context. The contestants often adopt fictional personae.

5 Mystic minstrals of Bengal who could be Vaishnavite Hindus or Sufi Muslims, much influenced by Tantra and Buddhism; the name's origins are debated; maybe from the Sanskrit *batul:* divinely inspired madness. Non-performing bauls follow rituals of cleansing the human body where god resides. Singer-performer bauls spread their wisdom through their songs. From his position on the fringes of society, the baul calls for social justice.

6 The five elements: fire, water, air, earth, space.

7 Julius (Abdul Karim) Germanicus is a well-known Hungarian Orientalist who was associated with Rabindranath Tagore's university, Visva-Bharati, Santiniketan, and published *Modern Movements in Islam* (Kolkata: Visva-Bharati, 1932). He also taught at Jamia Milia University, Delhi, and became a Muslim; he is currently professor and head, Department of Oriental and Islamic Studies, Budapest University.

Glossary

abba	father
adaab	form of salutation
amma	mother
apa	older sister
arati	worshipping Hindu gods and goddesses with lamps
attar	perfume
begum / begum saheba	commonly used to refer to a married woman of a respectable family
bhabi /bhabi saheba	sister-in-law
bhai / bhai saheb / bhaijan	brother
boro	eldest; usually used as a prefix, boro bhai
bu/bubu	sister
chacha	uncle
chachi	aunt; chacha's wife
chhoto	youngest, usually used as a prefix, chhoto bhai
dada /da	elder brother
dadaji	paternal grandfather
dadi / dadima	paternal grandmother
didi /di	elder sister
dulha-miyan	brother-in-law; sister's husband
ghat	the bank of a river or pond, usually paved, used for bathing, washing; also a pier
ghazal	short poem or song the theme of which is usually romantic
gua	betel nut
halwa	sweet made with semolina and ghee
jamai	son-in-law
jamdani	hand-woven sari of an elaborate design
kaka	paternal uncle who is younger than one's father
kakima	wife of kaka

kaviraj	Hindu doctor practising traditional Indian herbal medicine
khala	maternal aunt
khalamma	maternal aunt or grand-aunt
Khuda	Lord Almighty
mahaprasad	the offering given to a god which is later shared among devotees
mama	maternal uncle
maqtab	primary school for Muslims
mejo	sẹcond; usually used as a prefix, mejo bhai
mohanbhog	a sweet dish like halwa
murabba	glazed fruit, marinated in syrup
nana / nanaji	maternal grandfather
nanu/nani	maternal grandmother
oju	ritual ablution before namaz; also the act of washing
phuphu / phuphuamma	paternal aunt
pir	holy man, spiritual healer
pitha	traditional Indian sweet made of rice flour with different fillings
salaam	Muslim custom of touching an elder's feet as a mark of respect
sejo	third, usually used as a prefix, sejo bhai
zenana	the inner quarters of a Muslim household

Appendix

Sofia Khatun, B.A.: Satire on Polygamy

Translated by Adrita Mukherjee

We heard about Sofia Khatun from the book by Anisuzzaman, *Muslim Banglar Samayik Patra* (The Magazines of Muslim Bengal). Following a clue from that book, we traced an article written by Sofia Khatun, '*Bangla Sahitye Anudarata*' (The Conservative Nature of Bengali Literature) which was published in the Magh 1923 (B.S. 1329) of the *Bangiya Musalman Sahitya Patrika* (The Literary Magazine of Muslim Bengal). The B.A. degree after the author's name intrigued us; and the sharp wit of the piece roused further interest. Indeed, apart from the writings of Begum Rokeya Sakhawat Hossain, we have not found evidence of such acerbic wit in the writing of any other contemporary author.

Anisuzzaman also mentions in his book another magazine named *Annesa*, which was published from Chittagong. The editor of this magazine was one Begum Sofia Khatun.[1] Sonia Nishat Amin also mentions *Annesa* and Sofia Khatun in her book, but does not provide any other detail.[2] We found a few issues of *Annesa* at the Bangla Akademi library, Dhaka, which did not mention the B.A. degree after Sofia Khatun's name. Besides, we did not find any similarity between the somewhat conservative ideal of *Annesa* and the obviously educated and liberal mind that was reflected in the writing of Sofia Khatun, B.A.

Who then was 'Begum Sofia Khatun'? And who was 'Sofia Khatun, B.A.'? We have not found answers to these questions. We collected a few articles published under the name of 'Sofia Khatun, B.A.' for our research from magazines like *Sachitra Shishir, Bharatbarsha, Roop O Ranga*, and so on. All the pieces were written between 1923 and 1925 (B.S. 1329-1331).

The author seems to be one of the first graduates among Bengali Muslims. It is surprising that none of her contemporaries had written about such a woman, whose work reflects vast experience and a depth of analytical power. We have asked the author Umartul Fazl from Chittagong, the widow of the author Abul

Fazl, and she is unable to recall anyone like her. Mohammad Nasiruddin, too, never mentioned a highly educated Muslim woman like her, nor did Sofia Kamal remember such an author.

Sofia Khatun writes about her own life in articles published in *Sachitra Shishir*—but we have not been able to find a connecting link between these bits and pieces. For instance, in the essay *Amader Katha* (About Ourselves, published in *Bharatbarsha*, 1924 (B.S. 1330), she writes about her father taking her by the hand to Sister Nivedita who gave her lessons. In the essay *Pujor Smriti* (Memories of Durga Puja), published in *Sachitra Shishir*, Ashwin 1924 (B.S. 1331) she writes about her father's friend, the great scholar 'Jagannath Prasadji' from Benaras. In the essay *Bangalir Sahityanurag* (The Bengali's Devotion to Literature), however, she says, 'My father was an Afghan, and so was my mother.' This essay, published in the Sravan 1924 (B.S. 1331) issue of the *Bangiya Musalman Sahitya Patrika*, also mentions her younger brother who was an economist: 'My younger brother [was educated at] Oxford and the University of Berlin.'

We tried to follow these leads in our attempt to trace the author. We looked at the list of graduates of the University of Calcutta, and tried to find a Muslim economist of the time who had studied at Oxford and Berlin. We have, however, been unsuccessful in our search for Sofia Khatun.

At the end of our futile search, a thought has occurred to us—and this is only speculation on our part—that 'Sofia Khatun, B.A.' was perhaps a pseudonym used by a writer. Why did she disappear after writing for only two or three years? Even if it were a pseudonym, what had inspired the author to publish under the name of a Muslim woman? What would have been the purpose behind it? Maybe someone would be able to answer such questions. As an illustration of Sofia Khatun's writing we present one of her short essays.

We Need to Pass a Law

Please do not laugh when you read the above title—although it is a laughable matter indeed. It is a truth that cannot be disputed. The law I propose is to be used against the old men of our land who are desperate to get married. A young man has written me a letter from Hooghly jail: 'I heard recently that my great uncle (my mother's uncle) has got married about a month ago. The old man was unable to fulfil his long-nurtured desire as long as I was around. Now he is going about saying that he has done it as an act of kindness—in order to relieve a poor worried father of his burden of an unmarried daughter. My new 'great aunt' is fourteen years old. He paid 525 rupees for her. What a wonderful way of selling a girl! There is another young girl at home—the old man's own daughter, my youngest aunt, a widow, and exactly my age.

'Actually, my great uncle is my rival, in a way. He's got the power of money that I do not have. Just think—what won't a man do for money? Here I am, sitting inside the jail, shedding futile tears for the unfortunate girl who is sure to be widowed soon. Even my youngest sister is much older than her.'

Dear reader! Kindly spare a moment to think about this wretched old man. The better part of his life being over, he ought to be thinking of spiritual things—but look at his ways! Is it any use writing against them in the papers, or lampooning them? They do not even know what newspapers are. The only way, therefore, of putting a stop to this despicable practice is to pass a law which would ensure that no man above the age of fifty would be able to marry. Despite this law if they do marry, I think they ought to be put behind bars for at least a year, and we have to make sure that the imprisonment is rigorous. Maybe it isn't such a bad idea to make them work at oil-mills, taking the place of bullocks!

I should also mention something else here. The young man I referred to earlier has since then been socially ostracised thanks to the efforts of his great uncle. The reason for this is that he does not hesitate to eat food cooked by lower caste people or Muslims. He is actively involved in the Non-Cooperation movement, and does not support the caste system—this seems to be his crime. Indeed, isn't it time to start thinking about the villages of Bengal? To dally with a wife young enough to be your granddaughter while sternly advising your widowed daughter to observe the rigours of widowhood—if this is not the greatest torture on women, then what is the yardstick to measure the oppression on women in this cursed country? Would those who thought that women were not oppressed in our country become aware and at last open their eyes? What is the point of showing how bravely they can write, living in cities, far way from reality, as they do, railing against those who are educated and in particular against educated women? I would like to quote a couplet from Hafez here:

The fault you find in others and chide in them,
Search within yourself, and give it a name.

Is it right to point your finger when you could be blameworthy too?

One does not notice the prevalence of old men taking young wives in our own society, because there are many old women ready to marry the old men. In a way, this is not a bad thing. It does not happen frequently, however, in educated families. Nevertheless, it is not unusual for a man to take a second wife while he has a son old enough to get married. The reviewer of the story 'Nirupama' by Jaladhar babu writes in the Introduction that the plot of the story is unrealistic—but I am not prepared to agree with him. I happen to know that the father of one of the young Bengali novelists has recently taken part in such a wedding. I do not know if Jaladhar babu's story is inspired by this very person, but the author does have a reputation of writing stories based on real incidents.

If these men are unable to contain their carnal desires even in their old age, if they are so eager to make laughing stocks of themselves before their own family members—then I appeal to them to consider marrying the scores of women who have been widowed at a tender age. Why create a farce by marrying young girls? I have a question for old men who are impelled to re-marry: why enforce rigorous abstinence on women which they themselves are not capable of observing? Are the women made any different from men?

Sachitra Shishir, Agrahayan 1924 (B.S. 1331)

Notes

1 Anisuzzaman, *Muslim Banglar Samayik Patra* (Dhaka: Bangla Akademi, 1969): 347.

2 Sonia Nishat Amin, *The World of Muslim Women in Colonial Bengal, 1876-1939* (Leiden: E. J. Brill, 1996): 233-234.

Bibliography

Books in English

Abu-Lughod, Lila, ed., *Remaking Women: Feminism and Modernity in the Middle-East,* Princeton: Princeton University Press, 1998.

Ahmed, Leila, *Women and Gender in Islam: Historical Roots of a Modern Debate,* Yale: Yale University Press, 1992.

Ahmed, Rafiuddin, *The Bengal Muslims 1871-1906: A Quest for Identity,* Delhi: Oxford University Press, 1981.

Ahmed, Sufia, *The Muslim Community in Bengal, 1884-1912,* Dhaka: Oxford University Press, 1974.

Amin, Sonia Nishat, *The World of Muslim Women in Colonial Bengal 1876-1939,* Leiden: E. J. Brill, 1996.

Amin, Firdous, and Niaz Zaman, eds., *Infinite Variety: Women in Society and Literature,* Dhaka: University Press Ltd, 1994.

Borthwick, Meredith, *The Changing Role of Women in Bengal 1849-1905,* Princeton: Princeton University Press, 1984.

Hardy, Peter, *The Muslims of British India,* London: Cambridge University Press, 1972.

Hoodfar, Homa, *Between Marriage and the Market: Intimate Politics and Survival in Cairo,* Berkeley: University of California Press, 1997.

Ikramullah, Begum Shaista S., *From Purdah to Parliament,* London, Cresset Press, 1967.

Jahan, Roushan, ed., *Sultana's Dream and Selections from The Secluded Ones,* New York: The Feminist Press, 1988.

Jones, Kenneth W., ed., *Religious Controversy in British India: Dialogues in South Asian Languages,* New York: SUNY Press, 1992.

Karlekar, Malavika, *Voices from Within: Early Personal Narratives of Bengali Women,* Delhi: Oxford University Press, 1991.

Kaviraj, Narahari, *Wahabi and Farazi Rebels of Bengal,* Delhi: People's Publishing House, 1982.

Mahmood, Saba, *Politics of Piety: The Islamic Revival and the Feminist Subject*, Princeton: Princeton University Press, 2005

Mernissi, Fatima, *Beyond the Veil: Male-Female Dynamics in Modern Muslim Society*, Bloomington: Indiana University Press, 1987.

—, *The Veil and the Male Elite: A Feminist Interpretation of Women's Rights in Islam*, transl. by Mary Jo Lakeland, New York: Basic Books, 1992. Original French ed., Paris: Albin Michel, 1987.

—, *Women and Islam*, Delhi: Kali for Women, 1993.

—, *Islam and Democracy: Fear of the Modern World*, New York: Basic Books, 2002.

Metcalf, Barbara Daly, *Islamic Revival in British India: Deoband 1860-1900*, Princeton: Princeton University Press, 1982.

—, *Perfecting Women: Maulana Ashraf Ali Thanawi's Behisti Zewar: A Partial Translation with Commentary*, Delhi: Oxford University Press, 1992.

Minault, Gail, ed., *The Extended Family: Women and Political Participation in India and Pakistan*, Delhi: Chanakya Publications, 1981.

Moghissi, Hiadeh, *Feminism and Islamic Fundamentalism: The Limits of Postmodern Analysis*, London: Zed Press, 1999.

Najmabadi, Afsaneh, *Women with Mustaches and Men without Beards: Gender and Sexual Anxieties of Iranian Modernity*, Berkeley: University of California Press, 2005.

Roy, Asim, *The Islamic Syncretic Tradition in Bengal*, Princeton: Princeton University Press, 1983.

Roy, Bharati, ed., *From the Seams of History*, Delhi: Oxford University Press, 1996

Sarkar, Mahua, *Visible Histories, Disappearing Women: Producing Muslim Womanhood in Late Colonial Bengal*, Durham, NC: Duke University Press; Delhi: Zubaan Books, 2008.

Shaarawi, Huda, *Harem Years: The Memoirs of an Egyptian Feminist, 1879-1924*, translated by Margot Badran, New York: Feminist Press, 1987.

Tharu, Susie and K. Lalitha, eds., *Women Writing in India: 600 BC to the Present*,2 vols, Delhi: Oxford University Press, 1991;1993.

Wadud, Amina, *Qur'an and Woman: Rereading the Sacred Text from a Woman's Perspective*, New York: Oxford University Press, 1999. Original ed, Kuala Lumpur: Penerbit Fajar Bakati, 1992.

Books by the Authors in the anthology and their contemporaries

Chaudhurani, Faizunnessa, *Rupjalal,* Dhaka: Girish Jantra, published by Sheikh Munshi Mula, 1876.

Fazl, Umartul, *Priyodiner Smriti,* Dhaka: Muktodhara, 1987.

Hossain, Rokeya Sakhawat, *Motichur,* vol1, Kolkata: Nabanur Karjyalay, 1904.

—, *Motichur,* vol.2, Kolkata: Author, 1922.

—, *Padmarag,* Kolkata: Author, 1924.

Kamal, Sufia, *Keyar Kanta,* 1937; rpt, Dhaka: Anirban, 1992.

—, *Sanjher Maya,* 1938; rpt, Dhaka: Shahed Kamal, 1966.

—, *Ekaale Amader Kaal,* Dhaka: Jnan Prakashani, 1988.

Khanam, Fatema, *Saptarshi,* Dhaka: Bulbul Publishing House, 1964.

Khatun, Akhtar Mahal Syeda, *Niyantrita,* Dhaka: Raihan Begum, 1979.

Imam, Akhtar, *Amar Jibon Katha,* Dhaka: Unmesh Prakashan, 1993.

—, *Bileter Dingulo,* Dhaka: Unmesh Prakashan, 1997.

—, *Eden Theke Bethune,* Dhaka: Unmesh Prakashan, 1990.

Mahmud, Shamsunnahar, *Punyamoyee,* Kolkata: Bulbul Publishing House, 1925.

—, *Rokeya-Jibani,* 1938; rpt, Kolkata: Naya Udyog, 1996; Dhaka: Sahitya Prakash, 1996.

—, *Shishu Shiksha,* Kolkata: Bulbul Publishing House, 1939.

—, *Nazrulke Jemon Dekhechhi,* Kolkata: Nabajug Prakashani, 1958.

Quadir, Abdul, ed., *Begum Rokeya Rachanabali,* Dhaka: Bangla Academy, 1993.

Quaiyum, Md. Abdul, ed., *Nurunnesa Granthabali,* 1929 (BS 1336), Dhaka: Bangla Academy, 1970.

Quddus, Md. Abdul, ed., *Razia Khatun Chowdhuranir Rachana Sankalan,* Comilla: Rabeya Khatun Chowdhuri, 1982.

Rahman, Mrs. M., *Chanachur,* Hooghly: Kazi Mahmmudar Rahman, 1927 (BS 1334).

—, *Muktir Mulya,* Kolkata: North Bengal Publishing House (distributor; adverstised in 1952 (BS 1359)

Siddiqua, Mahmuda Khatun, *Aranyer Sur,* Dhaka: Adil Brothers and Co., 1963.

—, *Mon O Mrittika,* Dhaka: Nawroz Kitabistan, 1940.

—, *Pasharini,* Nadia: Haripada Gangopadhyay, 1931 (BS 1338).

Taifur, Sara, *Swarger Jyoti,* 1916; rpt, Dhaka: Bangla Academy, 1963.

Selected Books in Bengali

Ahmed, Wakil, *Unish Shataker Bangali Musalmaner Chinta Chetonar Dhara,* Dhaka: Bangla Academy, 1983.

Akhtar, Shaheen, *Sati O Swatantara: Bangla Sahitye Nari*, 3 vols, Dhaka: Dibya Prakash and Water Lily, 2007.

Akmam, Afroz, *Begum Rokeya : Sangrami Ek Protibimbo*, Dhaka: Mofarahus Satter, 2001.

Anisuzzaman, *Muslim Banglar Samayik Patra 1831-1930,* Dhaka: Bangla Academy, 1969.

—, *Bangali Nari : Sahitye O Somaje*, Dhaka: Sahitya Prakash, 2000.

—, *Muslim Manosh O Bangla Sahitya,* Dhaka: Papyrus, rpt, 2001 [1965].

Banu, Chhahifa, *Chhahifa Sangeet,* published by Abdul Jabbar of Srihatta (Sylhet), Saudagartula; printed by Muhammad Abdul Gani in Islamia Press, Srihatta Bandarbazaar, 1907 (BS 1314).

Begum, Maleka, *Ami Nari: Tinsha Bachharer (Atharo-Bish Shatak) Bangali Narir Itihash,* Dhaka: University Press Ltd, 2001.

—, *Joutuker Sanskriti*, Dhaka: University Press, 2006.

Chakrabarti, Sambuddha, *Andare Antare: Unish Shatake Bangali Bhadromahila,* Kolkata: Stree, 1995.

Hai, Abdul Muhammad, and Syed Ali Ahsan, *Bangla Sahityer Itibritto*, Dhaka: Ahmad Publishing House, 1994.

Hossain, Mir Mosharraf, *Mir Mosharraf Hossain Rachanabali,* Dhaka: Bangla Academy, 1985.

—, *Bibi Kulsumer Rojnamcha: Natun Tathye Natun Bhashye,* Dhaka: Shamsujjaman Khan, Abasar, 2004.

Mahmud, Moshfeka, *Patre Rokeya-Porichiti*, Dhaka : Sahitya Prakash, 1996.

Mannan, Kazi Abdul, *Unish Shataker Sahityapatra O Muslim Manas,* 2nd ed., Dhaka: Student Ways, 1967.

Maqsud, Syed Abul, *Pothikrit Naribadi Khairunnesa Khatun*, Dhaka : Sahitya Prakash, 1998.

Murshid, Ghulam, *Sankocher Biwbhalata: Adhunikotar Abhighate*

Bangaramanir Pratikriya, Dhaka: Bangla Academy, 1985.

—, *Rasasundari Theke Rokeya: Nari Pragatir Eksho Bachhar,* Dhaka: Bangla Academy, 1993.

Nasiruddin, Mohammad, *Bangla Sahitye Saogat Jug,* Dhaka: Nurjahan Begum, 1985.

Purokayastho, Nibedita Das, *Muktimanche Nari*, Dhaka : Prip Trust, 1999.

Rahaman, Najibar, *Anowara,* 1914; rpt, Dhaka: Ananda Prakashan, 1998.

—, *Goriber Meye,* 1914; rpt, Dhaka: Ananda Prakashan, 1998.

Roy, Bharati ed., *Shekaler Nari Shiksha: Bamabodhini Patrika 1270-1321,* Kolkata: Calcutta University, 1994.

Saleh, Tasneem, and Khorshed Alam, eds., *Kato Jihobar Kotha : Bangladesher Naribadi Golpo Sankalan*, Dhaka : Kshona, 2002.

Siraj, Syed Mustafa, *Aleek Manush*, 2nd ed., Kolkata: Dey's Publishing, 1994.

Uddin, Majir, *Bangla Sahitye Muslim Mahila,* Dhaka: University Press Ltd, 1985.

Zaman, Selina Bahar, *Kayek Chhatra Praner Patra*, Dhaka : Bulbul Publishing House, 2004.